S0-AVP-895

Rabindranath Tagore
Omnibus

III

Rabindranath Tagore Omnibus Contents

Volume-I

Volume-II

Volume-III

Rabindranath Tagore
Omnibus
III

Rupa & Co

Concept and Typeset Copyright © Rupa & Co. 2005

First in Rupa Paperback 2005
Third Impression 2007

Published by
Rupa • Co
7/16, Ansari Road, Daryaganj,
New Delhi 110 002

Sales Centres:

Allahabad Bangalore Chandigarh Chennai
Hyderabad Jaipur Kathmandu
Kolkata Mumbai Pune

All rights reserved.
No part of this publication may be reproduced,
stored in a retrieval system, or transmitted, in any form or by
any means, electronic, mechanical, photocopying, recording or
otherwise, without the prior permission of the copyright publishers.

Typeset by
Nikita Overseas Pvt. Ltd,
1410 Chiranjiv Tower,
43 Nehru Place,
New Delhi 110 019

Printed in India by
Gopsons Papers Ltd.
A-14 Sector 60
Noida 201 301

Contents

NATIONALISM

Nationalism in Japan

I

The worst form of bondage is the bondage of dejection, which keeps men hopelessly chained in loss of faith in themselves. We have been repeatedly told, with some justification, that Asia lives in the past—it is like a rich mausoleum which displays all its magnificence in trying to immortalise the dead. It was said of Asia that it could never move in the path of progress, its face was so inevitably turned backwards. We accepted this accusation, and came to believe it. In India, I know, a large section of our educated community, grown tired of feeling the humiliation of this charge against us, is trying with all its resources of self-deception to turn it into a matter of boasting. But boasting is only a masked shame, it does not truly believe in itself.

When things stood still like this, and we in Asia hypnotised ourselves into the belief that it could never by any possibility be otherwise, Japan rose from her dreams, and in giant strides left centuries of inaction behind, overtaking the present time in its foremost achievement. This has broken the spell under which we lay in torpor for ages, taking it to be the normal condition of certain races living in certain geographical limits. We forgot that in Asia great kingdoms were founded, philosophy, science, arts and literatures flourished, and all the great religions of the world had their cradles. Therefore it cannot be said that there is anything inherent in the soil and climate of Asia to produce mental inactivity and to atrophy the faculties which impel men to go forward. For centuries we did hold torches of civilisation in the East when the West slumbered in darkness, and that could never be the sign of sluggish minds or narrowness of vision.

Then fell the darkness of night upon all the lands of the East. The current of time seemed to stop at once, and Asia ceased to take any new food, feeding upon its own past, which is really feeding upon itself. The stillness seemed like death, and the great voice was silenced which sent forth messages of eternal truth that have saved man's life from pollution for generations, like the ocean of air that keeps the earth sweet, ever cleansing its impurities.

But life has its sleep, its periods of inactivity, when it loses its movements, takes no new food, living upon its past storage. Then it grows helpless, its muscles relaxed, and it easily lends itself to be jeered at for its stupor. In the rhythm of life, pauses there must be for the renewal of life. Life in its activity is ever spending itself, burning all its fuel. This extravagance cannot go on indefinitely, but is always followed by a passive stage, when all expenditure is stopped and all adventures abandoned in favour of rest and slow recuperation.

The tendency of mind is economical: it loves to form habits and move in grooves which save it the trouble of thinking anew at each of its steps. Ideals once formed make the mind lazy. It becomes afraid to risk its acquisitions in fresh endeavours. It tries to enjoy complete security by shutting up its belongings behind fortifications of habits. But this is really shutting oneself up from the fullest enjoyment of one's own possessions. It is miserliness. The living ideals must not lose their touch with the growing and changing life. Their real freedom is not within the boundaries of security, but on the high-road of adventures, full of the risk of new experiences.

One morning the whole world looked up in surprise when Japan broke through her walls of old habits in a night and came out triumphant. It was done in such an incredibly short time that it seemed like a change of dress and not like the building up of a new structure. She showed the confident strength of maturity, and the freshness and infinite potentiality of new life at the same moment. The fear was entertained that it was a mere freak of history, a child's game of Time, the blowing up of a soap-bubble, perfect in its rondure and colouring, hollow in its heart and without substance. But Japan has proved conclusively that this sudden revealment of her power is not a short-lived wonder, a chance product of time and tide, thrown up from the depth of obscurity to be swept away the next moment into a sea of oblivion.

The truth is that Japan is old and new at the same time. She has her legacy of ancient culture from the East—the culture that enjoins man to look for his true wealth and power in his inner soul, the culture that gives self-possession in the face of loss and danger, self-sacrifice without counting the cost or hoping for gain, defiance of death, acceptance of countless social obligations that we owe to men as social beings. In a word, modern Japan has come out of the immemorial East like a lotus blossoming in easy grace, all the while keeping its firm hold upon the profound depth from which it has sprung.

And Japan, the child of the Ancient East, has also fearlessly claimed all the gifts of the modern age for herself. She has shown her bold spirit in breaking through the confinements of habits, useless accumulations of the lazy mind, which seeks safety in its thrift and its locks and keys. Thus she has come in contact with the living time and has accepted with eagerness and aptitude the responsibilities of modern civilisation.

This it is which has given heart to the rest of Asia. We have seen that the life and the strength are there in us; only the dead crust has to be removed. We have seen that taking shelter in the dead is death itself, and only taking all the risk of life to the fullest extent is living.

I, for myself, cannot believe that Japan has become what she is by imitating the West. We cannot imitate life, we cannot simulate strength for long, nay, what is more, a mere imitation is a source of weakness. For it hampers our true nature; it is always in our way. It is like dressing our skeleton with another man's skin, giving rise to eternal feuds between the skin and the bones at every movement.

The real truth is that science is not man's nature, it is mere knowledge and training. By knowing the laws of the material universe you do not change your deeper humanity. You can borrow knowledge from others, but you cannot borrow temperament.

But at the imitative stage of our schooling we cannot distinguish between the essential and the non-essential, between what is transferable and what is not. It is something like the faith of the primitive mind in the magical properties of the accidents of outward forms which accompany some real truth. We are afraid of leaving out something valuable and efficacious by not swallowing the husk with the kernel. But while our greed delights in wholesale appropriation, it is the function of our vital nature to assimilate, which is the only true appropriation for a living organism. Where there is life it is sure to assert itself by its choice of acceptance and refusal according to its constitutional necessity. The living organism does not allow itself to grow into its food; it changes its food into its own body. And only thus can it grow strong and not by mere accumulation, or by giving up its personal identity.

Japan has imported her food from the West, but not her vital nature. Japan cannot altogether lose and merge herself in the scientific paraphernalia she has acquired from the West and be turned into a mere borrowed machine. She has her own soul, which must assert itself over all her requirements. That she is capable of doing so, and that the process of assimilation is going on, have been amply proved by the signs of vigorous health that she exhibits. And I earnestly hope that Japan may never lose her faith in her own soul, in the mere pride of her foreign acquisition. For that pride itself is a humiliation, ultimately leading to poverty and weakness. It is the pride of the fop who sets more store on his new head-dress than on his head itself.

The whole world waits to see what this great eastern nation is going to do with the opportunities and responsibilities she has accepted from the hands of the modern time. If it be a mere reproduction of the West, then the great expectation she has raised will remain unfulfilled. For there are grave questions that western civilisation has presented before the world but not completely answered. The conflict between the individual and the state, labour and capital, the man and the woman; the conflict between the greed of material gain and the spiritual life of man, the organised selfishness of nations and the higher ideals of humanity; the conflict between all the ugly complexities inseparable from giant organisations of commerce and state and the natural instincts of man crying for simplicity and beauty and fulness of leisure—all these have to be brought to a harmony in a manner not yet dreamt of.

We have seen this great stream of civilisation choking itself from debris carried by its innumerable channels. We have seen that with all its vaunted love of humanity it has proved itself the greatest menace to Man, far worse than the sudden outbursts of nomadic barbarism from which men suffered in the early ages of history. We have seen that, in spite of its boasted love of freedom, it has produced worse forms of slavery than ever were current in earlier societies—

slavery whose chains are unbreakable, either because they are unseen, or because they assume the names and appearance of freedom. We have seen, under the spell of its gigantic sordidness, man losing faith in all the heroic ideals of life which have made him great.

Therefore you cannot with a light heart accept the modern civilisation with all its tendencies, methods and structures, and dream that they are inevitable. You must apply your eastern mind, your spiritual strength, your love of simplicity, your recognition of social obligation, in order to cut out a new path for this great unwieldy car of progress, shrieking out its loud discords as it runs. You must minimise the immense sacrifice of man's life and freedom that it claims in its every movement. For generations you have felt and thought and worked, have enjoyed and worshipped in your own special manner; and this cannot be cast off like old clothes. It is in your blood, in the marrow of your bones, in the texture of your flesh, in the tissue of your brains; and it must modify everything you lay your hands upon, without your knowing, even against your wishes. Once you did solve the problems of man to your own satisfaction, you had your philosophy of life and evolved your own art of living. All this you must apply to the present situation, and out of it will arise a new creation and not a mere repetition, a creation which the soul of your people will own for itself and proudly offer to the world as its tribute to the welfare of man. Of all countries in Asia, here in Japan you have the freedom to use the materials you have gathered from the West according to your genius and your need. Therefore your responsibility is all the greater, for in your voice Asia shall answer the questions that Europe has submitted to the conference of Man. In your land the experiments will be carried on by which the East will change the aspects of modern civilisation, infusing life in it where it is a machine, substituting the human heart for cold expediency, not caring so much for power and success as for harmonious and living growth, for truth and beauty.

I cannot but bring to your mind those days when the whole of eastern Asia from Burma to Japan was united with India in the closest tie of friendship, the only natural tie which can exist between nations. There was a living communication of hearts, a nervous system evolved through which messages ran between us about the deepest needs of humanity. We did not stand in fear of each other; we had not to arm ourselves to keep each other in check; our relation was not that of self-interest, of exploration and spoliation of each other's pocket; ideas and ideals were exchanged, gifts of the highest love were offered and taken; no difference of languages and customs hindered us in approaching each other heart to heart; no pride of race or insolent consciousness of superiority, physical or mental, marred our relation; our arts and literatures put forth new leaves and flowers under the influence of this sunlight of united hearts, and races belonging to different lands and languages and histories acknowledged the highest unity of man and the deepest bond of love. May we not also remember that in those days of peace and goodwill, of men uniting for those supreme ends of life, your nature laid by for itself the balm of immortality which has helped your people to be born again in a new age, to be able to survive its old outworn structures and take on a new young body, to come out unscathed from the shock of the most wonderful revolution that the world has ever seen?

The political civilisation which has sprung up from the soil of Europe and is overrunning the whole world, like some prolific weed, is based upon exclusiveness. It is always watchful to keep the aliens at bay or to exterminate them. It is carnivorous and cannibalistic in its tendencies, it feeds upon the resources of other peoples and tries to swallow their whole future. It is always afraid of other races achieving eminence, naming it as a peril, and tries to thwart all symptoms of greatness outside its own boundaries, forcing down races of men who are weaker, to be eternally fixed in their weakness. Before this political civilisation came to its power and opened its hungry jaws wide enough to gulp down great continents of the earth, we had wars, pillages, changes of monarchy and consequent miseries, but never such a sight of fearful and hopeless voracity, such wholesale feeding of nation upon nation, such huge machines for turning great portions of the earth into mince-meat, never such terrible jealousies with all their ugly teeth and claws ready for tearing open each other's vitals. This political civilisation is scientific, not human. It is powerful because it concentrates all its forces upon one purpose, like a millionaire acquiring money at the cost of his soul. It betrays its trust, it weaves its meshes of lies without shame, it enshrines gigantic idols of greed in its temples, taking great pride in the costly ceremonials of its worship, calling this patriotism. And it can be safely prophesied that this cannot go on, for there is a moral law in this world which has its application both to individuals and to organised bodies of men. You cannot go on violating these laws in the name of your nation, yet enjoy their advantage as individuals. This public sapping of ethical ideals slowly reacts upon each member of society, gradually breeding weakness where it is not seen, and causing that cynical distrust of all things sacred in human nature, which is the true symptom of senility. You must keep in mind that this political civilisation, this creed of national patriotism, has not been given a long trial. The lamp of ancient Greece is extinct in the land where it was first lighted; the power of Rome lies dead and buried under the ruins of its vast empire. But the civilisation, whose basis is society and the spiritual ideal of man, is still a living thing in China and in India. Though it may look feeble and small, judged by the standard of the mechanical power of modern days, yet like small seeds it still contains life and will sprout and grow, and spread its beneficent branches, producing flowers and fruits when its time comes and showers of grace descend upon it from heaven. But ruins of skyscrapers of power, and broken machinery of greed, even God's rain is powerless to raise up again; for they were not of life, but went against life as a whole—they are relics of the rebellion that shattered itself to pieces against the eternal.

But the charge is brought against us that the ideals we cherish in the East are static, that they have not the impetus in them to move, to open out new vistas of knowledge and power, that the systems of philosophy which are the mainstays of the time-worn civilisations of the East despise all outward proofs, remaining stolidly satisfied in their subjective certainty. This proves that when our knowledge is vague we are apt to accuse of vagueness our object of knowledge itself. To a western observer our civilisation appears as all metaphysics, as to a deaf man piano-playing appears to be mere movements of fingers and no music. He cannot think that we have found some deep basis of reality upon which we have built our institutions.

Unfortunately all proofs of reality are in realisation. The reality of the scene before you depends only upon the fact that you can see, and it is difficult for us to prove to an unbeliever that our civilisation is not a nebulous system of abstract speculations, that it has achieved something which is a positive truth—a truth that can give man's heart its shelter and sustenance. It has evolved an inner sense—a sense of vision, the vision of the infinite reality in all finite things.

But he says, 'You do not make any progress; there is no movement in you.' I ask him, 'How do you know it? You have to judge progress according to its aim. A railway train makes its progress towards the terminus station—it is movement. But a full-grown tree has no definite movement of that kind; its progress is the inward progress of life. It lives, with its aspiration towards light tingling in its leaves and creeping in its silent sap.'

We also have lived for centuries; we still live, and we have our aspiration for a reality that has no end to its realisation— a reality that goes beyond death, giving it a meaning, that rises above all evils of life, bringing its peace and purity, its cheerful renunciation of self. The product of this inner life is a living product. It will be needed when the youth returns home weary and dust-laden, when the soldier is wounded, when the wealth is squandered away and pride is humbled, when man's heart cries for truth in the immensity of facts, and harmony in the contradiction of tendencies. Its value is not in its multiplication of materials, but in its spiritual fulfilment.

There are things that cannot wait. You have to rush and run and march if you must fight or take the best place in the market. You strain your nerves and are on the alert when you chase opportunities that are always on the wing. But there are ideals which do not play hide-and-seek with our life; they slowly grow from seed to flower, from flower to fruit; they require infinite space and heaven's light to mature, and the fruits that they produce can survive years of insult and neglect. The East with her ideals, in whose bosom are stored the ages of sunlight and silence of stars, can patiently wait till the West, hurrying after the expedient, loses breath and stops. Europe, while busily speeding to her engagements, disdainfully casts her glance from her carriage window at the reaper reaping his harvest in the field, and in her intoxication of speed cannot but think of him as slow and ever receding backwards. But the speed comes to its end; the engagement loses its meaning and the hungry heart clamours for food, till at last she comes to the lowly reaper reaping his harvest in the sun. For if the office cannot wait, or the buying and selling, or the craving for excitement, love waits, and beauty, and the wisdom of suffering and the fruits of patient devotion and reverent meekness of simple faith. And thus shall wait the East till her time comes.

I must not hesitate to acknowledge where Europe is great, for great she is without doubt. We cannot help loving her with all our heart and paying her the best homage of our admiration—the Europe who, in her literature and art, pours out an inexhaustible cascade of beauty and truth fertilising all countries and all time; the Europe who, with a mind which is titanic in its untiring power, is sweeping the height and the depth of the universe, winning her homage of knowledge from the infinitely great and the infinitely small, applying all the resources of her great intellect and heart in healing the sick and alleviating those miseries of man which up till now we were contented to accept in a spirit of hopeless resignation; the Europe who is making the earth yield more fruit than seemed possible, coaxing and compelling the great forces of nature into man's service. Such true greatness must have its motive power in spiritual strength. For only the spirit of man can defy all limitations, have faith in its ultimate success, throw its searchlight beyond the immediate and the apparent, gladly suffer martyrdom for ends which cannot be achieved in its lifetime and accept failure without acknowledging defeat. In the heart of Europe runs the purest stream of human love, of love of justice, of spirit of self-sacrifice for higher ideals. The Christian culture of centuries has sunk deep in her life's core. In Europe we have seen noble minds who have ever stood up for the rights of man irrespective of colour and creed; who have braved calumny and insult from their own people in fighting for humanity's cause and raising their voices against the mad orgies of militarism, against the rage for brutal retaliation or rapacity that sometimes takes possession of a whole people; who are always ready to make reparation for wrongs done in the past by their own nations and vainly attempt to stem the tide of cowardly injustice that flows unchecked because the resistance is weak and innocuous on the part of the injured. There are these knight-errants of modern Europe who have not lost their faith in the disinterested love of freedom, in the ideals which own no geographical boundaries or national self-seeking. These are there to prove that the fountainhead of the water of everlasting life has not run dry in Europe, and from thence she will have her rebirth time after time. Only there, where Europe is too consciously busy in building up her power, defying her deeper nature and mocking it, she is heaping up her iniquities to the sky, crying for God's vengeance and spreading the infection of ugliness, physical and moral, over the face of the earth with her heartless commerce heedlessly outraging man's sense of the beautiful and the good. Europe is supremely good in her beneficence where her face is turned to all humanity; and Europe is supremely evil in her maleficent aspect where her face is turned only upon her own interest, using all her power of greatness for ends which are against the infinite and eternal in Man.

Eastern Asia has been pursuing its own path, evolving its own civilisation, which was not political but social, not predatory and mechanically efficient but spiritual and based upon all the varied and deeper relations of humanity. The solutions of the life problems of peoples were thought out in seclusion and carried out behind the security of aloofness, where all the dynastic changes and foreign invasions hardly touched them. But now we are overtaken by the outside world, our seclusion is lost for ever. Yet this we must not regret, as a plant should never regret when the obscurity of its seed-time is broken. Now the time has come when we must make the world problem our own problem; we must bring the spirit of civilisation into harmony with the history of all nations of the earth; we must not, in foolish pride, still keep ourselves fast within the shell of the seed and the crust of the earth which protected and nourished our ideals; for these, the shell and the crust, were meant to be broken, so that life may spring up in all its vigour and beauty, bringing its offerings to the world in open light.

In this task of breaking the barrier and facing the world Japan has come out the first in the East. She has infused hope in the heart of all Asia. This hope provides the hidden fire which is needed for all works of creation. Asia now feels that she must prove her life by producing living work; she must not lie passively dormant, or feebly imitate the West, in the infatuation of fear and flattery. For this we offer our thanks to this Land of the Rising Sun and solemnly ask her to remember that she has the mission of the East to fulfil. She must infuse the sap of a fuller humanity into the heart of modern civilisation. She must never allow it to get choked with noxious undergrowth, but lead it up towards light and freedom, towards the pure air and broad space where it can receive, in the dawn of its day and the darkness of its night, heaven's inspiration. Let the greatness of her ideals become visible to all men like her snow-crowned Fuji rising from the heart of the country into the region of the infinite, supremely distinct from its surroundings, beautiful like a maiden in its magnificent sweep of curve, yet firm and strong and serenely majestic.

II

I have travelled in many countries and have met with men of all classes, but never in my travels did I feel the presence of the human so distinctly as in this land. In other great countries signs of man's power loomed large, and I saw vast organisations which showed efficiency in all their features. There, display and extravagance, in dress, in furniture, in costly entertainments, are startling. They seem to push you back into a corner, like a poor intruder at a feast; they are apt to make you envious, or take your breath away with amazement. There, you do not feel man as supreme; you are hurled against a stupendousness of things that alienate. But in Japan it is not the display of power or wealth that is the predominating element. You see everywhere emblems of love and admiration, and not mostly of ambition and greed. You see a people whose heart has come out and scattered itself in profusion in its commonest utensils of everyday life, in its social institutions, in its manners, which are carefully perfect, and in its dealings with things which are not only deft but graceful in every movement.

What has impressed me most in this country is the conviction that you have realised nature's secrets, not by methods of analytical knowledge, but by sympathy. You have known her language of lines, and music of colours, the symmetry in her irregularities, and the cadence in her freedom of movements; you have seen how she leads her immense crowds of things yet avoids all frictions, how the very conflicts in her creations break out in dance and music, how her exuberance has the aspect of the fulness of self-abandonment, and not a mere dissipation of display. You have discovered that nature reserves her power in forms of beauty; and it is this beauty which, like a mother, nourishes all the giant forces at her breast, keeping them in active vigour, yet in repose. You have known that energies of nature save themselves from wearing out by the rhythm of a perfect grace, and that she, with the tenderness of her curved lines, takes away fatigue from the world's muscles. I have felt that you have been able to assimilate these secrets into your life, and the truth which lies in the beauty of all things has passed into your souls. A mere knowledge of things can be had in a short enough time, but their spirit can only be acquired by centuries of training and self-control. Dominating nature from outside is a much simpler thing than making her your own in love's delight, which is a work of true genius. Your race has shown that genius, not by acquirement but by creation, not by display of things but by manifestation of its own inner being. This creative power there is in all nations, and it is ever active in getting hold of men's natures and giving them a form according to its ideals. But here, in Japan, it seems to have achieved its success, and deeply sunk into the minds of all men, and permeated their muscles and nerves. Your instincts have become true, your senses keen, and your hands have acquired natural skill. The genius of Europe has given her people the power of organisation, which has specially made itself manifest in politics and commerce and in co-ordinating scientific knowledge. The genius of Japan has given you the vision of beauty in nature and the power of realising it in your life.

All particular civilisation is the interpretation of particular human experience. Europe seems to have felt emphatically the conflict of things in the universe, which can only be brought under control by conquest. Therefore she is ever ready for fight, and the best portion of her attention is occupied in organising forces. But Japan has felt, in her world, the touch of some presence, which has evoked in her soul a feeling of reverent adoration. She does not boast of her mastery of nature, but to her she brings, with infinite care and joy, her offerings of love. Her relationship with the world is the deeper relationship of heart. This spiritual bond of love she has established with the hills of her country, with the sea and the streams, with the forests in all their flowery moods and varied physiognomy of branches; she has taken into her heart all the rustling whispers and sighing of the woodlands and sobbing of the waves; the sun and the moon she has studied in all the modulations of their lights and shades, and she is glad to close her shops to greet the seasons in her orchards and gardens and cornfields. This opening of the heart to the soul of the world is not confined to a section of your privileged classes; it is not the forced product of exotic culture, but it belongs to all your men and women of all conditions. This experience of your soul, in meeting a personality in the heart of the world, has been embodied in your civilisaton. It is a civilisation of human relationship. Your duty towards your state has naturally assumed the character of filial duty, your nation becoming one family with your Emperor as its head. Your national unity has not been evolved from the comradeship of arms for defensive and offensive purpose, or from partnership in raiding adventures, dividing among each member the danger and spoils of robbery. It is not an outcome of the necessity of organisation for some ulterior purpose, but it is an extension of the family and obligations of the heart in a wide field of space and time. The ideal of *maitri* is at the bottom of your culture—*maitri* with men and *maitri* with Nature. And the true expression of this love is in the language of beauty, which is so abundantly universal in this land. This is the reason why a stranger like myself, instead of feeling envy or humiliation before these manifestations of beauty, these creations of love, feels a readiness to participate in the joy and glory of such revealment of the human heart.

And this had made me all the more apprehensive of the change which threatens Japanese civilisation, as something like a menace to one's own person. For the huge heterogeneity of the modern age, whose only common bond is usefulness, is nowhere so pitifully exposed against the dignity and hidden power of reticent beauty as in Japan.

But the danger lies in this, that organised ugliness storms the mind and carries the day by its mass, by its aggressive persistence, but its power of mockery is directed against the deeper sentiments of the heart. Its harsh obtrusiveness makes it forcibly visible to us, overcoming our senses—and we bring sacrifices to its alter, as does a savage to the fetish which appears powerful because of its hideousness. Therefore its rivalry with things that are modest and profound and have the subtle delicacy of life is to be dreaded.

I am quite sure that there are men in your country who are not in sympathy with your inherited ideals, whose object is to gain and not to grow. They are loud in their boast that they have modernised Japan. While I agree with them so far as to say that the spirit of the race should harmonise with the spirit of the time, I must warn them that modernising is a mere affectation of modernism, just as an affectation of poesy is poetising. It is nothing but mimicry, only affectation is louder than the original, and it is too literal. One must bear in mind that those who have the true modern spirit need not modernise, just as those who are truly brave are not braggarts. Modernism is not in the dress of the Europeans, or in the hideous structures where their children are interned when they take their lessons, or in the square houses with flat, straight wall-surfaces, pierced with parallel lines of windows, where these people are caged in their lifetime; certainly modernism is not in their ladies' bonnets, carrying on them loads of incongruities. These are not modern, but merely European. True modernism is freedom of mind, not slavery of taste. It is independence of thought and action, not tutelage under European schoolmasters. It is science, but not its wrong application in life—a mere imitation of our science teachers who reduce it into a superstition, absurdly invoking its aid for all impossible purposes.

Life based upon mere science is attractive to some men, because it has all the characteristics of sport; it feigns seriousness, but is not profound. When you go a-hunting, the less pity you have the better; for your one object is to chase the game and kill it, to feel that you are the greater animal, that your method of destruction is thorough and scientific. And the life of science is that superficial life. It pursues success with skill and thoroughness, and takes no account of the higher nature of man. But those whose minds are crude enough to plan their lives upon the supposition that man is merely a hunter and his paradise the paradise of sportsmen will be rudely awakened in the midst of their trophies of skeletons and skulls.

I do not for a moment suggest that Japan should be unmindful of acquiring modern weapons of self-protection. But this should never be allowed to go beyond her instinct of self-preservation. She must know that the real power is not in the weapons themselves, but in the man who wields those weapons; and when he, in his eagerness for power, multiplies his weapons at the cost of his own soul, then it is he who is in even greater danger than his enemies.

Things that are living are so easily hurt; therefore they require protection. In nature, life protects itself within its coverings, which are built with life's own material. Therefore they are in harmony with life's growth, or else when the time comes they easily give way and are forgotten. The living man has his true protection in his spiritual ideals which have their vital connection with his life, and grow with his growth. But, unfortunately, all his armour is not living—some of it is made of steel, inert and mechanical. Therefore, while making use of it, man has to be careful to protect himself from its tyranny. If he is weak enough to grow smaller to fit himself to his covering, then it becomes a process of gradual suicide by shrinkage of the soul. And Japan must have a firm faith in the moral law of existence to be able to assert to herself that the western nations are following that path of suicide, where they are smothering their humanity under the immense weight of organisations in order to keep themselves in power and hold others in subjection.

What is dangerous for Japan is not the imitation of the outer features of the West, but the acceptance of the motive force of western nationalism as her own. Her social ideals are already showing signs of defeat at the hands of politics. I can see her motto, taken from science, 'Survival of the fittest', writ large at the entrance of her present day history—the motto whose meaning is, 'Help yourself, and never heed what it costs to others', the motto of the blind man who only believes in what he can touch, because he cannot see. But those who can see know that men are so closely knit that when you strike others the blow comes back to yourself. The moral law, which is the greatest discovery of man, is the discovery of this wonderful truth, that man becomes all the truer the more he realises himself in others. This truth has not only a subjective value, but is manifested in every department of our life. And nations who sedulously cultivate moral blindness as the cult of patriotism will end their existence in a sudden and violent death. In past ages we had foreign invasions, but they never touched the soul of the people deeply. They were merely the outcome of individual ambitions. The people themselves, being free from the responsibilities of the baser and more heinous side of those adventures, had all the advantage of the heroic and the human disciplines derived from them. This developed their unflinching loyalty, their single-minded devotion to the obligations of honour, their power of complete self-surrender and fearless acceptance of death and danger. Therefore the ideals, whose seats were in the hearts of the people, would not undergo any serious change owing to the policies adopted by the kings or generals. But now, where the spirit of western nationalism prevails, the whole people is being taught from boyhood to foster hatreds and ambitions by all kinds of means—by the manufacture of half-truths and untruths in history, by persistent misrepresentation of other races and the culture of unfavourable sentiments towards them, by setting up memorials of events, very often false, which for the sake of humanity should be speedily forgotten, thus continually brewing evil menace towards neighbours and nations other than their own. This is poisoning the very fountainhead of humanity. It is discrediting the ideals which were born of the lives of men who were our greatest and best. It is holding up gigantic selfishness as the one universal religion for all nations of the world. We can take anything else from the hands of science, but not this elixir of moral death. Never think for a moment that the hurts you inflict upon other races will not infect you, or that the enmities you sow around your homes will be a wall of protection to you for all time to come. To imbue the minds of the whole people with an abnormal vanity of its own superiority, to teach it to take pride in its moral callousness and ill-begotten wealth, to perpetuate the humiliation of defeated nations by exhibiting trophies won from war, and using these in schools in order to breed in children's minds contempt for others, is imitating the West where she has a festering sore, whose swelling is a swelling of disease eating into its vitality.

Our food crops, which are necessary for our sustenance, are products of centuries of selection and care. But the vegetation, which we have not to transform into our lives, does not require the patient thoughts of generations. It is not easy to get rid of weeds; but it is easy, by process of neglect, to ruin your food crops and let them revert to their primitive state of wildness. Likewise the culture, which has so kindly adapted itself to your soil—so intimate with life, so human— not only needed tilling and weeding in past ages, but still needs anxious work and watching. What is merely modern— as science and methods of organisation—can be transplanted; but what is vitally human has fibres so delicate, and roots so numerous and far-reaching, that it dies when moved from the soil. Therefore I am afraid of the rude pressure of the political ideals of the West upon your own. In political civilisation, the state is an abstraction and the relationship of men utilitarian. Because it has no root in sentiments, it is so dangerously easy to handle. Half a century has been enough for you to master this machine; and there are men among you whose fondness for it exceeds their love for the living ideals, which were born with the birth of your nation and nursed in your centuries. It is like a child who, in the excitement of his play, imagines he likes his play-things better than his mother.

Where man is at his greatest, he is unconscious. Your civilisation, whose mainspring is the bond of human relationship, has been nourished in the depth of a healthy life beyond reach of prying self-analysis. But a mere political relationship is all-conscious; it is an eruptive inflammation of aggressiveness. It has forcibly burst upon your notice. And the time has come when you have to be roused into full consciousness of the truth by which you live, so that you may not be taken unawares. The past has been God's gift to you; about the present, you must make your own choice.

So the questions you have to put to yourselves are these: 'Have we read the world wrong, and based our relation to it upon an ignorance of human nature? Is the instinct of the West right, where she builds her national welfare behind the barricade of a universal distrust of humanity?'

You must have detected a strong accent of fear whenever the West has discussed the possibility of the rise of an eastern race. The reason of it is this, that the power by whose help she thrives is an evil power; so long as it is held on her own side she can be safe, while the rest of the world trembles. The vital ambition of the present civilisation of Europe is to have the exclusive possession of the devil. All her armaments and diplomacy are directed upon this one object. But these costly rituals for invocation of the evil spirit lead through a path of prosperity to the brink of cataclysm. The furies of terror, which the West has let loose upon God's world, come back to threaten herself and goad her into preparations of more and more frightfulness; this gives her no rest, and makes her forget all else but the perils that she causes to others and incurs herself. To the worship of this devil of politics she sacrifices other countries as victims. She feeds upon their dead flesh and grows fat upon it, so long as the carcasses remain fresh—but they are sure to rot at last, and the dead will take their revenge by spreading pollution far and wide and poisoning the vitality of the feeder. Japan had all her wealth of humanity, her harmony of heroism and beauty, her depth of self-control and richness of self-expression; yet the western nations felt no respect for her till she proved that the bloodhounds of Satan are not only bred in the kennels of Europe but can also be domesticated in Japan and fed with man's miseries. They admit Japan's equality with themselves, only when they know that Japan also possesses the key to open the floodgate of hell-fire upon the fair earth whenever she chooses, and can dance in their own measure the devil dance of pillage, murder and ravishment of innocent women, while the world goes to ruin. We know that, in the early state of man's moral immaturity, he only feels reverence for the god whose malevolence he dreads. But is this the ideal of man which we can look up to with pride: after centuries of civilisation nations fearing each other like the prowling wild beasts of the night-time; shutting their doors of hospitality; combining only for purpose of aggression or defence; hiding in their holes their trade secrets, state secrets, secrets of their armaments; making peace-offerings to each other's barking dogs with the meat which does not belong to them; holding down fallen races which struggle to stand upon their feet; with their right hands dispensing religion to weaker peoples, while robbing them with their left—is there anything in this to make us envious? Are we to bend our knees to the spirit of this nationalism, which is sowing broadcast over all the world seeds of fear, greed, suspicion, unashamed lies of its diplomacy, and unctuous lies of its profession of peace and goodwill and universal brotherhood of Man? Can our minds be free from doubt when we rush to the western market to buy this foreign product in exchange for our own inheritance? I am aware how difficult it is to know one's self; and the man who is intoxicated furiously denies his drunkenness; yet the West herself is anxiously thinking of her problems and trying experiments. But she is like a glutton who has not the heart to give up his intemperance in eating, and fondly clings to the hope he can cure his nightmares of indigestion by medicine. Europe is not ready to give up her political inhumanity, with all the baser passions of man attendant upon it; she believes only in modification of systems, and not in change of heart.

We are willing to buy their machine-made systems, not with our hearts, but with our brains. We shall try them and build sheds for them, but not enshrine them in our homes or temples. There are races who worship the animals they kill; we can buy meat from them when we are hungry, but not the worship which goes with the killing. We must not vitiate our children's minds with the superstition that business is business, war is war, politics is politics. We must know that man's business has to be more than mere business, and so should be his war and politics. You had your own industry in Japan; how scrupulously honest and true it was, you can see by its products—by their grace and strength, their conscientiousness in details, where they can hardly be observed. But the tidal wave of falsehood has swept over your land from that part of the world where business is business, and honesty is followed merely as a best policy. Have you never felt shame when you see the trade advertisements, not only plastering the whole town with lies and exaggerations, but invading the green fields, where the peasants do their honest labour, and the hill-tops, which greet the first pure light of the morning?

It is so easy to dull our sense of honour and delicacy of mind with constant abrasion, while falsehoods stalk abroad with proud steps in the name of trade, politics and patriotism, that any protest against their perpetual intrusion into our lives is considered to be sentimentalism, unworthy of true manliness.

And it has come to pass that the children of those heroes who would keep their word at the point of death, who would disdain to cheat men for vulgar profit, who even in their fight would much rather court defeat than be dishonourable, have become energetic in dealing with falsehoods and do not feel humiliated by gaining advantage from them. And this has been effected by the charm of the word 'modern'. But if undiluted utility be modern, beauty is of all ages; if mean selfishness be modern, the human ideals are no new inventions. And we must know for certain that however modern may be the proficiency which cripples man for the sake of methods and machines, it will never live to be old.

But while trying to free our minds from the arrogant claims of Europe and to help ourselves out of the quick sands of our infatuation, we may go to the other extreme and bind ourselves with a wholesale suspicion of the West. The reaction of disillusionment is just as unreal as the first shock of illusion. We must try to come to that normal state of mind by which we can clearly discern our own danger and avoid it without being unjust towards the source of that danger. There is always the natural temptation in us of wishing to pay back Europe in her own coin, and return contempt for contempt and evil for evil. But that again would be to imitate Europe in one of her worst features, which comes out in her behaviour to people whom she describes as yellow or red, brown or black. And this is a point on which we in the East have to acknowledge our guilt and own that our sin has been as great, if not greater, when we insulted humanity by treating with utter disdain and cruelty men who belonged to a particular creed, colour or caste. It is really because we are afraid of our own weakness, which allows itself to be overcome by the sight of power, that we try to substitute for it another weakness which makes itself blind to the glories of the West. When we truly know that Europe which is great and good, we can effectively save ourselves from the Europe which is mean and grasping. It is easy to be unfair in one's judgement when one is faced with human miseries—and pessimism is the result of building theories while the mind is suffering. To despair of humanity is only possible if we lose faith in truth which brings to it strength, when its defeat is greatest, and calls out new life from the depth of its destruction. We must admit that there is a living soul in the West which is struggling unobserved against the hugeness of the organisations under which men, women and children are being crushed, and whose mechanical necessities are ignoring laws that are spiritual and human—the soul whose sensibilities refuse to be dulled completely by dangerous habits of heedlessness in dealings with races for whom it lacks natural sympathy. The West could never have risen to the eminence she has reached if her strength were merely the strength of the brute or of the machine. The divine in her heart is suffering from the injuries inflicted by her hands upon the world—and from this pain of her higher nature flows the secret balm which will bring healing to these injuries. Time after time she has fought against herself and has undone the chains which with her own hands she fastened round helpless limbs; and though she forced poison down the throat of a great nation at the point of the sword for gain of money, she herself woke up to withdraw from it, to wash her hands clean again. This shows hidden springs of humanity in spots which look dead and barren. It proves that the deeper truth in her nature, which can survive such a career of cruel cowardliness, is not greed, but reverence for unselfish ideals. It would be altogether unjust, both to us and to Europe, to say that she has fascinated the modern eastern mind by the mere exhibition of her power. Through the smoke of cannons and dust of markets the light of her moral nature has shone bright, and she has brought to us the ideal of ethical freedom, whose foundation lies deeper than social conventions and whose province of activity is world-wide.

The East has instinctively felt, even through her aversion, that she has a great deal to learn from Europe, not merely about the materials of power, but about its inner source, which is of the mind and of the moral nature of man. Europe has been teaching us the higher obligations of public good above those of the family and the clan, and the sacredness of law, which makes society independent of individual caprice, secures for it continuity of progress, and guarantees justice to all men of all positions in life. Above all things Europe has held high before our minds the banner of liberty, through centuries of martyrdom and achievement—liberty of conscience, liberty of thought and action, liberty in the ideals of art and literature. And because Europe has won our deep respect, she has become so dangerous for us where she is turbulently weak and false— dangerous like poison when it is served along with our best food. There is one safety for us upon which we hope we may count, and that is that we can claim Europe herself as our ally in our resistance to her temptations and to her violent encroachments; for she has ever carried her own standard of perfection, by which we can measure her falls and gauge her degrees of failure, by which we can call her before her own tribunal and put her to shame—the shame which is the sign of the true pride of nobleness.

But our fear is that the poison may be more powerful than the food, and what is strength in her today may not be a sign of health, but the contrary; for it may be temporarily caused by the upsetting of the balance of life. Our fear is that evil has a fateful fascination when it assumes dimensions which are colossal—and though at last it is sure to lose its centre of gravity by its abnormal disproportion, the mischief which it creates before its fall may be beyond reparation.

Therefore I ask you to have the strength of faith and clarity of mind to know for certain that the lumbering structure of modern progress, riveted by the iron bolts of efficiency, which runs upon the wheels of ambition, cannot hold together for long. Collisions are certain to occur, for it has to travel upon organised lines; it is too heavy to choose its own course freely, and once it is off the rails its endless train of vehicles is dislocated. A day will come when it will fall in a heap of ruin and cause serious obstruction to the traffic of the world. Do we not see signs of this even now? Does not the voice come to us through the din of war, the shrieks of hatred, the wailings of despair, through the churning of the unspeakable filth which has been accumulating for ages in the bottom of this nationalism—the voice which cries to our soul that the tower of national selfishness, which goes by the name of patriotism, which has raised its banner of treason against heaven, must totter and fall with a crash, weighed down by its own bulk, its flag kissing the dust, its light extinguished? My brothers, when the red light of conflagration sends up its crackle of laughter to the stars, keep your faith upon those stars and not upon the fire of destruction. For when the conflagration consumes itself and dies down, leaving its memorial in ashes, the eternal light will again shine in the East—the East which has been the birthplace of the morning sun of man's history. And who knows if that day has not already dawned, and the sun not risen, in the easternmost horizon of Asia? And I offer, as did my ancestor *rishis*, my salutation to that sunrise of the East, which is destined once again to illumine the whole world.

I know my voice is too feeble to raise itself above the uproar of this bustling time, and it is easy for any street urchin to fling against me the epithet of 'unpractical'. It will stick to my coat-tail, never to be washed away, effectively excluding me from the consideration of all respectable persons. I know what a risk one runs from the vigorously athletic crowds in being styled an idealist in these days, when thrones have lost their dignity and prophets have become an anachronism, when the sound that drowns all voices is the noise of the market-place. Yet when, one day, standing on the outskirts of Yokohama town bristling with its display of modern miscellanies, I watched the sunset in your southern sea, and saw its peace and majesty among your pine-clad hills—with the great Fujiyama growing faint against the golden horizon, like a god overcome with his own radiance—the music of eternity welled up through the evening silence, and I felt that the sky and the earth and the lyrics of the dawn and the dayfall are with the poets and idealists, and not with the marketmen robustly contemptuous of all sentiment—that, after all the forgetfulness of his divinity, man will remember again that heaven is always in touch with his world, which can never be abandoned for good to the hounding wolves of the modern era, scenting human blood and howling to the skies.

Nationalism in the West

Man's history is being shaped according to the difficulties it encounters. These have offered us problems and claimed their solutions from us, the penalty of non-fulfilment being death or degradation.

These difficulties have been different in different peoples of the earth, and in the manner of our overcoming them lies our distinction.

The Scythians of the earlier period of Asiatic history had to struggle with the scarcity of their natural resources. The easiest solution that they could think of was to organise their whole population, men, women, and children, into bands of robbers. And they were irresistible to those who were chiefly engaged in the constructive work of social co-operation.

But fortunately for man the easiest path is not his truest path. If his nature were not as complex as it is, if it were as simple as that of a pack of hungry wolves, then, by this time, those hordes of marauders would have overrun the whole earth. But man, when confronted with difficulties, has to acknowledge that he is man, that he has his responsibilities to the higher faculties of his nature, by ignoring which he may achieve success that is immediate, perhaps, but that will become a death-trap to him. For what are obstacles to the lower creatures are opportunities to the higher life of man.

To India has been given her problem from the beginning of history—it is the race problem. Races ethnologically different have in this country come into close contact. This fact has been and still continues to be the most important one is our history. It is our mission to face it and prove our humanity by dealing with it in the fullest truth. Until we fulfil our mission all other benefits will be denied us.

There are other peoples in the world who have to overcome obstacles in their physical surroundings, or the menace of their powerful neighbours. They have organised their power till they are not only reasonably free from the tyranny of Nature and human neighbours, but have a surplus of it left in their hands to employ against others. But in India, our difficulties being internal, our history has been the history of continual social adjustment and not that of organised power for defence and aggression.

Neither the colourless vagueness of cosmopolitanism, nor the fierce self-idolatry of nation-worship, is the goal of human history. And India has been trying to accomplish her task through social regulation of differences on the one hand, and the spiritual recognition of unity on the other. She has made grave errors in setting up the boundary walls too rigidly between races, in perpetuating in her classifications the results of inferiority; often she has crippled her children's minds and narrowed their lives in order to fit them into her social forms, but for centuries new experiments have been made and adjustments carried out.

Her mission has been like that of a hostess who has to provide proper accommodation for numerous guests, whose habits and requirements are different from one another. This gives rise to infinite complexities whose solution depends not merely upon tactfulness but upon sympathy and true realisation of the unity of man. Towards this realisation have worked, from the early time of the *Upanishads*[1] up to the present moment, a series of great spiritual teachers, whose one object has been to set at naught all differences of man by the overflow of our consciousness of God. In fact, our history has not been of the rise and fall of kingdoms, of fights for political supremacy. In our country records of these days have been despised and forgotten, for they in no way represent the true history of our people. Our history is that of our social life and attainment of spiritual ideals.

But we feel that our task is not yet done. The world-flood has swept over our country, new elements have been introduced, and wider adjustments are waiting to be made.

We feel this all the more because the teaching and example of the West have entirely run counter to what we think was given to India to accomplish. In the West the national machinery of commerce and politics turns out neatly compressed bales of humanity which have their use and high market value; but they are bound in iron hoops, labelled and separated off with scientific care and precision. Obviously God made man to be human, but this modern product has such marvellous square-cut finish, savouring of gigantic manufacture, that the Creator will find it difficult to recognise it as a thing of spirit and a creature made in His own divine image.

But I am anticipating. What I was about to say is this. Take it in whatever spirit you like, here is India, of about fifty centuries at least, who tried to live peacefully and think deeply, the India devoid of all politics, the India of no nations, whose one ambition has been to know this world as of soul, to live here every moment of her life in the meek spirit of adoration, in the glad consciousness of an eternal and personal relationship with it. It was upon this remote portion of

---

1. About 200 prose and verse treatises on metaphysical philosophy, dating from around 400 BC.

humanity, childlike in its manner, with the wisdom of the old, that the Nation of the West burst in.

Through all the fights and intrigues and deceptions of her earlier history India had remained aloof. Because her homes, her fields, her temples of worship, her schools, where her teachers and students lived together in the atmosphere of simplicity and devotion and learning, her village self-government with its simple laws and peaceful administration—all these truly belonged to her. But her thrones were not her concern. They passed over her head like clouds, now tinged with purple gorgeousness, now black with the threat of thunder. Often they brought devastations in their wake, but they were like catastrophes of nature whose traces are soon forgotten.

But this time it was different. It was not a mere drift over her surface of life—drift of cavalry and foot soldiers, richly caparisoned elephants, white tents and canopies, strings of patient camels bearing the loads of royalty, bands of kettle-drums and flutes, marble domes of mosques, palaces and tombs, like the bubbles of the foaming wine of extravagance; stories of treachery and loyal devotion, of changes of fortune, of dramatic surprises of fate. This time it was the Nation of the West driving its tentacles of machinery deep down into the soil.

Therefore I say to you, it is we who are called as witnesses to give evidence as to what our Nation has been to humanity. We had known the hordes of Mughals and Pathans who invaded India, but we had known them as human races, with their own religions and customs, likes and dislikes—we had never known them as a nation. We loved and hated them as the occasions arose; we fought for them and against them, talked with them in a language which was theirs as well as our own, and guided the destiny of the Empire in which we had our active share. But this time we had to deal, not with kings, not with human races, but with a nation—we, who are no nation ourselves.

Now let us, from our own experience, answer the question: what is this Nation?

A nation, in the sense of the political and economic union of a people, is that aspect which a whole population assumes when organised for a mechanical purpose. Society as such has no ulterior purpose. It is an end in itself. It is a spontaneous self-expression of man as a social being. It is a natural regulation of human relationships, so that men can develop ideals of life in co-operation with one another. It has also a political side, but this is only for a special purpose. It is for self-preservation. It is merely the side of power, not of human ideals. And in the early days it had its separate place in society, restricted to the professionals. But when with the help of science and the perfecting of organisation this power begins to grow and brings in harvests of wealth, then it crosses its boundaries with amazing rapidity. For then it goads all its neighbouring societies with greed of material prosperity, and consequent mutual jealousy, and by the fear of each other's growth into powerfulness. The time comes when it can stop no longer, for the competition grows keener, organisation grows vaster, and selfishness attains supremacy. Trading upon the greed and fear of man, it occupies more and more space in society, and at last becomes its ruling force.

It is just possible that you have lost through habit the consciousness that the living bonds of society are breaking up, and giving place to merely mechanical organisation. But one sees signs of it everywhere. It is owing to this that war has been declared between man and woman, because the natural thread is snapping which holds them together in harmony; because man is driven to professionalism, producing wealth for himself and others, continually turning the wheel of power for his own sake or for the sake of the universal officialdom, leaving woman alone to wither and to die or to fight her own battle unaided. And thus there, where co-operation is natural, has intruded competition. The very psychology of men and women about their mutual relation is changing and becoming the psychology of the primitive fighting elements, rather than of humanity seeking its completeness through the union based upon mutual self-surrender. For the elements which have lost their living bond of reality have lost the meaning of their existence. Like gaseous particles forced into a too narrow space, they come in continual conflict with each other till they burst the very arrangement which holds them in bondage.

Then look at those who call themselves anarchists, who resent the imposition of power, in any form whatever, upon the individual. The only reason for this is that power has become too abstract—it is a scientific product made in the political laboratory of the Nation, through the dissolution of personal humanity.

And what is the meaning of these strikes in the economic world, which like the prickly shrubs in a barren soil shoot up with renewed vigour each time they are cut down? What but that the wealth-producing mechanism is incessantly growing into vast stature, out of proportion to all other needs of society, and the full reality of man is more and more crushed under its weight? This state of things inevitably gives rise to eternal feuds among the elements freed from the wholeness and wholesomeness of human ideals, and interminable economic war is waged between capital and labour. For greed of wealth and power can never have a limit, and compromise of self-interest can never attain the final spirit of reconciliation. They must go on breeding jealousy and suspicion to the end— the end which only comes through some sudden catastrophe or a spiritual rebirth.

When this organisation of politics and commerce, whose other name is the Nation, becomes all-powerful at the cost of the harmony of the higher social life, then it is an evil day for humanity. When a father becomes a gambler and his obligations to his family take the secondary place in his mind, then he is no longer a man, but an automaton led by the power of greed. Then he can do things which, in his normal state of mind, he would be ashamed to do. It is the same thing with society. When it allows itself to be turned into a perfect organisation of power, then there are few crimes it is unable to perpetrate, because success is the object and justification of a machine, while goodness only is the end and purpose of man. When this engine of organisation begins to attain a vast size, and those who are mechanics are made into parts of the machine, then the personal man is eliminated to a phantom, everything becomes a revolution of policy carried out by the human parts of the machines, with no twinge of pity or moral responsibility. It may happen that even through this apparatus the moral nature of man tries to assert itself, but the whole series of ropes and pulleys creak and cry, the forces of the human heart become entangled among the forces of the human automaton, and only with difficulty can the moral purpose transmit itself into some tortured shape of result.

This abstract being, the Nation, is ruling India. We have seen in our country some brand of tinned food advertised as entirely made and packed without being touched by hand. This description applies to the governing of India, which is as little touched by the human hand as possible. The governors need not know our language, need not come into personal touch with us except as officials; they can aid or hinder our aspirations from a disdainful distance, they can lead us on a certain path of policy and then pull us back again with the manipulation of office red tape. The newspapers of England, in whose columns London street accidents are recorded with some decency of pathos, need take but the scantiest notice of calamities which happen in India over areas of land sometimes larger than the British Isles.

But we, who are governed, are not a mere abstraction. We, on our side, are individuals with living sensibilities. What comes to us in the shape of a mere bloodless policy may pierce into the very core of our life, may threaten the whole future of our people with a perpetual helplessness of emasculation, and yet may never touch the chord of humanity on the other side, or touch it in the most inadequately feeble manner. Such wholesale and universal acts of fearful responsibility man can never perform, with such a degree of systematic unawareness, where he is an individual human being. These only become possible where the man is represented by an octopus of abstractions, sending out its wriggling arms in all directions of space, and fixing its innumerable suckers even into the far-away future. In this reign of the nation, the governed are pursued by suspicions; and these are the suspicions of a tremendous mass of organised brain and muscle. Punishments are meted out which leave a trail of miseries across a large bleeding tract of the human heart, but these punishments are dealt by a mere abstract force in which a whole population of a distant country has lost its human personality.

I have not come here, however, to discuss the question as it affects my own country, but as it affects the future of all humanity. It is not a question of the British government, but of government by the Nation—the Nation which is the organised self-interest of a whole people, where it is least human and least spiritual. Our only intimate experience of the Nation is with the British Nation, and as far as the government by the Nation goes there are reasons to believe that it is one of the best. Then, again, we have to consider that the West is necessary to the East. We are complementary to each other because of our different outlooks upon life which have given us different aspects of truth. Therefore if it be true that the spirit of the West has come upon our fields in the guise of a storm it is nevertheless scattering living seeds that are immortal. And when in India we become able to assimilate in our life what is permanent in western civilisation we shall be in a position to bring about a reconciliation of these two great worlds. Then will come to an end the one-sided dominance which is galling. What is more, we have to recognise that the history of India does not belong to one particular race but to a process of creation to which various races of the world contributed—the Dravidians and the Aryans, the ancient Greeks and the Persians, the Mohammedans of the West and those of central Asia. Now at last has come the turn of the English to become true to this history and bring to it the tribute of their life, and we neither have the right nor the power to exclude this people from the building of the destiny of India. Therefore what I say about the Nation has more to do with the history of Man than specially with that of India.

This history has come to a stage when the moral man, the complete man, is more and more giving way, almost without knowing it, to make room for the political and the commercial man, the man of the limited purpose. This process, aided by the wonderful progress in science, is assuming gigantic proportion and power, causing the upset of man's moral balance, obscuring his human side under the shadow of soulless organisation. We have felt its iron grip at the root of our life, and for the sake of humanity we must stand up and give warning to all, that this nationalism is a cruel epidemic of evil that is sweeping over the human world of the present age and eating into its moral vitality.

I have a deep love and a great respect for the British race as human beings. It has produced great-hearted men, thinkers of great thoughts, doers of great deeds. It has given rise to a great literature. I know that these people love justice and freedom, and hate lies. They are clean in their minds, frank in their manners, true in their friendships; in their behaviour they are honest and reliable. The personal experience which I have had of their literary men has roused my admiration not merely for their power of thought or expression but for their chivalrous humanity. We have felt the greatness of this people as we feel the sun; but as for the Nation, it is for us a thick mist of a stifling nature covering the sun itself.

This government by the Nation is neither British nor anything else; it is an applied science and therefore more or less similar in its principles wherever it is used. It is like a hydraulic press, whose pressure is impersonal, and on that account completely effective. The amount of its power may vary in different engines. Some may even be driven by hand, thus leaving a margin of comfortable looseness in their tension, but in spirit and in method their differences are small. Our government might have been Dutch, or French, or Portuguese, and its essential features would have remained much the same as they are now. Only perhaps, in some cases, the organisation might not have been so densely perfect, and therefore some shreds of the human might still have been clinging to the wreck, allowing us to deal with something which resembles our own throbbing heart.

Before the Nation came to rule over us we had other governments which were foreign, and these, like all governments, had some element of the machine in them. But the difference between them and the government by the Nation is like the difference between the hand-loom and the power-loom. In the products of the hand-loom the magic of man's living fingers finds its expression, and its hum harmonises with the music of life. But the power-loom is relentlessly lifeless and accurate and monotonous in its production.

We must admit that during the personal government of former days there have been instances of tyranny, injustice, and extortion. They caused sufferings and unrest from which we are glad to be rescued. The protection of law is not only a boon, but it is a valuable lesson to us. It is teaching us the discipline which is necessary for the stability of civilisation and for continuity of progress. We are realising through it that there is a universal standard of justice to which all men, irrespective of their caste and colour, have their equal claim.

This reign of law in our present government in India has established order in this vast land inhabited by peoples different in their races and customs. It has made it possible for these peoples to come in closer touch with one another and cultivate a communion of aspiration.

But this desire for a common bond of comradeship among the different races of India has been the work of the spirit of the West, not that of the Nation of the West. Wherever in Asia the people have received the true lesson of the West it is in spite of the western Nation. Only because Japan had been able to resist the dominance of this western Nation could she acquire the benefit of western civilisation in fullest measure. Though China has been poisoned at the very spring of her moral and physical life by this Nation, her struggle to receive the best lessons of the West may yet be successful if not hindered by the Nation. It was only the other day that Persia woke up from her age-long sleep at the call of the West to be instantly trampled into stillness by the Nation. The same phenomenon prevails in this country also, where the people are hospitable, but the Nation has proved itself to be otherwise, making an Eastern guest feel humiliated to stand before you as a member of the humanity of his own motherland.

In India we are suffering from this conflict between the spirit of the West and the nation of the West. The benefit of western civilisation is doled out to us in a miserly measure by the nation, which tries to regulate the degree of nutrition as near the zero-point of vitality as possible. The portion of education allotted to us is so raggedly insufficient that it ought to outrage the sense of decency of western humanity. We have seen in these countries how the people are encouraged and trained and given every facility to fit themselves for the great movements of commerce and industry spreading over the world, while in India the only assistance we get is merely to be jeered at by the Nation for lagging behind. While depriving us of our opportunities and reducing our education to the minimum required for conducting a foreign government, this Nation pacifies its conscience by calling us names, by sedulously giving currency to the arrogant cynicism that the East is east and the West is west and never the twain shall meet. If we must believe our schoolmaster in his taunt that, after nearly two centuries of his tutelage, India not only remains unfit for self-government but unable to display originality in her intellectual attainments, must we ascribe it to something in the nature of western culture and our inherent incapacity to receive it or to the judicious niggardliness of the nation that has taken upon itself the white man's burden of civilising the East? That Japanese people have some qualities which we lack we may admit, but that our intellect is naturally unproductive compared to theirs we cannot accept even from them whom it is dangerous for us to contradict.

The truth is that the spirit of conflict and conquest is at the origin and in the centre of western nationalism; its basis is not social co-operation. It has evolved a perfect organisation of power, but not spiritual idealism. It is like the pack of predatory creatures that must have its victims. With all its heart it cannot bear to see its hunting-grounds converted into cultivated fields. In fact, these nations are fighting among themselves for the extension of their victims and their reserve forests. Therefore the western nation acts like a dam to check the free flow of western civilisation into the country of the No-Nation. Because this civilisation is the civilisation of power, therefore it is exclusive; it is naturally unwilling to open its sources of power to those whom it has selected for its purposes of exploitation.

But all the same, moral law is the law of humanity, and the exclusive civilisation which thrives upon others who are barred from its benefit carries its own death-sentence in its moral limitation. The slavery that it gives rise to unconsciously drains its own love of freedom dry. The helplessness with which it weighs down its world of victims exerts its force of gravitation every moment upon the power that creates it. And the greater part of the world which is being denuded of its self-sustaining life by the Nation will one day become the most terrible of all its burdens, ready to drag it down into the bottom of destruction. Whenever the Power removes all checks from its path to make its career easy, it triumphantly rides into its ultimate crash of death. Its moral brake becomes slacker every day without its knowing it, and its slippery path of ease becomes its path of doom.

Of all things in western civilisation, those which this western Nation has given us in a most generous measure are law and order. While the small feeding-bottle of our education is nearly dry, and sanitation sucks its own thumb in despair, the military organisation, the magisterial offices, the police, the Criminal Investigation Department, the secret spy system, attain to an abnormal girth in their waists, occupying every inch of our country. This is to maintain order. But is not this order merely a negative good? Is it not for giving people's life greater opportunities of the freedom of development? Its perfection is the perfection of an egg-shell, whose true value lies in the security it affords to the chick and its nourishment and not in the convenience it offers to the person at the breakfast table. Mere administration is unproductive; it is not creative, not being a living thing. It is a steam-roller, formidable in its weight and power, having its uses, but it does not help the soil to become fertile. When after its enormous toil it comes to offer us its boon of peace we can but murmur under our breath that 'peace is good, but not more than life, which is God's own great boon'.

On the other hand, our former governments were woefully lacking in many of the advantages of the modern government. But because those were not the governments by the Nation, their texture was loosely woven, leaving big gaps through which our own life sent its threads and imposed its designs. I am quite sure in those days we had things that were extremely distasteful to us. But we know that when we walk barefooted upon ground strewn with gravel, our feet come gradually to adjust themselves to the caprices of the inhospitable earth; while if the tiniest particle of gravel finds its lodgement inside our shoes we can never forget and forgive its intrusion. And these shoes are the government by the Nation—it is tight, it regulates our steps with a closed-up system, within which our feet have only the slightest liberty to make their own adjustments. Therefore, when you produce your statistics to compare the number of gravels which our feet had to encounter in former days with the paucity in the present regime, they hardly touch the real point. It is not a question of the number of outside obstacles but the comparative powerlessness of the individual to cope with them. This narrowness of freedom is an evil which is more radical, not because of its quantity but because of its nature. And we cannot but acknowledge this paradox: that while the spirit of the West marches under its banner of freedom, the nation of the West forges its iron chains of organisation which are the most relentless and unbreakable that have ever been manufactured in the whole history of man.

When the humanity of India was not under the government of the Organisation, the elasticity of change was great enough to encourage men of power and spirit to feel that they had their destinies in their own hands. The hope of the unexpected was never absent, and a freer play of imagination, on the part of both the governor and the governed, had its effect in the making of history. We were not confronted with a future, which was a dead white wall of granite blocks eternally guarding against the expression and extension of our own powers, the hopelessness of which lies in the reason that these powers are becoming atrophied at their very roots by the scientific process of paralysis. For every single individual in the country of the No-Nation is completely in the grip of a whole nation, whose tireless vigilance, being the vigilance of a machine, has not the human power to overlook or to discriminate. At the least pressing of its button the monster organisation becomes all eyes, whose ugly stare of inquisitiveness cannot be avoided by a single person amongst the immense multitude of the ruled. At the least turn of its screw, by the fraction of an inch, the grip is tightened to the point of suffocation around every man, woman and child of a vast population, for whom no escape is imaginable in their own country or even in any country outside their own.

It is the continual and stupendous dead pressure of the inhuman upon the living human under which the modern world is groaning. Not merely the subject races, but you who live under the delusion that you are free, are every day sacrificing your freedom and humanity to this fetish of nationalism, living in the dense poisonous atmosphere of world-wide suspicion and greed and panic.

I have seen in Japan the voluntary submission of the whole people to the trimming of their minds and clipping of their freedom by their government, which through various educational agencies regulates their thoughts, manufactures their feelings, becomes suspiciously watchful when they show signs of inclining towards the spiritual, leading them through a narrow path not towards what is true but what is necessary for the complete welding of them into one uniform mass according to its own recipe. The people accept this all pervading mental slavery with cheerfulness and pride because of their nervous desire to turn themselves into a machine of power, called the Nation, and emulate other machines in their collective worldliness.

When questioned as to the wisdom of its course, the newly converted fanatic of nationalism answers that 'so long as nations are rampant in this world we have not the option freely to develop our higher humanity. We must utilise every faculty that we possess to resist the evil by assuming it ourselves in the fullest degree. For the only brotherhood possible in the modern world is the brotherhood of hooliganism.' The recognition of the fraternal bond of love between Japan and Russia, which has lately been celebrated with an immense display of rejoicing in Japan, was not owing to any sudden recrudescence of the spirit of Christianity or of Buddhism, but it was a bond established according to the modern faith in a surer relationship of mutual menace of bloodshedding. Yes, one cannot but acknowledge that these facts are the facts of the world of the nation, and the only moral of it is that all the peoples of the earth should strain their physical, moral and intellectual resources to the utmost to defeat one another in the wrestling match of powerfulness. In ancient days Sparta paid all her attention to becoming powerful; she did become so by crippling her humanity, and died of the amputation.

But it is no consolation to us to know that the weakening of humanity from which the present age is suffering is not limited to the subject races, and that its ravages are even more radical because insidious and voluntary in peoples who are hypnotised into believing that they are free. This bartering of your higher aspirations of life for profit and power has been your own free choice, and I leave you there, at the wreckage of your soul, contemplating your protuberant prosperity. But will you never be called to answer for organising the instincts of self-aggrandisement of whole peoples into perfection and calling it good? I ask you: what disaster has there ever been in the history of man, in its darkest period, like this terrible disaster of the Nation fixing its fangs deep into the naked flesh of the world, taking permanent precautions against its natural relaxation?

You, the people of the West, who have manufactured this abnormality, can you imagine the desolating despair of this haunted world of suffering man possessed by the ghastly abstraction of the organising man? Can you put yourself into the position of the peoples, who seem to have been doomed to an eternal damnation of their own humanity, who not only must suffer continual curtailment of their manhood, but even raise their voices in paeans of praise for the benignity of a mechanical apparatus in its interminable parody of providence?

Have you not seen, since the commencement of the existence of the Nation, that the dread of it has been the one goblin-dread with which the whole world has been trembling? Wherever there is a dark corner, there is the suspicion of its secret malevolence; and people live in a perpetual distrust of their back where they have no eyes. Every sound of a footstep, every rustle of movement in the neighbourhood, sends a thrill of terror all around. And this terror is the parent of all that is base in man's nature. It makes one almost openly unashamed of inhumanity. Clever lies become matters of self-congratulation. Solemn pledges become a farce—laughable for their very solemnity. The Nation, with all its paraphernalia of power and prosperity, its flags and pious hymns, its blasphemous prayers in the churches, and the literary mock thunders of its patriotic bragging, cannot hide the fact that the Nation is the greatest evil for the Nation, that all its precautions are against it, and any new birth of its fellow in the world is always followed in its mind by the dread of a new peril. Its one wish is to trade on the feebleness of the rest of the world, like some insects that are bred in the paralysed flesh of victims kept just enough alive to make them toothsome and nutritious. Therefore it is ready to send its poisonous fluid into the vitals of the other living peoples who, not being nations, are harmless. For this the Nation has had and still has its richest pasture in Asia. Great China, rich with her ancient wisdom and social ethics, her discipline of industry and self-control, is like a whale awakening the lust of spoil in the heart of the Nation. She is already carrying in her quivering flesh harpoons sent by the unerring aim of the Nation, the creature of science and selfishness. Her pitiful attempt to shake off her traditions of humanity, her social ideals, and spend her last exhausted resources in drilling herself into modern efficiency, is thwarted at every step by the Nation. It is tightening its financial ropes round her, trying to drag her up on the shore and cut her into pieces, and then go and offer public thanksgiving to God for supporting the one existing evil and shattering the possibility of a new one. And for all this the Nation has been claiming the gratitude of history and all eternity for its exploitation, ordering its band of praise to be struck up from end to end of the world, declaring itself to be the salt of the earth, the flower of humanity, the blessing of God hurled with all His force upon the naked skulls of the world of No-Nations.

I know what your advice will be. You will say: form yourselves into a nation, and resist this encroachment of the Nation. But is this the true advice, that of a man to a man? Why should this be a necessity? I could well believe you if you had said: be more good, more just, more true in your relation to man; control your greed, make your life wholesome in its simplicity and let your consciousness of the divine in humanity be more perfect in its expression. But must you say that it is not the soul, but the machine, which is of the utmost value to ourselves, and that man's salvation depends upon his disciplining himself into a perfection of the dead rhythm of wheels and counterwheels, that machine must be pitted against machine, and nation against nation, in an endless bull-fight of politics?

You say: these machines will come into an agreement for their mutual protection, based upon a conspiracy of fear. But will this federation of steam-boilers supply you with a soul, a soul which has her conscience and her God? What is to happen to that larger part of the world where fear will have no hand in restraining you? Whatever safety they now enjoy, those countries of No-Nation, from the unbridled licence of forge and hammer and turn-screw, results from the mutual jealousy of the powers. But when, instead of being numerous separate machines they become riveted into one organised gregariousness of gluttony, commercial and political, what remotest chance of hope will remain for those others, who have lived and suffered, have loved and worshipped, have thought deeply and worked with meekness, but whose only crime has been that they have not organised?

But, you say, 'That does not matter, the unfit must go to the wall—they shall die, and this is science.'

No, for the sake of your own salvation, I say, they shall *live*, and this is truth. It is extremely bold of me to say so, but I assert that man's world is a moral world, not because we blindly agree to believe it, but because it is so in truth which would be dangerous for us to ignore. And this moral nature of man cannot be divided into convenient compartments for its preservation. You cannot secure it for your home consumption with protective tariff walls, while in foreign parts making it enormously accommodating in its free trade of licence.

Has not this truth already come home to you now, when this cruel war has driven its claws into the vitals of Europe, when her hoard of wealth is bursting into smoke and her humanity is shattered into bits on her battlefields? You ask in amazement: what has she done to deserve this? The answer is that the West has been systematically petrifying her moral nature in order to lay a solid foundation for her gigantic abstractions of efficiency. She has all along been starving the life of the personal man into that of the professional.

In your mediaeval age in Europe, the simple and the natural man, with all his violent passions and desires, was engaged in trying to find out a reconciliation in the conflict between the flesh and the spirit. All through the turbulent career of her vigorous youth the temporal and the spiritual forces both acted strongly upon her nature, and were moulding it into completeness of moral personality. Europe owes all her greatness in humanity to that period of discipline—the discipline of the man in his human integrity.

Then came the age of intellect, of science. We all know that intellect is impersonal. Our life and our heart are one with us, but our mind can be detached from the personal man and then only can it freely move in its world of thoughts. Our intellect is an ascetic who wears no clothes, takes no food, knows no sleep, has no wishes, feels no love or hatred or pity for human limitations, who only reasons unmoved through the vicissitudes of life. It burrows to the roots of things, because it has no personal concern with the thing itself. The grammarian walks straight through all poetry and goes to the root of words without obstruction, because he is seeking not reality, but law. When he finds the law, he is able to teach people how to master words. This is a power—the power which fulfils some special usefulness, some particular need of man.

Reality is the harmony which gives to the component parts of a thing the equilibrium of the whole. You break it, and have in your hands the nomadic atoms fighting against one another, therefore unmeaning. Those who covet power try to get mastery of these aboriginal fighting elements, and through some narrow channels force them into some violent service for some particular needs of man.

This satisfaction of man's needs is a great thing. It gives him freedom in the material world. It confers on him the benefit of a greater range of time and space. He can do things in a shorter time and occupies a larger space with more thoroughness of advantage. Therefore he can easily outstrip those who live in a world of a slower time and of space less fully occupied.

This progress of power attains more and more rapidity of pace. And, for the reason that it is a detached part of man, it soon outruns the complete humanity. The moral man remains behind, because it has to deal with the whole reality, not merely with the law of things, which is impersonal and therefore abstract.

Thus man, with his mental and material power far outgrowing his moral strength, is like an exaggerated giraffe whose head has suddenly shot up miles away from the rest of him, making normal communication difficult to establish. This greedy head, with its huge dental organisation, has been munching all the topmost foliage of the world, but the nourishment is too late in reaching his digestive organs, and his heart is suffering from want of blood. Of this present disharmony in man's nature the West seems to have been blissfully unconscious. The enormity of its material success has diverted all its attention towards self-congratulation on its bulk. The optimism of its logic goes on basing the calculations of its good fortune upon the indefinite prolongation of its railway lines towards eternity. It is superficial enough to think that all tomorrows are merely todays, with the repeated additions of twenty-four hours. It has no fear of the chasm, which is opening wider every day, between man's ever growing storehouses and the emptiness of his hungry humanity. Logic does not know that, under the lowest bed of endless strata of wealth and comforts, earthquakes are being hatched to restore the balance of the moral world; and one day the gaping gulf of spiritual vacuity will draw into its bottom the store of things that have their eternal love for the dust.

Man in his fulness is not powerful, but perfect. Therefore, to turn him into mere power, you have to curtail his soul as much as possible. When we are fully human, we cannot fly at one another's throats; our instincts of social life, our traditions of moral ideals stand in the way. If you want me to take to butchering human beings, you must break up that wholeness of my humanity through some discipline which makes my will dead, my thoughts numb, my movements automatic, and then from the dissolution of the complex personal man will come out that abstraction, that destructive force, which has no relation to human truth, and therefore can be easily brutal or mechanical. Take away man from his natural surroundings, from the fulness of his communal life, with all its living associations of beauty and love and social obligations, and you will be able to turn him into so many fragments of a machine for the production of wealth on a gigantic scale. Turn a tree into a log and it will burn for you, but it will never bear living flowers and fruit.

This process of dehumanising has been going on in commerce and politics. And out of the long birth-throes of mechanical energy has been born this fully developed apparatus of magnificent power and surprising appetite which has been christened in the West as the Nation. As I have hinted before, because of its quality of abstraction it has, with the greatest ease, gone far ahead of the complete moral man. And having the conscience of a ghost and the callous perfection of an automaton, it is causing disasters with which the volcanic dissipations of the youthful moon would be ashamed to be brought into comparison. As a result, the suspicion of man for man stings all the limbs of this civilisation like the hairs of the nettle. Each country is casting its net of espionage into the slimy bottom of the others, fishing for their secrets, the treacherous secrets which brew in the oozy depths of diplomacy. And what is their secret service but the nation's underground trade in kidnapping, murder and treachery and all the ugly crimes bred in the depth of rottenness? Because each nation has its own history of thieving and lies and broken faith, therefore there can only flourish international suspicion and jealousy, and international moral shame becomes anaemic to a degree of ludicrousness. The nation's bagpipe of righteous indignation has so changed its tune according to the variation of time and to the altered groupings of the alliances of diplomacy, that it can be enjoyed with amusement as the variety performance of the political music hall.

I am just coming from my visit to Japan, where I exhorted this young nation to take its stand upon the higher ideals of humanity and never to follow the West in its acceptance of the organised selfishness of Nationalism as its religion, never to gloat upon the feebleness of its neighbours, never to be unscrupulous in its behaviour to the weak, where it can be gloriously mean with impunity, while turning its right cheek of brighter humanity for the kiss of admiration to those who have the power to deal it a blow. Some of the newspapers praised my utterances for their poetical qualities, while adding with a leer that it was the poetry of a defeated people. I felt they were right. Japan had been taught in a modern school the lesson how to become powerful. The schooling is done and she must enjoy the fruits of her lessons. The West in the voice of her thundering cannon had said at the door of Japan: let there be a nation—and there was a Nation. And now that it *has* come into existence, why do you not feel in your heart of hearts a pure feeling of gladness and say that it is good? Why is it that I saw in an English paper an expression of bitterness at Japan's boasting of her superiority of civilisation—the thing that the British, along with other nations, have been carrying on for ages without blushing? Because the idealism of selfishness must keep itself drunk with a continual dose of self-laudation. But the same vices which seem so natural and innocuous in its own life make it surprised and angry at their unpleasantness when seen in other nations. Therefore, when you see the Japanese nation, created in your own image, launched in its career of national boastfulness, you shake your head and say, it is not good. Has it not been one of the causes that raise the cry on these shores for preparedness to meet one more power of evil with a greater power of injury? Japan protests that she has her *bushido*, that she can never be treacherous to America to whom she owes her gratitude. But you find it difficult to believe her—for the wisdom of the Nation is not in its faith in humanity but in its complete distrust. You say to yourself that it is not with Japan of the *bushido*, the Japan of the moral ideals, that you have to deal—it is with the abstraction of the popular selfishness, it is with the Nation; and Nation can only trust Nation where their interests coalesce, or at least do not conflict. In fact your instinct tells you that the advent of another people into the arena of nationality makes another addition to the evil which contradicts all that is highest in Man and proves by its success that unscrupulousness is the way to prosperity—and goodness is good for the weak and God is the only remaining consolation of the defeated.

Yes, this is the logic of the Nation. And it will never heed the voice of truth and goodness. It will go on its ring-dance of moral corruption, linking steel unto steel, and machine unto machine, trampling under its tread all the sweet flowers of simple faith and the living ideals of man.

But we delude ourselves into thinking that humanity in these modern days is more to the front than ever before. The reason for this self-delusion is because man is served with the necessaries of life in greater profusion and his physical ills are being alleviated with more efficacy. But the chief part of this is done, not by moral sacrifice, but by intellectual power. In quantity it is great, but it springs from the surface and spreads over the surface. Knowledge and efficiency are powerful in their outward effect, but they are the servants of man, not the man himself. Their service is like the service in a hotel, where it is elaborate, but the host is absent; it is more convenient than hospitable.

Therefore we must not forget that the scientific organisations vastly spreading in all directions are strengthening our power, but not our humanity. With the growth of power the cult of the self-worship of the Nation grows in ascendancy, and the individual willingly allows the Nation to take donkey-rides upon his back; and there happens the anomaly which must have such disastrous effects, that the individual worships with all sacrifices a god which is morally much inferior to himself. This could never have been possible if the god had been as real as the individual.

Let me give an illustration of this point. In some parts of India it has been enjoined as an act of great piety for a widow to go without food and water on a particular day every fortnight. This often leads to cruelty, unmeaning and inhuman. And yet men are not by nature cruel to such a degree. But this piety being a mere unreal abstraction completely deadens the moral sense of the individual, just as the man who would not hurt an animal unnecessarily would cause horrible suffering to a large number of innocent creatures when he drugs his feelings with the abstract idea of 'sport'! Because these ideas are creations of our intellect, because they are logical classifications, therefore they can so easily hide in their mist the personal man.

And the idea of the nation is one of the most powerful anaesthetics that man has invented. Under the influence of its fumes the whole people can carry out its systematic programme of the most virulent self-seeking without being in the least aware of its moral perversion—in fact can feel dangerously resentful if it is pointed out.

But can this go on indefinitely, continually producing barrenness of moral insensibility upon a large tract of our living nature? Can it escape its nemesis for ever? Has this giant power of mechanical organisation no limit in this world against which it may shatter itself all the more completely because of its terrible strength and velocity? Do you believe that evil can be permanently kept in check by competition with evil, and that conference of prudence can keep the devil chained in its makeshift cage of mutual agreement?

This European war of Nations is the war of retribution. Man, the person, must protest for his very life against the heaping up of things where there should be the heart, and systems and policies where there should flow living human relationship. The time has come when, for the sake of the whole outraged world, Europe should fully know in her own person the terrible absurdity of the thing called the Nation.

The Nation has thriven long upon mutilated humanity. Men, the fairest creations of God, came out of the National manufactory in huge numbers as war-making and money-making puppets, ludicrously vain of their pitiful perfection of mechanism. Human society grew more and more into a marionette show of politicians, soldiers, manufacturers and bureaucrats, pulled by wire arrangements of wonderful efficiency.

But the apotheosis of selfishness can never make its interminable breed of hatred and greed, fear and hypocrisy, suspicion and tyranny, an end in themselves. These monsters grow into huge shapes but never into harmony. And this Nation may grow on to an unimaginable corpulence, not of a living body, but of steel and steam and office buildings, till its deformity can contain no longer its ugly voluminousness—till it begins to crack and gape, breathe gas and fire in gasps, and its death-rattles sound in cannon roars. In this war the death-throes of the Nation have commenced. Suddenly, all its mechanism going mad, it has begun the dance of the Furies, shattering its own limbs, scattering them into the dust. It is the fifth act of the tragedy of the unreal.

Those who have any faith in Man cannot but fervently hope that the tyranny of the Nation will not be restored to all its former teeth and claws, to its far-reaching iron arms and its immense inner cavity, all stomach and no heart; that man will have his new birth, in the freedom of his individuality, from the enveloping vagueness of abstraction.

The veil has been raised, and in this frightful war the West has stood face to face with her own creation to which she had offered her soul. She must know what it truly is.

She had never let herself suspect what slow decay and decomposition were secretly going on in her moral nature, which often broke out in doctrines of scepticism, but still oftener and in still more dangerously subtle manner showed itself in her unconsciousness of the mutilation and insult that she had been inflicting upon a vast part of the world. Now she must know the truth nearer home.

And then there will come from her own children those who will break themselves free from the slavery of this illusion, this perversion of brotherhood founded upon self-seeking, those who will own themselves as God's children and as no bond-slaves of machinery, which turns souls into commodities and life into compartments, which, with its iron claws, scratches out the heart of the world and knows not what it has done.

And we of the No-Nations of the world, whose heads have been bowed to the dust, will know that this dust is more sacred than the bricks which build the pride of power. For this dust is fertile of life, and of beauty and worship. We shall thank God that we were made to wait in silence through the night of despair, had to bear the insult of the proud and the strong man's burden, yet all through it, though our hearts quaked with doubt and fear, never could we blindly believe in the salvation which machinery offered to man, but we held fast to our trust in God and the truth of the human soul. And we can still cherish the hope that, when power becomes ashamed to occupy its throne and is ready to make way for love, when the morning comes for cleansing the blood-stained steps of the Nation along the highroad of humanity, we shall be called upon to bring our own vessel of sacred water—the water of worship—to sweeten the history of man into purity, and with its sprinkling make the trampled dust of the centuries blessed with fruitfulness.

Nationalism in India

Our real problem in India is not political. It is social. This is a condition not only prevailing in India, but among all nations. I do not believe in an exclusive political interest. Politics in the West have dominated western ideals, and we in India are trying to imitate you. We have to remember that in Europe, where peoples had their racial unity from the beginning, and where natural resources were insufficient for the inhabitants, the civilisation has naturally taken on the character of political and commercial aggressiveness. For on the one hand they had no internal complications, and on the other they had to deal with neighbours who were strong and rapacious. To have perfect combination among themselves and a watchful attitude of animosity against others was taken as the solution of their problems. In former days they organised and plundered; in the present age the same spirit continues—and they organise and exploit the whole world.

But from the earliest beginnings of history India has had her own problem constantly before her—it is the race problem. Each nation must be conscious of its mission, and we in India must realise that we cut a poor figure when we try to be political, simply because we have not yet been finally able to accomplish what was set before us by our providence.

This problem of race unity which we have been trying to solve for so many years has likewise to be faced by you here in America. Many people in this country ask me what is happening to the caste distinctions in India. But when this question is asked me, it is usually done with a superior air. And I feel tempted to put the same question to our American critics with a slight modification: 'What have you done with the Red Indian and the Negro?' For you have not got over your attitude of caste towards them. You have used violent methods to keep aloof from other races, but until you have solved the question, here in America, you have no right to question India.

In spite of our great difficulty, however, India has done something. She has tried to make an adjustment of races, to acknowledge the real differences between them where these exist, and yet seek for some basis of unity. This basis has come through our saints, like Nanak, Kabir, Chaitanya[1] and others, preaching one God to all races of India.

In finding the solution of our problem we shall have helped to solve the world problem as well. What India has been, the whole world is now. The whole world is becoming one country through scientific facility. And the moment is arriving when you must also find a basis of unity which is not political. If India can offer to the world her solution, it will be a contribution to humanity. There is only one history— the history of man. All national histories are merely chapters in the larger one. And we are content in India to suffer for such a great cause.

Each individual has his self-love. Therefore his brute instinct leads him to fight with others in the sole pursuit of his self-interest. But man has also his higher instincts of sympathy

---

1. Nanak (1469-1533), Kabir (1440-1518),
   Chaitanya (1485-1533).

and mutual help. The people who are lacking in this higher moral power and who therefore cannot combine in fellowship with one another must perish or live in a state of degradation. Only those peoples have survived and achieved civilisation who have this spirit of co-operation strong in them. So we find that from the beginning of history men had to choose between fighting with one another and combining, between serving their own interest or the common interest of all.

In our early history, when the geographical limits of each country and also the facilities of communication were small, this problem was comparatively small in dimension. It was sufficient for men to develop their sense of unity within their area of segregation. In those days they combined among themselves and fought against others. But it was this moral spirit of combination which was the true basis of their greatness, and this fostered their art, science and religion. At that early time the most important fact that man had to take count of was the fact of the members of one particular race of men coming in close contact with one another. Those who truly grasped this fact through their higher nature made their mark in history.

The most important fact of the present age is that all the different races of men have come close together. And again we are confronted with two alternatives. The problem is whether the different groups of peoples shall go on fighting with one another or find out some true basis of reconciliation and mutual help; whether it will be interminable competition or co-operation.

I have no hesitation in saying that those who are gifted with the moral power of love and vision of spiritual unity, who have the least feeling of enmity against aliens, and the sympathetic insight to place themselves in the position of others, will be the fittest to take their permanent place in the age that is lying before us, and those who are constantly developing their instincts for fight and intolerance of aliens will be eliminated. For this is the problem before us, and we have to prove our humanity by solving it through the help of our higher nature. The gigantic organisations for hurting others and warding off their blows, for making money by dragging others back, will not help us. On the contrary, by their crushing weight, their enormous cost and their deadening effect upon living humanity, they will seriously impede our freedom in the larger life of a higher civilisation.

During the evolution of the Nation the moral culture of brotherhood was limited by geographical boundaries, because at that time those boundaries were true. Now they have become imaginary lines of tradition divested of the qualities of real obstacles. So the time has come when man's moral nature must deal with this great fact with all seriousness or perish. The first impulse of this change of circumstance has been the churning up of man's baser passions of greed and cruel hatred. If this persists indefinitely, and armaments go on exaggerating themselves to unimaginable absurdities, and machines and storehouses envelop this fair earth with their dirt and smoke and ugliness, then it will end in a conflagration of suicide. Therefore man will have to exert all his power of love and clarity of vision to make another great moral adjustment which will comprehend the whole world of men and not merely the fractional groups of nationality. The call has come to every individual in the present age to prepare himself and his surroundings for this dawn of a new era, when man shall discover his soul in the spiritual unity of all human beings.

If it is given at all to the West to struggle out of these tangles of the lower slopes to the spiritual summit of humanity then I cannot but think that it is the special mission of America to fulfil this hope of God and man. You are the country of expectation, desiring something else than what is. Europe has her subtle habits of mind and her conventions. But America, as yet, has come to no conclusions. I realise how much America is untrammelled by the traditions of the past, and I can appreciate that experimentalism is a sign of America's youth. The foundation of her glory is in the future, rather than in the past, and if one is gifted with the power of clairvoyance, one will be able to love the America that is to be.

America is destined to justify western civilisation to the East. Europe has lost faith in humanity, and has become distrustful and sickly. America, on the other hand, is not pessimistic or blasé. You know, as a people, that there is such a thing as a better and a best, and that knowledge drives you on. There are habits that are not merely passive but aggressively arrogant. They are not like mere walls, but are like hedges of stinging nettles. Europe has been cultivating these hedges of habits for long years, till they have grown round her dense and strong and high. The pride of her traditions has sent its roots deep into her heart. I do not wish to contend that it is unreasonable. But pride in every form breeds blindness at the end. Like all artificial stimulants its first effect is a heightening of consciousness, and then with the increasing dosage it muddles it and brings an exultation that is misleading. Europe has gradually grown hardened in her pride in all her outer and inner habits. She not only cannot forget that she is western, but she takes every opportunity to hurl this fact against others to humiliate them. This is why she is growing incapable of imparting to the East what is best in herself, and of accepting in a right spirit the wisdom that the East has stored for centuries.

In America national habits and traditions have not had time to spread their clutching roots round your hearts. You have constantly felt and complained of your disadvantages when you compared your nomadic restlessness with the settled traditions of Europe—the Europe which can show her picture of greatness to the best advantage because she can fix it against the background of the past. But in this present age of transition, when a new era of civilisation is sending its trumpet-call to all peoples of the world across an unlimited future, this very freedom of detachment will enable you to accept its invitation and to achieve the goal for which Europe began her journey but lost herself mid-way. For she was tempted out of her path by her pride of power and greed of possession.

Not merely your freedom from habits of mind in individuals, but also the freedom of your history from all unclean entanglements, fits you in your career of holding the banner of civilisation of the future. All the great nations of Europe have their victims in other parts of the world. This not only deadens their moral sympathy but also their intellectual sympathy, which is so necessary for the understanding of races which are different from one's own. Englishmen can never truly understand India, because their minds are not disinterested with regard to that country. If you compare England with Germany or France you will find she has produced the smallest number of scholars who have studied Indian literature and philosophy with any amount of sympathetic insight or thoroughness. This attitude of apathy and contempt is natural where the relationship is abnormal and founded upon national selfishness and pride. But your history has been disinterested, and that is why you have been able to help Japan in her lessons in western civilisation, and that is why China can look upon you with the best confidence in this, her darkest period of danger. In fact you are carrying all the responsibility of a great future because you are untrammelled by the grasping miserliness of a past. Therefore, of all countries of the earth, America has to be fully conscious of this future; her vision must not be obscured and her faith in humanity must be strong with the strength of youth.

A parallelism exists between America and India—the parallelism of welding together into one body various races.

In my country we have been seeking to find out something common to all races, which will prove their real unity. No nation looking for a mere political or commercial basis of unity will find such a solution sufficient. Men of thought and power will discover the spiritual unity, will realise it, and preach it.

India has never had a real sense of nationalism. Even though from childhood I had been taught that idolatry of the Nation is almost better than reverence for God and humanity, I believe I have outgrown that teaching, and it is my conviction that my countrymen will truly gain their India by fighting against the education which teaches them that a country is greater than the ideals of humanity.

The educated Indian at present is trying to absorb some lessons from history contrary to the lessons of our ancestors. The East, in fact, is attempting to take unto itself a history, which is not the outcome of its own living. Japan, for example, thinks she is getting powerful through adopting western methods but, after she has exhausted her inheritance, only the borrowed weapons of civilisation will remain to her. She will not have developed herself from within.

Europe has her past. Europe's strength therefore lies in her history. We in India must make up our minds that we cannot borrow other people's history, and that if we stifle our own we are committing suicide. When you borrow things that do not belong to your life, they only serve to crush your life.

And therefore I believe that it does India no good to compete with western civilisation in its own field. But we shall be more than compensated if, in spite of the insults heaped upon us, we follow our own destiny.

There are lessons which impart information or train our minds for intellectual pursuits. These are simple and can be acquired and used with advantage. But there are others which affect our deeper nature and change our direction of life. Before we accept them and pay their value by selling our own inheritance, we must pause and think deeply. In man's history there come ages of fireworks which dazzle us by their force and movement. They laugh not only at our modest household lamps but also at the eternal stars. But let us not for that provocation be precipitate in our desire to dismiss our lamps. Let us patiently bear our present insult and realise that these fireworks have splendour but not permanence, because of the extreme explosiveness which is the cause of their power, and also of their exhaustion. They are spending a fatal quantity of energy and substance compared to their gain and production.

Anyhow, our ideals have been evolved through our own history, and even if we wished we could only make poor fireworks of them because their materials are different from yours, as is also their moral purpose. If we cherish the desire of paying our all to buy a political nationality it will be as absurd as if Switzerland had staked her existence on her ambition to build up a navy powerful enough to compete with that of England. The mistake that we make is in thinking that man's channel of greatness is only one—the one which has made itself painfully evident for the time being by its depth of insolence.

We must know for certain that there is a future before us and that future is waiting for those who are rich in moral ideals and not in mere things. And it is the privilege of man to work for fruits that are beyond his immediate reach, and to adjust his life not in slavish conformity to the examples of some present success or even to his own prudent past, limited in its aspiration, but to an infinite future bearing in its heart the ideals of our highest expectations.

We must recognise that it is providential that the West has come to India. And yet someone must show the East to the

West, and convince the West that the East has her contribution to make to the history of civilisation. India is no beggar of the West. And yet even though the West may think she is, I am not for thrusting off western civilisation and becoming segregated in our independence. Let us have a deep association. If Providence wants England to be the channel of that communication, of that deeper association, I am willing to accept it with all humility. I have great faith in human nature, and I think the West will find its true mission. I speak bitterly of western civilisation when I am conscious that it is betraying its trust and thwarting its own purpose. The West must not make herself a curse to the world by using her power for her own selfish needs but, by teaching the ignorant and helping the weak, she should save herself from the worst danger that the strong is liable to incur by making the feeble acquire power enough to resist her intrusion. And also she must not make her materialism to be the final thing, but must realise that she is doing a service in freeing the spiritual being from the tyranny of matter.

I am not against one nation in particular, but against the general idea of all nations. What is the Nation?

It is the aspect of a whole people as an organised power. This organisation incessantly keeps up the insistence of the population on becoming strong and efficient. But this strenuous effort after strength and efficiency drains man's energy from his higher nature where he is self-sacrificing and creative. For thereby man's power of sacrifice is diverted from his ultimate object, which is moral, to the maintenance of this organisation, which is mechanical. Yet in this he feels all the satisfaction of moral exaltation and therefore becomes supremely dangerous to humanity. He feels relieved of the urging of his conscience when he can transfer his responsibility to this machine which is the creation of his intellect and not of his complete moral personality. By this device the people who love freedom perpetuate slavery in a large portion of the world with the comfortable feeling of pride in having done its duty; men who are naturally just can be cruelly unjust both in their act and their thought, accompanied by a feeling that they are helping the world to receive its deserts; men who are honest can blindly go on robbing others of their human rights for self-aggrandisement, all the while abusing the deprived for not deserving better treatment. We have seen in our everyday life even small organisations of business and profession produce callousness of feeling in men who are not naturally bad, and we can well imagine what a moral havoc it is causing in a world where whole peoples are furiously organising themselves for gaining wealth and power.

Nationalism is a great menace. It is the particular thing which for years has been at the bottom of India's troubles. And inasmuch as we have been ruled and dominated by a nation that is strictly political in its attitude, we have tried to develop within ourselves, despite our inheritance from the past, a belief in our eventual political destiny.

There are different parties in India, with different ideals. Some are struggling for political independence. Others think that the time has not arrived for that, and yet believe that India should have the rights that the English colonies have. They wish to gain autonomy as far as possible.

In the beginning of the history of political agitation in India there was not the conflict between parties which there is today. At that time there was a party known as the Indian Congress;[2] they had no real programme. They had a few grievances for redress by the authorities. They wanted larger representation in the Council House, and more freedom in Municipal Government. They wanted scraps of things, but they had no constructive ideal. Therefore I was lacking in

---

2. The Indian National Congress was founded in 1885.

enthusiasm for their methods. It was my conviction that what India most needed was constructive work coming from within herself. In this work we must take all risks and go on doing the duties which by right are ours, though in the teeth of persecution, winning moral victory at every step, by our failure and suffering. We must show those who are over us that we have in ourselves the strength of moral power, the power to suffer for truth. Where we have nothing to show, we have only to beg. It would be mischievous if the gifts we wish for were granted to us at once, and I have told my countrymen, time and again, to combine for the work of creating opportunities to give vent to our spirit of self-sacrifice, and not for the purpose of begging.

The party, however, lost power because the people soon came to realise how futile was the half policy adopted by them. The party split,[3] and there arrived the Extremists, who advocated independence of action, and discarded the begging method—the easiest method of relieving one's mind from his responsibility towards his country. Their ideals were based on western history. They had no sympathy with the special problems of India. They did not recognise the patent fact that there were causes in our social organisation which made the Indian incapable of coping with the alien. What should we do if, for any reason, England was driven away? We should simply be victims for other nations. The same social weaknesses would prevail. The thing we in India have to think of is this: to remove those social customs and ideals which have generated a want of self-respect and a complete dependence on those above us—a state of affairs which has been brought about entirely by the domination in India of the caste system, and the blind and lazy habit of relying upon

---

3. In 1907, at the annual session of the Indian National Congress, held at Surat.

the authority of traditions that are incongruous anachronisms in the present age.

Once again I draw your attention to the difficulties India has had to encounter and her struggle to overcome them. Her problem was the problem of the world in miniature. India is too vast in its area and too diverse in its races. It is many countries packed in one geographical receptacle. It is just the opposite of what Europe truly is; namely, one country made into many. Thus Europe in its culture and growth has had the advantage of the strength of the many as well as the strength of the one. India, on the contrary, being naturally many, yet adventitiously one, has all along suffered from the looseness of its diversity and the feebleness of its unity. A true unity is like a round globe; it rolls on, carrying its burden easily. But diversity is a many-cornered thing which has to be dragged and pushed with all force. Be it said to the credit of India that this diversity was not her own creation; she has had to accept it as a fact from the beginning of her history. In America and Australia, Europe has simplified her problem by almost exterminating the original population. Even in the present age this spirit of extermination is making itself manifest, in the inhospitable shutting out of aliens, by those who themselves were aliens in the lands they now occupy. But India tolerated difference of races from the first, and that spirit of toleration has acted all through her history.

Her caste system is the outcome of this spirit of toleration. For India has all along been trying experiments in evolving a social unity within which all the different peoples could be held together, while fully enjoying the freedom of maintaining their own differences. The tie has been as loose as possible, yet as close as the circumstances permitted. This has produced something like a United States of a social federation, whose common name is Hinduism.

India had felt that diversity of races there must be and should be, whatever may be its drawbacks, and you can never coerce nature into your narrow limits of convenience without paying one day very dearly for it. In this India was right; but what she failed to realise was that in human beings differences are not like the physical barriers of mountains, fixed for ever—they are fluid with life's flow, they are changing their courses and their shapes and volumes.

Therefore in her caste regulations India recognised differences, but not the mutability which is the law of life. In trying to avoid collisions she set up boundaries of immovable walls, thus giving to her numerous races the negative benefit of peace and order but not the positive opportunity of expansion and movement. She accepted nature where it produces diversity, but ignored it where it uses that diversity for its world-game of infinite permutations and combinations. She treated life in all truth where it is manifold, but insulted it where it is ever moving. Therefore Life departed from her social system and in its place she is worshipping with all ceremony the magnificent cage of countless compartments that she has manufactured.

The same thing happened where she tried to ward off the collisions of trade interests. She associated different trades and professions with different castes. This had the effect of allaying for good the interminable jealousy and hatred of competition—the competition which breeds cruelty and makes the atmosphere thick with lies and deception. In this also India laid all her emphasis upon the law of heredity, ignoring the law of mutation, and thus gradually reduced arts into crafts and genius into skill.

However, what western observers fail to discern is that in her caste system India in all seriousness accepted her responsibility to solve the race problem in such a manner as to avoid all friction, and yet to afford each race freedom within its boundaries. Let us admit India has not in this achieved a full measure of success. But this you must also concede: that the West, being more favourably situated as to homogeneity of races, has never given her attention to this problem, and whenever confronted with it she has tried to make it easy by ignoring it altogether. And this is the source of her anti-Asiatic agitations for depriving aliens of their right to earn their honest living on these shores. In most of your colonies you only admit them on condition of their accepting the menial positions of hewers of wood and drawers of water. Either you shut your doors against the aliens or reduce them into slavery. And this is your solution to the problem of race-conflict. Whatever may be its merits you will have to admit that it does not spring from the higher impulses of civilisation but from the lower passions of greed and hatred. You say this is human nature—and India also thought she knew human nature when she strongly barricaded her race distinctions by the fixed barriers of social gradations. But we have found out to our cost that human nature is not what it seems, but what it is in truth, which is in its infinite possibilities. And when we in our blindness insult humanity for its ragged appearance it sheds its disguise to disclose to us that we have insulted our God. The degradation which we cast upon others in our pride or self-interest degrades our own humanity—and this is the punishment which is most terrible, because we do not detect it till it is too late.

Not only in your relation with aliens but with the different sections of your own society you have not achieved harmony of reconciliation. The spirit of conflict and competition is allowed the full freedom of its reckless career. And because its genesis is the greed of wealth and power it can never come to any other end but to a violent death. In India the production of commodities was brought under the law of social adjustments. Its basis was co-operation, having for its object the perfect satisfaction of social needs. But in the West it is guided by the impulse of competition, whose end is the gain of wealth for individuals. But the individual is like the geometrical line; it is length without breadth. It has not got the depth to be able to hold anything permanently. Therefore its greed or gain can never come to finality. In its lengthening process of growth it can cross other lines and cause entanglements, but will ever go on missing the ideal of completeness in its thinness of isolation.

In all our physical appetites we recognise a limit. We know that to exceed that limit is to exceed the limit of health. But has this lust for wealth and power no bounds beyond which is death's dominion? In these national carnivals of materialism are not the western peoples spending most of their vital energy in merely producing things and neglecting the creation of ideals? And can a civilisation ignore the law of moral health and go on in its endless process of inflation by gorging upon material things? Man in his social ideals naturally tries to regulate his appetites, subordinating them to the higher purpose of his nature. But in the economic world our appetites follow no other restrictions but those of supply and demand which can be artificially fostered, affording individuals opportunities for indulgence in an endless feast of grossness. In India our social instincts imposed restrictions upon our appetites— maybe it went to the extreme of repression—but in the West the spirit of economic organisation with no moral purpose goads the people into the perpetual pursuit of wealth; but has this no wholesome limit?

The ideals that strive to take form in social institutions have two objects. One is to regulate our passions and appetites for the harmonious development of man, and the other is to help him to cultivate disinterested love for his fellow-creatures. Therefore society is the expression of those moral and spiritual aspirations of man which belong to his higher nature.

Our food is creative, it builds our body; but not so wine, which stimulates. Our social ideals create the human world, but when our mind is diverted from them to greed of power then in that state of intoxication we live in a world of abnormality where our strength is not health and our liberty is not freedom. Therefore political freedom does not give us freedom when our mind is not free. An automobile does not create freedom of movement, because it is a mere machine. When I myself am free I can use the automobile for the purpose of my freedom.

We must never forget in the present day that those people who have got their political freedom are not necessarily free; they are merely powerful. The passions which are unbridled in them are creating huge organisations of slavery in the disguise of freedom. Those who have made the gain of money their highest end are unconsciously selling their life and soul to rich persons or to the combinations that represent money. Those who are enamoured of their political power and gloat over their extension of dominion over foreign races gradually surrender their own freedom and humanity to the organisations necessary for holding other peoples in slavery. In the so-called free countries the majority of the people are not free; they are driven by the minority to a goal which is not even known to them. This becomes possible only because people do not acknowledge moral and spiritual freedom as their object. They create huge eddies with their passions, and they feel dizzily inebriated with the mere velocity of their whirling movement, taking that to be freedom. But the doom which is waiting to overtake them is as certain as death— for man's truth is moral truth and his emancipation is in the spiritual life.

The general opinion of the majority of the present-day nationalists in India is that we have come to a final completeness in our social and spiritual ideals, the task of the constructive work of society having been done several thousand years before we were born, and that now we are free to employ all our activities in the political direction. We never dream of blaming our social inadequacy as the origin of our present helplessness, for we have accepted as the creed of our nationalism that this social system has been perfected for all time to come by our ancestors, who had the superhuman vision of all eternity and supernatural power for making infinite provision for future ages. Therefore, for all our miseries and shortcomings, we hold responsible the historical surprises that burst upon us from outside. This is the reason why we think that our one task is to build a political miracle of freedom upon the quicksand of social slavery. In fact we want to dam up the true course of our own historical stream, and only borrow power from the sources of other peoples' history.

Those of us in India who have come under the delusion that mere political freedom will make us free have accepted their lessons from the West as the gospel truth and lost their faith in humanity. We must remember that whatever weakness we cherish in our society will become the source of danger in politics. The same inertia which leads us to our idolatry of dead forms in social institutions will create in our politics prison-houses with immovable walls. The narrowness of sympathy which makes it possible for us to impose upon a considerable portion of humanity the galling yoke of inferiority will assert itself in our politics in creating the tyranny of injustice.

When our nationalists talk about ideals they forget that the basis of nationalism is wanting. The very people who are upholding these ideals are themselves the most conservative in their social practice. Nationalists say, for example: look at Switzerland where, in spite of race differences, the people have solidified into a nation. Yet, remember that in Switzerland the races can mingle, they can intermarry, because they are of the same blood. In India there is no common birthright. And when we talk of western nationality we forgot that the nations there do not have that physical repulsion, one for the other, that we have between different castes. Have we an instance in the whole world where a people who are not allowed to mingle their blood shed their blood for one another except by coercion or for mercenary purposes? And can we ever hope that these moral barriers against our race amalgamation will not stand in the way of our political unity?

Then again we must give full recognition to this fact that our social restrictions are still tyrannical, so much so as to make men cowards. If a man tells me that he has heterodox ideas, but that he cannot follow them because he would be socially ostracised, I excuse him for having to live a life of untruth, in order to live at all. The social habit of mind which impels us to make the life of our fellow-being a burden to them where they differ from us even in such a thing as their choice of food, is sure to persist in our political organisation and result in creating engines of coercion to crush every rational difference which is the sign of life. And tyranny will only add to the inevitable lies and hypocrisy in our political life. Is the mere name of freedom so valuable that we should be willing to sacrifice for its sake our moral freedom?

The intemperance of our habits does not immediately show its effects when we are in the vigour of our youth. But it gradually consumes that vigour, and when the period of decline sets in then we have to settle accounts and pay off our debts, which leads us to insolvency. In the West you are still able to carry your head high, though your humanity is suffering every moment form its dipsomania of organising power. India also in the heyday of her youth could carry in her vital organs the dead weight of her social organisations stiffened to rigid perfection, but it has been fatal to her, and has produced a gradual paralysis of her living nature. And this is the reason why the educated community of India has become insensible of her social needs. They are taking the very immobility of our social structures as the sign of their perfection—and because the healthy feeling of pain is dead in the limbs of our social organism they delude themselves into thinking that it needs no ministration. Therefore they think that all their energies need their only scope in the political field. It is like a man whose legs have become shrivelled and useless, trying to delude himself that these limbs have grown still because they have attained their ultimate salvation, and all that is wrong about him is the shortness of his sticks.

So much for the social and the political regeneration of India. Now we come to her industries, and I am very often asked whether there is in India any industrial regeneration since the advent of the British government. It must be remembered that at the beginning of the British rule in India our industries were suppressed, and since then we have not met with any real help or encouragement to enable us to make a stand against the monster commercial organisations of the world. The nations have decreed that we must remain purely an agricultural people, even forgetting the use of arms for all time to come. Thus India is being turned into so many predigested morsels of food ready to be swallowed at any moment by any nation which has even the most rudimentary set of teeth in its head.

India therefore has very little outlet for her industrial originality. I personally do not believe in the unwieldy organisations of the present day. The very fact that they are ugly shows that they are in discordance with the whole creation. The vast powers of nature do not reveal their truth in hideousness, but in beauty. Beauty is the signature which the Creator stamps upon His works when He is satisfied with them. All our products that insolently ignore the laws of perfection and are unashamed in their display of ungainliness bear the perpetual weight of God's displeasure. So far as your commerce lacks the dignity of grace it is untrue. Beauty and her twin brother Truth require leisure and self-control for their growth. But the greed of gain has no time or limit to its capaciousness. Its one object is to produce and consume. It has pity neither for beautiful nature nor for living human beings. It is ruthlessly ready without a moment's hesitation to crush beauty and life out of them, moulding them into money. It is this ugly vulgarity of commerce which brought upon it the censure of contempt in our earlier days, when men had leisure to have an unclouded vision of perfection in humanity. Men in those times were rightly ashamed of the instinct of mere money-making. But in this scientific age money, by its very abnormal bulk, has won its throne. And when from its eminence of piled-up things it insults the higher instincts of man, banishing beauty and noble sentiments from its surroundings, we submit. For we in our meanness have accepted bribes from its hands and our imagination has grovelled in the dust before its immensity of flesh.

But its very unwieldiness and its endless complexities are its true signs of failure. The swimmer who is an expert does not exhibit his muscular force by violent movements, but exhibits some power which is invisible and which shows itself in perfect grace and reposefulness. The true distinction of man from animals is in his power and worth which are inner and invisible. But the present-day commercial civilisation of man is not only taking too much time and space but killing time and space. Its movements are violent; its noise is discordantly loud. It is carrying its own damnation because it is trampling into distortion the humanity upon which it stands. It is strenuously turning out money at the cost of happiness. Man is reducing himself to his minimum in order to be able to make amplest room for his organisations. He is deriding his human sentiments into shame because they are apt to stand in the way of his machines.

In our mythology we have the legend that the man who performs penances for attaining immortality has to meet with temptations sent by Indra, the Lord of the Immortals. If he is lured by them he is lost. The West has been striving for centuries after its goal of immortality. Indra has sent her the temptation to try her. It is the gorgeous temptation of wealth. She has accepted it, and her civilisation of humanity has lost its path in the wilderness of machinery.

This commercialism with its barbarity of ugly decorations is a terrible menace to all humanity, because it is setting up the ideal of power over that of perfection. It is making the cult of self-seeking exult in its naked shamelessness. Our nerves are more delicate than our muscles. Things that are the most precious in us are helpless as babes when we take away from them the careful protection which they claim from us for their very preciousness. Therefore, when the callous rudeness of power runs amuck in the broadway of humanity it scares away by its grossness the ideals which we have cherished with the martyrdom of centuries.

The temptation which is fatal for the strong is still more so for the weak. And I do not welcome it in our Indian life, even though it be sent by the Lord of the Immortals. Let our life be simple in its outer aspect and rich in its inner gain. Let our civilisation take its firm stand upon its basis of social co-operation and not upon that of economic exploitation and conflict. How to do it in the teeth of the drainage of our lifeblood by the economic dragons is the task set before the thinkers of all oriental nations who have faith in the human soul. It is a sign of laziness and impotency to accept conditions imposed upon us by others who have other ideals than ours. We should actively try to adapt the world powers to guide our history to its own perfect end.

From the above you will know that I am not an economist. I am willing to acknowledge that there is a law of demand and supply and an infatuation of man for more things than are good for him. And yet I will persist in believing that there is such a thing as the harmony of completeness in humanity, where poverty does not take away his riches, where defeat may lead him to victory, death to immortality, and where in the compensation of Eternal Justice those who are the last may yet have their insult transmuted into a golden triumph.

MASHI AND OTHER STORIES

Mashi

I

'Mashi!'[1]

'Try to sleep, Jotin, it is getting late.'

'Never mind if it is. I have not many days left. I was thinking that Mani should go to her father's house.——I forget where he is now.'

'Sitarampur.'

'Oh yes! Sitarampur. Send her there. She should not remain any longer near a sick man. She herself is not strong.'

'Just listen to him! How can she bear to leave you in this state?'

'Does she know what the doctors——?'

'But she can see for herself! The other day she cried her eyes out at the merest hint of having to go to her father's house.'

We must explain that in this statement there was a slight distortion of truth, to say the least of it. The actual talk with Mani was as follows:—

'I suppose, my child, you have got some news from your father? I thought I saw your cousin Anath here.'

---

1. The maternal aunt is addressed as Mashi.

'Yes! Next Friday will be my little sister's *annaprashan*[2] ceremony. So I'm thinking——'

'All right, my dear. Send her a gold necklace. It will please your mother.'

'I'm thinking of going myself. I've never seen my little sister, and I want to ever so much.'

'Whatever do you mean? You surely don't think of leaving Jotin alone? Haven't you heard what the doctor says about him?'

'But he said that just now there's no special cause for——'

'Even if he did, you can see his state.'

'This is the first girl after three brothers, and she's a great favourite.——I have heard that it's going to be a grand affair. If I don't go, mother will be very——'

'Yes, yes! I don't understand your mother. But I know very well that your father will be angry enough if you leave Jotin just now.'

'You'll have to write a line to him saying that there is no special cause for anxiety, and that even if I go, there will be no——'

'You're right there; it will certainly be no great loss if you do go. But remember, if I write to your father, I'll tell him plainly what is in my mind.'

'Then you needn't write. I shall ask my husband, and he will surely——'

'Look here, child, I've borne a good deal from you, but if you do that, I won't stand it for a moment. Your father knows you too well for you to deceive him.'

When Mashi had left her, Mani lay down on her bed in a bad temper.

---

2. The *annaprashan* ceremony takes place when a child is first given rice. Usually it receives its name on that day.

Her neighbour and friend came and asked what was the matter.

'Look here! What a shame it is! Here's my only sister's *annaprashan* coming, and they don't want to let me go to it!'

'Why! Surely you're never thinking of going, are you, with your husband so ill?'

'I don't do anything for him, and I couldn't if I tried. It's so deadly dull in this house, that I tell you frankly I can't bear it.'

'You are a strange woman!'

'But I can't pretend, as you people do, and look glum lest any one should think ill of me.'

'Well, tell me your plan.'

'I must go. Nobody can prevent me.'

'Isss! What an imperious young woman you are!'

II

Hearing that Mani had wept at the mere thought of going to her father's house, Jotin was so excited that he sat up in bed. Pulling his pillow towards him, he leaned back, and said: 'Mashi, open this window a little, and take that lamp away.'

The still night stood silently at the window like a pilgrim of eternity; and the stars gazed in, witnesses through untold ages of countless death-scenes.

Jotin saw his Mani's face traced on the background of the dark night, and saw those two big dark eyes brimming over with tears, as it were for all eternity.

Mashi felt relieved when she saw him so quiet, thinking he was asleep.

Suddenly he started up, and said: 'Mashi, you all thought that Mani was too frivolous ever to be happy in our house. But you see now——'

'Yes, I see now, my Baba,[3] I was mistaken—but trial tests a person.'

'Mashi!'

'Do try to sleep, dear!'

'Let me think a little, let me talk. Don't be vexed, Mashi!'

'Very well.'

'Once, when I used to think I could not win Mani's heart, I bore it silently. But you——'

'No, dear, I won't allow you to say that; I also bore it.'

'Our minds, you know, are not clods of earth which you can possess by merely picking up. I felt that Mani did not know her own mind, and that one day at some great shock——'

'Yes, Jotin, you are right,'

'Therefore I never took much notice of her waywardness.'

Mashi remained silent, suppressing a sigh. Not once, but often she had seen Jotin spending the night on the verandah wet with the splashing rain, yet not caring to go into his bedroom. Many a day he lay with a throbbing head, longing, she knew, that Mani would come and soothe his brow, while Mani was getting ready to go to the theatre. Yet when Mashi went to fan him, he sent her away petulantly. She alone knew what pain lay hidden in that distress. Again and again she had wanted to say to Jotin: 'Don't pay so much attention to that silly child, my dear; let her learn to want,—to cry for things.' But these things cannot be said, and are apt to be misunderstood. Jotin had in his heart a shrine set up to the goddess Woman, and there Mani had her throne. It was hard for him to imagine that his own fate was to be denied his share of the wine of love poured out by that divinity. Therefore the worship went on, the sacrifice was offered, and the hope of a boon never ceased.

---

3. Baba literally means Father, but is often used by elders as a term of endearment. In the same way 'Ma' is used.

Mashi imagined once more that Jotin was sleeping, when he cried out suddenly:

'I know you thought that I was not happy with Mani, and therefore you were angry with her. But Mashi, happiness is like those stars. They don't cover all the darkness; there are gaps between. We make mistakes in life and we misunderstand, and yet there remain gaps through which truth shines. I do not know whence comes this gladness that fills my heart to-night.'

Mashi began gently to soothe Jotin's brow, her tears unseen in the dark.

'I was thinking, Mashi, she's so young! What will she do when I am——?'

'Young, Jotin? She's old enough. I too was young when I lost the idol of my life, only to find him in my heart for ever. Was that any loss, do you think? Besides, is happiness absolutely necessary?'

'Mashi, it seems as if just when Mani's heart shows signs of awakening I have to——'

'Don't you worry about that, Jotin. Isn't it enough if her heart awakes?'

Suddenly Jotin recollected the words of a village minstrel's song which he had heard long before:

*O my heart! you woke not when the man of my heart
    came to my door.*
At the sound of his departing steps you woke up.
Oh, you woke up in the dark!

'Mashi, what is the time now?'

'About nine.'

'So early as that! Why, I thought it must be at least two or three o'clock. My midnight, you know, begins at sundown. But why did you want me to sleep, then?'

'Why, you know how late last night you kept awake talking; so to-day you must get to sleep early.'

'Is Mani asleep?'

'Oh no, she's busy making some soup for you.'

'You don't mean to say so, Mashi? Does she——?'

'Certainly! Why, she prepares all your food, the busy little woman.'

'I thought perhaps Mani could not——'

'It doesn't take long for a woman to learn such things. With the need it comes of itself.'

'The fish soup, that I had in the morning, had such a delicate flavour, I thought you had made it.'

'Dear me, no! Surely you don't think Mani would let me do anything for you? Why, she does all your washing herself. She knows you can't bear anything dirty about you. If only you could see your sitting-room, how spick and span she keeps it! If I were to let her haunt your sick-room, she would wear herself out. But that's what she really wants to do.'

'Is Mani's health, then——?'

'The doctors think she should not be allowed to visit the sick-room too often. She's too tender-hearted.'

'But, Mashi, how do you prevent her from coming?'

'Because she obeys me implicitly. But still I have constantly to be giving her news of you.'

The stars glistened in the sky like tear-drops. Jotin bowed his head in gratitude to his life that was about to depart, and when Death stretched out his right hand towards him through the darkness, he took it in perfect trust.

Jotin sighed, and, with a slight gesture of impatience, said:

'Mashi, if Mani is still awake, then, could I—if only for a——?'

'Very well! I'll go and call her.'

'I won't keep her long, only for five minutes. I have something particular to tell her.'

Mashi, sighing, went out to call Mani. Meanwhile Jotin's pulse began to beat fast. He knew too well that he had never been able to have an intimate talk with Mani. The two instruments were tuned differently and it was not easy to play them in unison. Again and again, Jotin had felt pangs of jealousy on hearing Mani chattering and laughing merrily with her girl companions. Jotin blamed only himself, —why couldn't he talk irrelevant trifles as they did? Not that he could not, for with his men friends he often chatted on all sorts of trivialities. But the small talk that suits men is not suitable for women. You can hold a philosophical discourse in monologue, ignoring your inattentive audience altogether, but small talk requires the co-operation of at least two. The bagpipes can be played singly, but there must be a pair of cymbals. How often in the evenings had Jotin, when sitting on the open verandah with Mani, made some strained attempts at conversation, only to feel the thread snap. And the very silence of the evening felt ashamed. Jotin was certain that Mani longed to get away. He had even wished earnestly that a third person would come. For talking is easy with three, when it is hard for two.

He began to think what he should say when Mani came. But such manufactured talk would not satisfy him. Jotin felt afraid that these five minutes of to-night would be wasted. Yet, for him, there were but few moments left for intimate talk.

III

'What's this, child, you're not going anywhere, are you?'

'Of course, I'm going to Sitarampur.'

'What do you mean? Who is going to take you?'

'Anath.'

'Not to-day, my child, some other day.'

'But the compartment has already been reserved.'

'What does that matter? That loss can easily be borne. Go to-morrow, early in the morning.'

'Mashi, I don't hold by your inauspicious days. What harm if I do go to-day?'

'Jotin wants to have a talk with you.'

'All right! there's still some time. I'll just go and see him.'

'But you mustn't say that you are going.'

'Very well, I won't tell him, but I shan't be able to stay long. To-morrow is my sister's *annaprashan,* and I must go to-day.'

'Oh, my child! I beg you to listen to me this once. Quiet your mind for a while and sit by him. Don't let him see your hurry.'

'What can I do? The train won't wait for me. Anath will be back in ten minutes. I can sit by him till then.'

'No, that won't do. I shall never let you go to him in that frame of mind....Oh, you wretch! the man you are torturing is soon to leave this world; but I warn you, you will remember this day till the end of your days! That there is a God! that there is a God! you will some day understand!'

'Mashi, you mustn't curse me like that.'

'Oh, my darling boy! my darling! why do you go on living longer? There is no end to this sin, yet I cannot check it!'

Mashi after delaying a little returned to the sick-room, hoping by that time Jotin would be asleep. But Jotin moved in his bed when she entered. Mashi exclaimed:

'Just look what she has done!'

'What's happened? Hasn't Mani come? Why have you been so long, Mashi?'

'I found her weeping bitterly because she had allowed the milk for your soup to get burnt! I tried to console her, saying, "Why, there's more milk to be had!" But that she could be so careless about the preparation of *your* soup made her wild. With great trouble I managed to pacify her and put her to bed. So I haven't brought her to-day. Let her sleep it off.'

Though Jotin was pained when Mani didn't come, yet he felt a certain amount of relief. He had half feared that Mani's bodily presence would do violence to his heart's image of her. Such things had happened before in his life. And the gladness of the idea that Mani was miserable at burning *his* milk filled his heart to overflowing.

'Mashi!'

'What is it, Baba?'

'I feel quite certain that my days are drawing to a close. But I have no regrets. Don't grieve for me.'

'No, dear, I won't grieve. I don't believe that only life is good and not death.'

'Mashi, I tell you truly that death seems sweet.'

Jotin, gazing at the dark sky, felt that it was Mani herself who was coming to him in Death's guise. She had immortal youth and the stars were flowers of blessing, showered upon her dark tresses by the hand of the World-Mother. It seemed as if once more he had his first sight of his bride under the veil of darkness.[4] The immense night became filled with the loving gaze of Mani's dark eyes. Mani, the bride of this house, the little girl, became transformed into a world-image, —her throne on the altar of the stars at the confluence of life and death. Jotin said to himself with clasped hands: 'At last the veil is raised, the covering is rent in this deep darkness. Ah, beautiful one! How often have you wrung my heart, but no longer shall you forsake me!'

IV

'I'm suffering, Mashi, but nothing like you imagine. It seems to me as if my pain were, gradually separating itself from my

4. The bride and the bridegroom see each other's face for the first time at the marriage ceremony under a veil thrown over their heads.

life. Like a laden boat, it was so long being towed behind, but the rope has snapped, and now it floats away with all my burdens. Still I can see it, but it is no longer mine....But, Mashi, I've not seen Mani even once for the last two days!'

'Jotin, let me give you another pillow.'

'It almost seems to me, Mashi, that Mani also has left me like that laden boat of sorrow which drifts away.'

'Just sip some pomegranate juice, dear! Your throat must be getting dry.'

'I wrote my will yesterday; did I show it to you? I can't recollect.'

'There's no need to show it to me, Jotin.'

'When mother died, I had nothing of my own. You fed me and brought me up. Therefore I was saying—'

'Nonsense, child! I had only this house and a little property. You earned the rest.'

'But this house——?'

'That's nothing. Why, you've added to it so much that it's difficult to find out where my house was!'

'I'm sure Mani's love for you is really——'

'Yes, yes! I know that, Jotin. Now you try to sleep.'

'Though I have bequeathed all my property to Mani, it is practically yours, Mashi. She will never disobey you.'

'Why are you worrying so much about that, dear?'

'All I have I owe to you. When you see my will don't think for a moment that——'

'What do you mean, Jotin? Do you think I shall mind for a moment because you give to Mani what belongs to you? Surely I'm not so mean as that?'

'But you also will have——'

'Look here, Jotin, I shall get angry with you. You want to console me with money!'

'Oh, Mashi, how I wish I could give you something better than money!'

'That you have done, Jotin!—more than enough. Haven't I had you to fill my lonely house? I must have won that great good-fortune in many previous births! You have given me so much that now, if my destiny's due is exhausted, I shall not complain. Yes, yes! Give away everything in Mani's name,— your house, your money, your carriage, and your land—such burdens are too heavy for me!'

'Of course I know you have lost your taste for the enjoyments of life, but Mani is so young that——'

'No! you mustn't say that. If you want to leave her your property, it is all right, but as for enjoyment—'

'What harm if she does enjoy herself, Mashi?'

'No, no, it will be impossible. Her throat will become parched, and it will be dust and ashes to her.'

Jotin remained silent. He could not decide whether it was true or not, and whether it was a matter of regret or otherwise, that the world, would become distasteful to Mani for want of him. The stars seemed to whisper in his heart:

'Indeed it is true. We have been watching for thousands of years, and know that all these great preparations for enjoyment are but vanity.'

Jotin sighed and said: 'We cannot leave behind us what is really worth giving.'

'It's no trifle you are giving, dearest. I only pray she may have the power to know the value of what is given her.'

'Give me a little more of that pomegranate juice. Mashi, I'm thirsty. Did Mani come to me yesterday, I wonder?'

'Yes, she came, but you were asleep. She sat by your head, fanning you for a long time, and then went away to get your clothes washed.'

'How wonderful! I believe I was dreaming that very moment that Mani was trying to enter my room. The door was slightly open, and she was pushing against it, but it wouldn't open. But, Mashi, you're going too far,—you ought to let her see that I am dying; otherwise my death will be a terrible shock to her.'

'Baba, let me put this shawl over your feet; they are getting cold.'

'No, Mashi, I can't bear anything over me like that.'

'Do you know, Jotin, Mani made this shawl for you? When she ought to have been asleep, she was busy at it. It was finished only yesterday.'

Jotin took the shawl, and touched it tenderly with his hands. It seemed to him that the softness of the wool was Mani's own. Her loving thoughts had been woven night after night with its threads. It was not made merely of wool, but also of her touch. Therefore, when Mashi drew that shawl over his feet, it seemed as if, night after night, Mani had been caressing his tired limbs.

'But, Mashi, I thought Mani didn't know how to knit,— at any rate she never liked it.'

'It doesn't take long to learn a thing. Of course I had to teach her. Then there are a good many mistakes in it.'

'Let there be mistakes; we're not going to send it to the Paris Exhibition. It will keep my feet warm in spite of its mistakes.'

Jotin's mind began to picture Mani at her task, blundering and struggling, and yet patiently going on night after night. How sweetly pathetic it was! And again he went over the shawl with his caressing fingers.

'Mashi, is the doctor downstairs?'

'Yes, he will stay here to-night.'

'But tell him it is useless for him to give me a sleeping draught. It doesn't bring me real rest and only adds to my pain. Let me remain properly awake. Do you know, Mashi, that my wedding took place on the night of the full moon in the month of *Baisakh*? To-morrow will be that day, and the stars of that very night will be shining in the sky. Mani perhaps has forgotten. I want to remind her of it to-day; just call her to me for a minute or two....Why do you keep silent? I suppose the doctor has told you I am so weak that any excitement will——but I tell you truly, Mashi, to-night, if I can have only a few minutes' talk with her, there will be no need for any sleeping draughts. Mashi, don't cry like that! I am quite well. To-day my heart is full as it has never been in my life before. That's why I want to see Mani. No, no, Mashi, I can't bear to see you crying! You have been so quiet all these last days. Why are you so troubled to-night?'

'Oh, Jotin, I thought that I had exhausted all my tears, but I find there are plenty left. I can't bear it any longer.'

'Call Mani. I'll remind her of our wedding night, so that to-morrow she may——'

'I'm going, dear, Shombhu will wait at the door. If you want anything, call him.'

Mashi went to Mani's bedroom and sat down on the floor crying, —'Oh come, come once, you heartless wretch! Keep his last request who has given you his all! Don't kill him who is already dying!'

Jotin hearing the sound of footsteps started up saying, 'Mani!'

'I am Shombhu. Did you call me?'

'Ask your mistress to come?'

'Ask whom?'

'Your mistress.'

'She has not yet returned.'

'Returned? From where?'

'From Sitarampur.'

'When did she go?'

'Three days ago.'

For a moment Jotin felt numb all over, and his head began to swim. He slipped down from the pillows, on which he was reclining, and kicked off the woollen shawl that was over his feet.

When Mashi came back after a long time, Jotin did not mention Mani's name, and Mashi thought he had forgotten all about her.

Suddenly Jotin cried out: 'Mashi, did I tell you about the dream I had the other night?'

'Which dream?'

'That in which Mani was pushing the door, and the door wouldn't open more than an inch. She stood outside unable to enter. Now I know that Mani has to stand outside my door till the last.'

Mashi kept silent. She realised that the heaven she had been building for Jotin out of falsehood had toppled down at last. If sorrow comes, it is best to acknowledge it.—When God strikes, we cannot avoid the blow.

'Mashi, the love I have got from you will last through all my births. I have filled this life with it to carry it with me. In the next birth, I am sure you will be born as my daughter, and I shall tend you with all my love.'

'What are you saying, Jotin? Do you mean to say I shall be born again as a woman? Why can't you pray that I should come to your arms as a son?'

'No, no, not a son! You will come to my house in that wonderful beauty which you had when you were young. I can even imagine how I shall dress you.'

'Don't talk so much, Jotin, but try to sleep.'

'I shall name you "Lakshmi".'

'But that is an old-fashioned name, Jotin!'

'Yes, but you are my old-fashioned Mashi. Come to my house again with those beautiful old-fashioned manners.'

'I can't wish that I should come and burden your home with the misfortune of a girl-child!'

'Mashi, you think me weak, and are wanting to save me all trouble.'

'My child, I am a woman, so I have my weakness. Therefore I have tried all my life to save you from all sorts of trouble,— only to fail.'

'Mashi, I have not had time in this life to apply the lessons I have learnt. But they will keep for my next birth. I shall show them what a man is able to do. I have learnt how false it is always to be looking after oneself.'

'Whatever you may say, darling, you have never grasped anything for yourself, but given everything to others.'

'Mashi, I can boast of one thing at any rate. I have never been a tyrant in my happiness, or tried to enforce my claims by violence. Because lies could not content me, I have had to wait long. Perhaps truth will be kind to me at last.—Who is that, Mashi, who is that?'

'Where? There's no one there, Jotin!'

'Mashi, just go and see in the other room. I thought I——'

'No, dear! I don't see anybody.'

'But it seemed quite clear to me that——'

'No, Jotin, it's nothing. So keep quiet! The doctor is coming now.'

When the doctor entered, he said:

'Look here, you mustn't stay near the patient so much, you excite him. You go to bed, and my assistant will remain with him.'

'No, Mashi, I can't let you go.'

'All right, Baba! I will sit quietly in that corner.'

'No, no! you must sit by my side. I can't let go your hand, not till the very end. I have been made by your hand, and only from your hand shall God take me.'

'All right,' said the doctor, 'you can remain there. But, Jotin Babu, you must not talk to her. It's time for you to take your medicine.'

'Time for my medicine? Nonsense! The time for that is over. To give medicine now is merely to deceive; besides I am not afraid to die. Mashi, Death is busy with his physic; why do you add another nuisance in the shape of a doctor? Send him away, send him away! It is you alone I need now! No one else, none whatever! No more falsehood!'

'I protest, as a doctor, this excitement is doing you harm.'

'Then go, doctor, don't excite me any more!—Mashi, has he gone?....That's good! Now come and take my head in your lap.'

'All right, dear! Now, Baba, try to sleep!'

'No, Mashi, don't ask me to sleep. If I sleep, I shall never wake. I still need to keep awake a little longer. Don't you hear a sound? Somebody is coming.'

V

'Jotin dear, just open your eyes a little. She has come. Look once and see!'

'Who has come? A dream?'

'Not a dream, darling! Mani has come with her father.'

'Who are you?'

'Can't you see? This is your Mani!'

'Mani? Has that door opened?'

'Yes, Baba, it is wide open.'

'No, Mashi, not that shawl! not *that* shawl! That shawl is a fraud!'

'It is not a shawl, Jotin! It is our Mani, who has flung herself on your feet. Put your hand on her head and bless her. Don't cry like that, Mani! There will be time enough for that. Keep quiet now for a little.'

The Skeleton

In the room next to the one in which we boys used to sleep, there hung a human skeleton. In the night it would rattle in the breeze which played about its bones. In the day these bones were rattled by us. We were taking lessons in osteology from a student in the Campbell Medical School, for our guardians were determined to make us masters of all the sciences. How far they succeeded we need not tell those who know us; and it is better hidden from those who do not.

Many years have passed since then. In the meantime the skeleton has vanished from the room, and the science of osteology from our brains, leaving no trace behind.

The other day, our house was crowded with guests, and I had to pass the night in the same old room. In these now unfamiliar surroundings, sleep refused to come, and, as I tossed from side to side, I heard all the hours of the night chimed, one after another, by the church clock near by. At length the lamp in the corner of the room, after some minutes of choking and spluttering, went out altogether. One or two bereavements had recently happened in the family, so the going out of the lamp naturally led me to thoughts of death. In the great arena of nature, I thought, the light of a lamp losing itself in eternal darkness, and the going out of the light of our little human lives, by day or by night, were much the same thing.

My train of thought recalled to my mind the skeleton. While I was trying to imagine what the body which had clothed it could have been like, it suddenly seemed to me that something was walking round and round my bed, groping along the walls of the room. I could hear its rapid breathing. It seemed as if it was searching for something which it could not find, and pacing round the room with ever-hastier steps. I felt quite sure that this was a mere fancy of my sleepless, excited brain; and that the throbbing of the veins in my temples was really the sound which seemed like running footsteps. Nevertheless, a cold shiver ran all over me. To get rid of this hallucination, I called out aloud: 'Who is there?' The footsteps seemed to stop at my bedside, and the reply came: 'It is I. I have come to look for that skeleton of mine.'

It seemed absurd to show any fear before the creature of my own imagination; so, clutching my pillow a little more tightly, I said in a casual sort of way: 'A nice business for this time of night! Of what use will that skeleton be to you now?'

The reply seemed to come almost from my mosquito-curtain itself. 'What a question! In that skeleton were the bones that encircled my heart; the youthful charm of my six-and-twenty years bloomed about it. Should I not desire to see it once more?'

'Of course,' said I, 'a perfectly reasonable desire. Well, go on with your search, while I try to get a little sleep.'

Said the voice: 'But I fancy you are lonely. All right; I'll sit down a while, and we will have a little chat. Years ago I used to sit by men and talk to them. But during the last thirty-five years I have only moaned in the wind in the burning-places of the dead. I would talk once more with a man as in the old times.'

I felt that some one sat down just near my curtain. Resigning myself to the situation, I replied with as much cordiality as

I could summon. 'That will be very nice indeed. Let us talk of something cheerful.'

'The funniest thing I can think of is my own life-story. Let me tell you that.'

The church clock chimed the hour of two.

'When I was in the land of the living, and young, I feared one thing like death itself, and that was my husband. My feelings can be likened only to those of a fish caught with a hook. For it was as if a stranger had snatched me away with the sharpest of hooks from the peaceful calm of my childhood's home—and from him I had no means of escape. My husband died two months after my marriage, and my friends and relations moaned pathetically on my behalf. My husband's father, after scrutinising my face with great care, said to my mother-in-law: "Do you not see, she has the evil eye?"—Well, are you listening? I hope you are enjoying the story?'

'Very much indeed!' said I. 'The beginning is extremely humorous.'

'Let me proceed then. I came back to my father's house in great glee. People tried to conceal it from me, but I know well that I was endowed with a rare and radiant beauty. What is your opinion?'

'Very likely,' I murmured. 'But you must remember that I never saw you.'

'What! Not seen me? What about that skeleton of mine? Ha! ha! ha! Never mind. I was only joking. How can I ever make you believe that those two cavernous hollows contained the brightest of dark, languishing eyes? And that the smile which was revealed by those ruby lips had no resemblance whatever to the grinning teeth which you used to see? The mere attempt to convey to you some idea of the grace, the charm, the soft, firm, dimpled curves, which in the fulness of youth were growing and blossoming over those dry old bones makes me smile; it also makes me angry. The most eminent doctors of my time could not have dreamed of the bones of that body of mine as materials for teaching osteology. Do you know, one young doctor that I knew of, actually compared me to a golden *champak* blossom. It meant that to him the rest of human kind was fit only to illustrate the science of physiology, that I was a flower of beauty. Does any one think of the skeleton of a *champak* flower?

'When I walked, I felt that, like a diamond scattering splendour, my every movement set waves of beauty radiating on every side. I used to spend hours gazing on my hands— hands which could gracefully have reined the liveliest of male creatures.

'But that stark and staring old skeleton of mine has borne false-witness to you against me, while I was unable to refute the shameless libel. That is why of all men I hate you most! I feel I would like once for all to banish sleep from your eyes with a vision of that warm rosy loveliness of mine, to sweep out with it all the wretched osteological stuff of which your brain is full.'

'I could have sworn by your body,' cried I, 'if you had it still, that no vestige of osteology has remained in my head, and that the only thing that it is now full of is a radiant vision of perfect loveliness, glowing against the black background of night. I cannot say more than that.'

'I had no girl-companions,' went on the voice. 'My only brother had made up his mind not to marry. In the zenana I was alone. Alone I used to sit in the garden under the shade of the trees, and dream that the whole world was in love with me; that the stars with sleepless gaze were drinking in my beauty; that the wind was languishing in sighs as on some pretext or other it brushed past me; and that the lawn on which my feet rested, had it been conscious, would have lost consciousness against their touch. It seemed to me that all the young men in the world were as blades of grass at my feet; and my heart, I know not why, used to grow sad.

'When my brother's friend, Shekhar, had passed out of the Medical College, he became our family doctor. I had already often seen him from behind a curtain. My brother was a strange man, and did not care to look on the world with open eyes. It was not empty enough for his taste; so he gradually moved away from it, until he was quite lost in an obscure corner. Shekhar was his one friend, so he was the only young man I could ever get to see. And when I held my evening court in my garden, then the host of imaginary young men whom I had at my feet were each one a Shekhar.——— Are you listening? What are you thinking of?'

I sighed as I replied: 'I was wishing I was Shekhar!'

'Wait a bit. Hear the whole story first. One day, in the rains, I was feverish. The doctor came to see me. That was our first meeting. I was reclining opposite the window, so that the blush of the evening sky might temper the pallor of my complexion. When the doctor, coming in, looked up into my face, I put myself into his place, and gazed at myself in imagination. I saw in the glorious evening light that delicate wan face laid like a drooping flower against the soft white pillow, with the unrestrained curls playing over the forehead, and the bashfully lowered eyelids casting a pathetic shade over the whole countenance.

'The doctor, in a tone bashfully low, asked my brother: "Might I feel her pulse?"

'I put out a tired, well-rounded wrist from beneath the coverlet. "Ah!" thought I, as I looked on it, "If only there had been a sapphire bracelet."[1] I have never before seen a doctor so awkward about feeling a patient's pulse. His fingers trembled

---

1. Widows are supposed to dress in white only, without ornaments or jewellery.

as they felt my wrist. He measured the heat of my fever, I gauged the pulse of his heart.——Don't you believe me?'

'Very easily,' said I; 'the human heart-beat tells its tale.'

'After I had been taken ill and restored to health several times, I found that the number of the courtiers who attended my imaginary evening reception began to dwindle till they were reduced to only one! And at last in my little world there remained only one doctor and one patient.

'In these evenings I used to dress myself[2] secretly in a canary-coloured *sari;* twine about the braided knot into which I did my hair a garland of white jasmine blossoms; and with a little mirror in my hand betake myself to my usual seat under the trees.

'Well! Are you perhaps thinking that the sight of one's own beauty would soon grow wearisome? Ah no! for I did not see myself with my own eyes. I was then one and also two. I used to see myself as though I were the doctor; I gazed, I was charmed, I fell madly in love. But, in spite of all the caresses I lavished on my self, a sigh would wander about my heart, moaning like the evening breeze.

'Anyhow, from that time I was never alone. When I walked I watched with downcast eyes the play of my dainty little toes on the earth, and wondered what the doctor would have felt had he been there to see. At mid-day the sky would be filled with the glare of the sun, without a sound, save now and then the distant cry of a passing kite. Outside our garden-walls the hawker would pass with his musical cry of "Bangles for sale, crystal bangles." And I, spreading a snow-white sheet on the lawn, would lie on it with my head on my arm. With studied carelessness the other arm would rest lightly on the soft sheet, and I would imagine to myself that some one had caught sight

---

2. See the previous note.

of the wonderful pose of my hand, that some one had clasped it in both of his and imprinted a kiss on its rosy palm, and was slowly walking away.—What if I ended the story here? How would it do?'

'Not half a bad ending,' I replied thoughtfully. 'It would no doubt remain a little incomplete, but I could easily spend the rest of the night putting in the finishing touches.'

'But that would make the story too serious. Where would the laugh come in? Where would be the skeleton with its grinning teeth?

'So let me go on. As soon as the doctor had got a little practice, he took a room on the ground floor of our house for a consulting-chamber. I used to then sometimes ask him jokingly about medicines and poisons, and how much of this drug or that would kill a man. The subject was congenial and he would wax eloquent. These talks familiarised me with the idea of death; and so love and death were the only two things that filled my little world. My story is now nearly ended—there is not much left.'

'Not much of the night is left either,' I muttered.

'After a time I noticed that the doctor had grown strangely absent-minded, and it seemed as if he were ashamed of something which he was trying to keep from me. One day he came in, somewhat smartly dressed, and borrowed my brother's carriage for the evening.

'My curiosity became too much for me, and I went up to my brother for information. After some talk beside the point, I at last asked him: "By the way, Dada,[3] where is the doctor going this evening in your carriage?"

'My brother briefly replied: "To his death."

"Oh, do tell me," I importuned. "Where is he really going?"

---

3. Elder brother.

"To be married," he said, a little more explicitly.

"Oh, indeed!" said I, as I laughed long and loudly.

'I gradually learnt that the bride was an heiress, who would bring the doctor a large sum of money. But why did he insult me by hiding all this from me? Had I ever begged and prayed him not to marry. Because it would break my heart? Men are not to be trusted. I have known only one man in all my life, and in a moment I made this discovery.

'When the doctor came in after his work and was ready to start, I said to him, rippling with laughter the while: "Well, doctor, so you are to be married to-night?"

'My gaiety not only made the doctor lose countenance; it thoroughly irritated him.

'"How is it," I went on, "That there is no illumination, no band of music?"

'With a sigh he replied: "Is marriage then such a joyful occasion?"

'I burst out into renewed laughter. "No, no," said I, "this will never do. Who ever heard of a wedding without lights and music?"

'I bothered my brother about it so much that he at once ordered all the trappings of a gay wedding.

'All the time I kept on gaily talking of the bride, of what would happen, of what I would do when the bride came home. "And, doctor," I asked, "will you still go on feeling pulses?" Ha! ha! ha! Though the inner workings of people's, especially men's, minds are not visible, still I can take my oath that these words were piercing the doctor's bosom like deadly darts.

'The marriage was to be celebrated late at night. Before starting, the doctor and my brother were having a glass of wine together on the terrace, as was their daily habit. The moon had just risen.

'I went up smiling, and said: "Have you forgotten your wedding, doctor? It is time to start."

'I must here tell you one little thing. I had meanwhile gone down to the dispensary and got a little powder, which at a convenient opportunity I had dropped unobserved into the doctor's glass.

'The doctor, draining his glass at a gulp, in a voice thick with emotion, and with a look that pierced me to the heart, said: "Then I must go."

'The music struck up. I went into my room and dressed myself in my bridal-robes of silk and gold. I took out my jewellery and ornaments from the safe and put them all on; I put the red mark of wifehood on the parting in my hair. And then under the tree in the garden I prepared my bed.

'It was a beautiful night. The gentle south wind was kissing away the weariness of the world. The scent of jasmine and *bela* filled the garden with rejoicing.

'When the sound of the music began to grow fainter and fainter; the light of the moon to get dimmer and dimmer; the world with its lifelong associations of home and kin to fade away from my perceptions like some illusion—then I closed my eyes, and smiled.

'I fancied that when people came and found me they would see that smile of mine lingering on my lips like a trace of rose-coloured wine, that when I thus slowly entered my eternal bridal-chamber I should carry with me this smile, illuminating my face. But alas for the bridal-chamber! Alas for the bridal-robes of silk and gold! When I woke at the sound of a rattling within me, I found three urchins learning osteology from my skeleton. Where in my bosom my joys and griefs used to throb, and the petals of youth to open one by one, there the master with his pointer was busy naming my bones. And as to that last smile, which I had so carefully rehearsed, did you see any sign of that?

'Well, well, how did you like the story?'

'It has been delightful,' said I.

At this point the first crow began to caw. 'Are you there?' I asked. There was no reply.

The morning light entered the room.

The Auspicious Vision

Kantichandra was young; yet after his wife's death he sought no second partner, and gave his mind to the hunting of beasts and birds. His body was long and slender, hard and agile; his sight keen; his aim unerring. He dressed like a countryman, and took with him Hira Singh the wrestler, Chakkanlal, Khan Saheb the musician, Mian Saheb, and many others. He had no lack of idle followers.

In the month of *Agrahayan* Kanti had gone out shooting near the swamp of Nydighi with a few sporting companions. They were in boats, and an army of servants, in boats also, filled the bathing-ghats. The village women found it well-nigh impossible to bathe or to draw water. All day long, land and water trembled to the firing of the guns; and every evening musicians killed the chance of sleep.

One morning as Kanti was seated in his boat cleaning a favourite gun, he suddenly started at what he thought was the cry of wild duck. Looking up, he saw a village maiden, coming to the water's edge, with two white ducklings clasped to her breast. The little stream was almost stagnant. Many weeds choked the current. The girl put the birds into the water and watched them anxiously. Evidently the presence of the sportsmen was the cause of her care and not the wildness of the ducks.

The girl's beauty had a rare freshness—as if she had just come from Vishwakarma's[1] workshop. It was difficult to guess her age. Her figure was almost a woman's, but her face was so childish that clearly the world had left no impression there. She seemed not to know herself that she had reached the threshold of youth.

Kanti's gun-cleaning stopped for a while. He was fascinated. He had not expected to see such a face in such a spot. And yet its beauty suited its surroundings better than it would have suited a palace. A bud is lovelier on the bough than in a golden vase. That day the blossoming reeds glittered in the autumn dew and morning sun, and the fresh, simple face set in the midst was like a picture of festival to Kanti's enchanted mind. Kalidas has forgotten to sing how Siva's Mountain-Queen herself sometimes has come to the young Ganges, with just such ducklings in her breast. As he gazed, the maiden started in terror, and hurriedly took back the ducks into her bosom with a half-articulate cry of pain. In another moment, she had left the river-bank and disappeared into the bamboo thicket hard by. Looking round, Kanti saw one of his men pointing an unloaded gun at the ducks. He at once went up to him, wrenched away his gun, and bestowed on his cheek a prodigious slap. The astonished humourist finished his joke on the floor. Kanti went on cleaning his gun.

But curiosity drove Kanti to the thicket wherein he had seen the girl disappear. Pushing his way through, he found himself in the yard of a well-to-do householder. On one side was a row of conical thatched barns, on the other a clean cow-shed, at the end of which grew a *zizyph* bush. Under the bush was seated the girl he had seen that morning, sobbing over a wounded dove, into whose yellow beak she was trying to wring a little water from the moist corner of

---

1. The divine craftsman in Hindu mythology.

her garment. A grey cat, its fore-paws on her knee, was looking eagerly at the bird, and every now and then, when it got too forward, she kept it in its place by a warning tap on the nose.

This little picture, set in the peaceful mid-day surrounding of the householder's yard, instantly impressed itself on Kanti's sensitive heart. The checkered light and shade, flickering beneath the delicate foliage of the *zizyph*, played on the girl's lap. Not far off a cow was chewing the cud, and lazily keeping off the flies with slow movements of its head and tail. The north wind whispered softly in the rustling bamboo thickets. And she who at dawn on the river-bank had looked like the Forest Queen, now in the silence of noon showed the eager pity of the Divine Housewife. Kanti, coming in upon her with his gun, had a sense of intrusion. He felt like a thief caught red-handed. He longed to explain that it was not he who had hurt the dove. As he wondered how he should begin, there came a call of 'Sudha!' from the house. The girl jumped up. 'Sudha!' came the voice again. She took up her dove, and ran within. 'Sudha,'[2] thought Kanti, 'what an appropriate name!'

Kanti returned to the boat, handed his gun to his men, and went over to the front door of the house. He found a middle-aged Brahmin, with a peaceful, clean-shaven face, seated on a bench outside, and reading a devotional book. Kanti saw in his kindly, thoughtful face something of the tenderness which shone in the face of the maiden.

Kanti saluted him, and said: 'May I ask for some water, sir? I am very thirsty.' The elder man welcomed him with eager hospitality, and, offering him a seat on the bench, went inside and fetched with his own hands a little brass plate of sugar wafers and a bell-metal vessel full of water.

---

2. *Sudha* means nectar, ambrosia.

After Kanti had eaten and drunk, the Brahmin begged him to introduce himself. Kanti gave his own name, his father's name, and the address of his home, and then said in the usual way: 'If I can be of any service, sir, I shall deem myself fortunate.'

'I require no service, my son,' said Nabin Banerji; 'I have only one care at present.'

'What is that, sir?' said Kanti.

'It is my daughter, Sudha, who is growing up (Kanti smiled as he thought of her babyish face), and for whom I have not yet been able to find a worthy bridegroom. If I could only see her well married, all my debt to this world would be paid. But there is no suitable bridegroom here, and I cannot leave my charge of Gopinath here, to search for a husband elsewhere.'

'If you would see me in my boat, sir, we would have a talk about the marriage of your daughter.' So saying, Kanti repeated his salute and went back. He then sent some of his men into the village to inquire, and in answer heard nothing but praise of the beauty and virtues of the Brahmin's daughter.

When next day the old man came to the boat on his promised visit, Kanti bent low in salutation, and begged the hand of his daughter for himself. The Brahmin was so much overcome by this undreamed-of piece of good fortune—for Kanti not only belonged to a well-known Brahmin family, but was also a landed proprietor of wealth and position—that at first he could hardly utter a word in reply. He thought there must have been some mistake, and at length mechanically repeated: 'You desire to marry my daughter?'

'If you will deign to give her to me,' said Kanti.

'You mean Sudha?' he asked again.

'Yes,' was the reply.

'But will you not first see and speak to her——?'

Kanti, pretending he had not seen her already, said: 'Oh, that we shall do at the moment of the Auspicious Vision.'[3]

In a voice husky with emotion the old man said: 'My Sudha is indeed a good girl, well skilled in all the household arts. As you are so generously taking her on trust, may she never cause you a moment's regret. This is my blessing!'

The brick-built mansion of the Mazumdars had been borrowed for the wedding ceremony, which was fixed for next *Magh*, as Kanti did not wish to delay. In due time the bridegroom arrived on his elephant, with drums and music and with a torchlight procession, and the ceremony began.

When the bridal couple were covered with the scarlet screen for the rite of the Auspicious Vision, Kanti looked up at his bride. In that bashful, downcast face, crowned with the wedding coronet and bedecked with sandal paste, he could scarcely recognise the village maiden of his fancy, and in the fullness of his emotion a mist seemed to becloud his eyes.

At the gathering of women in the bridal chamber, after the wedding ceremony was over, an old village dame insisted that Kanti himself should take off his wife's bridal veil. As he did so he started back. It was not the same girl.

Something rose from within his breast and pierced into his brain. The light of the lamps seemed to grow dim, and darkness to tarnish the face of the bride herself.

At first he felt angry with his father-in-law. The old scoundrel had shown him one girl, and married him to another. But on calmer reflection he remembered that the old man had not shown him any daughter at all—that it was all his own

---

3. After betrothal, the prospective bride and bridegroom are not supposed to see each other again till that part of the wedding ceremony which is called *Auspicious Vision*.

fault. He thought it best not to show his arrant folly to the world, and took his place again with apparent calmness.

He could swallow the powder; he could not get rid of its taste. He could not bear the merry-makings of the festive throng. He was in a blaze of anger with himself as well as with everybody else.

Suddenly he felt the bride, seated by his side, give a little start and a suppressed scream; a leveret, scampering into the room, had brushed across her feet. Close upon it followed the girl he had seen before. She caught up the leveret into her arms, and began to caress it with an affectionate murmuring. 'Oh, the mad girl!' cried the women as they made signs to her to leave the room. She heeded them not, however, but came and unconcernedly sat in front of the wedded pair, looking into their faces with a childish curiosity. When a maidservant came and took her by the arm to lead her away, Kanti hurriedly interposed, saying, 'Let her be.'

'What is your name?' he then went on to ask her.

The girl swayed backwards and forwards but gave no reply. All the women in the room began to titter.

Kanti put another question: 'Have those ducklings of yours grown up?'

The girl stared at him as unconcernedly as before.

The bewildered Kanti screwed up courage for another effort, and asked tenderly after the wounded dove, but with no avail. The increasing laughter in the room betokened an amusing joke.

At last Kanti learned that the girl was deaf and dumb, the companion of all the animals and birds of the locality. It was but by chance that she rose the other day when the name of Sudha was called.

Kanti now received a second shock. A black screen lifted from before his eyes. With a sigh of intense relief, as of escape from calamity, he looked once more into the face of his bride.

Then came the true Auspicious Vision. The light from his heart and from the smokeless lamps fell on her gracious face; and he saw it in its true radiance, knowing that Nabin's blessing would find fulfilment.

The Supreme Night

I used to go to the same dame's school with Surabala and play at marriage with her. When I paid visits to her house, her mother would pet me, and setting us side by side would say to herself: 'What a lovely pair!'

I was a child then, but I could understand her meaning well enough. The idea became rooted in my mind that I had a special right to Surabala above that of people in general. So it happened that, in the pride of ownership, at times I punished and tormented her; and she, too, fagged for me and bore all my punishments without complaint. The village was wont to praise her beauty; but in the eyes of a young barbarian like me that beauty had no glory;—I knew only that Surabala had been born in her father's house solely to bear my yoke, and that therefore she was the particular object of my neglect.

My father was the land-steward of the Chaudhuris, a family of *zemindars*. It was his plan, as soon as I had learnt to write a good hand, to train me in the work of estate management and secure a rent collectorship for me somewhere. But in my heart I disliked the proposal. Nilratan of our village had run away to Calcutta, had learnt English there, and finally became the *Nazir*[1] of the District Magistrate; *that* was my life's ideal: I was secretly determined to be the

---

1. Superintendent of bailiffs.

Head Clerk of the Judge's Court, even if I could not become the Magistrate's *Nazir*.

I saw that my father always treated these court officers with the greatest respect. I knew from my childhood that they had to be propitiated with gifts of fish, vegetables, and even money. For this reason I had given a seat of high honour in my heart to the court underlings, even to the bailiffs. These are the gods worshipped in our Bengal,—a modern miniature edition of the 330 millions of deities of the Hindu pantheon. For gaining material success, people have more genuine faith in *them* than in the good Ganesh, the giver of success; hence the people now offer to these officers everything that was formerly Ganesh's due.

Fired by the example of Nilratan, I too seized a suitable opportunity and ran away to Calcutta. There I first put up in the house of a village acquaintance, and afterwards got some funds from my father for my education. Thus I carried on my studies regularly.

In addition, I joined political and benevolent societies. I had no doubt whatever that it was urgently necessary for me to give my life suddenly for my country. But I knew not how such a hard task could be carried out. Also no one showed me the way.

But, nevertheless, my enthusiasm did not abate at all. We country lads had not learnt to sneer at everything like the precocious boys of Calcutta, and hence our faith was very strong. The 'leaders' of our associations delivered speeches, and we went begging for subscriptions from door to door in the hot blaze of noon without breaking our fast; or we stood by the roadside distributing hand-bills, or arranged the chairs and benches in the lecture-hall, and, if anybody whispered a word against our leader, we got ready to fight him. For these things the city boys used to laugh at us as provincials.

I had come to Calcutta to be a *Nazir* or a Head Clerk, but I was preparing to become a Mazzini or a Garibaldi.

At this time Surabala's father and my father laid their heads together to unite us in marriage. I had come to Calcutta at the age of fifteen; Surabala was eight years old then. I was now eighteen, and in my father's opinion I was almost past the age of marriage. But it was my secret vow to remain unmarried all my life and to die for my country; so I told my father that I would not marry before I had finished my education.

In two or three months I learnt that Surabala had been married to a pleader named Ram Lochan. I was then busy collecting subscriptions for raising fallen India, and this news did not seem worth my thought.

I had matriculated, and was about to appear at the Intermediate Examination, when my father died. I was not alone in the world, but had to maintain my mother and two sisters. I had therefore to leave college and look out for employment. After a good deal of exertion I secured the post of second master in the matriculation school of a small town in the Noakhali District.

I thought, here is just the work for me! By my advice and inspiration I shall train up every one of my pupils as a general for future India.

I began to work, and then found that the impending examination was a more pressing affair than the future of India. The headmaster got angry whenever I talked of anything outside grammar or algebra. And in a few months my enthusiasm, too, flagged.

I am no genius. In the quiet of the home I may form vast plans; but when I enter the field of work, I have to bear the yoke of the plough on my neck like the Indian bullock, get my tail twisted by my master, break clods all day, patiently and with bowed head, and then at sunset have to be satisfied if I can get any cud to chew. Such a creature has not the spirit to prance and caper.

One of the teachers lived in the school-house, to guard against fires. As I was a bachelor, this work was thrown on me. I lodged in a thatched shed close to the large cottage in which the school sat.

The school-house stood at some distance from the inhabited portion of the town, and beside a big tank. Around it were betel-nut, cocoa-nut, and *madar* trees, and very near to the school building two large ancient *nim* trees grew close together, and cast a cool shade around.

One thing I have forgotten to mention, and indeed I had not so long considered it worth mentioning. The local Government pleader, Ram Lochan Ray, lived near our school. I also knew that his wife—my early playmate, Surabala—lived with him.

I got acquainted with Ram Lochan Babu. I cannot say whether he knew that I had known Surabala in childhood. I did not think fit to mention the fact at my first introduction to him. Indeed, I did not clearly remember that Surabala had been ever linked with my life in any way.

One holiday I paid a visit to Ram Lochan Babu. The subject of our conversation has gone out of my mind; probably it was the unhappy condition of present-day India. Not that he was very much concerned or heart-broken over the matter; but the subject was such that one could freely pour forth one's sentimental sorrow over it for an hour or two while puffing at one's *hooka*.

While thus engaged, I heard in a side-room the softest possible jingle of bracelets, crackle of dress, and footfall; and I felt certain that two curious eyes were watching me through a small opening of the window.

All at once there flashed upon my memory a pair of eyes,——a pair of large eyes, beaming with trust, simplicity, and girlhood's love,—black pupils—thick dark eyelashes,—a calm fixed gaze. Suddenly some unseen force squeezed my heart in an iron grip, and it throbbed with intense pain.

I returned to my house, but the pain clung to me. Whether I read, wrote, or did any other work, I could not shake that weight off my heart; a heavy load seemed to be always swinging from my heart-strings.

In the evening, calming myself a little, I began to reflect: 'What ails me?' From within came the question: 'Where is *your* Surabala now?' I replied: 'I gave her up of my free will. Surely I did not expect her to wait for me for ever.'

But something kept saying: '*Then* you could have got her merely for the asking. *Now* you have not the right to look at her even once, do what you will. That Surabala of your boyhood may come very close to you; you may hear the jingle of her bracelets; you may breathe the air embalmed by the essence of her hair,—but there will always be a wall between you two.'

I answered: 'Be it so. What is Surabala to me?'

My heart rejoined: 'To-day Surabala is nobody to you. But what might she not have been to you?'

Ah! that's true. *What* might she not have been to me? Dearest to me of all things, closer to me than the world besides, the sharer of all my life's joys and sorrows, she might have been. And now, she is so distant, so much of a stranger, that to look on her is forbidden, to talk with her is improper, and to think of her is a sin!—while this Ram Lochan, coming suddenly from nowhere, has muttered a few set religious texts, and in one swoop has carried off Surabala from the rest of mankind!

I have not come to preach a new ethical code, or to revolutionise society; I have no wish to tear asunder domestic ties. I am only expressing the exact working of my mind, though it may not be reasonable. I could not by any means banish from my mind the sense that Surabala, reigning there within shelter of Ram Lochan's home, was mine far more than his. The thought was, I admit, unreasonable and improper,— but it was not unnatural.

Thereafter I could not set my mind to any kind of work. At noon when the boys in my class hummed, when Nature outside simmered in the sun, when the sweet scent of the *nim* blossoms entered the room on the tepid breeze, I then wished,— I know not what I wished for; but this I can say, that I did not wish to pass all my life in correcting the grammar exercises of those future hopes of India.

When school was over, I could not bear to live in my large lonely house; and yet, if any one paid me a visit, it bored me. In the gloaming as I sat by the tank and listened to the meaningless breeze sighing through the betel and cocoa-nut palms, I used to muse that human society is a web of mistakes; nobody has the sense to do the right thing at the right time, and when the chance is gone we break our hearts over vain longings.

I could have married Surabala and lived happily. But I must be a Garibaldi,—and I ended by becoming the second master of a village school! And pleader Ram Lochan Ray, who had no special call to be Surabala's husband,—to whom, before his marriage, Surabala was no wise different from a hundred other maidens,—has very quietly married her, and is earning lots of money as Government pleader; when his dinner is badly cooked he scolds Surabala, and when he is in good humour he gives her a bangle! He is sleek and fat, tidily dressed, free from every kind of worry; *he* never passes his evenings by the tank gazing at the stars and sighing.

Ram Lochan was called away from our town for a few days by a big case elsewhere. Surabala in her house was as lonely as I was in my school building.

I remember it was a Monday. The sky was overcast with

clouds from the morning. It began to drizzle at ten o'clock. At the aspect of the heavens our headmaster closed the school early. All day the black detached clouds began to run about in the sky as if making ready for some grand display. Next day, towards afternoon, the rain descended in torrents, accompanied by storm. As the night advanced the fury of wind and water increased. At first the wind was easterly; gradually it veered, and blew towards the south and south-west.

It was idle to try to sleep on such a night. I remembered that in this terrible weather Surabala was alone in her house. Our school was much more strongly built than her bungalow. Often and often did I plan to invite her to the school-house, while I meant to pass the night alone by the tank. But I could not summon up courage for it.

When it was half-past one in the morning, the roar of the tidal wave was suddenly heard,—the sea was rushing on us! I left my room and ran towards Surabala's house. In the way stood one embankment of our tank, and as I was wading to it the flood already reached my knees. When I mounted the bank, a second wave broke on it. The highest part of the bank was more than seventeen feet above the plain.

As I climbed up the bank, another person reached it from the opposite side. Who she was, every fibre of my body knew at once, and my whole soul was thrilled with the consciousness. I had no doubt that she too, had recognised me.

On an island some three yards in area stood we two; all else was covered with water.

It was a time of cataclysm; the stars had been blotted out of the sky; all the lights of the earth had been darkened; there would have been no harm if we had held converse *then*. But we could not bring ourselves to utter a word; neither of us made even a formal inquiry after the other's health. Only we stood gazing at the darkness. At our feet swirled the dense, black, wild, roaring torrent of death.

To-day Surabala has come to *my* side, leaving the whole world. To-day she has none besides *me*. In our far-off childhood this Surabala had come from some dark primeval realm of mystery, from a life in another orb, and stood by my side on this luminous peopled earth; and to-day, after a wide span of time, she has left that earth, so full of light and human beings, to stand alone by *my* side amidst this terrible desolate gloom of Nature's death-convulsion. The stream of birth had flung that tender bud before me, and the flood of death had wafted the same flower, now in full bloom, to *me* and to none else. One more wave and we shall be swept away from this extreme point of the earth, torn from the stalks on which we now sit apart, and made one in death.

May that wave never come! May Surabala live long and happily, girt round by husband and children, household and kinsfold! This one night, standing on the brink of Nature's destruction, I have tasted eternal bliss.

The night wore out, the tempest ceased, the flood abated; without a word spoken, Surabala went back to her house, and I, too, returned to my shed without having uttered a word.

I reflected: True, I have become no *Nazir* or Head Clerk, nor a Garibaldi; I am only the second master of a beggarly school. But one night had for its brief space beamed upon my whole life's course.

That one night, out of all the days and nights of my allotted span, has been the supreme glory of my humble existence.

Raja and Rani

Bipin Kisore was born 'with a golden spoon in his mouth'; hence he knew how to squander money twice as well as how to earn it. The natural result was that he could not live long in the house where he was born.

He was a delicate young man of comely appearance, an adept in music, a fool in business, and unfit for life's handicap. He rolled along life's road like the wheel of Jagannath's car. He could not long command his wonted style of magnificent living.

Luckily, however, Raja Chittaranjan, having got back his property from the Court of Wards, was intent upon organising an Amateur Theatre Party. Captivated by the prepossessing looks of Bipin Kisore and his musical endowments, the Raja gladly 'admitted him into his crew.'

Chittaranjan was a B.A. He was not given to any excesses. Though the son of a rich man, he used to dine and sleep at appointed hours and even at appointed places. And he suddenly became enamoured of Bipin like one unto drink. Often did meals cool and nights grow old while he listened to Bipin and discussed with him the merits of operatic compositions. The Dewan remarked that the only blemish in the otherwise perfect character of his master was his inordinate fondness for Bipin Kisore.

Rani Basanta Kumari raved at her husband, and said that he was wasting himself on a luckless baboon. The sooner she could do away with him, the easier she would feel.

The Raja was much pleased in his heart at this seeming jealousy of his youthful wife. He smiled, and thought that women-folk know only one man upon the earth—him whom they love; and never think of other men's desserts. That there may be many whose merits deserve regard, is not recorded in the scriptures of women. The only good man and the only object of a woman's favours is he who has blabbered into her ears the matrimonial incantations. A little moment behind the usual hour of her husband's meals is a world of anxiety to her, but she never cares a brass button if her husband's dependents have a mouthful or not. This inconsiderate partiality of the softer sex might be cavilled at, but to Chittaranjan it did not seem unpleasant. Thus, he would often indulge in hyperbolic laudations of Bipin in his wife's presence, just to provoke a display of her delightful fulminations.

But what was sport to the 'royal' couple, was death to poor Bipin. The servants of the house, as is their wont, took their cue from the Rani's apathetic and wilful neglect of the wretched hanger-on, and grew more apathetic and wilful still. They contrived to forget to look after his comforts, to Bipin's infinite chagrin and untold sufferings.

Once the Rani rebuked the servant Puté, and said: 'You are always shirking work; what do you do all through the day?' 'Pray, madam, the whole day is taken up in serving Bipin Babu under the Maharaja's orders,' stammered the poor valet.

The Rani retorted: 'Your Bipin Babu is a great Nawab, eh?' This was enough for Puté. He took the hint. From the very next day he left Bipin Babu's orts as they were, and at times forgot to cover the food for him. With unpractised hands Bipin often scoured his own dishes and not unfrequently went without meals. But it was not in him to whine and report to the Raja. It was not in him to lower himself by petty squabblings with menials. He did not mind it; he took everything in good part. And thus while the Raja's favours grew, the Rani's disfavour intensified, and at last knew no bounds.

Now the opera of *Subhadraharan* was ready after due rehearsal. The stage was fitted up in the palace court-yard. The Raja acted the part of 'Krishna,' and Bipin that of 'Arjuna.' Oh, how sweetly he sang! How beautiful he looked! The audience applauded in transports of joy.

The play over, the Raja came to the Rani and asked her how she liked it. The Rani replied: 'Indeed, Bipin acted the part of "Arjuna" gloriously! He does look like the scion of a noble family. His voice is rare!' The Raja said jocosely: 'And how do I look? Am I not fair? Have I not a sweet voice?' 'Oh, yours is a different case!' added the Rani, and again fell to dilating on the histrionic abilities of Bipin Kisore.

The tables were now turned. He who used to praise, now began to deprecate. The Raja, who was never weary of indulging in high-sounding panegyrics of Bipin before his consort, now suddenly fell reflecting that, after all, unthinking people made too much of Bipin's actual merits. What was extraordinary about his appearance of voice? A short while before he himself was one of those unthinking men, but in a sudden and mysterious way he developed symptoms of thoughtfulness!

From the day following, every good arrangement was made for Bipin's meals. The Rani told the Raja: 'It is undoubtedly wrong to lodge Bipin Babu with the petty officers of the Raj in the *Kachari*[1]; for all he now is, he was once a man of means.' The Raja ejaculated curtly: 'Ha!' and turned the subject. The Rani proposed that there might be another

---

1. *Kachari*, generally anglicised as *cuteberry*: officers and courts.

performance on the occasion of the first-rice ceremony of the 'royal' weanling. The Raja heard and heard her not.

Once on being reprimanded by the Raja for not properly laying his cloth, the servant Puté replied: 'What can I do? According to the Rani's behests I have to look after Bipin Babu and wait on him the livelong day.' This angered the Raja, and he exclaimed, highly nettled. 'Pshaw! Bipin Babu is a veritable Nawab, I see! Can't he cleanse his own dishes himself?' The servant, as before, took his cue, and Bipin lapsed back into his former wretchedness.

The Rani liked Bipin's songs—they were sweet—there was no gainsaying it. When her husband sat with Bipin to the wonted discourses of sweet music of an evening, she would listen from behind the screen in an adjoining room. Not long afterwards, the Raja began again his old habit of dining and sleeping at regular hours. The music came to an end. Bipin's evening services were no more needed.

Raja Chittaranjan used to look after his *zemindari* affairs at noon. One day he came earlier to the *zenana*, and found his consort reading something. On his asking her what she read, the Rani was a little taken aback, but promptly replied: 'I am conning over a few songs from Bipin Babu's song-book. We have not had any music since you tired abruptly of your musical hobby.' Poor woman! It was she who had herself made no end of efforts to eradicate the hobby from her husband's mind.

On the morrow the Raja dismissed Bipin—without a thought as to how and where the poor fellow would get a morsel henceforth!

Nor was this the only matter of regret to Bipin. He had been bound to the Raja by the dearest and most sincere tie of attachment. He served him more for affection than for pay. He was fonder of his friend than of the wages he received. Even after deep cogitation, Bipin could not ascertain the cause of the Raja's sudden estrangement. 'Tis Fate! all is Fate!' Bipin said to himself. And then, silently and bravely, he heaved a deep sigh, picked up his old guitar, put it up in the case, paid the last two coins in his pocket as a farewell *bakshish* to Puté, and walked out into the wide wide world where he had not a soul to call his friend.

The Trust Property

I

Brindaban Kundu came to his father in a rage and said: 'I am off this moment.'

'Ungrateful wretch!' sneered the father, Jaganath Kundu. 'When you have paid me back all that I have spent on your food and clothing, it will be time enough to give yourself these airs.'

Such food and clothing as was customary in Jaganath's household could not have cost very much. Our *rishis* of old managed to feed and clothe themselves on an incredibly small outlay. Jaganath's behaviour showed that his ideal in these respects was equally high. That he could not fully live up to it was due partly to the bad influence of the degenerate society around him, and partly to certain unreasonable demands of Nature in her attempt to keep body and soul together.

So long as Brindaban was single, things went smoothly enough, but after his marriage he began to depart from the high and rarefied standard cherished by his sire. It was clear that the son's ideas of comfort were moving away from the spiritual to the material, and imitating the ways of the world. He was unwilling to put up with the discomforts of heat and cold, thirst and hunger. His minimum of food and clothing rose apace.

Frequent were the quarrels between the father and the son. At last Brindaban's wife became seriously ill and a *kabiraj*[1] was called in. But when the doctor prescribed a costly medicine for his patient, Jaganath took it as a proof of sheer incompetence, and turned him out immediately. At first Brindaban besought his father to allow the treatment to continue; then he quarrelled with him about it, but to no purpose. When his wife died, he abused his father and called him a murderer.

'Nonsense!' said the father. 'Don't people die even after swallowing all kinds of drugs? If costly medicines could save life, how is it that kings and emperors are not immortal? You don't expect your wife to die with more pomp and ceremony than did your mother and your grandmother before her, do you?'

Brindaban might really have derived a great consolation from these words, had he not been overwhelmed with grief and incapable of proper thinking. Neither his mother nor his grandmother had taken any medicine before making their exit from this world, and this was the time-honoured custom of the family. But, alas, the younger generation was unwilling to die according to ancient custom. The English had newly come to the country at the time we speak of. Even in those remote days, the good old folks were horrified at the unorthodox ways of the new generation, and sat speechless, trying to draw comfort from their *hookas*.

Be that as it may, the modern Brindaban said to his old fogy of a father: 'I am off.'

The father instantly agreed, and wished publicly that, should he ever give his son one single pice in future, the gods might reckon his act as shedding the holy blood of cows. Brindaban in his turn similarly wished that, should he ever

---

1. Country doctor, unqualified by any medical training.

accept anything from his father, his act might be held as bad as matricide.

The people of the village looked upon this small revolution as a great relief after a long period of monotony. And when Jaganath disinherited his only son, every one did his best to console him. All were unanimous in the opinion that to quarrel with a father for the sake of a wife was possible only in these degenerate days. And the reason they gave was sound too. 'When your wife dies,' they said, 'you can find a second one without delay. But when your father dies, you can't get another to replace him for love or money.' Their logic no doubt was perfect, but we suspect that the utter hopelessness of getting another father did not trouble the misguided son very much. On the contrary, he looked upon it as a mercy.

Nor did separation from Brindaban weigh heavily on the mind of his father. In the first place, his absence from home reduced the household expenses. Then, again, the father was freed from a great anxiety. The fear of being poisoned by his son and heir had always haunted him. When he ate his scanty fare, he could never banish the thought of poison from his mind. This fear had abated somewhat after the death of his daughter-in-law, and, now that the son was gone, it disappeared altogether.

But there was one tender spot in the old man's heart. Brindaban had taken away with him his four-year-old son, Gokul Chandra. Now, the expense of keeping the child was comparatively small, and so Jaganath's affection for him was without a drawback. Still, when Brindaban took him away, his grief, sincere as it was, was mingled at first with calculation as to how much he would save a month by the absence of the two, how much the sum would come to in the year, and what would be the capital to bring it in as interest.

But the empty house, without Gokul Chandra in it to make mischief, became more and more difficult for the old man to live in. There was no one now to play tricks upon him when he was engaged in his *puja*,[2] no one to snatch away his food and eat it, no one to run away with his ink-pot, when he was writing up his accounts. His daily routine of life, now uninterrupted, became an intolerable burden to him. He bethought that this unworried peace was endurable only in the world to come. When he caught sight of the holes made in his quilt by his grandchild, and the pen-and-ink sketches executed by the same artist on his rush-mat, his heart was heavy with grief. Once upon a time he had reproached the boy bitterly because he had torn his *dhoti* into pieces within the short space of two years; now tears stood in Jaganath's eyes as he gazed upon the dirty remnants lying in the bedroom. He carefully put them away in his safe, and registered a vow that, should Gokul ever come back again, he should not be reprimanded even if he destroyed one *dhoti* a year.

But Gokul did not return, and poor Jaganath aged rapidly. His empty home seemed emptier every day.

No longer could the old man stay peacefully at home. Even in the middle of the day, when all respectable folks in the village enjoyed their after-dinner siesta, Jaganath might be seen roaming over the village, *hooka*, in hand. The boys, at sight of him, would give up their play, and, retiring in a body to a safe distance, chant verses composed by a local poet, praising the old gentleman's economical habits. No one ventured to say his real name, lest he should have to go without his meal that day[3]—and so people gave him names after their own fancy. Elderly people called him Jaganash,[4]

---

2. A ceremonial worship.
3. It is a superstition current in Bengal that if a man pronounces the name of a very miserly individual, he has to go without his meal that day.
4. Jaganath is the Lord of Festivity, and *Jaganash* would mean the despoiler of it.

but the reason why the younger generation preferred to call him a vampire was hard to guess. It may be that the bloodless, dried-up skin of the old man had some physical resemblance to the vampire's.

II

One afternoon, when Jaganath was rambling as usual through the village lanes shaded by mango topes, he saw a boy, apparently a stranger, assuming the captaincy of the village boys and explaining to them the scheme of some new prank. Won by the force of his character and the startling novelty of his ideas, the boys had all sworn allegiance to him. Unlike the others, he did not run away from the old man as he approached, but came quite close to him and began to shake his own *chadar*. The result was that a live lizard sprang out of it on the old man's body, ran down his back and off towards the jungle. Sudden fright made the poor man shiver from head to foot, to the great amusement of the other boys, who shouted with glee. Before Jaganath had gone far, cursing and swearing, the *gamcha* on his shoulder suddenly disappeared, and the next moment it was seen on the head of the new boy, transformed into a turban.

The novel attentions of this manikin came as a great relief to Jaganath. It was long since any boy had taken such freedom with him. After a good deal of coaxing and many fair promises, he at last persuaded the boy to come to him, and this was the conversation which followed:

'What's your name, my boy?'

'Nitai Pal.'

'Where's your home?'

'Won't tell.'

'Who's your father?'

'Won't tell.'

'Why won't you?'

'Because I have run away from home.'

'What made you do it?'

'My father wanted to send me to school'.

It occurred to Jaganath that it would be useless extravagance to send such a boy to school, and his father must have been an unpractical fool not to have thought so.

'Well, well,' said Jaganath, 'how would you like to come and stay with me?'

'Don't mind,' said the boy, and forthwith he installed himself in Jaganath's house. He felt as little hesitation as though it were the shadow of a tree by the wayside. And not only that. He began to proclaim his wishes as regards his food and clothing with such coolness that you would have thought he had paid his reckoning in full beforehand; and, when anything went wrong, he did not scruple to quarrel with the old man. It had been easy enough for Jaganath to get the better of his own child; but now, where another man's child was concerned, he had to acknowledge defeat.

III

The people of the village marvelled when Nitai Pal was unexpectedly made so much of by Jaganath. They felt sure that the old man's end was near, and the prospect of his bequeathing all his property to this unknown brat made their hearts sore. Furious with envy, they determined to do the boy an injury, but the old man took care of him as though he was a rib in his breast.

At times, the boy threatened that he would go away, and the old man used to say to him temptingly: 'I will leave you all the property I possess.' Young as he was, the boy fully understood the grandeur of this promise.

The village people then began to make inquiries after the father of the boy. Their hearts melted with compassion for the agonised parents, and they declared that the son must be a rascal to cause them so much suffering. They heaped abuses on his head, but the heat with which they did it betrayed envy rather than a sense of justice.

One day the old man learned from a wayfarer that one Damodar Pal was seeking his lost son, and was even now coming towards the village. Nitai, when he heard this, became very restless and was ready to run away, leaving his future wealth to take care of itself. Jaganath reassured him, saying: 'I mean to hide you where nobody can find you—not even the village people themselves.'

This whetted the curiosity of the boy and he said: 'Oh, where? Do show me.'

'People will know, if I show you now. Wait till it is night,' said Jaganath.

The hope of discovering the mysterious hiding-place delighted Nitai. He planned to himself how, as soon as his father had gone away without him, he would have a bet with his comrades, and play hide-and-seek. Nobody would be able to find him. Wouldn't it be fun? His father, too, would ransack the whole village, and not find him—that would be rare fun also.

At noon, Jaganath shut the boy up in his house, and disappeared for some time. When he came home again, Nitai worried him with questions.

No sooner was it dark than Nitai said: 'Grandfather, shall we go now?'

'It isn't night yet,' replied Jaganath.

A little while later the boy exclaimed: 'It is night now, grandfather; come let's go.'

'The village people haven't gone to bed yet,' whispered Jaganath.

Nitai waited but a moment, and said: 'They have gone to bed now, grandfather; I am sure they have. Let's start now.'

The night advanced. Sleep began to weigh heavily on the eyelids of the poor boy, and it was a hard struggle for him to keep awake. At midnight, Jaganath caught hold of the boy's arm, and left the house, groping through the dark lanes of the sleeping village. Not a sound disturbed the stillness, except the occasional howl of a dog, when all the other dogs far and near would join in chorus, or perhaps the flapping of a night-bird, scared by the sound of human footsteps at that unusual hour. Nitai trembled with fear, and held Jaganath fast by the arm.

Across many a field they went, and at last came to a jungle, where stood a dilapidated temple without a god in it. 'What, here!' exclaimed Nitai in a tone of disappointment. It was nothing like what he had imagined. There was not much mystery about it. Often, since running away from home, he had passed nights in deserted temples like this. It was not a bad place for playing hide-and-seek; still it was quite possible that his comrades might track him there.

From the middle of the floor inside, Jaganath removed a slab of stone, and an underground room with a lamp burning in it was revealed to the astonished eyes of the boy. Fear and curiosity assailed his little heart. Jaganath descended by a ladder and Nitai followed him.

Looking around, the boy saw that there were brass *ghurras*[5] on all sides of him. In the middle lay spread an *assan*,[6] and in front of it were arranged vermilion, sandal paste, flowers, and other articles of *puja*. To satisfy his curiosity the boy dipped his hand into some of the *ghurras*, and drew out their contents. They were rupees and gold *mohurs*.

Jaganath, addressing the boy, said: 'I told you, Nitai, that I would give you all my money. I have not got much,—these

---

5. A water-pot holding about three gallons of water.
6. A prayer carpet.

ghurras are all that I possess. These I will make over to you
to-day.'

The boy jumped with delight. 'All?' he exclaimed; 'you
won't take back a rupee, will you?'

'If I do,' said the old man in solemn tones, 'may my hand
be attacked with leprosy. But there is one condition. If ever
my grandson, Gokul Chandra, or his son, or his grandson,
or his great-grandson or any of his progeny should happen
to pass this way, then you must make over to him, or to them,
every rupee and every *mohur* here.'

The boy thought that the old man was raving. 'Very well,'
he replied.

'Then sit on this *assan*,' said Jaganath.

'What for?'

'Because *puja* will be done to you.'

'But why?' said the boy, taken aback.

'This is the rule.'

The boy squatted on the *assan* as he was told. Jaganath
smeared his forehead with sandal paste, put a mark of vermilion
between his eyebrows, flung a garland of flowers round his
neck, and began to recite *mantras*.[7]

To sit there like a god, and hear *mantras* recited, made
poor Nitai feel very uneasy. 'Grandfather,' he whispered.

But Jaganath did not reply, and went on muttering his
incantations.

Finally, with great difficulty he dragged each *ghurra*
before the boy and made him repeat the following vow after
him.

'I do solemnly promise that I will make over all this
treasure to Gokul Chandra Kundu, the son of Brindaban
Kundu, the grandson of Jaganath Kundu, or to the son or to
the grandson or to the great-grandson of the said Gokul

---

7. Incantations.

Chandra Kundu, or to any other progeny of his who may be the rightful heir.'

The boy repeated this over and over again, until he felt stupefied, and his tongue began to grow stiff in his mouth. When the ceremony was over, the air of the cave was laden with the smoke of the earthern lamp and the breath-poison of the two. The boy felt that the roof of his mouth had become dry as dust, and his hands and feet were burning. He was nearly suffocated.

The lamp became dimmer and dimmer, and then went out altogether. In the total darkness that followed, Nitai could hear the old man climbing up the ladder. 'Grandfather, where are you going to?' said he, greatly distressed.

'I am going now,' replied Jaganath; 'you remain here. No one will be able to find you. Remember the name Gokul Chandra, the son of Brindaban, and the grandson of Jaganath.'

He then withdrew the ladder. In a stifled, agonised voice the boy implored: 'I want to go back to father.'

Jaganath replaced the slab. He then knelt down and placed his ear on the stone. Nitai's voice was heard once more— 'Father'—and then came a sound of some heavy object falling with a bump—and then—everything was still.

Having thus placed his wealth in the hands of a *yak*,[8] Jaganath began to cover up the stone with earth. Then he piled broken bricks and loose mortar over it. On the top of all he planted turfs of grass and jungle weeds. The night was almost spent, but he could not tear himself away from the spot. Now and again he placed his ear to the ground, and tried to listen. It seemed to him that from far far below— from the abysmal depth of the earth's interior—came a wailing.

---

8. *Yak* or *Yaksa* is a supernatural being described in Sanskrit mythology and poetry. In Bengal, *Yak* has come to mean a ghostly custodian of treasure, under such circumstances as in this story.

It seemed to him that the night-sky was flooded with that one sound, that the sleeping humanity of all the world was awake, and was sitting on its beds, trying to listen.

The old man in his frenzy kept on heaping earth higher and higher. He wanted somehow to stifle that sound, but still he fancied he could hear 'Father.'

He struck the spot with all his might and said: 'Be quiet—people might hear you.' But still he imagined he heard 'Father.'

The sun lighted up the eastern horizon. Jaganath then left the temple, and came into the open fields.

There, too, somebody called out 'Father.' Startled at the sound, he turned back and saw his son at his heels.

'Father,' said Brindaban, 'I hear my boy is hiding himself in your house. I must have him back.'

With eyes dilated and distorted mouth, the old man leaned forward and exclaimed: 'Your boy?'

'Yes, my boy Gokul. He is Nitai Pal now, and I myself go by the name of Damodar Pal. Your *fame* has spread so widely in the neighbourhood, that we were obliged to cover up our origin lest people should have refused to pronounce our names.'

Slowly the old man lifted both his arms above his head. His fingers began to twitch convulsively, as though he was trying to catch hold of some imaginary object in the air. He then fell on the ground.

When he came to his senses again, he dragged his son towards the ruined temple. When they were both inside it, he said: 'Do you hear any wailing sound?'

'No, I don't,' said Brindaban.

'Just listen very carefully. Do you hear anybody calling out "Father"?'

'No.'

This seemed to relieve him greatly.

From that day forward, he used to go about asking people: 'Do you hear any wailing sound?' They laughed at the raving dotard.

About four years later, Jaganath lay on his death-bed. When the light of this world was gradually fading away from his eyes, and his breathing became more and more difficult, he suddenly sat up in a state of delirium. Throwing both his hands in the air he seemed to grope about for something, muttering: 'Nitai, who has removed my ladder?'

Unable to find the ladder to climb out of his terrible dungeon, where there was no light to see and no air to breathe, he fell on his bed once more, and disappeared into that region where no one has ever been found out in the world's eternal game of hide-and-seek.[9]

---

9. The incidents described in this story, now happily a thing of the past, were by no means rare in Bengal at one time. Our author, however, slightly departs from the current accounts. Such criminally superstitious practices were resorted to by miserly persons under the idea that they themselves would re-acquire the treasure in a future state of existence. 'When you see me in a future birth passing this way, you must make over all this treasure to me. Guard it till then and stir not,'—was the usual promise exacted from the victim before he became *yak*. Many were the 'true' stories we heard in childhood of people becoming suddenly rich by coming across ghostly custodians of wealth belonging to them in a past birth.

The Riddle Solved

I

Krishna Gopal Sircar, *zemindar* of Jhikrakota, made over his estates to his eldest son, and retired to Kasi, as befits a good Hindu, to spend the evening of his life in religious devotion. All the poor and the destitute of the neighbourhood were in tears at the parting. Everyone declared that such piety and benevolence were rare in these degenerate days.

His son, Bipin Bihari, was a young man well educated after the modern fashion, and had taken the degree of Bachelor of Arts. He sported a pair of spectacles, wore a beard, and seldom mixed with others. His private life was unsullied. He did not smoke, and never touched cards. He was a man of stern disposition, though he looked soft and pliable. This trait of his character soon came home to his tenantry in diverse ways. Unlike his father, he would on no account allow the remission of one single pice out of the rents justly due to him. In no circumstances would he grant any tenant one single day's grace in paying up.

On taking over the management of the property, Bipin Bihari discovered that his father had allowed a large number of Brahmins to hold land entirely rent-free, and a larger number at rents much below the prevailing rates. His father was incapable of resisting the importunate solicitation of others—such was the weakness of his character.

Bipin Bihari said this could never be. He could not abandon the income of half his property—and he reasoned with himself thus: *Firstly,* the persons who were in actual enjoyment of the concessions and getting fat at his expense were a lot of worthless people, and wholly undeserving of charity. Charity bestowed on such objects only encouraged idleness. *Secondly,* living nowadays had become much costlier than in the days of his ancestors. Wants had increased apace. For a gentleman to keep up his position had become four times as expensive as in days past. So he could not afford to scatter gifts right and left as his father had done. On the contrary, it was his bounden duty to call back as many of them as he possibly could.

So Bipin Bihari lost no time in carrying into effect what he conceived to be his duty. He was a man of strict principles.

What had gone out of his grasp, returned to him little by little. Only a very small portion of his father's grants did he allow to remain undisturbed, and he took good care to arrange that even those should not be deemed permanent.

The wails of the tenants reached Krishna Gopal at Benares through the post. Some even made a journey to that place to represent their grievances to him in person. Krishna Gopal wrote to his son intimating his displeasure. Bipin Bihari replied, pointing out that the times had changed. In former days, he said, the *zemindar,* was compensated for the gifts he made by the many customary presents he received from his tenantry. Recent statutes had made all such impositions illegal. The *zemindar* had now to rest content with just the stipulated rent, and nothing more. 'Unless,' he continued, 'We keep a strict watch over the payment of our just dues, what will be left to us? Since the tenants won't give us anything extra now, how can we allow them concessions? Our relations must henceforth be strictly commercial. We shall be ruined if we go on making gifts and endowments, and the preservation of our property and the keeping up of our position will be rendered very difficult.'

Krishna Gopal became uneasy at finding that times should have changed so much. 'Well, well,' he murmured to himself, 'the younger generation knows best, I suppose. Our old-fashioned methods won't do now. If I interfere, my son might refuse to manage the property, and insist on my going back. No, thank you—I would rather not. I prefer to devote the few days that are left me to the service of my God.'

II

So things went on. Bipin Bihari put his affairs in order after much litigation in the Courts, and by less constitutional methods outside. Most of the tenants submitted to his will out of fear. Only a fellow called Asimuddin, son of Mirza Bibi, remained refractory.

Bipin's displeasure was keenest against this man. He could quite understand his father having granted rent-free lands to Brahmins, but why this Mohammedan should be holding so much land, some free and some at rents lower than the prevailing rates, was a riddle to him. And what was he? The son of a low Mohammedan widow, giving himself air and defying the whole world, simply because he had learnt to read and write a little at the village school. To Bipin it was intolerable.

He made inquiries of his clerks about Asimuddin's holdings. All that they could tell him was that Babu Krishna Gopal himself had made these grants to the family many years back, but they had no idea as to what his motive might have been. They imagined, however, that perhaps the widow won the compassion of the kind-hearted *zemindar*, by representing to him her woe and misery.

To Bipin these favours seemed to be utterly undeserved. He had not seen the pitiable condition of these people in days gone by. Their comparative ease at the present day and their arrogance drove him to the conclusion that they had impudently swindled his tender-hearted father out of a part of his lawful income.

Asimuddin was a stiff-necked sort of a fellow, too. He vowed that he would lay down his life sooner than give up an inch of his land. Then came open hostilities.

The poor old widow tried her best to pacify her son. 'It is no good fighting with the *zemindar*,' she would often say to him. 'His kindness has kept us alive so long; let us depend upon him still though he may curtail his favours. Surrender to him part of the lands as he desires.'

'Oh, mother!' protested Asimuddin. 'What do you know of these matters, pray?'

One by one, Asimuddin lost the cases instituted against him. The more he lost, the more his obstinacy increased. For the sake of his all, he staked all that was his.

One afternoon, Mirza Bibi collected some fruits and vegetables from her little garden, and unknown to her son went and sought an interview with Bipin Babu. She looked at him with a tenderness maternal in its intensity, and spoke: 'May Allah bless you, my son. Do not destroy Asim—it wouldn't be right of you. To your charge I commit him. Take him as though he were one whom it is your duty to support— as though he were a ne'er-do-well younger brother of yours. Vast is your wealth—don't grudge him a small particle of it, my son.'

This assumption of familiarity on the part of the garrulous old woman annoyed Bipin not a little. 'What do you know of these things, my good woman?' he condescended to say. 'If you have any representations to make, send your son to me.'

Being assured for the second time that she knew nothing about these affairs, Mirza Bibi returned home, wiping her eyes with her apron all the way, and offering her silent prayers to Allah.

III

The litigation dragged its weary length from the Criminal to the Civil courts, and thence to the High Court, where at last Asimuddin met with a partial success. Eighteen months passed in this way. But he was a ruined man now—plunged in debts up to his very ears. His creditors took this opportunity to execute the decrees they had obtained against him. A date was fixed for putting up to auction every stick and stone that he had left.

It was Monday. The village market had assembled by the side of a tiny river, now swollen by the rains. Buying and selling were going on, partly on the bank and partly in the boats moored there. The hubbub was great. Among the commodities for sale jack-fruits preponderated, it being the month of *Asadh. Hilsa* fish were seen in large quantities also. The sky was cloudy. Many of the stall-holders, apprehending a downpour, had stretched, a piece of cloth overhead, across bamboo poles put up for the purpose.

Asimuddin had come too—but he had not a copper with him. No shopkeepers allowed him credit nowadays. He therefore had brought a brass *thali*[1] and a *dao*[2] with him. These he would pawn, and then buy what he needed.

Towards evening, Bipin Babu was out for a walk attended by two or three retainers armed with *lathis*.[3] Attracted by the noise, he directed his steps towards the market. On his arrival,

1. *Thali:* plate.
2. *Dao:* knife.
3. *Lathis:* sticks.

he stopped awhile before the stall of Dwari, the oilman, and made kindly inquiries about his business. All on a sudden, Asimuddin raised his *dao* and ran towards Bipin Babu, roaring like a tiger. The market people caught hold of him half-way, and quickly disarmed him. He was forthwith given in custody to the police. Business in the market then went on as usual.

We cannot say that Bipin Babu was not inwardly pleased at this incident. It is intolerable that the creature we are hunting down should turn and show fight. 'The *badmash*,' Bipin chuckled; 'I have got him at last.'

The ladies of Bipin Babu's house, when they heard the news, exclaimed with horror: 'Oh, the ruffian! What a mercy they seized him in time!' They found consolation in the prospect of the man being punished as he richly deserved.

In another part of the village the same evening the widow's humble cottage, devoid of bread and bereft of her son, became darker than death. Others dismissed the incident of the afternoon from their minds, sat down to their meals, retired to bed and went to sleep, but to the widow the event loomed larger than anything else in this wide world. But, alas, who was there to combat it? Only a bundle of wearied bones and a helpless mother's heart trembling with fear.

IV

Three days have passed in the meanwhile. Tomorrow the case would come up for trial before a Deputy Magistrate. Bipin Babu would have to be examined as a witness. Never before this did a *zemindar* of Jhikrakota appear in the witness-box, but Bipin did not mind.

The next day at the appointed hour, Bipin Babu arrived at the Court in a palanquin in great state. He wore a turban on his head, and a watch-chain dangled on his breast. The Deputy Magistrate invited him to a seat on the daïs, beside his own. The Court-room was crowded to suffocation. So great a sensation had not been witnessed in this Court for many a year.

When the time for the case to be called drew near, a *chaprassi* came and whispered something in Bipin Babu's ear. He got up very agitated and walked out, begging the Deputy Magistrate to excuse him for a few minutes.

Outside he saw his old father a little way off, standing under a *banian* tree, barefooted and wrapped in a piece of *namabali*.[4] A string of beads was in his hand. His slender form shone with a gentle lustre, and tranquil compassion seemed to radiate from his forehead.

Bipin, hampered by his close-fitting trousers and his flowing *chapkan*, touched his father's feet with his forehead. As he did this his turban came off and kissed his nose, and his watch, popping out of his pocket, swung to and fro in the air. Bipin hurriedly straightened his turban, and begged his father to come to his pleader's house close by.

'No, thank you,' Krishna Gopal replied, 'I will tell you here what I have got to say.'

A curious crowd had gathered by this time. Bipin's attendants pushed them back.

Then Krishna Gopal said: 'You must do what you can to get Asim acquitted, and restore him the lands that you have taken away from him.'

'Is it for this, father,' said Bipin, very much surprised, 'that you have come all the way from Benares? Would you tell me why you have made these people the objects of your special favour?'

'What would you gain by knowing it, my boy?'

But Bipin persisted. 'It is only this, father,' he went on; 'I have revoked many a grant because I thought the tenants were not deserving. There were many Brahmins among them,

---

4. A garment with the name of Krishna printed over it.

but of them you never said a word. Why are you so keen about these Mohammedans now? After all that has happened, if I drop this case against Asim, and give him back his lands, what shall I say to the people?'

Krishna Gopal kept silence for some moments. Then, passing the beads through his shaky fingers with rapidity, he spoke with a tremulous voice: 'Should it be necessary to explain your conduct to people, you may tell them that Asimuddin is my son—and your brother.'

'What?' exclaimed Bipin in painful surprise 'From a Musalman's womb?'

'Even so, my son,' was the calm reply.

Bipin stood there for some time in mute astonishment. Then he found words to say: 'Come home, father; we will talk about it afterwards.'

'No, my son,' replied the old man, 'having once relinquished the world to serve my God, I cannot go home again. I return hence. Now I leave you to do what your sense of duty may suggest.' He then blessed his son, and, checking his tears with difficulty, walked off with tottering steps.

Bipin was dumbfounded, not knowing what to say nor what to do. 'So, such was the piety of the older generation,' he said to himself. He reflected with pride how much better he was than his father in point of education and morality. This was the result, he concluded, of not having a principle to guide one's actions.

Returning to the Court, he saw Asimuddin outside between two constables, awaiting his trial. He looked emaciated and worn out. His lips were pale and dry, and his eyes unnaturally bright. A dirty piece of cloth worn to shreds covered him. 'This my brother!' Bipin shuddered at the thought.

The Deputy Magistrate and Bipin were friends and the case ended in a fiasco. In a few days Asimuddin was restored to his former condition. Why all this happened, he could not understand. The village people were greatly surprised also.

However, the news of Krishna Gopal's arrival just before the trial soon got abroad. People began to exchange meaningful glances. The pleaders in their shrewdness guessed the whole affair. One of them, Ram Taran Babu, was beholden to Krishna Gopal for his education and his start in life. Somehow or other he had always suspected that the virtue and piety of his benefactor were shams. Now he was fully convinced that, if a searching inquiry were made, all 'pious' men might be found out. 'Let them tell their beads as much as they like,' he thought with glee, 'everybody in this world is just as bad as myself. The only difference between a good and a bad man is that the good practise dissimulation while the bad don't.' The revelation that Krishna Gopal's far-famed piety, benevolence, and magnanimity were nothing but a cloak of hypocrisy, settled a difficulty that had oppressed Ram Taran Babu for many years. By what process of reasoning, we do not know, the burden of gratitude was greatly lifted off his mind. It was a vast relief to him!

The Elder Sister

I

Having described at length the misdeeds of an unfortunate woman's wicked, tyrannical husband, Tara, the woman's neighbour in the village, very shortly declared her verdict: 'Fire be to such a husband's mouth.'

At this Joygopal Babu's wife felt much hurt; it did not become womankind to wish, in any circumstances whatever, a worse species of fire than that of a cigar in a husband's mouth.

When, therefore, she mildly disapproved the verdict, hard-hearted Tara cried with redoubled vehemence: "Twere better to be a widow seven births over than the wife of such a husband,' and saying this she broke up the meeting and left.

Sasi said within herself: 'I can't imagine any offence in a husband that could so harden the heart against him.' Even as she turned the matter over in her mind, all the tenderness of her loving soul gushed forth towards her own husband now abroad. Throwing herself with outstretched arms on that part of the bed whereon her husband was wont to lie, she kissed the empty pillow, caught the smell of her husband's head, and, shutting the door, brought out from a wooden box an old and almost faded photograph with some letters in his handwriting, and sat gazing upon them. Thus she passed the hushed noontide alone in her room, musing of old memories and shedding tears of sadness.

It was no new yoke this between Sasikala and Joygopal. They had been married at an early age and had children. Their long companionship had made the days go by in an easy, commonplace sort of way. On neither side had there been any symptoms of excessive passion. They had lived together nearly sixteen years without a break, when her husband was suddenly called away from home on business, and then a great impulse of love awoke in Sasi's soul. As separation strained the tie, love's knot grew tighter, and the passion, whose existence Sasi had not felt, now made her throb with pain.

So it happened that after so many long years, and at such an age, and being the mother of children, Sasi, on this spring noon, in her lonely chamber, lying on the bed of separation, began to dream the sweet dream of a bride in her budding youth. That love of which hitherto she had been unconscious suddenly aroused her with its murmuring music. She wandered a long way up the stream, and saw many a golden mansion and many a grove on either bank; but no foothold could she find now amid the vanished hopes of happiness. She began to say to herself that, when next she met her husband, life should not be insipid nor should the spring come in vain. How very often, in idle disputation or some petty quarrel, had she teased her husband! With all the singleness of a penitent heart she vowed that she would never show impatience again, never oppose her husband's wishes, bear all his commands, and with a tender heart submit to whatever he wished of good or ill; for the husband was all-in-all, the husband was the dearest object of love, the husband was divine.

Sasikala was the only and much-petted daughter of her parents. For this reason, though he had only a small property of his own, Joygopal had no anxieties about the future. His father-in-law had enough to support them in a village with royal state.

And then in his old age a son was born untimely to Sasikala's father. To tell the truth, Sasi was very sore in her mind at this unlooked-for, improper, and unjust action of her parents; nor was Joygopal particularly pleased.

The parents' love centred in this son of their advanced years, and when the newly arrived, diminutive, sleepy brother-in-law seized with his two weak tiny fists all the hopes and expectations of Joygopal, Joygopal found a place in a tea-garden in Assam.

His friends urged him to look for employment hard-by, but whether out of a general feeling of resentment, or knowing the chances of rapid rise in a tea-garden, Joygopal would not pay heed to anybody. He sent his wife and children to his father-in-law's, and left for Assam. It was the first separation between husband and wife in their married life.

This incident made Sasikala very angry with her baby brother. The soreness which may not pass the lips is felt the more keenly within. When the little fellow sucked and slept at his ease, his big sister found a hundred reasons, such as the rice is cold, the boys are too late for school, to worry herself and others, day and night, with her petulant humours.

But in a short time the child's mother died. Before her death, she committed her infant son to her daughter's care.

Then did the motherless child easily conquer his sister's heart. With loud whoops he would fling himself upon her, and with right good-will try to get her mouth, nose, eyes within his own tiny mouth; he would seize her hair within his little fists and refuse to give it up; awaking before the dawn, he would roll over to her side and thrill her with his soft touch, and babble like a noisy brook; later on, he would call her *jiji* and *jijima*, and in hours of work and rest, by doing forbidden things, eating forbidden food, going to forbidden places, would set up a regular tyranny over her; then Sasi could resist no longer. She surrendered herself completely to this wayward little tyrant. Since the child had no mother, his influence over her became the greater.

II

The child was named Nilmani. When he was two years old his father fell seriously ill. A letter reached Joygopal asking him to come as quickly as possible. When after much trouble he got leave and arrived, Kaliprasanna's last hour had come.

Before he died Kaliprasanna entrusted Joygopal with the charge of his son, and left a quarter of his estate to his daughter.

So Joygopal gave up his appointment, and came home to look after his property.

After a long time husband and wife met again. When a material body breaks it may be put together again. But when two human beings are divided, after a long separation, they never re-unite at the same place, and to the same time; for the mind is a living thing, and moment by moment it grows and changes.

In Sasi reunion stirred a new emotion. The numbness of age-long habit in their old marriage was entirely removed by the longing born of separation, and she seemed to win her husband much more closely than before. Had she not vowed in her mind that whatever days might come, and how long so ever they might be, she would never let the brightness of this glowing love for her husband be dimmed.

Of this reunion, however, Joygopal felt differently. When they were constantly together before he had been bound to his wife by his interests and idiosyncrasies. His wife was then a living truth in his life, and there would have been a great rent in the web of his daily habit if she were left out. Consequently Joygopal found himself in deep waters at first when he went abroad. But in time this breach in habit was patched up by a new habit.

And this was not all. Formerly his days went by in the most indolent and careless fashion. For the last two years, the stimulus of bettering his condition had stirred so powerfully in his breast that he had nothing else in his thoughts. As compared with the intensity of this new passion, his old life seemed like an unsubstantial shadow. The greatest changes in a woman's nature are wrought by love; in a man's, by ambition.

Joygopal, when he returned after two years, found his wife not quite the same as of old. To her life his infant brother-in-law had added a new breadth. This part of her life was wholly unfamiliar to him—here he had no communion with his wife. His wife tried hard to share her love for the child with him, but it cannot be said that she succeeded. Sasi would come with the child in her arms, and hold him before her husband with a smiling face—Nilmani would clasp Sasi's neck, and hide his face on her shoulder, and admit no obligation of kindred. Sasi wished that her little brother might show Joygopal all the arts he had learnt to capture a man's mind. But Joygopal was not very keen about it. How could the child show any enthusiasm? Joygopal could not at all understand what there was in the heavy-pated, grave-faced, dusky child that so much love should be wasted on him.

Women quickly understand the ways of love. Sasi at once understood that Joygopal did not care for Nilmani. Henceforth she used to screen her brother with the greatest care—to keep him away from the unloving, repelling look of her husband. Thus the child came to be the treasure of her secret care, the object of her isolated love.

Joygopal was greatly annoyed when Nilmani cried; so Sasi would quickly press the child to her breast, and with her whole heart and soul try to soothe him. And when Nilmani's cry happened to disturb Joygopal's sleep at night, and Joygopal with an expression of displeasure, and in a tortured spirit, growled at the child, Sasi felt humbled and fluttered like a guilty thing. Then she would take up the child in her lap, retire to a distance, and in a voice of pleading love, with such endearments as 'my gold, my treasure, my jewel,' lull him to sleep.

Children will fall out for a hundred things. Formerly in such cases, Sasi would punish her children, and side with her brother, for he was motherless. Now the law changed with the judge. Nilmani had often to bear heavy punishment without fault and without inquiry. This wrong went like a dagger to Sasi's heart; so she would take her punished brother into her room, and with sweets and toys, and by caressing and kissing him, solace as much as she could his stricken heart.

Thus the more Sasi loved Nilmani, the more Joygopal was annoyed with him. On the other hand, the more Joygopal showed his contempt for Nilmani, the more would Sasi bathe the child with the nectar of her love.

And when Joygopal behaved harshly to his wife, Sasi would minister to him silently, meekly, and with loving-kindness. But inwardly they hurt each other, moment by moment, about Nilmani.

The hidden clash of a silent conflict like this is far harder to bear than an open quarrel.

III

Nilmani's head was the largest part of him. It seemed as if the Creator had blown through a slender stick a big bubble at its top. The doctors feared sometimes that the child might be as frail and as quickly evanescent as a bubble. For a long time he could neither speak nor walk. Looking at his sad grave face, you might think that his parents had unburdened all the sad weight of their advanced years upon the head of this little child.

With his sister's care and nursing, Nilmani passed the period of danger, and arrived at his sixth year.

In the month of *Kartik*, on the *bhaiphota*[1] day, Sasi had dressed Nilmani up as a little Babu, in coat and *chadar* and red-bordered *dhoti*, and was giving him the 'brother's mark,' when her outspoken neighbour Tara came in and, for one reason or another, began a quarrel.

''Tis no use,' cried she, 'giving the "brother's mark" with so much show and ruining the brother in secret.'

At this Sasi was thunderstruck with astonishment, rage, and pain. Tara repeated the rumour that Sasi and her husband had conspired together to put the minor Nilmani's property up for sale for arrears of rent, and to purchase it in the name of her husband's cousin. When Sasi heard this, she uttered a curse that those who could spread such a foul lie might be stricken with leprosy in the mouth. And then she went weeping to her husband, and told him of the gossip. Joygopal said: 'Nobody can be trusted in these days. Upen is my aunt's son, and I felt quite safe in leaving him in charge of the property. He could not have allowed the *taluk* Hasilpur to fall into arrears and purchase it himself in secret, if I had had the least inkling about it.'

'Won't you sue then?' asked Sasi in astonishment.

'Sue one's cousin!' said Joygopal. 'Besides, it would be useless, a simple waste of money.'

It was Sasi's supreme duty to trust her husband's word, but Sasi could not. At last her happy home, the domesticity

---

1. Lit. the 'brother's mark.' A beautiful and touching ceremony in which a Hindu sister makes a mark of sandalwood paste on the forehead of her brother and utters a formula, 'putting the barrier in Yama's doorway' (figurative for wishing long life). On these occasions, the sisters entertain their brothers and make them presents of clothes, etc.

of her love seemed hateful to her. That home life which had once seemed her supreme refuge was nothing more than a cruel snare of self-interest, which had surrounded them, brother and sister, on all sides. She was a woman, single-handed, and she knew not how she could save the helpless Nilmani. The more she thought, the more her heart filled with terror, loathing, and an infinite love for her imperilled little brother. She thought that, if she only knew how, she would appear before the *Lat Saheb*,[2] nay, write to the Maharani herself, to save her brother's property. The Maharani would surely not allow Nilmani's *taluk*[3] of Hasilpur, with an income of seven hundred and fifty-eight rupees a year, to be sold.

When Sasi was thus thinking of bringing her husband's cousin to book by appealing to the Maharani herself, Nilmani was suddenly seized with fever and convulsions.

Joygopal called in the village doctor. When Sasi asked for a better doctor, Joygopal said: 'Why, Matilal isn't a bad sort.'

Sasi fell at his feet, and charged him with an oath on her own head; whereupon Joygopal said: 'Well, I shall send for the doctor from town.'

Sasi lay with Nilmani in her lap, nor would Nilmani let her out of his sight for a minute; he clung to her lest by some pretence she should escape; even while he slept he would not loosen his hold of her dress.

Thus the whole day passed, and Joygopal came after nightfall to say that the doctor was not at home; he had gone to see a patient at a distance. He added that he himself had to leave that very day on account of a lawsuit, and that he had told Matilal, who would regularly call to see the patient.

At night Nilmani wandered in his sleep. As soon as the morning dawned, Sasi, without the least scruple, took a boat

2. The Viceroy.
3. Land.

with her sick brother, and went straight to the doctor's house. The doctor was at home—he had not left the town. He quickly found lodgings for her, and having installed her under the care of an elderly widow, undertook the treatment of the boy.

The next day Joygopal arrived. Blazing with fury, he ordered his wife to return home with him at once.

'Even if you cut me to pieces, I won't return,' replied his wife. 'You all want to kill my Nilmani, who has no father, no mother, none other than me, but I will save him.'

'Then you remain here, and don't come back to my house,' cried Joygopal indignantly.

Sasi at length fired up. '*Your* house! Why, 'tis my brother's!'

'All right, we'll see,' said Joygopal. The neighbours made a great stir over this incident. 'If you want to quarrel with your husband,' said Tara, 'do so at home. What is the good of leaving your house? After all, Joygopal is your husband.'

By spending all the money she had with her, and selling her ornaments, Sasi saved her brother from the jaws of death. Then she heard that the big property which they had in Dwarigram, where their dwelling-house stood, the income of which was more than Rs.1500 a year, had been transferred by Joygopal into his own name with the help of the *zemindar*. And now the whole property belonged to them, not to her brother.

When he had recovered from his illness, Nilmani would cry plaintively: 'Let us go home, sister.' His heart was pining for his nephews and nieces, his companions. So he repeatedly said: 'Let us go home, sister, to that old house of ours.' At this Sasi wept. Where was their home?

But it was no good crying. Her brother had no one else besides herself in the world. Sasi thought of this, wiped her tears, and, entering the *zenana* of the Deputy Magistrate, Tarini Babu, appealed to his wife. The Deputy Magistrate knew Joygopal. That a woman should forsake her home, and engage in a dispute with her husband regarding matters of property, greatly incensed him against Sasi. However, Tarini Babu kept Sasi diverted, and instantly wrote to Joygopal. Joygopal put his wife and brother-in-law into a boat by force, and brought them home.

Husband and wife, after a second separation, met again for the second time! The decree of Prajapati![4]

Having got back his old companions after a long absence, Nilmani was perfectly happy. Seeing his unsuspecting joy, Sasi felt as if her heart would break.

IV

The Magistrate was touring in the Mofussil during the cold weather and pitched his tent within the village to shoot. The Saheb met Nilmani on the village *maidan*. The other boys gave him a wide berth, varying Chanakya's couplet a little, and adding the Saheb to the list of 'the clawed, the toothed, and the horned beasts.' But grave-natured Nilmani in imperturbable curiosity serenely gazed at the Saheb.

The Saheb was amused and came up and asked in Bengali: 'You read at the *pathasala*?'

The boy silently nodded. 'What *pustaks*[5] do you read?' asked the Saheb.

As Nilmani did not understand the word *pustak*, he silently fixed his gaze on the Magistrate's face. Nilmani told his sister the story of his meeting the Magistrate with great enthusiasm.

At noon, Joygopal, dressed in trousers, *chapkan*,[6] and *pagri*,[7] went to pay his salams to the Saheb. A crowd of suitors,

---

4. The Hindu god of marriage.
5. A literary word for books. The colloquial will be *boi*.
6. A *chapkan* is a long coat.
7. Turban.

chaprassies,[8] and constables stood about him. Fearing the heat, the Saheb had seated himself at a court-table outside the tent, in the open shade, and placing Joygopal in a chair, questioned him about the state of the village. Having taken the seat of honour in open view of the community, Joygopal swelled inwardly, and thought it would be a good thing if any of the Chakrabartis or Nandis came and saw him there.

At this moment, a woman, closely veiled, and accompanied by Nilmani, came straight up to the Magistrate. She said: 'Saheb, into your hands I resign my helpless brother. Save him.' The Saheb, seeing the large-headed, solemn boy, whose acquaintance he had already made, and thinking that the woman must be of a respectable family, at once stood up and said: 'Please enter the tent.'

The woman said: 'What I have to say I will say here.'

Joygopal writhed and turned pale. The curious villagers thought it capital fun, and pressed closer. But the moment the Saheb lifted his cane they scampered off.

Holding her brother by the hand, Sasi narrated the history of the orphan from the beginning. As Joygopal tried to interrupt now and then, the Magistrate thundered with a flushed face, '*Chup rao,*' and with the tip of his cane motioned to Joygopal to leave the chair and stand up.

Joygopal, inwardly raging against Sasi, stood speechless. Nilmani nestled up close to his sister, and listened awe-struck.

When Sasi had finished her story, the Magistrate put a few questions to Joygopal, and on hearing his answers, kept silence for a long while, and then addressed Sasi thus: 'My good woman, though this matter may not come up before me, still rest assured I will do all that is needful about it. You can return home with your brother without the least misgiving.'

---

8. Servants.

Sasi said: 'Saheb, so long as he does not get back his own home, I dare not take him there. Unless you keep Nilmani with you none else will be able to save him.'

'And what would you do?' queried the Saheb.

'I will retire to my husband's house,' said Sasi; 'there is nothing to fear for me.'

The Saheb smiled a little, and, as there was nothing else to do, agreed to take charge of this lean, dusty, grave, sedate, gentle Bengali boy whose neck was ringed with amulets.

When Sasi was about to take her leave, the boy clutched her dress. 'Don't be frightened, *baba,*—come,' said the Saheb. With tears streaming behind her veil, Sasi said: 'Do go, my brother, my darling brother—you will meet your sister again!'

Saying this she embraced him and stroked his head and back, and releasing her dress, hastily withdrew; and just then the Saheb put his left arm round him. The child wailed out: 'Sister oh, my sister!' Sasi turned round at once, and with outstretched arm made a sign of speechless solace, and with a bursting heart withdrew.

Again in that old, ever-familiar house husband and wife met. The decree of Prajapati!

But this union did not last long. For soon after the villagers learnt one morning that Sasi had died of cholera in the night, and had been instantly cremated.

None uttered a word about it. Only neighbour Tara would sometimes be on the point of bursting out, but people would shut up her mouth, saying, 'Hush!'

At parting, Sasi gave her word to her brother they would meet again. Where that word was kept none can tell.

Subha

When the girl was given the name of Subhashini,[1] who could have guessed that she would prove dumb? Her two elder sisters were Sukeshini[2] and Suhasini,[3] and for the sake of uniformity her father named his youngest girl Subhashini. She was called Subha for short.

Her two elder sisters had been married with the usual cost and difficulty, and now the youngest daughter lay like a silent weight upon the heart of her parents. All the world seemed to think that, because she did not speak, therefore she did not feel; it discussed her future and its own anxiety freely in her presence. She had understood from her earliest childhood that God had sent her like a curse to her father's house, so she withdrew herself from ordinary people, and tried to live apart. If only they would all forget her she felt she could endure it. But who can forget pain? Night and day her parents' minds were aching on her account. Especially her mother looked upon her as a deformity in herself. To a mother a daughter is a more closely intimate part of herself than a son can be; and a fault in her is a source of personal shame. Banikantha, Subha's father, loved her rather better than his

1. Sweetly speaking.
2. Lovely-locked.
3. Sweetly smiling.

other daughters; her mother regarded her with aversion as a stain upon her own body.

If Subha lacked speech, she did not lack a pair of large dark eyes, shaded with long lashes; and her lips trembled like a leaf in response to any thought that rose in her mind.

When we express our thought in words, the medium is not found easily. There must be a process of translation, which is often inexact, and then we fall into error. But black eyes need no translating; the mind itself throws a shadow upon them. In them thought opens or shuts, shines forth, or goes out in darkness, hangs steadfast like the setting moon, or, like the swift and restless lightning, illumines all quarters of the sky. They who from birth have had no other speech than the trembling of their lips learn a language of the eyes, endless in expression, deep as the sea, clear as the heavens, wherein play dawn and sunset, light and shadow. The dumb have a lonely grandeur like Nature's own. Wherefore the other children almost dreaded Subha, and never played with her. She was silent and companionless as noontide.

The hamlet where she lived was Chandipur. Its river, small for a river of Bengal, kept to its narrow bounds like a daughter of the middle class. This busy streak of water never overflowed its banks, but went about its duties as though it were a member of every family in the villages beside it. On either side were houses and banks shaded with trees. So stepping from her queenly throne, the river-goddess became a garden deity of each home; and forgetful of herself, performed her task of endless benediction with swift and cheerful foot.

Banikantha's house looked upon the stream. Every hut and stack in the place could be seen by the passing boatmen. I know not if amid these signs of worldly wealth any one noticed the little girl who, when her work was done, stole away to the waterside, and sat there. But here Nature fulfilled her want of speech, and spoke for her. The murmur of the brook, the voice of the village folk, the songs of the boatmen, the crying of the birds and rustle of trees mingled, and were one with the trembling of her heart. They became one vast wave of sound, which beat upon her restless soul. This murmur and movement of Nature were the dumb girl's language; that speech of the dark eyes, which the long lashes shaded, was the language of the world about her. From the trees, where the cicadas chirped, to the quiet stars there was nothing but signs and gestures, weeping and sighing. And in the deep mid-noon, when the boatmen and fisherfolk had gone to their dinner, when the villagers slept, and birds were still, when the ferry-boats were idle, when the great busy world paused in its toil, and became suddenly a lonely, awful giant, then beneath the vast impressive heavens there were only dumb Nature and a dumb girl, sitting very silent—one under the spreading sunlight, the other where a small tree cast its shadow.

But Subha was not altogether without friends. In the stall were two cows, Sarbbashi and Panguli. They had never heard their names from her lips, but they knew her footfall. Though she had no words, she murmured lovingly and they understood her gentle murmuring better than all speech. When she fondled them or scolded or coaxed them, they understood her better than men could do. Subha would come to the shed, and throw her arms round Sarbbashi's neck; she would rub her cheek against her friend's, and Panguli would turn her great kind eyes and lick her face. The girl paid them three regular visits every day, and others that were irregular. Whenever she heard any words that hurt her, she would come to these dumb friends out of due time. It was as though they guessed her anguish of spirit from her quiet look of sadness. Coming close to her, they would rub their horns softly against her arms, and in dumb, puzzled fashion try to comfort her. Besides these two, there were goats and a kitten; but Subha had not the same equality of friendship with them, though they showed the same attachment. Every time it got a chance, night or day, the kitten would jump into her lap, and settle down to slumber, and show its appreciation of an aid to sleep as Subha drew her soft fingers over its neck and back.

Subha had a comrade also among the higher animals, and it is hard to say what were the girl's relations with him, for he could speak, and his gift of speech left them without any common language. He was the youngest boy of the Gosains, Pratap by name, an idle fellow. After long effort, his parents had abandoned the hope that he would ever make his living. Now losers have this advantage, that, though their own folk disapprove of them, they are generally popular with every one else. Having no work to chain them, they become public property. Just as every town needs an open space where all may breathe, so a village needs two or three gentlemen of leisure, who can give time to all; so that, if we are lazy and want a companion, one is to hand.

Pratap's chief ambition was to catch fish. He managed to waste a lot of time this way, and might be seen almost any afternoon so employed. It was thus most often that he met Subha. Whatever he was about, he liked a companion; and, when one is catching fish, a silent companion is best of all. Pratap respected Subha for her taciturnity, and, as every one called her Subha, he showed his affection by calling her Su. Subha used to sit beneath a tamarind, and Pratap, a little distance off, would cast his line. Pratap took with him a small allowance of betel, and Subha prepared it for him. And I think that, sitting and gazing a long while, she desired ardently to bring some great help to Pratap, to be of real aid, to prove by any means that she was not a useless burden to the world. But there was nothing to do. Then she turned to the Creator in prayer for some rare power, that by an astonishing miracle she might startle Pratap into exclaiming: 'My! I never dreamt our Su could have done this!'

Only think! if Subha had been a water nymph, she might have risen slowly from the river, bringing the gem of a snake's crown to the landingplace. Then Pratap, leaving his paltry fishing, might dive into the lower world, and see there, on a golden bed in a palace of silver, whom else but dumb little Su, Banikantha's child? Yes, our Su, the only daughter of the king of that shining city of jewels! But that might not be, it was impossible. Not that anything is really impossible, but Su had been born, not into the royal house of Patalpur,[4] but into Banikantha's family, and she knew no means of astonishing the Gosains' boy.

Gradually she grew up. Gradually she began to find herself. A new inexpressible consciousness like a tide from the central places of the sea, when the moon is full, swept through her. She saw herself, questioned herself, but no answer came that she could understand.

Once upon a time, late on a night of full moon, she slowly opened her door, and peeped out timidly. Nature, herself at full moon, like lonely Subha, was looking down on the sleeping earth. Her strong young life beat within her; joy and sadness filled her being to its brim; she reached the limits even of her own illimitable, loneliness, nay, passed beyond them. Her heart was heavy, and she could not speak! At the skirts of this silent, troubled Mother there stood a silent troubled girl.

The thought of her marriage filled her parents with an anxious care. People blamed them, and even talked of making them outcasts. Banikantha was well off; they had fish-curry twice daily; and consequently he did not lack enemies. Then the women interfered, and Bani went away for a few days. Presently he returned, and said: 'We must go to Calcutta.'

They got ready to go to this strange country. Subha's heart was heavy with tears, like a mistwrapt dawn. With a

---

4. The Lower World.

vague fear that had been gathering for days, she dogged her father and mother like a dumb animal. With her large eyes wide open, she scanned their faces as though she wished to learn something. But not a word did they vouchsafe. One afternoon in the midst of all this, as Pratap was fishing, he laughed: 'So then, Su, they have caught your bridegroom, and you are going to be married! Mind you don't forget me altogether!' Then he turned his mind again to his fish. As a stricken doe looks in the hunter's face, asking in silent agony: 'What have I done to you?' so Subha looked at Pratap. That day she sat no longer beneath her tree. Banikantha, having finished his nap, was smoking in his bedroom when Subha dropped down at his feet and burst out weeping as she gazed towards him. Banikantha tried to comfort her, and his cheek grew wet with tears.

It was settled that on the morrow they should go to Calcutta. Subha went to the cow-shed to bid farewell to her childhood's comrades. She fed them with her hand; she clasped their necks; she looked into their faces, and tears fell fast from the eyes which spoke for her. That night was the tenth of the moon. Subha left her room, and flung herself down on her grassy couch beside her dear river. It was as if she threw her arms about Earth, her strong, silent mother, and tried to say: 'Do not let me leave you, mother. Put your arms about me, as I have put mine about you, and hold me fast.'

One day in a house in Calcutta, Subha's mother dressed her up with great care. She imprisoned her hair, knotting it up in laces, she hung her about with ornaments, and did her best to kill her natural beauty. Subha's eyes filled with tears. Her mother, fearing they would grow swollen with weeping, scolded her harshly, but the tears disregarded the scolding. The bridegroom came with a friend to inspect the bride. Her parents were dizzy with anxiety and fear when they saw the god arrive to select the beast for his sacrifice. Behind the stage, the mother called her instructions aloud, and increased her daughter's weeping twofold, before she sent her into the examiner's presence. The great man, after scanning her a long time, observed: 'Not so bad.'

He took special note of her tears, and thought she must have a tender heart. He put it to her credit in the account, arguing that the heart, which to-day was distressed at leaving her parents, would presently prove a useful possession. Like the oyster's pearls, the child's tears only increased her value, and he made no other comment.

The almanac was consulted, and the marriage took place on an auspicious day. Having delivered over their dumb girl into another's hands, Subha's parents returned home. Thank God! Their caste in this and their safety in the next world were assured! The bridegroom's work lay in the west, and shortly after the marriage he took his wife thither.

In less than ten days every one knew that the bride was dumb! At least, if any one did not, it was not her fault, for she deceived no one. Her eyes told them everything, though no one understood her. She looked on every hand; she found no speech: she missed the faces, familiar from birth, of those who had understood a dumb girl's language. In her silent heart there sounded an endless, voiceless weeping, which only the Searcher of Hearts could hear.

Using both eyes and ears *this* time, her lord made another careful examination, and married a second wife who could speak.

The Postmaster

The postmaster first took up his duties in the village of Ulapur. Though the village was a small one, there was an indigo factory near by, and the proprietor, an Englishman, had managed to get a post office established.

Our postmaster belonged to Calcutta. He felt like a fish out of water in this remote village. His office and living-room were in a dark thatched shed, not far from a green, slimy pond, surrounded on all sides by a dense growth.

The men employed in the indigo factory had no leisure; moreover, they were hardly desirable companions for decent folk. Nor is a Calcutta boy an adept in the art of associating with others. Among strangers he appears either proud or ill at ease. At any rate, the postmaster had but little company; nor had he much to do.

At times he tried his hand at writing a verse or two. That the movement of the leaves and the clouds of the sky were enough to fill life with joy—such were the sentiments to which he sought to give expression. But God knows that the poor fellow would have felt it as the gift of a new life if some genie of the *Arabian Nights* had in one night swept away the trees, leaves and all, and replaced them with a macadamised road, hiding the clouds from view with rows of tall houses.

The postmaster's salary was small. He had to cook his own meals, which he used to share with Ratan, an orphan girl of the village, who did odd jobs for him.

When in the evening the smoke began to curl up from the village cow-sheds,[1] and the cicadas chirped in every bush; when the *faquirs* of the Baül sect sang their shrill songs in their daily meeting-place; when any poet, who had attempted to watch the movement of the leaves in the dense bamboo thickets, would have felt a ghostly shiver run down his back, the postmaster would light his little lamp, and call out 'Ratan.'

Ratan would sit outside waiting for this call, and, instead of coming in at once, would reply: 'Did you call me, sir?'

'What are you doing?' the postmaster would ask.

'I must be going to light the kitchen fire,' would be the answer.

And the postmaster would say: 'Oh, let the kitchen fire be for awhile; light me my pipe first.'

At last Ratan would enter, with puffed-out cheeks, vigorously blowing into a flame a live coal to light the tobacco. This would give the postmaster an opportunity of conversing. 'Well, Ratan,' perhaps he would begin 'do you remember anything of your mother?' That was a fertile subject. Ratan partly remembered, and partly didn't. Her father had been fonder of her than her mother; him she recollected more vividly. He used to come home in the evening after his work, and one or two evenings stood out more clearly than others, like pictures in her memory. Ratan would squat on the floor near the postmaster's feet, as memories crowded in upon her. She called to mind a little brother that she had—and how on some bygone cloudy day she had played at fishing with him on the edge of the pond, with a twig for a make-believe fishing-rod. Such little incidents would drive out greater events

---

1. Smoky fires are lit in the cow-sheds to drive off mosquitoes.

from her mind. Thus, as they talked, it would often get very late, and the postmaster would feel too lazy to do any cooking at all. Ratan would then hastily light the fire, and toast some unleavened bread, which, with the cold remnants of the morning meal, was enough for their supper.

On some evenings, seated at his desk in the corner of the big empty shed, the postmaster too would call up memories of his own home, of his mother and his sister, of those for whom in his exile his heart was sad,—memories which were always haunting him, but which he could not talk about with the men of the factory, though he found himself naturally recalling them aloud in the presence of the simple little girl. And so it came about that the girl would allude to his people as mother, brother, and sister,[2] as if she had known them all her life. In fact, she had a complete picture of each one of them painted in her little heart.

One noon, during a break in the rains, there was a cool soft breeze blowing; the smell of the damp grass and leaves in the hot sun felt like the warm breathing of the tired earth on one's body. A persistent bird went on all the afternoon repeating the burden of its one complaint in Nature's audience chamber.

The postmaster had nothing to do. The shimmer of the freshly washed leaves, and the banked-up remnants of the retreating rain-clouds were sights to see; and the postmaster was watching them, and thinking to himself: 'Oh, if only some kindred soul were near—just one loving human being whom I could hold near my heart!' This was exactly, he went on to think, what that bird was trying to say, and it was the same feeling which the murmuring leaves were striving to express. But no one knows, or would believe, that such an idea might

---

2. Family servants call the master and mistress, father and mother, and the children, elder brothers and sisters.

also take possession of an ill-paid village postmaster in the deep, silent mid-day interval of his work.

The postmaster sighed, and called out, 'Ratan.' Ratan was then sprawling beneath the guava-tree, busily engaged in eating unripe guavas. At the voice of her master, she ran up breathlessly, saying: 'Were you calling me, Dada?'[3] 'I was thinking,' said the postmaster, 'of teaching you to read,' and then for the rest of the afternoon he taught her the alphabet.

Thus, in a very short time, Ratan had got as far as the double consonants.

It seemed as though the showers of the season would never end. Canals, ditches, and hollows were all overflowing with water. Day and night the patter of rain was heard, and the croaking of frogs. The village roads became impassable, and marketing had to be done in punts.

One heavily clouded morning, the postmaster's little pupil had been long waiting outside the door for her call, but, not hearing it as usual, she took up her dog-eared book, and slowly entered the room. She found her master stretched out on his pallet, and, thinking he was resting, she was about to retire on tip-toe, when she suddenly heard her name—'Ratan!' She turned at once and asked: 'Were you sleeping, Dada?' The postmaster in a plaintive voice said: 'I am not well. Feel my hand; is it very hot?'

In the loneliness of his exile, and in the gloom of the rains, his ailing body needed a little tender nursing. He longed to remember the touch on the forehead of soft hands with tinkling bracelets, to imagine the presence of loving womanhood, the nearness of mother and sister. And the exile was not disappointed. Ratan ceased to be a little girl. She at once stepped into the post of mother, called in the village doctor, gave the patient his pills at the proper intervals, sat

---

3. Dada = elder brother.

up all night by his pillow, cooked his gruel for him, and every now and then asked: 'Are you feeling a little better, Dada?'

It was some time before the postmaster, with weakened body, was able to leave his sick-bed. 'No more of this,' said he with decision. 'I must get a transfer.' He at once wrote off to Calcutta an application for a transfer, on the ground of the unhealthiness of the place.

Relieved from her duties as nurse, Ratan again took up her old place outside the door. But she no longer heard the same old call. She would sometimes peep inside furtively to find the postmaster sitting on his chair, or stretched on his pallet, and staring absent-mindedly into the air. While Ratan was awaiting her call, the postmaster was awaiting a reply to his application. The girl read her old lessons over and over again—her great fear was lest, when the call came, she might be found wanting in the double consonants. At last, after a week, the call did come one evening. With an overflowing heart Ratan rushed into the room with her—'Were you calling me, Dada?'

The postmaster said: 'I am going away tomorrow, Ratan.'

'Where are you going, Dada?'

'I am going home.'

'When will you come back?'

'I am not coming back.'

Ratan asked no other question. The postmaster, of his own accord, went on to tell her that his application for a transfer had been rejected, so he had resigned his post, and was going home.

For a long time neither of them spoke another word. The lamp went on dimly burning, and from a leak in one corner of the thatch water dripped steadily into an earthen vessel on the floor beneath it.

After a while Ratan rose, and went off to the kitchen to prepare the meal; but she was not so quick about it as on other days. Many new things to think of had entered her little brain. When the postmaster had finished his supper, the girl suddenly asked him: 'Dada, will you take me to your home?'

The postmaster laughed. 'What an idea!' said he; but he did not think it necessary to explain to the girl wherein lay the absurdity.

That whole night, in her waking and in her dreams, the postmaster's laughing reply haunted her—'What an idea!'

On getting up in the morning, the postmaster found his bath ready. He had stuck to his Calcutta habit of bathing in water drawn and kept in pitchers, instead of taking a plunge in the river as was the custom of the village. For some reason or other, the girl could not ask him about the time of his departure, so she had fetched the water from the river long before sunrise, that it should be ready as early as he might want it. After the bath came a call for Ratan. She entered noiselessly, and looked silently into her master's face for orders. The master said: 'You need not be anxious about my going away, Ratan; I shall tell my successor to look after you.' These words were kindly meant, no doubt: but inscrutable are the ways of a woman's heart!

Ratan had borne many a scolding from her master without complaint, but these kind words she could not bear. She burst out weeping, and said: 'No, no, you need not tell anybody anything at all about me; I don't want to stay on here.'

The postmaster was dumbfounded. He had never seen Ratan like this before.

The new incumbent duly arrived, and the postmaster, having given over charge, prepared to depart. Just before starting he called Ratan, and said: 'Here is something for you; I hope it will keep you for some little time.' He brought out from his pocket the whole of his months' salary, retaining only a trifle for his travelling expenses. Then Ratan fell at his feet and cried: 'Oh, Dada, I pray you, don't give me anything, don't in any way trouble about me,' and then she ran away out of sight.

The postmaster heaved a sigh, took up his carpet bag, put his umbrella over his shoulder, and, accompanied by a man carrying his many-coloured tin trunk, he slowly made for the boat.

When he got in and the boat was under way, and the rain-swollen river, like a stream of tears welling up from the earth, swirled and sobbed at her bows, then he felt a sort of pain at heart; the grief-stricken face of a village girl seemed to represent for him the great unspoken pervading grief of Mother Earth herself. At one time he had an impulse to go back, and bring away along with him that lonesome waif, forsaken of the world. But the wind had just filled the sails, the boat had got well into the middle of the turbulent current, and already the village was left behind, and its outlying burning-ground came in sight.

So the traveller, borne on the breast of the swift-flowing river, consoled himself with philosophical reflections on the numberless meetings and partings going on in the world—on death, the great parting, from which none returns.

But Ratan had no philosophy. She was wandering about the post office in a flood of tears. It may be that she had still a lurking hope in some corner of her heart that her Dada would return, and that is why she could not tear herself away. Alas for the foolish human heart!

The River Stairs

If you wish to hear of days gone by, sit on this step of mine, and lend your ears to the murmur of the rippling water.

The month of *Ashwin* (September) was about to begin. The river was in full flood. Only four of my steps peeped above the surface. The water had crept up to the low-lying parts of the bank, where the *kachu* plant grew dense beneath the branches of the mango grove. At that bend of the river, three old brick-heaps towered above the water around them. The fishing-boats, moored to the trunks of the *babla* trees on the bank, rocked on the heaving flow-tide at dawn. The path of tall grasses on the sandbank had caught the newly risen sun; they had just begun to flower, and were not yet in full bloom.

The little boats puffed out their tiny sails on the sunlit river. The Brahmin priest had come to bathe with his ritual vessels. The women arrived in twos and threes to draw water. I knew this was the time of Kusum's coming to the bathing-stairs.

But that morning I missed her. Bhuban and Swarno mourned at the *ghat*.[1] They said that their friend had been led away to her husband's house, which was a place far away from the river, with strange people, strange houses, and strange roads.

---

1. Bathing-place.

In time she almost faded out of my mind. A year passed. The women at the *ghat* now rarely talked of Kusum. But one evening I was startled by the touch of the long familiar feet. Ah, yes, but those feet were now without anklets, they had lost their old music.

Kusum had become a widow. They said that her husband had worked in some far-off place, and that she had met him only once or twice. A letter brought her the news of his death. A widow at eight years old, she had rubbed out the wife's red mark from her forehead, stripped off her bangles, and come back to her old home by the Ganges. But she found few of her old playmates there. Of them, Bhuban, Swarno, and Amala were married, and gone away; only Sarat remained, and she too, they said, would be wed in December next.

As the Ganges rapidly grows to fulness with the coming of the rains, even so did Kusum day by day grow to the fulness of beauty and youth. But her dull-coloured robe, her pensive face, and quiet manners drew a veil over her youth, and hid it from men's eyes as in a mist. Ten years slipped away, and none seemed to have noticed that Kusum had grown up.

One morning such as this, at the end of a far-off September, a tall, young, fair-skinned Sanyasi, coming I know not whence, took shelter in the Shiva temple in front of me. His arrival was noised abroad in the village. The women left their pitchers behind, and crowded into the temple to bow to the holy man.

The crowd increased day by day. The Sanyasi's fame rapidly spread among the women kind. One day he would recite the *Bhagbat,* another day he would expound the *Gita,* or hold forth upon a holy book in the temple. Some sought him for counsel, some for spells, some for medicines.

So months passed away. In April, at the time of the solar eclipse, vast crowds came here to bathe in the Ganges. A fair was held under the *babla* tree. Many of the pilgrims went to visit the Sanyasi, and among them were a party of women from the village where Kusum had been married.

It was morning. The Sanyasi was counting his beads on my steps, when all of a sudden one of the women pilgrims nudged another, and said: 'Why! He is our Kusum's husband!' Another parted her veil a little in the middle with two fingers and cried out: 'Oh dear me! So it is! He is the younger son of the Chatterji family of our village!' Said a third, who made little parade of her veil: 'Ah! he has got exactly the same brow, nose, and eyes!' Yet another woman, without turning to the Sanyasi, stirred the water with her pitcher, and sighed: 'Alas! That young man is no more; he will not come back. Bad luck to Kusum!'

But, objected one, 'He had not such a big beard'; and another, 'He was not so thin'; or 'He was most probably not so tall.' That settled the question for the time, and the matter spread no further.

One evening, as the full moon arose, Kusum came and sat upon my last step above the water, and cast her shadow upon me.

There was no other at the *ghat* just then. The crickets were chirping about me. The din of brass gongs and bells had ceased in the temple—the last wave of sound grew fainter and fainter, until it merged like the shade of a sound in the dim groves of the farther bank. On the dark water of the Ganges lay a line of glistening moonlight. On the bank above, in bush and hedge, under the porch of the temple, in the base of ruined houses, by the side of the tank, in the palm grove, gathered shadows of fantastic shapes. The bats swung from the *chhatim* boughs. Near the houses the loud clamour of the jackals rose and sank into silence.

Slowly the Sanyasi came out of the temple. Descending a few steps of the *ghat* he saw a woman sitting alone, and was about to go back, when suddenly Kusum raised her head, and looked behind her. The veil slipped away from her. The moonlight fell upon her face, as she looked up.

The owl flew away hooting over their heads. Starting at the sound, Kusum came to herself and put the veil back on her head. Then she bowed low at the Sanyasi's feet.

He gave her blessing and asked: 'Who are you?' She replied: 'I am called Kusum.'

No other word was spoken that night. Kusum went slowly back to her house which was hard by. But the Sanyasi remained sitting on my steps for long hours that night. At last when the moon passed from the east to the west, and the Sanyasi's shadow, shifting from behind, fell in front of him, he rose up and entered the temple.

Henceforth I saw Kusum come daily to bow at his feet. When he expounded the holy books, she stood in a corner listening to him. After finishing his morning service, he used to call her to himself and speak on religion. She could not have understood it all; but, listening attentively in silence, she tried to understand it. As he directed her, so she acted implicitly. She daily served at the temple—ever alert in the god's worship—gathering flowers for the puja, and drawing water from the Ganges to wash the temple floor.

The winter was drawing to its close. We had cold winds. But now and then in the evening the warm spring breeze would blow unexpectedly from the south; the sky would lose its chilly aspect; pipes would sound, and music be heard in the village after a long silence. The boatmen would set their boats drifting down the current, stop rowing, and begin to sing the songs of Krishna. This was the season.

Just then I began to miss Kusum. For some time she had given up visiting the temple, the *ghat*, or the Sanyasi.

What happened next I do not know, but after a while the two met together on my steps one evening.

With downcast looks, Kusum asked: 'Master, did you send for me?'

'Yes, why do I not see you? Why have you grown neglectful of late in serving the gods?'

She kept silent.

'Tell me your thoughts without reserve.'

Half averting her face, she replied: 'I am a sinner, Master, and hence I have failed in the worship.'

The Sanyasi said: 'Kusum, I know there is unrest in your heart.'

She gave a slight start, and, drawing the end of her sari over her face, she sat down on the step at the Sanyasi's feet, and wept.

He moved a little away, and said: 'Tell me what you have in your heart, and I shall show you the way to peace.'

She replied in a tone of unshaken faith, stopping now and then for words: 'If you bid me, I must speak out. But, then, I cannot explain it clearly. You, Master, must have guessed it all. I adored one as a god, I worshipped him, and the bliss of that devotion filled my heart to fulness. But one night I dreamt that the lord of my heart was sitting in a garden somewhere, clasping my right hand in his left, and whispering to me of love. The whole scene did not appear to me at all strange. The dream vanished, but its hold on me remained. Next day when I beheld him he appeared in another light than before. That dream-picture continued to haunt my mind. I fled far from him in fear, and the picture clung to me. Thenceforth my heart has known no peace,—all has grown dark within me!'

While she was wiping her tears and telling this tale, I felt that the Sanyasi was firmly pressing my stone surface with his right foot.

Her speech done, the Sanyasi said:

'You must tell me whom you saw in your dream.'

With folded hands, she entreated: 'I cannot.'

He insisted: 'You must tell me who he was.'

Wringing her hands she asked: 'Must I tell it?'

He replied: 'Yes, you must.'

Then crying, 'You are he, Master!' she fell on her face on my stony bosom, and sobbed.

When she came to herself, and sat up, the Sanyasi said slowly: 'I am leaving this place to-night that you may not see me again. Know that I am a Sanyasi, not belonging to this world. *You* must forget me.'

Kusum replied in a low voice: 'It will be so, Master.'

The Sanyasi said: 'I take my leave.'

Without a word more Kusum bowed to him, and placed the dust of his feet on her head. He left the place.

The moon set; the night grew dark. I heard a splash in the water. The wind raved in the darkness, as if it wanted to blow out all the stars of the sky.

The Castaway

Towards evening the storm was at its height. From the terrific downpour of rain, the crash of thunder, and the repeated flashes of lightning, you might think that a battle of the gods and demons was raging in the skies. Black clouds waved like the Flags of Doom. The Ganges was lashed into a fury, and the trees of the gardens on either bank swayed from side to side with sighs and groans.

In a closed room of one of the riverside houses at Chandernagore, a husband and his wife were seated on a bed spread on the floor, intently discussing. An earthen lamp burned beside them.

The husband, Sharat, was saying: 'I wish you would stay on a few days more; you would then be able to return home quite strong again.'

The wife, Kiran, was saying: 'I have quite recovered already. It will not, cannot possibly, do me any harm to go home now.'

Every married person will at once understand that the conversation was not quite so brief as I have reported it. The matter was not difficult, but the arguments for and against did not advance it towards a solution. Like a rudderless boat, the discussion kept turning round and round the same point; and at last it threatened to be overwhelmed in a flood of tears.

Sharat said: 'The doctor thinks you should stop here a few days longer.'

Kiran replied: 'Your doctor knows everything!'

'Well,' said Sharat, 'you know that just now all sorts of illness are abroad. You would do well to stop here a month or two more.'

'And at this moment I suppose every one in this place is perfectly well!'

What had happened was this: Kiran was a universal favourite with her family and neighbours, so that, when she fell seriously ill, they were all anxious. The village wiseacres thought it shameless for her husband to make so much fuss about a mere wife and even to suggest a change of air, and asked if Sharat supposed that no woman had ever been ill before, or whether he had found out that the folk of the place to which he meant to take her were immortal. Did he imagine that the writ of Fate did not run there? But Sharat and his mother turned a deaf ear to them, thinking that the little life of their darling was of greater importance than the united wisdom of a village. People are wont to reason thus when danger threatens their loved ones. So Sharat went to Chandernagore, and Kiran recovered, though she was still very weak. There was a pinched look on her face which filled the beholder with pity, and made his heart tremble, as he thought how narrowly she had escaped death.

Kiran was fond of society and amusement; the loneliness of her riverside villa did not suit her at all. There was nothing to do, there were no interesting neighbours, and she hated to be busy all day with medicine and dieting. There was no fun in measuring doses and making fomentations. Such was the subject discussed in their closed room on this stormy evening.

So long as Kiran deigned to argue, there was a chance of a fair fight. When she ceased to reply, and with a toss of her head disconsolately looked the other way, the poor man was disarmed. He was on the point of surrendering unconditionally when a servant shouted a message through the shut door.

Sharat got up, and, opening the door, learnt that a boat had been upset in the storm, and that one of the occupants, a young Brahmin boy, had succeeded in swimming ashore in their garden.

Kiran was at once her own sweet self, and set to work to get out some dry clothes for the boy. She then warmed a cup of milk, and invited him to her room.

The boy had long curly hair, big expressive eyes, and no sign yet of hair on the face. Kiran, after getting him to drink some milk, asked him all about himself.

He told her that his name was Nilkanta, and that he belonged to a theatrical troupe. They were coming to play in a neighbouring villa when the boat had suddenly foundered in the storm. He had no idea what had become of his companions. He was a good swimmer, and had just managed to reach the shore.

The boy stayed with them. His narrow escape from a terrible death made Kiran take a warm interest in him. Sharat thought the boy's appearance at this moment rather a good thing, as his wife would now have something to amuse her, and might be persuaded to stay on for some time longer. Her mother-in-law, too, was pleased at the prospect of profiting their Brahmin guest by her kindness. And Nilkanta himself was delighted at his double escape from his master and from the other world, as well as at finding a home in this wealthy family.

But in a short while Sharat and his mother changed their opinion, and longed for his departure. The boy found a secret pleasure in smoking Sharat's hookas; he would calmly go off in pouring rain with Sharat's best silk umbrella for a stroll through the village, and make friends with all whom he met.

Moreover, he had got hold of a mongrel village dog which he petted so recklessly that it came indoors with muddy paws, and left tokens of its visit on Sharat's spotless bed. Then he gathered about him a devoted band of boys of all sorts and sizes, and the result was that not a solitary mango in the neighbourhood had a chance of ripening that season.

There is no doubt that Kiran had a hand in spoiling the boy. Sharat often warned her about it, but she would not listen to him. She made a dandy of him with Sharat's cast-off clothes, and gave him new ones too. And because she felt drawn towards him, and also had a curiosity to know more about him, she was constantly calling him to her own room. After her bath and mid-day meal Kiran would be seated on the bedstead with her betel-leaf box by her side; and while her maid combed and dried her hair, Nilkanta would stand in front and recite pieces out of his repertory with appropriate gesture and song, his elf-locks waving wildly. Thus the long afternoon hours passed merrily away. Kiran would often try to persuade Sharat to sit with her as one of the audience, but Sharat, who had taken a cordial dislike to the boy, refused, nor could Nilkanta do his part half so well when Sharat was there. His mother would sometimes be lured by the hope of hearing sacred names in the recitation; but love of her mid-day sleep speedily overcame devotion, and she lay lapped in dreams.

The boy often got his ears boxed and pulled by Sharat, but as this was nothing to what he had been used to as a member of the troupe, he did not mind it in the least. In his short experience of the world he had come to the conclusion that, as the earth consisted of land and water, so human life was made up of eatings and beatings, and that the beatings largely predominated.

It was hard to tell Nilkanta's age. If it was about fourteen or fifteen, then his face was too old for his years; if seventeen or eighteen, then it was too young. He was either a man too early or a boy too late. The fact was that, joining the theatrical band when very young, he had played the parts of Radhika, Damayanti, Sita and Bidya's Companion. A thoughtful Providence so arranged things that he grew to the exact stature that his manager required, and then growth ceased. Since every one saw how small he was, and he himself felt small, he did not receive due respect for his years. These causes, natural and artificial, combined to make him sometimes seem immature for seventeen years, and at other times a lad of fourteen but far too knowing for seventeen. And as no sign of hair appeared on his face, the confusion became greater. Either because he smoked or because he used language beyond his years, his lips puckered into lines that showed him to be old and hard; but innocence and youth shone in his large eyes. I fancy that his heart remained young, but the hot glare of publicity had been a forcing-house that ripened untimely his outward aspect.

In the quiet shelter of Sharat's house and garden at Chandernagore, Nature had leisure to work her way unimpeded. He had lingered in a kind of unnatural youth, but now he silently and swiftly overpassed that stage. His seventeen or eighteen years came to adequate revelation. No one observed the change, and its first sign was this, that when Kiran treated him like a boy, he felt ashamed. When the gay Kiran one day proposed that he should play the part of lady's companion, the idea of woman's dress hurt him, though he could not say why. So now, when she called for him to act over again his old characters he disappeared. It never occurred to him that he was even now not much more than a lad-of-all-work in a strolling company. He even made up his mind to pick up a little education from Sharat's factor. But, because Nilkanta was the pet of his master's wife, the factor could not endure the sight of him. Also, his restless training made it impossible for him to keep his mind long engaged; presently, the alphabet did a misty dance before his eyes. He would sit long enough with an open book on his lap, leaning against a *champak* bush beside the Ganges. The waves sighed below, boats floated past, birds flitted and twittered restlessly above. What thoughts passed through his mind as he looked down on that book he alone knew, if indeed he did know. He never advanced from one word to another, but the glorious thought that he was actually reading a book filled his soul with exultation. Whenever a boat went by, he lifted his book, and pretended to be reading hard, shouting at the top of his voice. But his energy dropped as soon as the audience was gone.

Formerly he sang his songs automatically, but now their tunes stirred in his mind. Their words were of little import, and full of trifling alliteration. Even the little meaning they had was beyond his comprehension; yet when he sang—

> *Twice-born[1] bird, ah! wherefore stirred*
> *To wrong our royal lady?*
> *Goose, ah! say why wilt thou slay*
> *Her in forest shady?*

then he felt as if transported to another world, and to far other folk. This familiar earth and his own poor life became music, and he was transformed. That tale of goose and king's daughter flung upon the mirror of his mind a picture of surpassing beauty. It is impossible to say what he imagined he himself was, but the destitute little slave of the theatrical troupe faded from his memory.

When with evening the child of want lies down, dirty and hungry, in his squalid home, and hears of prince and princess and fabled gold, then in the dark hovel with its dim flickering candle, his mind springs free from her bonds of poverty and

---

1. Once in the egg, and again once out of the egg.

misery, and walks in fresh beauty and glowing raiment, strong beyond all fear of hindrance, through that fairy realm where all is possible.

Even so, this drudge of wandering players fashioned himself and his world anew, as he moved in spirit amid his songs. The lapping water, rustling leaves, and calling birds; the goddess who had given shelter to him, the helpless, the Godforsaken; her gracious, lovely face, her exquisite arms with their shining bangles, her rosy feet as soft as flower-petals; all these by some magic became one with the music of his song. When the singing ended, the mirage faded, and Nilkanta of the stage appeared again, with his wild elf-locks. Fresh from the complaints of his neighbour, the owner of the despoiled mango-orchard, Sharat would come and box his ears, and cuff him. The boy Nilkanta, the misleader of adoring youths, went forth once more, to make ever new mischief by land and water and in the branches that are above the earth.

Shortly after the advent of Nilkanta, Sharat's younger brother, Satish, came to spend his college vacation with them. Kiran was hugely pleased at finding a fresh occupation. She and Satish were of the same age, and the time passed pleasantly in games and quarrels and makings-up and laughter and even tears. Suddenly she would clasp him over the eyes, from behind, with vermilion-stained hands, she would write 'monkey' on his back, and sometimes bolt the door on him from outside amidst peals of laughter. Satish in his turn did not take things lying down; he would take her keys and rings, he would put pepper among her betel; he would tie her to the bed when she was not looking.

Meanwhile, heaven only knows what possessed poor Nilkanta. He was suddenly filled with a bitterness which he must avenge on somebody or something. He thrashed his devoted boy-followers for no fault, and sent them away crying. He would kick his pet mongrel till it made the skies resound with its whinings. When he went out for a walk, he would litter his path with twigs and leaves beaten from the roadside shrubs with his cane.

Kiran liked to see people enjoying good fare. Nilkanta had an immense capacity for eating, and never refused a good thing, however often it was offered. So Kiran liked to send for him to have his meals in her presence, and ply him with delicacies, happy in the bliss of seeing this Brahmin boy eat to satiety. After Satish's arrival she had much less spare time on her hands, and was seldom present when Nilkanta's meals were served. Before her absence made no difference to the boy's appetite, and he would not rise till he had drained his cup of milk, and rinsed it thoroughly with water.[2]

But now, if Kiran was not present to ask him to try this and that, he was miserable, and nothing tasted right. He would get up without eating much, and say to the serving-maid in a choking voice: 'I am not hungry.' He thought in imagination that the news of his repeated refusal, 'I am not hungry,' would reach Kiran, he pictured her concern, and hoped that she would send for him, and press him to eat. But nothing of the sort happened. Kiran never knew, and never sent for him; and the maid finished whatever he left. He would then put out the lamp in his room and throw himself on his bed in the darkness, burying his head in the pillow in a paroxysm of sobs. What was his grievance? Against whom? And from whom did he expect redress? At last, when none else came, Mother Sleep soothed with her soft caresses the wounded heart of the motherless lad.

Nilkanta came to the unshakable conviction that Satish was poisoning Kiran's mind against him. If Kiran was absent-minded,

2. A habit which was relic from his days of poverty, when milk was too rare a luxury to allow of even its stains in the cup being wasted.

and had not her usual smile, he would jump to the conclusion that some trick of Satish had made her angry with him. He took to praying to the gods, with all the fervour of his hate, to make him at the next rebirth Satish, and Satish him. He had an idea that a Brahmin's wrath could never be in vain; and the more he tried to consume Satish with the fire of his curses, the more did his own heart burn within him. And upstairs he would hear Satish laughing and joking with his sister-in-law.

Nilkanta never dared openly to show his enmity to Satish. But he would contrive a hundred petty ways of causing him annoyance. When Satish went for a swim in the river, and left his soap on the steps of the bathing-place, on coming back for it he would find that it had disappeared. Once he found his favourite striped tunic floating past him on the water, and thought it had been blown away by the wind.

One day Kiran, desiring to entertain Satish, sent for Nilkanta to recite as usual, but he stood there in gloomy silence. Quite surprised, Kiran asked him what was the matter. But he remained silent. And when again pressed by her to repeat some particular favourite piece of hers he answered: 'I don't remember,' and walked away.

At last the time came for their return home. Everybody was busy packing up. Satish was going with them. But to Nilkanta nobody said a word. The question whether he was to go or not seemed not to have occurred to anybody.

The question, as a matter of fact, had been raised by Kiran, who had proposed to take him along with them. But her husband and his mother and brother had all objected so strenuously that she let the matter drop. A couple of days before they were to start, she sent for the boy, and with kind words advised him to go back to his own home.

So many days had he felt neglected that this touch of kindness was too much for him; he burst into tears. Kiran's eyes were also brimming over. She was filled with remorse at the thought that she had created a tie of affection, which could not be permanent.

But Satish was much annoyed at the blubbering of this overgrown boy. 'Why does the fool stand there howling instead of speaking?' said he. When Kiran scolded him for an unfeeling creature, he replied: 'Sister mine, you do not understand. You are too good and trustful. This fellow turns up from the Lord knows where, and is treated like a king. Naturally the tiger has no wish to become a mouse again.[3] And he has evidently discovered that there is nothing like a tear or two to soften your heart.'

Nilkanta hurriedly left the spot. He felt he would like to be a knife to cut Satish to pieces: a needle to pierce him through and through; a fire to burn him to ashes. But Satish was not even scarred. It was only his own heart that bled and bled.

Satish had brought with him from Calcutta a grand inkstand. The inkpot was set in a mother-of-pearl boat drawn by a German-silver goose supporting a penholder. It was a great favourite of his, and he cleaned it carefully every day with an old silk handkerchief. Kiran would laugh and, tapping the silver bird's beak, would say—

Twice-born bird, ah! wherefore stirred
To wrong our royal lady?

and the usual war of words would break out between her and her brother-in-law.

The day before they were to start, the inkstand was missing, and could nowhere be found. Kiran smiled, and said: 'Brother-in-law, your goose has flown off to look for your Damayanti.'[4]

---

3. A reference to a folk-story of a saint who turned a pet mouse into a tiger.
4. To find Satish a wife.

But Satish was in a great rage. He was certain that Nilkanta had stolen it—for several people said they had seen him prowling about the room the night before. He had the accused brought before him. Kiran also was there. 'You have stolen my inkstand, you thief!' he blurted out. 'Bring it back at once.' Nilkanta had always taken punishment from Sharat, deserved or undeserved, with perfect equanimity. But, when he was called a thief in Kiran's presence, his eyes blazed with a fierce anger, his breast swelled, and his throat choked. If Satish had said another word he would have flown at him like a wild cat, and used his nails like claws.

Kiran was greatly distressed at the scene, and taking the boy into another room said in her sweet, kind way: 'Nilu, if you really have taken that inkstand give it to me quietly, and I shall see that no one says another word to you about it.' Big tears coursed down the boy's cheeks, till at last he hid his face in his hands, and wept bitterly. Kiran came back from the room, and said: 'I am sure Nilkanta has not taken the inkstand.' Sharat and Satish were equally positive that no other than Nilkanta could have done it.

But Kiran said determinedly: 'Never.'

Sharat wanted to cross-examine the boy, but his wife refused to allow it.

Then Satish suggested that his room and box should be searched. And Kiran said; 'If you dare do such a thing I will never, never forgive you. You shall not spy on the poor innocent boy.' And as she spoke, her wonderful eyes filled with tears. That settled the matter, and effectually prevented any further molestation of Nilkanta!

Kiran's heart overflowed with pity at this attempted outrage on a homeless lad. She got two new suits of clothes and a pair of shoes, and with these and a banknote in her hand she quietly went into Nilkanta's room in the evening. She intended to put these parting presents into his box as a surprise. The box itself had been her gift.

From her bunch of keys she selected one that fitted, and noiselessly opened the box. It was so jumbled up with odds and ends that the new clothes would not go in. So she thought she had better take everything out and pack the box for him. At first knives, tops, kite-flying reels, bamboo twigs, polished shells for peeling green mangoes, bottoms of broken tumblers and such like things dear to a boy's heart were discovered. Then there came a layer of linen, clean and otherwise. And from under the linen there emerged the missing inkstand, goose and all!

Kiran, with flushed face, sat down helplessly with the inkstand in her hand, puzzled and wondering.

In the meantime, Nilkanta had come into the room from behind without Kiran knowing it. He had seen the whole thing, and thought that Kiran had come like a thief to catch him in his thieving,—and that his deed was out. How could he ever hope to convince her that he was not a thief, and that only revenge had prompted him to take the inkstand, which he meant to throw into the river at the first chance? In a weak moment he had put it in his box instead. 'He was not a thief,' his heart cried out, 'not a thief!' Then what was he? What could he say? He had stolen, and yet he was not a thief! He could never explain to Kiran how grievously wrong she was in taking him for a thief; how could he bear the thought that she had tried to spy on him?

At last Kiran with a deep sigh replaced the inkstand in the box, and, as if she were the thief herself, covered it up with the linen and the trinkets as they were before; and at the top she placed the presents together with the banknote which she had brought for him.

The next day the boy was nowhere to be found. The villagers had not seen him; the police could discover no trace of him. Said Sharat: 'Now, as a matter of curiosity, let us have a look at his box.' But Kiran was obstinate in her refusal to allow that to be done.

She had the box brought up to her own room; and taking out the inkstand alone, threw it into the river.

The whole family went home. In a day the garden became desolate. And only that starving mongrel of Nilkanta's remained prowling along the river-bank, whining and whining as if its heart would break.

Saved

Gouri was the beautiful, delicately nurtured child of an old and wealthy family. Her husband, Paresh, had recently by his own efforts improved his straitened circumstances. So long as he was poor, Gouri's parents had kept their daughter at home, unwilling to surrender her to privation; so she was no longer young when at last she went to her husband's house. And Paresh never felt quite that she belonged to him. He was an advocate in a small western town, and had no close kinsman with him. All his thought was about his wife, so much so that sometimes he would come home before the rising of the Court. At first Gouri was at a loss to understand why he came back suddenly. Sometimes, too, he would dismiss one of the servants without reason; none of them ever suited him long. Especially if Gouri desired to keep any particular servant because he was useful, that man was sure to be got rid of forthwith. The high-spirited Gouri greatly resented this, but her resentment only made her husband's behaviour still stranger.

At last when Paresh, unable to contain himself any longer, began in secret to cross-question the maid about her, the whole thing reached his wife's ears. She was a woman of few words; but her pride raged within like a wounded lioness at these insults, and this mad suspicion swept like a destroyer's sword between them. Paresh, as soon as he saw that his wife understood his motive felt no more delicacy about taxing Gouri to her face; and the more his wife treated it with silent contempt, the more did the fire of his jealousy consume him.

Deprived of wedded happiness, the childless Gouri betook herself to the consolations of religion. She sent for Paramananda Swami, the young preacher of the Prayer-House hard by, and, formally acknowledging him as her spiritual preceptor, asked him to expound the *Gita* to her. All the wasted love and affection of her woman's heart was poured out in reverence at the feet of her Guru.

No one had any doubts about the purity of Paramananda's character. All worshiped him. And because Paresh did not dare to hint at any suspicion against him, his jealousy ate its way into his heart like a hidden cancer.

One day some trifling circumstance made the poison overflow. Paresh reviled Paramananda to his wife as a hypocrite, and said: 'Can you swear that you are not in love with this crane that plays the ascetic?'

Gouri sprang up like a snake that has been trodden on, and, maddened by his suspicion, said with bitter irony: 'And what if I am?' At this Paresh forthwith went off to the Court-house, and locked the door on her.

In a white heat of passion at this last outrage, Gouri got the door open somehow, and left the house.

Paramananda was poring over the scriptures in his lonely room in the silence of noon. All at once, like a flash of lightning out of a cloudless sky, Gouri broke in upon his reading.

'You here?' questioned her Guru in surprise.

'Rescue me, O my lord Guru,' said she, 'from the insults of my home life, and allow me to dedicate myself to the service of your feet.'

With a stern rebuke, Paramananda sent Gouri back home. But I wonder whether he ever again took up the snapped thread of his reading.

Paresh, finding the door open, on his return home, asked: 'Who has been here?'

'No one!' his wife replied. 'I have been to the house of my Guru.'

'Why?' asked Paresh, pale and red by turns. 'Because I wanted to.'

From that day Paresh had a guard kept over the house, and behaved so absurdly that the tale of his jealousy was told all over the town.

The news of the shameful insults that were daily heaped on his disciple disturbed the religious meditations of Paramananda. He felt he ought to leave the place at once; at the same time he could not make up his mind to forsake the tortured woman. Who can say how the poor ascetic got through those terrible days and nights?

At last one day the imprisoned Gouri got a letter. 'My child,' it ran, 'it is true that many holy women have left the world to devote themselves to God. Should it happen that the trials of this world are driving your thoughts away from God, I will with God's help rescue his handmaid for the holy service of his feet. If you desire, you may meet me by the tank in your garden at two o'clock to-morrow afternoon.'

Gouri hid the letter in the loops of her hair. At noon next day when she was undoing her hair before her bath she found that the letter was not there. Could it have fallen on to the bed and got into her husband's hands, she wondered. At first she felt a kind of fierce pleasure in thinking that it would enrage him; and then she could not bear to think that this letter, worn as a halo of deliverance on her head, might be defiled by the touch of insolent hands.

With swift steps she hurried to her husband's room. He lay groaning on the floor, with eyes rolled back and foaming mouth. She detached the letter from his clenched fist, and sent quickly for a doctor.

The doctor said it was a case of apoplexy. The patient had died before his arrival.

That very day, as it happened, Paresh had an important appointment away from home. Paramananda had found this out, and accordingly had made his appointment with Gouri. To such a depth had he fallen!

When the widowed Gouri caught sight from the window of her Guru stealing like a thief to the side of the pool, she lowered her eyes as at a lightning flash. And in that flash she saw clearly what a fall his had been.

The Guru called: 'Gouri.'

'I am coming,' she replied.

When Paresh's friends heard of his death and came to assist in the last rites, they found the dead body of Gouri lying beside that of her husband. She had poisoned herself. All were lost in admiration of the wifely loyalty she had shown in her *sati*, a loyalty rare indeed in these degenerate days.

My Fair Neighbour

My feelings towards the young widow who lived in the next house to mine were feelings of worship, at least, that is what I told to my friends and myself. Even my nearest intimate, Nabin, knew nothing of the real state of my mind. And I had a sort of pride that I could keep my passion pure by thus concealing it in the inmost recesses of my heart. She was like a dew-drenched *sephali*-blossom, untimely fallen to earth. Too radiant and holy for the flower-decked marriage-bed, she had been dedicated to Heaven.

But passion is like the mountain stream, and refuses to be enclosed in the place of its birth; it must seek an outlet. That is why I tried to give expression to my emotions in poems; but my unwilling pen refused to desecrate the object of my worship.

It happened curiously that just at this time my friend Nabin was afflicted with a madness of verse. It came upon him like an earthquake. It was the poor fellow's first attack, and he was equally unprepared for rhyme and rhythm. Nevertheless he could not refrain, for he succumbed to the fascination, as a widower to his second wife.

So Nabin sought help from me. The subject of his poems was the old, old one, which is ever new: his poems were all addressed to the beloved one. I slapped his back in jest, and asked him: 'Well, old chap, who is she?'

Nabin laughed, as he replied: 'That I have not yet discovered!'

I confess that I found considerable comfort in bringing help to my friend. Like a hen brooding on a duck's egg, I lavished all the warmth of my pent-up passion on Nabin's effusions. So vigorously did I revise and improve his crude productions, that the larger part of each poem became my own.

Then Nabin would say in surprise: 'That is just what I wanted to say, but could not. How on earth do you manage to get hold of all these fine sentiments?'

Poet-like, I would reply: 'They come from my imagination; for, as you know, truth is silent, and it is imagination only which waxes eloquent. Reality represses the flow of feeling like a rock; imagination cuts out a path for itself.'

And the poor puzzled Nabin would say: 'Y-e-s, I see, of course'; and then after some thought would murmur again: 'Yes, yes, you are right!'

As I have already said, in my own love there was a feeling of reverential delicacy which prevented me from putting it into words. But with Nabin as a screen, there was nothing to hinder the flow of my pen; and a true warmth of feeling gushed out into these vicarious poems.

Nabin in his lucid moments would say: 'But these are yours! Let me publish them over your name.'

'Nonsense!' I would reply. 'They are yours, my dear fellow; I have only added a touch or two here and there.'

And Nabin gradually came to believe it.

I will not deny that, with a feeling akin to that of the astronomer gazing into the starry heavens, I did sometimes turn my eyes towards the window of the house next door. It is also true that now and again my furtive glances would be rewarded with a vision. And the least glimpse of the pure light of that countenance would at once still and clarify all that was turbulent and unworthy in my emotions.

But one day I was startled. Could I believe my eyes? It was a hot summer afternoon. One of the fierce and fitful nor'-westers was threatening. Black clouds were massed in the north-west corner of the sky; and against the strange and fearful light of that background my fair neighbour stood, gazing out into empty space. And what a world of forlorn longing did I discover in the far-away look of those lustrous black eyes! Was there then, perchance, still some living volcano within the serene radiance of that moon of mine? Alas! that look of limitless yearning, which was winging its way through the clouds like an eager bird, surely sought—not heaven—but the nest of some human heart!

At the sight of the unutterable passion of that look I could hardly contain myself. I was no longer satisfied with correcting crude poems. My whole being longed to express itself in some worthy action. At last I thought I would devote myself to making widow-remarriage popular in my country. I was prepared not only to speak and write on the subject, but also to spend money on its cause.

Nabin began to argue with me. 'Permanent widowhood,' said he, 'has in it a sense of immense purity and peace; a calm beauty like that of the silent places of the dead shimmering in the wan light of the eleventh moon.[1] Would not the mere possibility of remarriage destroy its divine beauty?'

Now this sort of sentimentality always makes me furious. In time of famine, if a well-fed man speaks scornfully of food, and advises a starving man at point of death to glut his hunger on the fragrance of flowers and the song of birds, what are we to think of him? I said with some heat: 'Look here, Nabin, to the artist a ruin may be a beautiful object; but houses are built not only for the contemplations of artists, but that people may live therein; so they have to be kept in repair in

---

1. The eleventh day of the moon is a day of fasting and penance.

spite of artistic susceptibilities. It is all very well for you to idealise widowhood from your safe distance, but you should remember that within widowhood there is a sensitive human heart, throbbing with pain and desire.'

I had an impression that the conversion of Nabin would be a difficult matter, so perhaps I was more impassioned than I need have been. I was somewhat surprised to find at the conclusion of my little speech that Nabin after a single thoughtful sigh completely agreed with me. The even more convincing peroration which I felt I might have delivered was not needed!

After about a week Nabin came to me, and said that if I would help him he was prepared to lead the way by marrying a widow himself.

I was overjoyed. I embraced him effusively, and promised him any money that might be required for the purpose. Then Nabin told me his story.

I learned that Nabin's loved one was not an imaginary being. It appeared that Nabin, too, had for some time adored a widow from a distance, but had not spoken of his feelings to any living soul. Then the magazines in which Nabin's poems, or rather *my* poems, used to appear had reached the fair one's hands; and the poems had not been ineffective.

Not that Nabin had deliberately intended, as he was careful to explain, to conduct love-making in that way. In fact, said he, he had no idea that the widow knew how to read. He used to post the magazine, without disclosing the sender's name addressed to the widow's brother. It was only a sort of fancy of his, a concession to his, hopeless passion. It was flinging garlands before a deity; it is not the worshipper's affair whether the god knows or not, whether he accepts or ignores the offering.

And Nabin particularly wanted me to understand that he had no definite end in view when on diverse pretexts he sought and made the acquaintance of the widow's brother. Any near relation of the loved one needs must have a special interest for the lover.

Then followed a long story about how an illness of the brother at last brought them together. The presence of the poet himself naturally led to much discussion of the poems; nor was the discussion necessarily restricted to the subject out of which it arose.

After his recent defeat in argument at my hands, Nabin had mustered up courage to propose marriage to the widow. At first he could not gain her consent. But when he had made full use of my eloquent words, supplemented by a tear or two of his own, the fair one capitulated unconditionally. Some money was now wanted by her guardian to make arrangements.

'Take it at once,' said I.

'But,' Nabin went on, 'you know it will be some months before I can appease my father sufficiently for him to continue my allowance. How are we to live in the meantime?' I wrote out the necessary cheque without a word, and then said: 'Now tell me who she is. You need not look on me as a possible rival, for I swear I will not write poems to her; and even if I do I will not send them to her brother, but to you!'

'Don't be absurd,' said Nabin; 'I have not kept back her name because I feared your rivalry! That fact is, she was very much perturbed at taking this unusual step, and had asked me not to talk about the matter to my friends. But it no longer matters, now that everything has been satisfactorily settled. She lived at No. 19, the house next to yours.'

If my heart had been an iron boiler it would have burst. 'So she has no objection to remarriage?' I simply asked.

'Not at the present moment,' replied Nabin with a smile.

'And was it the poems alone which wrought the magic change?'

'Well, my poems were not so bad, you know,' said Nabin, 'were they?'

I swore mentally.

But at whom was I to swear? At him? At myself. At Providence? All the same, I swore.

THE HOME AND THE WORLD

Chapter I

Bimala's Story

I

Mother, to-day there comes back to my mind the vermilion mark[1] at the parting of your hair, the sari[2] which you used to wear, with its wide red border, and those wonderful eyes of yours, full of depth and peace. They came at the start of my life's journey, like the first streak of dawn, giving me golden provision to carry me on my way.

The sky which gives light is blue, and my mother's face was dark, but she had the radiance of holiness, and her beauty would put to shame all the vanity of the beautiful.

Every one says that I resemble my mother. In my childhood I used to resent this. It made me angry with my mirror. I thought that it was God's unfairness which was wrapped round my limbs,—that my dark features were not my due, but had come to me by some misunderstanding. All that remained for me to ask of my God in reparation was, that

---

1. The mark of Hindu wifehood and the symbol of all the devotion that it implies.
2. The sari is the dress of the Hindu woman.

I might grow up to be a model of what woman should be, as one reads it in some epic poem.

When the proposal came for my marriage, an astrologer was sent, who consulted my palm and said, 'This girl has good signs. She will become an ideal wife.'

And all the women who heard it said: 'No wonder, for she resembles her mother.'

I was married into a Rajah's house. When I was a child, I was quite familiar with the description of the Prince of the fairy story. But my husband's face was not of a kind that one's imagination would place in fairyland. It was dark, even as mine was. The feeling of shrinking, which I had about my own lack of physical beauty, was lifted a little; at the same time a touch of regret was left lingering in my heart.

But when the physical appearance evades the scrutiny of our senses and enters the sanctuary of our hearts, then it can forget itself. I know, from my childhood's experience, how devotion is beauty itself, in its inner aspect. When my mother arranged the different fruits, carefully peeled by her own loving hands, on the white stone plate, and gently waved her fan to drive away the flies while my father sat down to his meals, her service would lose itself in a beauty which passed beyond outward forms. Even in my infancy I could feel its power. It transcended all debates, or doubts, or calculations: it was pure music.

I distinctly remember after my marriage, when, early in the morning, I would cautiously and silently get up and take the dust[3] of my husband's feet without waking him, how at

---

3. Taking the dust of the feet is a formal offering of reverence and is done by lightly touching the feet of the revered one and the one's own head with the same hand. The wife does not ordinarily do this to the husband.

such moments I could feel the vermilion mark upon my forehead shining out like the morning star.

One day, he happened to awake, and smiled as he asked me: 'What is that, Bimala? What *are* you doing?'

I can never forget the shame of being detected by him. He might possibly have thought that I was trying to earn merit secretly. But no, no! That had nothing to do with merit. It was my woman's heart, which must worship in order to love.

My father-in-law's house was old in dignity from the days of the *Badshahs*. Some of its manners were of the Moguls and Pathans, some of its customs of Manu and Parashar. But my husband was absolutely modern. He was the first of the house to go through a college course and take his M.A. degree. His elder brother had died young, of drink, and had left no children. My husband did not drink and was not given to dissipation. So foreign to the family was this abstinence, that to many it hardly seemed decent! Purity, they imagined, was only becoming in those on whom fortune had not smiled. It is the moon which has room for stains, not the stars.

My husband's parents had died long ago, and his old grandmother was mistress of the house. My husband was the apple of her eye, the jewel on her bosom. And so he never met with much difficulty in overstepping any of the ancient usages. When he brought in Miss Gilby, to teach me and be my companion, he stuck to his resolve in spite of the poison secreted by all the wagging tongues at home and outside.

My husband had then just got through his B.A. examination and was reading for his M.A. degree; so he had to stay in Calcutta to attend college. He used to write to me almost every day, a few lines only, and simple words, but his bold, round handwriting would look up into my face, oh, so tenderly! I kept his letters in a sandalwood box and covered them every day with the flowers I gathered in the garden.

At that time the Prince of the fairy tale had faded, like the moon in the morning light. I had the Prince of my real world enthroned in my heart. I was his queen. I had my seat by his side. But my real joy was, that my true place was at his feet.

Since then, I have been educated, and introduced to the modern age in its own language, and therefore these words that I write seem to blush with shame in their prose setting. Except for my acquaintance with this modern standard of life, I should know, quite naturally, that just as my being born a woman was not in my own hands, so the element of devotion in woman's love is not like a hackneyed passage quoted from a romantic poem to be piously written down in round hand in a schoolgirl's copy-book.

But my husband would not give me any opportunity for worship. That was his greatness. They are cowards who claim absolute devotion from their wives as their right; that is a humiliation for both.

His love for me seemed to overflow my limits by its flood of wealth and service. But my necessity was more for giving than for receiving; for love is a vagabond, who can make his flowers bloom in the wayside dust, better than in the crystal jars kept in the drawing-room.

My husband could not break completely with the old-time traditions which prevailed in our family. It was difficult, therefore, for us to meet at any hour of the day we pleased.[4] I knew exactly the time that he could come to me, and therefore our meeting had all the care of loving preparation. It was like the rhyming of a poem; it had to come through the path of the metre.

---

4. It would not be reckoned good form for the husband to be continually going into the zenana, except at particular hours for meals or rest.

After finishing the day's work and taking my afternoon bath, I would do up my hair and renew my vermilion mark and put on my sari, carefully crinkled; and then, bringing back my body and mind from all distractions of household duties, I would dedicate it at this special hour, with special ceremonies, to one individual. That time, each day, with him was short; but it was infinite.

My husband used to say, that man and wife are equal in love because of their equal claim on each other. I never argued the point with him, but my heart said that devotion never stands in the way of true equality; it only raises the level of the ground of meeting. Therefore the joy of the higher equality remains permanent; it never slides down to the vulgar level of triviality.

My beloved, it was worthy of you that you never expected worship from me. But if you had accepted it, you would have done me a real service. You showed your love by decorating me, by educating me, by giving me what I asked for, and what I did not. I have seen what depth of love there was in your eyes when you gazed at me. I have known the secret sigh of pain you suppressed in your love for me. You loved my body as if it were a flower of paradise. You loved my whole nature as if it had been given you by some rare providence.

Such lavish devotion made me proud to think that the wealth was all my own which drove you to my gate. But vanity such as this only checks the flow of free surrender in a woman's love. When I sit on the queen's throne and claim homage, then the claim only goes on magnifying itself; it is never satisfied. Can there be any real happiness for a woman in merely feeling that she has power over a man? To surrender one's pride in devotion is woman's only salvation.

It comes back to me to-day how, in the days of our happiness, the fires of envy sprung up all around us. That was only natural, for had I not stepped into my good fortune by a mere chance, and without deserving it? But providence does not allow a run of luck to last for ever, unless its debt of honour be fully paid, day by day, through many a long day, and this made secure. God may grant us gifts, but the merit of being able to take and hold them must be our own. Alas for the boons that slip through unworthy hands!

My husband's grandmother and mother were both renowned for their beauty. And my widowed sister-in-law was also of a beauty rarely to be seen. When, in turn, fate left them desolate, the grandmother vowed she would not insist on having beauty for her remaining grandson when he married. Only the auspicious marks with which I was endowed gained me an entry into this family,—otherwise, I had no claim to be here.

In this house of luxury, but few of its ladies had received their meed of respect. They had, however, got used to the ways of the family, and managed to keep their heads above water, buoyed up by their dignity as Ranis of an ancient house, in spite of their daily tears being drowned in the foam of wine, and by the tinkle of the dancing girls' anklets. Was the credit due to me that my husband did not touch liquor, nor squander his manhood in the markets of woman's flesh? What charm did I know to soothe the wild and wandering mind of men? It was my good luck, nothing else. For fate proved utterly callous to my sister-in-law. Her festivity died out, while yet the evening was early, leaving the light of her beauty shining in vain over empty halls,—burning and burning, with no accompanying music!

His sister-in-law affected a contempt for my husband's modern notions. How absurd to keep the family ship, laden with all the weight of its time-honoured glory, sailing under the colours of his slip of a girl-wife alone! Often have I felt the lash of scorn. 'A thief who had stolen a husband's love!' 'A sham hidden in the shamelessness of her new-fangled finery!' The many coloured garments of modern fashion with which my husband loved to adorn me roused jealous wrath. 'Is not she ashamed to make a show-window of herself,—and with her looks, too!'

My husband was aware of all this, but his gentleness knew no bounds. He used to implore me to forgive her.

I remember I once told him: 'Women's minds are so petty, so crooked!' 'Like the feet of Chinese women,' he replied. 'Has not the pressure of society cramped them into pettiness and crookedness? They are but pawns of the fate which gambles with them. What responsibility have they of their own?'

My sister-in-law never failed to get from my husband whatever she wanted. He did not stop to consider whether her requests were right or reasonable. But what exasperated me most was that she was not grateful for this. I had promised my husband that I would not talk back at her, but this set me raging all the more, inwardly. I used to feel that goodness has a limit, which, if passed, somehow seems to make men cowardly. Shall I tell the whole truth? I have often wished that my husband had the manliness to be a little less good.

My sister-in-law, the Bara Rani,[5] was still young and had no pretensions to saintliness. Rather, her talk and jest and laugh inclined to be forward. The young maids with whom she surrounded herself were also impudent to a degree. But there was none to gainsay her,—for was not this the custom of the house? It seemed to me that my good fortune in having

---

5. *Bara* = Senior; *Chota* = Junior. In joint families of rank, though the widows remain entitled only to a life-interest in their husbands' share, their rank remains to them according to seniority, and the titles 'Senior' and 'Junior' continue to distinguish the elder and younger branches, even though the junior branch be the one in power.

a stainless husband was a special eyesore to her. He, however, felt more the sorrow of her lot than the defects of her character.

II

My husband was very eager to take me out of purdah.[6]

One day I said to him: 'What do I want with the outside world?'

'The outside world may want you,' he replied.

'If the outside world has got on so long without me, it may go on for some time longer. It need not pine to death for want of me.'

'Let it perish, for all I care! That is not troubling me. I am thinking about myself.'

'Oh, indeed. Tell me, what about yourself?'

My husband was silent, with a smile.

I knew his way, and protested at once: 'No, you are not going to run away from me like that! I want to have this out with you.'

'Can one ever finish a subject with words?'

'Do stop speaking in riddles. Tell me...'

'What I want is, that I should have you, and you should have me, more fully in the outside world. That is where and are still in debt to each other.'

'Is anything wanting, then, in the love we have here at home?'

'Here you are wrapped up in me. You know neither what you have, nor what you want.'

'I cannot bear to hear you talk like this.'

'I would have you come into the heart of the outer world and meet reality. Merely going on with your household duties,

---

6. The seclusion of the zenana, and all the customs peculiar to it, are designated by the general term 'Purdah,' which means Screen.

living all your life in the world of household conventions and the drudgery of household tasks,—you were not made for that! If we meet, and recognise each other, in the real world, then only will our love be true.'

'If there be any drawback here to our full recognition of each other, then I have nothing to say. But as for myself, I feel no want.'

'Well, even if the drawback is only on my side, why shouldn't you help to remove it?'

Such discussions repeatedly occurred. One day he said: 'The greedy man who is fond of his fish stew has no compunction in cutting up the fish according to his need. But the man who loves the fish wants to enjoy it in the water; and if that is impossible he waits on the bank; and even if he comes back home without a sight of it he has the consolation of knowing that the fish is all right. Perfect gain is the best of all; but if that is impossible, then the next best gain is perfect losing.'

I never liked the way my husband had of talking on this subject, but that is not the reason why I refused to leave the zenana. His grandmother was still alive. My husband had filled more than a hundred and twenty per cent of the house with the twentieth century, against her taste; but she had borne it uncomplaining. She would have borne it, likewise, if the daughter-in-law[7] of the Rajah's house had left its seclusion. She was even prepared for this happening. But I did not consider it important enough to give her the pain of it. I have read in books that we are called 'caged birds.' I cannot speak for others, but I had so much in this cage of mine that there was not room for it in the universe,—at least that is what I then felt.

---

7. The prestige of the daughter-in-law is of the first importance in a Hindu household of rank.—*Tr.*

The grandmother, in her old age, was very fond of me. At the bottom of her fondness was the thought that, with the conspiracy of favourable stars which attended me, I had been able to attract my husband's love. Were not men naturally inclined to plunge downwards? None of the others, for all their beauty, had been able to prevent their husbands going headlong into the burning depths which consumed and destroyed them. She believed that I had been the means of extinguishing this fire, so deadly to the men of the family. So she kept me in the shelter of her bosom, and trembled if I was in the least bit unwell.

His grandmother did not like the dresses and ornaments my husband brought from European shops to deck me with. But she reflected: 'Men will have some absurd hobby or other, which is sure to be expensive. It is no use trying to check their extravagance; one is glad enough if they stop short of ruin. If my Nikhil had not been busy dressing up his wife there is no knowing whom else he might have spent his money on!' So whenever any new dress of mine arrived she used to send for my husband and make merry over it.

Thus it came about that it was her taste which changed. The influence of the modern age fell so strongly upon her, that her evenings refused to pass if I did not tell her stories out of English books.

After his grandmother's death, my husband wanted me to go and live with him in Calcutta. But I could not bring myself to do that. Was not this our House, which she had kept under her sheltering care through all her trials and troubles? Would not a curse come upon me if I deserted it and went off to town? This was the thought that kept me back, as her empty seat reproachfully looked up at me. That noble lady had come into this house at the age of eight, and had died in her seventy-ninth year. She had not spent a happy life. Fate had hurled shaft after shaft at her breast, only to draw out more and more the imperishable spirit within. This great house was hallowed with her tears. What should I do in the dust of Calcutta, away from it?

My husband's idea was that this would be a good opportunity for leaving to my sister-in-law the consolation of ruling over the household, giving our life, at the same time, more room to branch out in Calcutta. That is just where my difficulty came in. She had worried my life out, she ill brooked my husband's happiness, and for this she was to be rewarded! And what of the day when we should have to come back here? Should I then get back my seat at the head?

'Why do you want that seat?' my husband would say. 'Are there not more precious things in life?'

Men never understand these things. They have their nests in the outside world; they little know the whole of what the household stands for. In these matters they ought to follow womanly guidance. Such were my thoughts at that time.

I felt the real point was, that one ought to stand up for one's rights. To go away, and leave everything in the hands of the enemy, would be nothing short of owning defeat.

But why did not my husband compel me to go with him to Calcutta? I know the reason. He did not use his power, just because he had it.

III

If one had to fill in, little by little, the gap between day and night, it would take an eternity to do it. But the sun rises and the darkness is dispelled,—a moment is sufficient to overcome an infinite distance.

One day there came the new era of *Swadeshi*[8] in Bengal; but as to how it happened, we had no distinct vision. There

---

8. The Nationalist movement, which began more as an economic than a political one, having as its main object the encouragement of indigenous industries.—*Tr.*

was no gradual slope connecting the past with the present. For that reason, I imagine, the new epoch came in like a flood, breaking down the dykes and sweeping all our prudence and fear before it. We had no time even to think about, or understand, what had happened, or what was about to happen.

My sight and my mind, my hopes and my desires, became red with the passion of this new age. Though, up to this time, the walls of the home—which was the ultimate world to my mind—remained unbroken, yet I stood looking over into the distance, and I heard a voice from the far horizon, whose meaning was not perfectly clear to me, but whose call went straight to my heart.

From the time my husband had been a college student he had been trying to get the things required by our people produced in our own country. There are plenty of date trees in our district. He tried to invent an apparatus for extracting the juice and boiling it into sugar and treacle. I heard that it was a great success, only it extracted more money than juice. After a while he came to the conclusion that our attempts at reviving our industries were not succeeding for want of a bank of our own. He was, at the time, trying to teach me political economy. This alone would not have done much harm, but he also took it into his head to teach his countrymen ideas of thrift, so as to pave the way for a bank; and then he actually started a small bank. Its high rate of interest, which made the villagers flock so enthusiastically to put in their money, ended by swamping the bank altogether.

The old officers of the estate felt troubled and frightened. There was jubilation in the enemy's camp. Of all the family, only my husband's grandmother remained unmoved. She would scold me, saying: 'Why are you all plaguing him so? Is it the fate of the estate that is worrying you? How many times have I seen this estate in the hands of the court receiver! Are men like women? Men are born spendthrifts and only know how to waste. Look here, child, count yourself fortunate that your husband is not wasting himself as well!'

My husband's list of charities was a long one. He would assist to the bitter end of utter failure any one who wanted to invent a new loom or rice-husking machine. But what annoyed me most was the way that Sandip Babu used to fleece him on the pretext of *Swadeshi* work. Whenever he wanted to start a newspaper, or travel about preaching the Cause, or take a change of air by the advice of his doctor, my husband would unquestioningly supply him with the money. This was over and above the regular living allowance which Sandip Babu also received from him. The strangest part of it was that my husband and Sandip Babu did not agree in their opinions.

As soon as the *Swadeshi* storm reached my blood, I said to my husband: 'I must burn all my foreign clothes.'

'Why burn them?' said he. 'You need not wear them as long as you please.'

'As long as I please! Not in this life...'

'Very well, do not wear them for the rest of your life, then. But why this bonfire business?'

'Would you thwart me in my resolve?'

'What I want to say is this: Why not try to build up something? You should not waste even a tenth part of your energies in this destructive excitement.'

'Such excitement will give us the energy to build.'

'That is as much as to say, that you cannot light the house unless you set fire to it.'

Then there came another trouble. When Miss Gilby first came to our house there was a great flutter, which afterwards calmed down when they got used to her. Now the whole thing was stirred up afresh. I had never bothered myself before as to whether Miss Gilby was European or Indian, but I began to do so now. I said to my husband:

'We must get rid of Miss Gilby.'

He kept silent.

I talked to him wildly, and he went away sad at heart.

After a fit of weeping, I felt in a more reasonable mood when we met at night. 'I cannot,' my husband said, 'look upon Miss Gilby through a mist of abstraction, just because she is English. Cannot you get over the barrier of her name after such a long acquaintance? Cannot you realise that she loves you?'

I felt a little ashamed and replied with some sharpness: 'Let her remain. I am not over-anxious to send her away.'

And Miss Gilby remained.

But one day I was told that she had been insulted by a young fellow on her way to church. This was a boy whom we were supporting. My husband turned him out of the house. There was not a single soul, that day, who could forgive my husband for that act,—not even I. This time Miss Gilby left of her own accord. She shed tears when she came to say good-bye, but my mood would not melt. To slander the poor boy so,—and such a fine boy, too, who would forget his daily bath and food in his enthusiasm for *Swadeshi*.

My husband escorted Miss Gilby to the railway station in his own carriage. I was sure he was going too far. When exaggerated accounts of the incident gave rise to a public scandal, which found its way to the newspapers, I felt he had been rightly served.

I had often become anxious at my husband's doings, but had never before been ashamed; yet now I had to blush for him! I did not know exactly, nor did I care, what wrong poor Noren might, or might not, have done to Miss Gilby, but the idea of sitting in judgement on such a matter at such a time! I should have refused to damp the spirit which prompted young Noren to defy the Englishwoman. I could not but look upon it as a sign of cowardice in my husband, that he should fail to understand this simple thing. And so I blushed for him.

And yet it was not that my husband refused to support *Swadeshi*, or was in any way against the Cause. Only he had not been able whole-heartedly to accept the spirit of *Bande Mataram*.[9]

'I am willing,' he said, 'to serve my country; but my worship I reserve for Right which is far greater than my country. To worship my country as a god is to bring a curse upon it.'

---

9. Lit.: Hail Mother; the opening words of a song by Bankim Chatterjee, the famous Bengali novelist. The song has now become the national anthem, and *Bande Mataram* the national cry, since the days of the *Swadeshi* movement.—*Tr.*

Chapter II

Bimala's Story

IV

This was the time when Sandip Babu with his followers came to our neighbourhood to preach *Swadeshi*.

There is to be a big meeting in our temple pavilion. We women are sitting there, on one side behind a screen. Triumphant shouts of *Bande Mataram* come nearer: and to them I am thrilling through and through. Suddenly a stream of barefooted youths in turbans, clad in ascetic ochre, rushes into the quadrangle, like a silt-reddened freshet into a dry river-bed at the first burst of the rains. The whole place is filled with an immense crowd, through which Sandip Babu is borne, seated in a big chair hoisted on the shoulders of ten or twelve of the youths.

Bande Mataram! Bande Mataram! Bande Mataram! It seems as though the skies would be rent and scattered into a thousand fragments.

I had seen Sandip Babu's photograph before. There was something in his features which I did not quite like. Not that he was bad-looking,—far from it: he had a splendidly handsome face. Yet, I know not why, it seemed to me, in spite of all its brilliance, that too much of base alloy had gone into its making. The light in his eyes somehow did not shine true. That was why I did not like it when my husband unquestioningly gave in to all his demands. I could bear the waste of money; but it vexed me to think that he was imposing on my husband, taking advantage of friendship. His bearing was not that of an ascetic, nor even of a person of moderate means, but foppish all over. Love of comfort seemed to ... any number of such reflections come back to me to-day, but let them be.

When, however, Sandip Babu began to speak that afternoon, and the hearts of the crowd swayed and surged to his words, as though they would break all bounds, I saw him wonderfully transformed. Especially when his features were suddenly lit up by a shaft of light from the slowly setting sun, as it sunk below the roof-line of the pavilion, he seemed to me to be marked out by the gods as their messenger to mortal men and women.

From beginning to end of his speech, each one of his utterances was a stormy outburst. There was no limit to the confidence of his assurance. I do not know how it happened, but I found I had impatiently pushed away the screen from before me and had fixed my gaze upon him. Yet there was none in that crowd who paid any heed to my doings. Only once, I noticed, his eyes, like stars in fateful Orion, flashed full on my face.

I was utterly unconscious of myself. I was no longer the lady of the Rajah's house, but the sole representative of Bengal's womanhood. And he was the champion of Bengal. As the sky had shed its light over him, so he must receive the consecration of a woman's benediction....

It seemed clear to me that, since he had caught sight of me, the fire in his words had flamed up more fiercely. Indra's[1]

---

1. The Jupiter Pluvius of Hindu Mythology.

steed refused to be reined in, and there came the roar of
thunder and the flash of lighting. I said within myself that
his language had caught fire from my eyes; for we women
are not only the deities of the household fire, but the flame
of the soul itself.

I returned home that evening radiant with a new pride
and joy. The storm within me had shifted my whole being
from one centre to another. Like the Greek maidens of old,
I fain would cut off my long, resplendent tresses to make a
bowstring for my hero. Had my outward ornaments been
connected with my inner feelings, then my necklet, my armlets,
my bracelets, would all have burst their bonds and flung
themselves over that assembly like a shower of meteors. Only
some personal sacrifice, I felt, could help me to bear the
tumult of my exaltation.

When my husband came home later, I was trembling lest
he should utter a sound out of tune with the triumphant paean
which was still ringing in my ears, lest his fanaticism for truth
should lead him to express disapproval of anything that had
been said that afternoon. For then I should have openly defied
and humiliated him. But he did not say a word, ... which I
did not like either.

He should have said: 'Sandip has brought me to my
senses. I now realise how mistaken I have been all this time.'

I somehow felt that he was spitefully silent, that he
obstinately refused to be enthusiastic. I asked how long Sandip
Babu was going to be with us.

'He is off to Rangpur early to-morrow morning,' said my
husband.

'Must it be to-morrow?'

'Yes, he is already engaged to speak there.'

I was silent for a while and then asked again:

'Could he not possibly stay a day longer?'

'That may hardly be possible, but why?'

'I want to invite him to dinner and attend on him myself.'

My husband was surprised. He had often entreated me to be present when he had particular friends to dinner, but I had never let myself be persuaded. He gazed at me curiously, in silence, with a look I did not quite understand.

I was suddenly overcome with a sense of shame. 'No, no,' I exclaimed, 'that would never do!'

'Why not!' said he. 'I will ask him myself, and if it is at all possible he will surely stay on for to-morrow.'

It turned out to be quite possible.

I will tell the exact truth. That day I reproached my Creator because he had not made me surpassingly beautiful,— not to steal any heart away, but because beauty is glory. In this great day the men of the country should realise its goddess in its womanhood. But, alas, the eyes of men fail to discern the goddess, if outward beauty be lacking. Would Sandip Babu find the *Shakti* of the Motherland manifest in me? Or would he simply take me to be an ordinary, domestic woman?

That morning I scented my flowing hair and tied it in a loose knot, bound by a cunningly intertwined red silk ribbon. Dinner, you see, was to be served at midday, and there was no time to dry my hair after my bath and do it up plaited in the ordinary way. I put on a gold-bordered white *sari,* and my short-sleeve muslin jacket was also gold-bordered.

I felt that there was a certain restraint about my costume and that nothing could well have been simpler. But my sister-in-law, who happened to be passing by, stopped dead before me, surveyed me from head to foot and with compressed lips smiled a meaning smile. When I asked her the reason, 'I am admiring your get-up!' she said.

'What is there so entertaining about it?' I enquired, considerably annoyed.

'It's superb,' she said. 'I was only thinking that one of those low-necked English bodices would have made it perfect.'

Not only her mouth and eyes, but her whole body seemed to ripple with suppressed laughter as she left the room.

I was very, very angry, and wanted to change everything and put on my everyday clothes. But I cannot tell exactly why I could not carry out my impulse. Women are the ornaments of society,—thus I reasoned with myself,—and my husband would never like it, if I appeared before Sandip Babu unworthily clad.

My idea had been to make my appearance after they had sat down to dinner. In the bustle of looking after the serving the first awkwardness would have passed off. But dinner was not ready in time, and it was getting late. Meanwhile my husband had sent for me to introduce the guest.

I was feeling horribly shy about looking Sandip Babu in the face. However, I managed to recover myself enough to say: 'I am so sorry dinner is getting late.'

He boldly came and sat right beside me as he replied: 'I get a dinner of some kind every day but the Goddess of Plenty keeps behind the scenes. Now that the goddess herself has appeared, it matters little if the dinner lags behind.'

He was just as emphatic in his manners as he was in his public speaking. He had no hesitation and seemed to be accustomed to occupy, unchallenged, his chosen seat. He claimed the right to intimacy so confidently, that the blame would seem to belong to those who should dispute it.

I was in terror lest Sandip Babu should take me for a shrinking, old-fashioned bundle of inanity. But, for the life of me, I could not sparkle in repartees such as might charm or dazzle him. What could have possessed me, I angrily wondered, to appear before him in such an absurd way?

I was about to retire when dinner was over, but Sandip Babu, as bold as ever, placed himself in my way.

'You must not,' he said, 'think me greedy. I was not the dinner that kept me staying on, it was your invitation. If you

were to run away now, that would not be playing fair with
your guest.'

If he had not said these words with a careless ease, they
would have been out of tune. But, after all, he was such a
great friend of my husband that I was like his sister.

While I was struggling to climb up this high wave of
intimacy, my husband came to the rescue, saying: 'Why not
come back to us after you have taken your dinner?'

'But you must give your word,' said Sandip Babu, 'before
we let you off.'

'I will come,' said I, with a slight smile.

'Let me tell you,' continued Sandip Babu, 'why I cannot
trust you. Nikhil has been married these nine years, and all
this while you have eluded me. If you do this again for another
nine years, we shall never meet again.'

I took up the spirit of his remark as I dropped my voice
to reply: 'Why even then should we not meet?'

'My horoscope tells me I am to die early. None of my
forefathers have survived their thirtieth year. I am now
twenty-seven.'

He knew this would go home. This time there must have
been a shade of concern in my low voice as I said: 'The
blessings of the whole country are sure to avert the evil
influence of the stars.'

'Then the blessings of the country must be voiced by its
goddess. This is the reason for my anxiety that you should
return, so that my talisman may begin to work from to-day.'

Sandip Babu had such a way of taking things by storm
that I got no opportunity of resenting what I never should
have permitted in another.

'So,' he concluded with a laugh, 'I am going to hold this
husband of yours as a hostage till you come back.'

As I was coming away, he exclaimed: 'May I trouble you
for a trifle?'

I started and turned round.

'Don't be alarmed,' he said. 'It's merely a glass of water. You might have noticed that I did not drink any water with my dinner. I take it a little later.'

Upon this I had to make a show of interest and ask him the reason. He began to give the history of his dyspepsia. I was told how he had been a martyr to it for seven months, and how, after the usual course of nuisances, which included different allopathic and homoeopathic misadventures, he had obtained the most wonderful results by indigenous methods.

'Do you know,' he added, with a smile, 'God has built even my infirmities in such a manner that they yield only under the bombardment of *Swadeshi* pills.'

My husband, at this, broke his silence. 'You must confess,' said he, 'that you have as immense an attraction for foreign medicine as the earth has for meteors. You have three shelves in your sitting-room full of...'

Sandip Babu broke in: 'Do you know what they are? They are the punitive police. They come, not because they are wanted, but because they are imposed on us by the rule of this modern age, exacting fines and inflicting injuries.'

My husband could not bear exaggerations, and I could see he disliked this. But all ornaments are exaggerations. They are not made by God, but by man. Once I remember in defence of some untruth of mine I said to my husband: 'Only the trees and beasts and birds tell unmitigated truths, because these poor things have not the power to invent. In this men show their superiority to the lower creatures, and women beat even men. Neither is a profusion of ornament unbecoming for a woman, nor a profusion of untruth.'

As I came out into the passage leading to the zenana I found my sister-in-law, standing near a window overlooking the reception rooms, peeping through the venetian shutter.

'You here?' I asked in surprise.
'Eavesdropping!' she replied.

V

When I returned, Sandip Babu was tenderly apologetic. 'I am afraid we have spoilt your appetite,' he said.

I felt greatly ashamed. Indeed, I had been too indecently quick over my dinner. With a little calculation, it would become quite evident that my non-eating had surpassed the eating. But I had no idea that any one could have been deliberately calculating.

I suppose Sandip Babu detected my feeling of shame, which only augmented it. 'I was sure,' he said, 'that you had the impulse of the wild deer to run away, but it is a great boon that you took the trouble to keep your promise with me.'

I could not think of any suitable reply and so I sat down, blushing and uncomfortable, at one end of the sofa. The vision that I had of myself, as the *Shakti* of Womanhood, incarnate, crowning Sandip Babu simply with my presence, majestic and unashamed, failed me altogether.

Sandip Babu deliberately started a discussion with my husband. He knew that his keen wit flashed to the best effect in an argument. I have often since observed, that he never lost an opportunity for a passage at arms whenever I happened to be present.

He was familiar with my husband's views on the cult of *Bande Mataram*, and began in a provoking way: 'So you do not allow that there is room for an appeal to the imagination in patriotic work?'

'It has its place, Sandip, I admit, but I do not believe in giving it the whole place. I would know my country in its frank reality, and for this I am both afraid and ashamed to make use of hypnotic texts of patriotism.'

'What you call hypnotic texts I call truth. I truly believe my country to be my God. I worship Humanity. God manifests Himself both in man and in his country.'

'If that is what you really believe, there should be no difference for you between man and man, and so between country and country.'

'Quite true. But my powers are limited, so my worship of Humanity is continued in the worship of my country.'

'I have nothing against your worship as such, but how is it you propose to conduct your worship of God by hating other countries in which He is equally manifest?'

'Hate is also an adjunct of worship. Arjuna won Mahadeva's by wrestling with him. God will be with us in the end, if we are prepared to give Him battle.'

'If that be so, then those who are serving and those who are harming the country are both His devotees. Why, then, trouble to preach patriotism?'

'In the case of one's own country, it is different. There the heart clearly demands worship.'

'If you push the same argument further you can say that since God is manifested in us, our *self* has to be worshipped before all else; because our natural instinct claims it.'

'Look here, Nikhil, this is all merely dry logic. Can't you recognise that there is such a thing as feeling?'

'I tell you the truth, Sandip,' my husband replied. 'It is my feelings that are outraged, whenever you try to pass off injustice as a duty, and unrighteousness as a moral idea. The fact, that I am incapable of stealing, is not due to my possessing logical faculties, but to my having some feeling of respect for myself and love for ideals.'

I was raging inwardly. At last I could keep silent no longer. 'Is not the history of every country,' I cried, 'whether England, France, Germany, or Russia, the history of stealing for the sake of one's own country?'

'They have to answer for these thefts; they are doing so even now; their history is not yet ended.'

'At any rate,' interposed Sandip Babu, 'why should we not follow suit? Let us first fill our country's coffers with stolen goods and then take centuries, like these other countries, to answer for them, if we must. But, I ask you, where do you find this "answering" in history?'

'When Rome was answering for her sin no one knew it. All that time, there was apparently no limit to her prosperity. But do you not see one thing: how these political bags of theirs are bursting with lies and treacheries, breaking their backs under their weight?'

Never before had I any opportunity of being present at a discussion between my husband and his men friends. Whenever he argued with me I could feel his reluctance to push me into a corner. This arose out of the very love he bore me. Today for the first time I saw his fencer's skill in debate.

Nevertheless, my heart refused to accept my husband's position. I was struggling to find some answer, but it would not come. When the word 'righteousness' comes into an argument, it sounds ugly to say that a thing can be too good to be useful.

All of a sudden Sandip Babu turned to me with the question: 'What do you say to this?'

'I do not care about fine distinctions,' I broke out. 'I will tell you broadly what I feel. I am only human. I am covetous. I would have good things for my country. If I am obliged, I would snatch them and filch them. I have anger. I would be angry for my country's sake. If necessary, I would smite and slay to avenge her insults. I have my desire to be fascinated, and fascination must be supplied to me in bodily shape by my country. She must have some visible symbol casting its spell upon my mind. I would make my country a Person, and call her Mother, Goddess, Durga,—for whom I would redden the earth with sacrificial offerings. I am human, not divine.'

Sandip Babu leapt to his feet with uplifted arms and shouted 'Hurrah!'—The next moment he corrected himself and cried: '*Bande Mataram.*'

A shadow of pain passed over the face of my husband. He said to me in a very gentle voice: 'Neither am I divine: I am human. And therefore I dare not permit the evil which is in me to be exaggerated into an image of my country,— never, never!'

Sandip Babu cried out: 'See, Nikhil, how in the heart of a woman Truth takes flesh and blood. Woman knows how to be cruel: her virulence is like a blind storm. It is beautifully fearful. In man it is ugly, because it harbours in its centre the gnawing worms of reason and thought. I tell you, Nikhil, it is our women who will save the country. This is not the time for nice scruples. We must be unswervingly, unreasoningly brutal. We must sin. We must give our women red sandal paste with which to anoint and enthrone our sin. Don't you remember what the poet says:

> Come, Sin, O beautiful Sin,
> Let thy stinging red kisses pour down fiery red wine into our blood.
> Sound the trumpet of imperious evil
> And cross our forehead with the wreath of exulting lawlessness,
> O Deity of Desecration,
> Smear our breasts with the blackest mud of disrepute, unashamed.

Down with that righteousness, which cannot smilingly bring rack and ruin.'

When Sandip Babu, standing with his head high, insulted at a moment's impulse all that men have cherished as their highest, in all countries and in all times, a shiver went right through my body.

But, with a stamp of his foot, he continued his declamation: 'I can see that you are that beautiful spirit of fire, which burns the home to ashes and lights up the larger world with its flame. Give to us the indomitable courage to go to the bottom of Ruin itself. Impart grace to all that is baneful.'

It was not clear to whom Sandip Babu addressed his last appeal. It might have been She whom he worshipped with his *Bande Mataram*. It might have been the Womanhood of his country. Or it might have been its representative, the woman before him. He would have gone further in the same strain, but my husband suddenly rose from his seat and touched him lightly on the shoulder saying: 'Sandip, Chandranath Babu is here.'

I started and turned round, to find an aged gentleman at the door, calm and dignified, in doubt as to whether he should come in or retire. His face was touched with a gentle light like that of the setting sun.

My husband came up to me and whispered: 'This is my master, of whom I have so often told you. Make your obeisance to him.'

I bent reverently and took the dust of his feet. He gave me his blessing saying: 'May God protect you always, my little mother.'

I was sorely in need of such a blessing at that moment.

Nikhil's Story

I

One day I had the faith to believe that I should be able to bear whatever came from my God. I never had the trial. Now I think it has come.

I used to test my strength of mind by imagining all kinds of evil which might happen to me—poverty, imprisonment, dishonour, death,—even Bimala's. And when I said to myself that I should be able to receive these with firmness, I am sure I did not exaggerate. Only I could never even imagine one thing, and to-day it is that of which I am thinking, and wondering whether I can really bear it. There is a thorn somewhere pricing in my heart, constantly giving me pain while I am about my daily work. It seems to persist even when I am asleep. The very moment I wake up in the morning, I find that the bloom has gone from the face of the sky. What is it? What has happened?

My mind has become so sensitive, that even my past life, which came to me in the disguise of happiness, seems to wring my very heart with its falsehood; and the shame and sorrow which are coming close to me are losing their cover of privacy, all the more because they try to veil their faces. My heart has become all eyes. The things that should not be seen, the things I do not want to see,—these I must see.

The day has come at last when my ill-starred life has to reveal its destitution in a long-drawn series of exposures. This penury, all unexpected, has taken its seat in the heart where plenitude seemed to reign. The fees which I paid to delusion for just nine years of my youth have now to be returned with interest to Truth till the end of my days.

What is the use of straining to keep up my pride? What harm if I confess that I have something lacking in me? Possibly it is that unreasoning forcefulness which women love to find in men. But is strength a mere display of muscularity? Must strength have no scruples in treading the weak underfoot?

But why all these arguments? Worthiness cannot be earned merely by disputing about it. And I am unworthy, unworthy, unworthy.

What if I *am* unworthy? The true value of love is this, that it can ever bless the unworthy with its own prodigality. For the worthy there are many rewards on God's earth, but God has specially reserved love for the unworthy.

Up till now Bimala was my home-made Bimala, the product of the confined space and the daily routine of small duties. Did the love which I received from her, I asked myself, come from the deep spring of her heart, or was it merely like the daily provision of pipe water pumped up by the municipal steam-engine of society?

I longed to find Bimala blossoming fully in all her truth and power. But the thing I forgot to calculate was, that one must give up all claims based on conventional rights, if one would find a person freely revealed in truth.

Why did I fail to think of this? Was it because of the husband's pride of possession over his wife? No. It was because I placed the fullest trust upon love. I was vain enough to think that I had the power in me to bear the sight of truth in its awful nakedness. It was tempting Providence, but still I clung to my proud determination to come out victorious in the trial.

Bimala had failed to understand me in one thing. She could not fully realise that I held as weakness all imposition of force. Only the weak dare not be just. They shirk their responsibility of fairness and try quickly to get at results through the short-cuts of injustice. Bimala has no patience with patience. She loves to find in men the turbulent, the angry, the unjust. Her respect must have its element of fear.

I had hoped that when Bimala found herself free in the outer world she would be rescued from her infatuation for tyranny. But now I feel sure that this infatuation is deep down in her nature. Her love is for the boisterous. From the tip of her tongue to the pit of her stomach she must tingle with red pepper in order to enjoy the simple fare of life. But my determination was, never to do my duty with frantic impetuosity, helped on by the fiery liquor of excitement. I know Bimala finds it difficult to respect me for this, taking my scruples for feebleness,—and she is quite angry with me because I am not running amuck crying *Bande Mataram*.

For the matter of that, I have become unpopular with all my countrymen because I have not joined them in their carousals. They are certain that either I have a longing for some title, or else that I am afraid of the police. The police on their side suspect me of harbouring some hidden design and protesting too much in my mildness.

What I really feel is this, that those who cannot find food for their enthusiasm in a knowledge of their country as it actually is, or those who cannot love men just because they are men,—who needs must shout and deify their country in order to keep up their excitement,—these love excitement more than their country.

To try to give our infatuation a higher place than Truth is a sign of inherent slavishness. Where our minds are free we find ourselves lost. Our moribund vitality must have for its rider either some fantasy, or some one in authority, or a sanction from the pundits, in order to make it move. So long as we are impervious to truth and have to be moved by some hypnotic stimulus, we must know that we lack the capacity for self-government. Whatever may be our condition, we shall either need some imaginary ghost or some actual medicine-man to terrorise over us.

The other day when Sandip accused me of lack of imagination, saying that this prevented me from realising my country in a visible image, Bimala agreed with him. I did not say anything in my defence, because to win in argument does not lead to happiness. Her difference of opinion is not due to any inequality of intelligence, but rather to dissimilarity of nature.

They accuse me of being unimaginative,—that is, according to them, I may have oil in my lamp, but no flame. Now this is exactly the accusation which I bring against them. I would say to them: 'You are dark, even as the flints are. You must come to violent conflicts and make a noise in order to produce your sparks. But their disconnected flashes merely assist, your pride, and not your clear vision.'

I have been noticing for some time that there is a gross cupidity about Sandip. His fleshly feelings make him harbour delusions about his religion and impel him into a tyrannical attitude in his patriotism. His intellect is keen, but his nature is coarse, and so he glorifies his selfish lusts under high-sounding names. The cheap consolations of hatred are as urgently necessary for him as the satisfaction of his appetites. Bimala has often warned me, in the old days, of his hankering after money. I understood this, but I could not bring myself to haggle with Sandip. I felt ashamed even to own to myself that he was trying to take advantage of me.

It will, however, be difficult to explain to Bimala to-day that Sandip's love of country is but a different phase of his covetous self-love. Bimala's hero-worship of Sandip makes me hesitate all the more to talk to her about him, lest some touch of jealousy may lead me unwittingly into exaggeration. It may be that the pain at my heart is already making me see a distorted picture of Sandip. And yet it is better perhaps to speak out than to keep my feelings gnawing within me.

II

I have known my master these thirty years. Neither calumny, nor disaster, nor death itself has any terrors for him. Nothing could have saved me, born as I was into the traditions of this family of ours, but that he has established his own life in the centre of mine, with its peace and truth and spiritual vision, thus making it possible for me to realise goodness in its truth.

My master came to me that day and said: 'Is it necessary to detain Sandip here any longer?'

His nature was so sensitive to all omens of evil that he had at once understood. He was not easily moved, but that day he felt the dark shadow of trouble ahead. Do I not know how well he loves me?

At tea-time I said to Sandip: 'I have just had a letter from Rangpur. They are complaining that I am selfishly detaining you. When will you be going there?'

Bimala was pouring out the tea. Her face fell at once. She threw just one enquiring glance at Sandip.

'I have been thinking,' said Sandip, 'that this wandering up and down means a tremendous waste of energy. I feel that if I could work from a centre I could achieve more permanent results.'

With this he looked up at Bimala and asked: 'Do you not think so too?'

Bimala hesitated for a reply and then said: 'Both ways seem good,—to do the work from a centre, as well as by travelling about. That in which you find greater satisfaction is the way for you.'

'Then let me speak out my mind,' said Sandip. 'I have never yet found any one source of inspiration suffice me for good. That is why I have been constantly moving about, rousing enthusiasm in the people, from which in turn I draw my own store of energy. To-day you have given me the message of my country. Such fire I have never beheld in any man. I shall be able to spread the fire of enthusiasm in my country by borrowing it from you. No, do not be ashamed. Your are far above all modesty and diffidence. You are the Queen Bee of our hive, and we the workers shall rally around you. You shall be our centre, our inspiration.'

Bimala flushed all over with bashful pride and her hand shook as she went on pouring out the tea.

Another day my master came to me and said: 'Why don't you two go up to Darjeeling for a change? You are not looking well. Have you been getting enough sleep?'

I asked Bimala in the evening whether she would care to have a trip to the Hills. I knew she had a great longing to see the Himalayas. But she refused.... The country's Cause, I suppose!

I must not lose my faith: I shall wait. The passage from the narrow to the larger world is stormy. When she is familiar with this freedom, then I shall know where my place is. If I discover that I do not fit in with the arrangement of the outer world, then I shall not quarrel with my fate, but silently take my leave.... Use force? But for what? Can force prevail against Truth?

Sandip's Story

I

The impotent man says: 'That which has come to my share is mine.' And the weak man assents. But the lesson of the whole world is: 'That is really mine which I can snatch away.' My country does not become mine simply because it is the country of my birth. It becomes mine on the day when I am able to win it by force.

Every man has a natural right to possess, and therefore greed is natural. It is not in the wisdom of nature that we should be content to be deprived. What my mind covets, my surroundings must supply. This is the only true understanding between our inner and outer nature in this world. Let moral ideals remain merely for those poor anaemic creatures of starved desire whose grasp is weak. Those who can desire with all their soul and enjoy with all their heart, those who have no hesitation or scruple, it is they who are the anointed of Providence. Nature spreads out her richest and loveliest treasures for their benefit. They swim across streams, leap over walls, kick open doors, to help themselves to whatever is worth taking. In such a getting one can rejoice; such wresting as this gives value to the thing taken.

Nature surrenders herself, but only to the robber. For she delights in this forceful desire, this forceful abduction. And so she does not put the garland of her acceptance round the lean, scraggy neck of the ascetic. The music of the wedding march is struck. The time of the wedding I must not let pass. My heart therefore is eager. For, who is the bridegroom? It is I. The bridegroom's place belongs to him who, torch in hand, can come in time. The bridegroom in Nature's wedding hall comes unexpected and uninvited.

Ashamed? No, I am never ashamed! I ask for whatever I want, and I do not always wait to ask before I take it. Those who are deprived by their own diffidence dignify their privation by the name of modesty. The world into which we are born is the world of reality. When a man goes away from the market of real things with empty hands and empty stomach, merely filling his bag with big sounding words, I wonder why he ever came into this hard world at all. Did these men get their appointment from the epicures of the religious world, to play set tunes on sweet, pious texts in that pleasure garden where blossom airy nothings? I neither affect those tunes nor do I find any sustenance in those blossoms.

What I desire, I desire positively, superlatively. I want to knead it with both my hands and both my feet; I want to smear it all over my body; I want to gorge myself with it to the full. The scrannel pipes of those who have worn themselves out by their moral fastings, till they have become flat and pale like starved vermin infesting a long-deserted bed, will never reach my ear.

I would conceal nothing, because that would be cowardly. But if I cannot bring myself to conceal when concealment is needful, that also is cowardly. Because you have your greed, you build your walls. Because I have my greed, I break through them. You use your power: I use my craft. These are the realities of life. On these depend kingdoms and empires and all the great enterprises of men.

As for those *avatars* who come down from their paradise to talk to us in some holy jargon—their words are not real. Therefore, in spite of all the applause they get, these sayings of theirs only find a place in the hiding corners of the weak. They are despised by those who are strong, the rulers of the world. Those who have had the courage to see this have won success, while those poor wretches who are dragged one way by nature and the other way by these *avatars*, they set one foot in the boat of the real and the other in the boat of the unreal, and thus are in a pitiable plight, able neither to advance nor to keep their place.

There are many men who seem to have been born only with an obsession to die. Possibly there is a beauty, like that of a sunset, in this lingering death in life which seems to fascinate them. Nikhil lives this kind of life, if life it may be called. Years ago, I had a great argument with him on this point.

'It is true,' he said, 'that you cannot get anything except by force. But then what *is* this force? And then also, what *is* this getting? The strength I believe in is the strength of renouncing.'

'So you,' I exclaimed, 'are infatuated with the glory of bankruptcy.'

'Just as desperately as the chick is infatuated about the bankruptcy of its shell,' he replied. 'The shell is real enough, yet it is given up in exchange for intangible light and air. A sorry exchange, I suppose you would call it?'

When once Nikhil gets onto metaphor, there is no hope of making him see that he is merely dealing with words, not with realities. Well, well, let him be happy with his metaphors. We are the flesh-eaters of the world; we have teeth and nails; we pursue and grab and tear. We are not satisfied with chewing in the evening the cud of the grass we have eaten in the morning. Anyhow, we cannot allow your metaphor-mongers to bar the door to our sustenance. In that case we shall simply steal or rob, for we must live.

People will say that I am starting some novel theory, just because those who are moving in this world are in the habit of talking differently though they are really acting up to it all the time. Therefore they fail to understand, as I do, that this is the only working moral principle. In point of fact, I know that my idea is not an empty theory at all, for it has been proved in practical life. I have found that my way always wins over the hearts of women, who are creatures of this world of reality and do not roam about in cloud-land, as men do, in idea-filled balloons.

Women find in my features, my manner, my gait, my speech, a masterful passion,—not a passion dried thin with the heat of asceticism, not a passion with its face turned back at every step in doubt and debate, but a full-blooded passion. It roars and rolls on, like a flood, with the cry: *'I want, I want I want.'* Women feel, in their own heart of hearts, that this indomitable passion is the lifeblood of the world, acknowledging no law but itself, and therefore victorious. For this reason they have so often abandoned themselves to be swept away on the flood-tide of my passion, recking naught as to whether it takes them to life or to death. This power which wins these women is the power of mighty men, the power which wins the world of reality.

Those who imagine the greater desirability of another world merely shift their desires from the earth to the skies. It remains to be seen how high their gushing fountain will play, and for how long. But this much is certain: women were not created for these pale creatures,—these lotus-eaters of idealism.

'Affinity!' When it suited my need, I have often said that God has created special pairs of men and women, and that the union of such is the only legitimate union, higher than all unions made by law. The reason of it is, that though man wants to follow nature, he can find no pleasure in it unless he screens himself with some phrase,—and that is why this world is so over-flowing with lies.

'Affinity!' Why should there be only one? There may be affinity with thousands. It was never in my agreement with nature that I should overlook all my innumerable affinities for the sake of only one. I have discovered many in my own life up to now, yet that has not closed the door to one more,— and that one is clearly visible to my eyes. She has also discovered her own affinity to me.

And then?

Then, if I do not win I am a coward.

Chapter III

Bimala's Story

VI

I wonder what could have happened to my feeling of shame. The fact is, I had no time to think about myself. My days and nights were passing in a whirl, like an eddy with myself in the centre. No gap was left for hesitation or delicacy to enter.

One day my sister-in-law remarked to my husband: 'Up to now the women of this house have been kept weeping. Here comes the men's turn.'

'We must see that they do not miss it,' she continued, turning to me. 'I see you are out for the fray, Chota[1] Rani! Hurl your shafts straight at their hearts.'

Her keen eyes looked me up and down. Not one of the colours into which my toilet, my dress, my manners, my speech, had blossomed out had escaped her. I am ashamed to speak of it to-day, but I felt no shame then. Something within me was at work of which I was not even conscious. I used to overdress, it is true, but more like an automaton, with no particular design. No doubt I knew which effort of

---

1. Bimala, the younger brother's wife, was the *Chota* or Junior Rani.

mine would prove specially pleasing to Sandip Babu, but that required no intuition, for he would discuss it openly before all of them.

One day he said to my husband: 'Do you know, Nikhil, when I first saw our Queen Bee, she was sitting there so demurely in her gold-bordered *sari*. Her eyes were gazing enquiringly into space, like stars which had lost their way, just as if she had been for ages standing on the edge of some darkness, looking out for something unknown. But when I saw her, I felt a quiver run through me. It seemed to me that the gold border of her *sari* was her own inner fire flaming out and twining round her. That is the flame we want, visible fire! Look here, Queen Bee, you really must do us the favour of dressing once more as a living flame.'

So long I had been like a small river at the border of a village. My rhythm and my language were different from what they are now. But the tide came up from the sea, and my breast heaved; my banks gave way and the great drum-beats of the sea waves echoed in my mad current. I could not understand the meaning of that sound in my blood. Where was that former self of mine? Whence came foaming into me this surging flood of glory? Sandip's hungry eyes burnt like the lamps of worship before my shrine. All his gaze proclaimed that I was a wonder in beauty and power; and the loudness of his praise, spoken and unspoken, drowned all other voices in my world. Had the Creator created me afresh, I wondered? Did he wish to make up now for neglecting me so long? I who before was plain had become suddenly beautiful. I who before had been of no account now felt in myself all the splendour of Bengal itself.

For Sandip Babu was not a mere individual. In him was the confluence of millions of minds of the country. When he called me the Queen Bee of the hive, I was acclaimed with a chorus of praise by all our patriot workers. After that, the loud jests of my sister-in-law could not touch me any longer. My relations with all the world underwent a change. Sandip Babu made it clear how all the country was in need of me. I had no difficulty in believing this at the time, for I felt that I had the power to do everything. Divine strength had come to me. It was something which I had never felt before, which was beyond myself. I had no time to question it to find out what was its nature. It seemed to belong to me, and yet to transcend me. It comprehended the whole of Bengal.

Sandip Babu would consult me about every little thing touching the Cause. At first I felt very awkward and would hang back, but that soon wore off. Whatever I suggested seemed to astonish him. He would go into raptures and say: 'Men can only think. You women have a way of understanding without thinking. Woman was created out of God's own fancy. Man, He had to hammer into shape.'

Letters used to come to Sandip Babu from all parts of the country which were submitted to me for my opinion. Occasionally he disagreed with me. But I would not argue with him. Then after a day or two,—as if a new light had suddenly dawned upon him,—he would send for me and say: 'It was my mistake. Your suggestion was the correct one.' He would often confess to me that wherever he had taken steps contrary to my advice he had gone wrong. Thus I gradually came to be convinced that behind whatever was taking place was Sandip Babu, and behind Sandip Babu was the plain common sense of a woman. The glory of a great responsibility filled my being.

My husband had no place in our counsels. Sandip Babu treated him as a younger brother, of whom personally one may be very fond and yet have no use for his business advice. He would tenderly and smilingly talk about my husband's childlike innocence, saying that his curious doctrine and perversities of mind had a flavour of humour which made them all the more lovable. It was seemingly this very affection for Nikhil which led Sandip Babu to forbear from troubling him with the burden of the country.

Nature has many anodynes in her pharmacy, which she secretly administers when vital relations are being insidiously severed, so that none may know of the operation, till at last one awakes to know what a great rent has been made. When the knife was busy with my life's most intimate tie, my mind was so clouded with fumes of intoxicating gas that I was not in the least aware of what a cruel thing was happening. Possibly this is woman's nature. When her passion is roused she loses her sensibility for all that is outside it. When, like the river, we women keep to our banks, we give nourishment with all that we have: when we overflow them we destroy with all that we are.

Sandip's Story

II

I can see that something has gone wrong. I got an inkling of it the other day.

Ever since my arrival, Nikhil's sitting-room had become a thing amphibious,—half women's apartment, half men's: Bimala had access to it from the zenana, it was not barred to me from the outer side. If we had only gone slow, and made use of our privileges with some restraint, we might not have fallen foul of other people. But we went ahead so vehemently that we could not think of the consequences.

Whenever Bee comes into Nikhil's room, I somehow get to know of it from mine. There are the tinkle of bangles and other little sounds; the door is perhaps shut with a shade of unnecessary vehemence; the bookcase is a trifle stiff and creaks if jerked open. When I enter I find Bee, with her back to the door, ever so busy selecting a book from the shelves. And as I offer to assist her in this difficult task she starts and protests; and then we naturally get on to other topics.

The other day, on an inauspicious[2] Thursday afternoon, I sallied forth from my room at the call of these same sounds. There was a man on guard in the passage. I walked on without

---

2. According to the Hindu calendar.—*Tr*

so much as glancing at him, but as I approached the door he put himself in my way saying: 'Not that way, sir.'

'Not that way! Why?'

'The Rani Mother is there.'

'Oh, very well. Tell your Rani Mother that Sandip Babu wants to see her.'

'That cannot be, sir. It is against orders.'

I felt highly indignant. 'I order you!' I said in a raised voice. 'Go and announce me.'

The fellow was somewhat taken aback at my attitude. In the meantime I had neared the door. I was on the point of reaching it, when he followed after me and took me by the arm saying: 'No, sir, you must not.'

What! To be touched by a flunkey! I snatched away my arm and gave the man a sounding blow. At this moment Bee came out of the room to find the man about to insult me.

I shall never forget the picture of her wrath! That Bee is beautiful is a discovery of my own. Most of our people would see nothing in her. Her tall, slim figure these boors would call 'lanky.' But it is just this lithesomeness of hers that I admire,—like an up-leaping fountain of life, coming direct out of the depths of the Creator's heart. Her complexion is dark, but it is the lustrous darkness of a sword-blade, keen and scintillating.

'Nanku!' she commanded, as she stood in the doorway, pointing with her finger, 'leave us.'

'Do not be angry with him,' said I. 'If it is against orders, it is I who should retire.'

Bee's voice was still trembling as she replied: 'You must not go. Come in.'

It was not a request, but again a command! I followed her in, and taking a chair fanned myself with a fan which was on the table. Bee scribbled something with a pencil on a sheet of paper and, summoning a servant handed it to him saying: 'Take this to the Maharaja.'

'Forgive me,' I resumed. 'I was unable to control myself, and hit that man of yours.'

'You served him right,' said Bee.

'But it was not the poor fellow's fault, after all. He was only obeying his orders.'

Here Nikhil came in, and as he did so I left my seat with a rapid movement and went and stood near the window with my back to the room.

'Nanku, the guard, has insulted Sandip Babu,' said Bee to Nikhil.

Nikhil seemed to be so genuinely surprised that I had to turn round and stare at him. Even an outrageously good man fails in keeping up his pride of truthfulness before his wife,— if she be the proper kind of woman.

'He insolently stood in the way when Sandip Babu was coming in here,' continued Bee. 'He said he had orders....'

'Whose orders?' asked Nikhil.

'How am I to know?' exclaimed Bee impatiently, her eyes brimming over with mortification.

Nikhil sent for the man and questioned him. 'It was not my fault,' Nanku repeated sullenly. 'I had my orders.'

'Who gave you the order?'

'The Bara Rani Mother.'

We were all silent for a while. After the man had left, Bee said: 'Nanku must go!'

Nikhil remained silent. I could see that his sense of justice would not allow this. There was no end to his qualms. But this time he was up against a touch problem. Bee was not the woman to take things lying down. She would have to get even with her sister-in-law by punishing this fellow. And as Nikhil remained silent, her eyes flashed fire. She knew not how to pour her scorn upon her husband's feebleness of spirit. Nikhil left the room after a while without another word.

The next day Nanku was not to be seen. On enquiry, I learnt that he had been sent off to some other part of the estates, and that his wages had not suffered by such transfer.

I could catch glimpses of the ravages of the storm raging over this, behind the scenes. All I can say is, that Nikhil is a curious creature, quite out of the common.

The upshot was, that after this Bee began to send for me to the sitting-room, for a chat, without any contrivance, or pretence of its being an accident. Thus from bare suggestion we came to broad hint: the implied came to be expressed. The daughter-in-law of a princely house lives in a starry region so remote from the ordinary outsider that there is not even a regular road for his approach. What a triumphal progress of Truth was this which, gradually but persistently, thrust aside veil after veil of obscuring custom, till at length Nature herself was laid bare.

Truth? Of course it was the truth! The attraction of man and woman for each other is fundamental. The whole world of matter, from the speck of dust upwards, is ranged on its side. And yet men would keep it hidden away out of sight, behind a tissue of words; and with homemade sanctions and prohibitions make of it a domestic utensil. Why, it's as absurd as melting down the solar system to make a watch-chain for one's son-in-law![3]

When, in spite of all, reality awakes at the call of what is but naked truth, what a gnashing of teeth and beating of breasts is there! But can one carry on a quarrel with a storm? It never takes the trouble to reply, it only gives a shaking.

I am enjoying the sight of this truth, as it gradually reveals itself. These tremblings of steps, these turnings of the face, are sweet to me: and sweet are the deceptions which deceive not only others, but also Bee herself. When Reality has to

3. The son-in-law is the pet of a Hindu household.

meet the unreal, deception is its principal weapon; for its enemies always try to shame Reality by calling it gross, and so it needs must hide itself, or else put on some disguise. The circumstances are such that it dare not frankly avow: 'Yes, I am gross, because I am true. I am flesh. I am passion. I am hunger, unashamed and cruel.'

All is now clear to me. The curtain flaps, and through it I can see the preparations for the catastrophe. The little red ribbon, which peeps through the luxuriant masses of her hair, with its flush of secret longing, it is the lolling tongue of the red storm cloud. I feel the warmth of each turn of her *sari*, each suggestion of her raiment, of which even the wearer may not be fully conscious.

Bee was not conscious, because she was ashamed of the reality; to which men have given a bad name, calling it Satan; and so it has to steal into the garden of paradise in the guise of a snake, and whisper secrets into the ears of man's chosen consort and make her rebellious; then farewell to all ease; and after that comes death!

My poor little Queen Bee is living in a dram. She knows not which way she is treading. It would not be safe to awaken her before the time. It is best for me to pretend to be equally unconscious.

The other day, at dinner, she was gazing at me in a curious sort of way, little realising what such glances mean! As my eyes met hers, she turned away with a flush. 'You are surprised at my appetite,' I remarked. 'I can hide everything, except that I am greedy! Anyhow, why trouble to blush for me, since I am shameless?'

This only made her colour more furiously, as she stammered: 'No, no, I was only …'

'I know,' I interrupted. 'Women have a weakness for greedy men; for it is this greed of ours which gives them the upper hand. The indulgence which I have always received at their hands has made me all the more shameless. I do not mind your watching the good things disappear, not one bit. I mean to enjoy every one of them.'

The other day I was reading an English book in which sex-problems were treated in an audaciously realistic manner. I had left it lying in the sitting-room. As I went there the next afternoon, for something or other, I found Bee seated with this book in her hand. When she heard my footsteps she hurriedly put it down and placed another book over it—a volume of Mrs. Hemans's poems.

'I have never been able to make out,' I began, 'why women are so shy about being caught reading poetry. We men—lawyers, mechanics, or what not,—may well feel ashamed. If we must read poetry, it should be at dead of night, within closed doors. But you women are so akin to poesy. The Creator Himself is a lyric poet, and Jayadeva[4] must have practised the divine art seated at His feet.'

Bee made no reply, but only blushed uncomfortably. She made as if she would leave the room. Whereupon I protested: 'No, no, pray read on. I will just take a book I left here, and run away.' With which I took up my book from the table. 'Lucky you did not think of glancing over its pages,' I continued, 'or you would have wanted to chastise me.'

'Indeed! Why?' asked Bee.

'Because it is not poetry,' said I. 'Only blunt things, bluntly put, without any finicking niceness. I wish Nikhil would read it.'

Bee frowned a little as she murmured: 'What makes you wish that?'

'He is a man, you see, one of us. My only quarrel with him is that he delights in a misty vision of this world. Have

---

4. A Vaishnava poet (Sanskrit) whose lyrics of the adoration of the Divinity serve as well to express all shades of human passion.—*Tr.*

you not observed how this trait of his makes him look on *Swadeshi* as if it was some poem of which the metre must be kept correct at every step? We, with the clubs of our prose, are the iconoclasts of metre.'

'What has your book to do with *Swadeshi*?'

'You would know if you only read it. Nikhil wants to go by made-up maxims, in *Swadeshi* as in everything else; so he knocks up against human nature at every turn, and then falls to abusing it. He never will realise that human nature was created long before phrases were, and will survive them too.'

Bee was silent for a while and then gravely said: 'Is it not part of human nature to try and rise superior to itself?'

I smiled inwardly. 'These are not your words,' I thought to myself. 'You have learnt them from Nikhil. *You* are a healthy human being. Your flesh and blood have responded to the call of reality. You are burning in every vein with life-fire,—do I not know it? How long should they keep you cool with the wet towel of moral precepts?'

'The weak are in the majority,' I said aloud. 'They are continually poisoning the ears of men by repeating these shibboleths. Nature has denied them strength,—it is thus that they try to enfeeble others.'

'We women are weak,' replied Bimala. 'So I suppose we must join in the conspiracy of the weak.'

'Women weak!' I exclaimed with a laugh. 'Men belaud you as delicate and fragile, so as to delude you into thinking yourselves weak. But it is you women who are strong. Men make a great outward show of their so-called freedom, but those who know their inner minds are aware of their bondage. They have manufactured scriptures with their own hands to bind themselves; with their very idealism the have made golden fetters of women to wind round their body and mind. If men had not that extraordinary faculty of entangling themselves in meshes of their own contriving, nothing could have kept them bound. But as for you women, you have desired to conceive reality with body and soul. You have given birth to reality. You have suckled reality at your breasts.'

Bee was well read for a woman, and would not easily give in to my arguments. 'If that were true,' she objected, 'men would not have found women attractive.'

'Women realise the danger,' I replied, 'They know that men love delusions, so they give them full measure by borrowing their own phrases. They know that man, the drunkard, values intoxication more than food, and so they try to pass themselves off as an intoxicant. As a matter of fact, but for the sake of man, woman has no need for any make-believe.'

'Why, then, are you troubling to destroy the illusion?'

'For freedom. I want the country to be free. I want human relations to be free.'

III

I was aware that it is unsafe suddenly to awake a sleep-walker. But I am so impetuous by nature, a halting gait does not suit me. I knew I was overbold that day. I knew that the first shock of such ideas is apt to be almost intolerable. But with women it is always audacity that wins.

Just as we were getting on nicely, who should walk in but Nikhil's old tutor Chandranath Babu. The world would have been not half a bad place to live in but for these schoolmasters, who make one want to quit it in disgust. The Nikhil type wants to keep the world always a school. This incarnation of a school turned up that afternoon at the psychological moment.

We all remain schoolboys in some corner of our hearts, and I, even I, felt somewhat pulled up. As for poor Bee, she at once took her place solemnly, like the topmost girl of the class on the front bench. All of a sudden she seemed to remember that she had to face her examination.

Some people are so like eternal pointsmen lying in wait by the line, to shunt one's train of thought from one rail to another.

Chandranath Babu had no sooner come in than he cast about for some excuse to retire, mumbling: 'I beg your pardon, I...'

Before he could finish, Bee went up to him and made a profound obeisance, saying: 'Pray do not leave us, sir. Will you not take a seat?' She looked like a drowning person clutching at him for support,—the little coward!

But possibly I was mistaken. It is quite likely that there was a touch of womanly wile in it. She wanted, perhaps, to raise her value in my eyes. She might have been pointedly saying to me: 'Please don't imagine for a moment that I am entirely overcome by you. My respect for Chandranath Babu is even greater.'

Well, indulge in your respect by all means! Schoolmasters thrive on it. But not being one of them, I have no use for that empty compliment.

Chandranath Babu began to talk about *Swadeshi*. I thought I would let him go on with his monologues. There is nothing like letting an old man talk himself out. It makes him feel that he is winding up the world, forgetting all the while how far away the real world is from his wagging tongue.

But even my worst enemy would not accuse me of patience. And when Chandranath Babu went on to say: 'If we expect to gather fruit where we have sown no seed, then we ...' I had to interrupt him.

'Who wants fruit?' I cried. 'We go by the Author of the *Gita* who says that we are concerned only with the doing, not with the fruit of our deeds.'

'What is it then that you *do* want?' asked Chandranath Babu.

'Thorns!' I exclaimed, 'which cost nothing to plant.'

'Thorns do not obstruct others only,' he replied. 'They have a way of hurting one's own feet.'

'That is all right for a copy-book,' I retorted. 'But the real thing is that we have this burning at heart. Now we have only to cultivate thorns for others' soles; afterwards when they hurt us we shall find leisure to repent. But why be frightened even of That? When at last we have to die it will be time enough to get cold. While we are on fire let us seethe and boil.'

Chandranath Babu smiled. 'Seethe by all means,' he said, 'but do not mistake it for work, or heroism. Nations which have got on in the world have done so by action, not by ebullition. Those who have always lain in dread of work, when with a start they awake to their sorry plight, they look to short cuts and scamping for their deliverance.'

I was girding up my loins to deliver a crushing reply, when Nikhil came back. Chandranath Babu rose, and looking towards Bee, said: 'Let me go now, my little mother, I have some work to attend to.'

As he left, I showed Nikhil the book in my hand. 'I was telling Queen Bee about this book,' I said.

Ninety-nine per cent of people have to be deluded with lies, but it is easier to delude this perpetual pupil of the schoolmaster with the truth. He is best cheated openly. So, in playing with him, the simplest course was to lay my cards on the table.

Nikhil read the title on the cover, but said nothing. 'These writers,' I continued, 'are busy with their rooms, sweeping away the dust of epithets with which men have covered up this world of ours. So, as I was saying, I wish you would read it.'

'I have read it,' said Nikhil.

'Well, what do you say?'

'It is all very well for those who really care to think, but poison for those who shirk thought.'

'What do you mean?'

'Those who preach "Equal Rights of Property" should not be thieves. For, if they are, they would be preaching lies. When passion is in the ascendant, this kind of book is not rightly understood.'

'Passion,' I replied, 'is the street lamp which guides us. To call it untrue is as hopeless as to expect to see better by plucking out our natural eyes.'

Nikhil was visibly growing excited. 'I accept the truth of passion,' he said, 'only when I recognise the truth of restraint. By pressing what we want to see right into our eyes we only injure them: we do not see. So does the violence of passion, which would leave no space between the mind and its object, defeat its purpose.'

'It is simply your intellectual foppery,' I replied, 'which makes you indulge in moral delicacy, ignoring the savage side of truth. This merely helps you to mystify things, and so you fail to do your work with any degree of strength.'

'The intrusion of strength,' said Nikhil impatiently, 'where strength is out of place, does not help you in your work.... But why are we arguing about these things? Vain arguments only brush off the fresh bloom of truth.'

I wanted Bee to join in the discussion, but she had not said a word up to now. Could I have given her too rude a shock, leaving her assailed with doubts and wanting to learn her lesson afresh from the schoolmaster? Still, a thorough shaking up is essential. One must begin by realising that things supposed to be unshakable can be shaken.

'I am glad I had this talk with you,' I said to Nikhil, 'for I was on the point of lending this book to Queen Bee to read.'

'What harm?' said Nikhil. 'If I could read the book, why not Bimala too? All I want to say is, that in Europe people look at everything from the view-point of science. But man is neither mere physiology, nor biology, nor psychology, nor even sociology. For God's sake don't forget that. Man is infinitely more than the natural science of himself. You laugh at me, calling me the schoolmaster's pupil, but that is what you are, not I. You want to find the truth of man from your science teachers, and not from your own inner being.'

'But why all this excitement?' I mocked.

'Because I see you are bent on insulting man and making him petty.'

'Where on earth do you see all that?'

'In the air, in my outraged feelings. You would go on wounding the great, the unselfish, the beautiful in man.'

'What mad idea is this of yours.'

Nikhil suddenly stood up. 'I tell you plainly, Sandip,' he said, 'man may be wounded unto death, but he will not die. This is the reason why I am ready to suffer all, knowing all, with eyes open.'

With these words he hurriedly left the room.

I was staring blankly at his retreating figure, when the sound of a book, falling from the table, made me turn to find Bee following him with quick, nervous steps, making a detour to avoid passing too near me.

A curious creature, that Nikhil! He feels the danger threatening his home, and yet why does he not turn me out? I know, he is waiting for Bimal to give him the cue. If Bimal tells him that their mating has been a misfit, he will bow his head and admit that it may have been a blunder! He has not the strength of mind to understand that to acknowledge a mistake is the greatest of all mistakes. He is a typical example of how ideas make for weakness. I have not seen another like him,—so whimsical a product of nature! He would hardly do as a character in a novel or drama, to say nothing of real life.

And Bee? I am afraid her dram-life is over from to-day. She has at length understood the nature of the current which is bearing her along. Now she must either advance or retreat, open-eyed. The chances are she will now advance a step, and then retreat a step. But that does not disturb me. When one is on fire, this rushing to and fro makes the blaze all the fiercer. The fright she has got will only fan her passion.

Perhaps I had better not say much to her, but simply select some modern books for her to read. Let her gradually come to the conviction that to acknowledge and respect passion as the supreme reality, is to be modern,—not to be ashamed of it, not to glorify restraint. If she finds shelter in some such word as 'modern,' she will find strength.

Be that as it may, I must see this out to the end of the Fifth Act. I cannot, unfortunately, boast of being merely a spectator, seated in the royal box, applauding now and again. There is a wrench at my heart, a pang in every nerve. When I have put out the light and am in my bed, little touches, little glances, little words flit about and fill the darkness. When I get up in the morning, I thrill with lively anticipations, my blood seems to course through me to the strains of music....

There was a double photo-frame on the table with Bee's photograph by the side of Nikhil's. I had taken out hers. Yesterday I showed Bee the empty side and said: 'Theft becomes necessary only because of miserliness, so its sin must be divided between the miser and the thief. Do you not think so?'

'It was not a good one,' observed Bee simply, with a little smile.

'What is to be done?' said I. 'A portrait cannot be better than a portrait. I must be content with it, such as it is.'

Bee took up a book and began to turn over the pages. 'If you are annoyed,' I went on, 'I must make a shift to fill up the vacancy.'

To-day I have filled it up. This photograph of mine was taken in my early youth. My face was then fresher, and so was my mind. Then I still cherished some illusions about this world and the next. Faith deceives men, but it has one great merit: it imparts a radiance to the features.

My portrait now reposes next to Nikhil's, for are not the two of us old friends?

Chapter IV

Nikhil's Story

III

I was never self-conscious. But nowadays I often try to take an outside view,—to see myself as Bimal sees me. What a dismally solemn picture it makes, my habit of taking things too seriously!

Better, surely, to laugh away the world than flood it with tears. That is, in fact, how the world gets on. We relish our food and rest, only because we can dismiss, as so many empty shadows, the sorrows scattered everywhere, both in the home and in the outer world. If we took them as true, even for a moment, where would be our appetite, our sleep?

But I cannot dismiss myself as one of these shadows, and so the load of my sorrow lies eternally heavy on the heart of my world.

Why not stand out aloof in the highway of the universe, and feel yourself to be part of the all? In the midst of the immense, age-long concourse of humanity, what is Bimal to you? Your wife? What is a wife? A bubble of a name blown big with your own breath, so carefully guarded night and day, yet ready to burst at any pin-prick from outside.

My wife,—and so, forsooth, my very own! If she says: 'No, I am myself,'—am I to reply: 'How can that be? Are you not mine?'

'My wife,'—Does that amount to an argument, much less the truth? Can one imprison a whole personality within that name?

My wife!—Have I not cherished in this little world all that is purest and sweetest in my life, never for a moment letting it down from my bosom to the dust? What incense of worship, what music of passion, what flowers of my spring and of my autumn, have I not offered up at its shrine? If, like a toy paper-boat, she be swept along into the muddy waters of the gutter,—would I not also...?

There it is again, my incorrigible solemnity! Why 'muddy'? What 'gutter'? Names, called in a fit of jealousy, do not change the facts of the world. If Bimal is not mine, she is not; and no fuming, or fretting, or arguing will serve to prove that she is. If my heart is breaking—let it break! That will not make the world bankrupt,—nor even me; for man is so much greater than the things he loses in this life. This very ocean of tears has its other shore, else none would have ever wept.

But then there is Society to be considered...which let Society consider! If I weep it is for myself, not for Society. If Bimal, should say she is not mine, what care I where my Society wife may be?

Suffering there must be; but I must save myself, by any means in my power, from one form of self-torture: I must never think that my life loses its value because of any neglect it may suffer. The full value of my life does not all go to buy my narrow domestic world; its great commerce does not stand or fall with some petty success or failure in the bartering of my personal joys and sorrows.

The time has come when I must divest Bimala of all the ideal decorations with which I decked her. It was owing to my own weakness that I indulged in such idolatry. I was too greedy. I created an angel of Bimala, in order to exaggerate my own enjoyment. But Bimala is what she is. It is preposterous to expect that she should assume the role of an angel for my pleasure. The Creator is under no obligation to supply me with angels, just because I have an avidity for imaginary perfection.

I must acknowledge that I have merely been an accident in Bimala's life. Her nature, perhaps, can only find true union with one like Sandip. At the same time, I must not, in false modesty, accept my rejection as my desert. Sandip certainly has attractive qualities, which had their sway also upon myself; but, yet, I feel sure, he is not a greater man than I. If the wreath of victory falls to his lot to-day, and I am overlooked, then the dispenser of the wreath will be called to judgement.

I say this in no spirit of boasting. Sheer necessity has driven me to the pass, that to secure myself from utter desolation I must recognise all the value that I truly possess. Therefore, through the terrible experience of suffering let there come upon me the joy of deliverance,—deliverance from self-distrust.

I have come to distinguish what is really in me from what I foolishly imagined to be there. The profit and loss account has been settled, and that which remains is myself,—not a crippled self, dressed in rags and tatters, not a sick self to be nursed on invalid diet, but a spirit which has gone through the worst, and has survived.

My master passed through my room a moment ago and said with his hand on my shoulder: 'Get away to bed, Nikhil, the night is far advanced.'

The fact is, it has become so difficult for me to go to bed till late,—till Bimala is fast asleep. In the day-time we meet, and even converse, but what am I to say when we are alone

together, in the silence of the night?—so ashamed do I feel
in mind and body.

'How is it, sir, you have not yet retired?' I asked in my
turn. My master smiled a little, as he left me, saying: 'My
sleeping days are over. I have now attained the waking age.'

I had written thus far, and was about to rise to go off
bedwards when, through the window before me, I saw the
heavy pall of July cloud suddenly part a little, and a big star
shine through. It seemed to say to me: 'Dreamland ties are
made, and dreamland ties are broken, but I am here for
ever,—the everlasting lamp of the bridal night.'

All at once my heart was full with the thought that my
Eternal Love was steadfastly waiting for me through the ages,
behind the veil of material things. Through many a life, in
many a mirror, have I seen her image,—broken mirrors,
crooked mirrors, dusty mirrors. Whenever I have sought to
make the mirror my very own, and shut it up within my box,
I have lost sight of the image. But what of that. What have
I to do with the mirror, or even the image?

My beloved, your smile shall never fade, and every dawn
there shall appear fresh for me the vermilion mark on your
forehead!

'What childish cajolery of self-deception,' mocks some
devil from his dark corner,—'silly prattle to make children
quiet!'

That may be. But millions and millions of children, with
their million cries, have to be kept quiet. Can it be that all
this multitude is quieted with only a lie? No, my Eternal Life
cannot deceive me, for she is true!

She is true; that is why I have seen her and shall see her
so often, even in my mistakes, even through the thickest mist
of tears. I have seen her and lost her in the crowd of life's
marketplace and found her again; and I shall find her once
more when I have escaped through the loophole of death.

Ah, cruel one, play with me no longer! If I have failed to track you by the marks of your footsteps on the way, by the scent of your tresses lingering in the air, make me not weep for that forever. The unveiled star tells me not to fear. That which is eternal must always be there.

Now let me go and see my Bimala. She must have spread her tired limbs on the bed, limp after her struggles, and be asleep. I will leave a kiss on her forehead without waking her,—that shall be the flower-offering of my worship. I believe I could forget everything after death,—all my mistakes, all my sufferings,—but some vibration of the memory of that kiss would remain; for the wreath which is being woven out of the kisses of many a successive birth is to crown the Eternal Beloved.

As the gong of the watch rang out, sounding the hour of two, my sister-in-law came into the room. 'Whatever are you doing, brother dear?'[1] she cried. 'For pity's sake go to bed and stop worrying so. I cannot bear to look on that awful shadow of pain on your face.' Tears welled up in her eyes and overflowed as she entreated me thus.

I could not utter a word, but took the dust of her feet, as I went off to bed.

---

1. When a relationship is established by marriage, or by mutual understanding arising out of special friendship or affection, the persons so related call each other in terms of such relationship, and not by name.—Tr.

Bimala's Story

VII

At first I suspected nothing, feared nothing; I simply felt dedicated to my country. What a stupendous joy there was in this unquestioning surrender. Verily had I realised how, in thoroughness of self-destruction, man can find supreme bliss.

For aught I know, this frenzy of mine might have come to a gradual, natural end. But Sandip Babu would not have it so, he would insist on revealing himself. The tone of his voice became as intimate as a touch, every look flung itself on its knees in beggary. And, through it all, there burned a passion which in its violence made as though it would tear me up by the roots, and drag me along by the hair.

I will not shirk the truth. This cataclysmal desire drew me by day and by night. It seemed desperately alluring,—this making havoc of myself. What a shame it seemed, how terrible, and yet how sweet! Then there was my overpowering curiosity, to which there seemed no limit. He of whom I knew but little, who never could assuredly be mine, whose youth flared so vigorously in a hundred points of flame—of, the mystery of his seething passions, so immense, so tumultuous!

I began with a feeling of worship, but that soon passed away. I ceased even to respect Sandip; on the contrary, I began over again under my eyes. Things were arranged in the cabinets in one kind of order; I pulled them all out and rearranged them in a different way. I found no time that afternoon even to do up my hair; I hurriedly tied it into a loose knot, and went and worried everybody, fussing about the store-room. The stores seemed short, and pilfering must have been going on of late, but I could not muster up the courage to take any particular person to task,—for might not the thought have crossed somebody's mind: 'Where were your eyes all these days!'

In short, I behaved that day as one possessed. The next day I tried to do some reading. What I read I have no idea, but after a spell of absent-mindedness I found I had wandered away, book in hand, along the passage leading towards the outer apartments, and was standing by a window looking out upon the verandah running along the row of rooms on the opposite side of the quadrangle. One of these rooms, I felt, had crossed over to another shore, and the ferry had ceased to ply. I felt like the ghost of myself of two days ago, doomed to remain where I was, and yet not really there, blankly looking out for ever.

As I stood there, I saw Sandip come out of his room into the verandah, a newspaper in his hand. I could see that he looked extraordinarily disturbed. The courtyard, the railings, in front, seemed to rouse his wrath. He flung away his newspaper with a gesture which seemed to want to rend the space before him.

I felt I could no longer keep my vow. I was about to move on towards the sitting-room, when I found my sister-in-law behind me. 'O Lord, this beats everything!' she ejaculated, as she glided away. I could not proceed to the outer apartments.

The next morning when my maid came calling, 'Rani Mother, it is getting late for giving out the stores,' I flung the keys to her, saying, 'Tell Harimati to see to it, ' and went on with some embroidery of English pattern on which I was engaged, seated near the window.

Then came a servant with a letter. 'From Sandip Babu,' said he. What unbounded boldness! What must the messenger have thought? There was a tremor within my breast as I opened the envelope. There was no address on the letter, only the words: *An urgent matter—touching the Cause. Sandip.*

I flung aside the embroidery. I was up on my feet in a moment, giving a touch or two to my hair by the mirror. I kept the *sari* I had on, changing only my jacket,—for one of my jackets had its associations.

I had to pass through one of the verandahs, where my sister-in-law used to sit in the morning slicing betel-nut. I refused to feel awkward. 'Whither away, Chota Rani?' she cried.

'To the sitting-room outside.'

'So early! A matinée, eh?'

And, as I passed on without further reply, she hummed after me a flippant song.

IX

When I was about to enter the sitting-room, I saw Sandip immersed in an illustrated catalogue of British Academy pictures, with his back to the door. He has a great notion of himself as an expert in matters of Art.

One day my husband said to him: 'If the artists ever want a teacher, they need never lack for one so long as you are there.' It had not been my husband's habit to speak cuttingly, but latterly there has been a change and he never spares Sandip.

'What makes you suppose that artists need no teachers?' Sandip retorted.

'Art is a creation,' my husband replied. 'So we should humbly be content to receive our lessons about Art from the work of the artist.'

Sandip laughed at this modesty, saying: 'You think that meekness is a kind of capital which increases your wealth the more you use it. It is my conviction that those who lack pride only float about like water reeds which have no roots in the soil.'

My mind used to be full of contradictions when they talked thus. On the one hand I was eager that my husband should win in argument and that Sandip's pride should be shamed. Yet, on the other, it was Sandip's unabashed pride which attracted me so. It shone like a precious diamond, which knows no diffidence, and sparkles in the face of the sun itself.

I entered the room. I knew Sandip could hear my footsteps as I went forward, but he pretended not to, and kept his eyes on the book.

I dreaded his Art talks, for I could not overcome my delicacy about the pictures he talked of, and the things he said, and had much ado in putting on an air of overdone insensibility to hide my qualms. So, I was almost on the point of retracing my steps, when, with a deep sigh, Sandip raised his eyes, and affected to be startled at the sight of me. 'Ah, you have come!' he said.

In his words, in his tone, in his eyes, there was a world of suppressed reproach, as if the claims he had acquired over me made my absence, even for these two or three days, a grievous wrong. I knew this attitude was an insult to me, but, alas, I had not the power to resent it.

I made no reply, but though I was looking another way, I could not help feeling that Sandip's plaintive gaze had planted itself right on my face, and would take no denial. I did so wish he would say something, so that I could shelter myself behind his words. I cannot tell how long this went on, but at last I could stand it no longer. 'What is this matter,' I asked, 'you are wanting to tell me about?'

Sandip again affected surprise as he said: 'Must there always be some matter? Is friendship by itself a crime? Oh, Queen Bee, to think that you should make so light of the greatest thing on earth! Is the heart's worship to be shut out like a stray cur?'

There was again that tremor within me. I could feel the crisis coming, too importunate to be put off. Joy and fear struggled for the mastery. Would my shoulders, I wondered, be broad enough to stand its shock, or would it not leave me overthrown, with my face in the dust?

I was trembling all over. Steadying myself with an effort I repeated: 'You summoned me for something touching the Cause, so I have left my household duties to attend to it.'

'That is just what I was trying to explain,' he said, with a dry laugh. 'Do you not know that I come to worship? Have I not told you that, in you, I visualise the *Shakti* of our country? The Geography of a country is not the whole truth. No one can give up his life for a map! When I see you before me, then only do I realise how lovely my country is. When you have anointed me with your own hands, then shall I know I have the sanction of my country; and if, with that in my heart, I fall fighting, it shall not be on the dust of some map-made land, but on a lovingly spread skirt—do you know what kind of skirt?—like that of the earthen-red *sari* you wore the other day, with a broad blood-red border. Can I ever forget it? Such are the visions which give vigour to life, and joy to death!'

Sandip's eyes took fire as he went on, but whether it was the fire of worship, or of passion, I could not tell. I was reminded of the day on which I first heard him speak, when I could not be sure whether he was a person, or just a living flame.

I had not the power to utter a word. You cannot take shelter behind the walls of decorum when in a moment the fire leaps up and, with the flash of its sword and the roar of its laughter, destroys all the miser's stores. I was in terror lest he should forget himself and take me by the hand. For he shook like a quivering tongue of fire; his eyes showered scorching sparks on me.

'Are you for ever determined,' he cried after a pause, 'to make gods of your petty household duties,—you who have it in you to send us to life or to death? Is this power of yours to be kept veiled in a zenana? Cast away all false shame, I pray you; snap your fingers at the whispering around. Take your plunge to-day into the freedom of the outer world.'

When, in Sandip's appeals, his worship of the country gets to be subtly interwoven with his worship of me, then does my blood dance, indeed, and the barriers of my hesitation totter. His talks about Art and Sex, his distinctions between Real and Unreal, had but clogged my attempts at response with some revolting nastiness. This, however, now burst again into a glow before which my repugnance faded away. I felt that my resplendent womanhood made me indeed a goddess. Why should not its glory flash from my forehead with visible brilliance? Why does not my voice find a word, some audible cry, which would be like a sacred spell to my country for its fire initiation?

All of a sudden my maid Khema rushed into the room, dishevelled. 'Give me my wages and let me go,' she screamed. 'Never in all my life have I been so...' The rest of her speech was drowned in sobs.

'What is the matter?'

Thako, the Bara Rani's maid, it appeared, had for no rhyme or reason reviled her in unmeasured terms. She was in such a state, it was no manner of use trying to pacify her by saying I would look into the matter afterwards.

The slime of domestic life that lay beneath the lotus bank of womanhood came to the surface. Rather than allow Sandip a prolonged vision of it, I had to hurry back within.

X

My sister-in-law was absorbed in her betel-nuts, the suspicion of a smile playing about her lips, as if nothing untoward had happened. She was still humming the same song.

'Why has your Thako been calling poor Khema names?' I burst out.

'Indeed? The wretch! I will have her broomed out of the house. What a shame to spoil your morning out like this! As for Khema, where are the hussy's manners to go and disturb you when you are engaged? Anyhow, Chota Rani, don't you worry yourself with these domestic squabbles. Leave them to me, and return to your friend.'

How suddenly the wind in the sails of our mind veers round! This going to meet Sandip outside seemed, in the light of the zenana code, such an extraordinarily out-of-the-way thing to do that I went off to my own room, at a loss for a reply. I knew this was my sister-in-law's doing and that she had egged her maid on to contrive this scene. But I had brought myself to such an unstable poise that I dared not have my fling.

Why, it was only the other day that I found I could not keep up to the last the unbending hauteur with which I had demanded from my husband the dismissal of the man Nanku. I felt suddenly abashed when the Bara Rani came up and said: 'It is really all my fault, brother dear. We are old-fashioned folk, and I did not quite like the ways of your Sandip Babu, so I only told the guard ... but how was I to know that our Chota Rani would take this as an insult?—I thought it would be the other way about! Just my incorrigible silliness!'

The thing which seems so glorious when viewed from the heights of the country's cause, looks so muddy when seen from the bottom. One begins by getting angry, and then feels disgusted.

I shut myself into my room, sitting by the window, thinking how easy life would be if only one could keep in harmony with one's surroundings. How simply the senior Rani sits in her verandah with her betel-nuts and how inaccessible to me has become my natural seat beside my daily duties! Where will it all end, I asked myself? Shall I ever recover, as from a delirium, and forget it all; or am I to be dragged to depths from which there can be no escape in this life? How on earth did I manage to let my good fortune escape me, and spoil my life so? Every wall of this bedroom of mine, which I first entered nine years ago as a bride, stares at me in dismay.

When my husband came home, after his M.A. examination, he brought for me this orchid belonging to some far-away land beyond the seas. From beneath these few little leaves sprang such a cascade of blossoms, it looked as if they were pouring forth from some overturned urn of Beauty. We decided, together, to hang it here, over this window. It flowered only that once, but we have always been in hope of its doing so once more. Curiously enough I have kept on watering it these days, from force of habit, and it is still green.

It is now four years since I framed a photograph of my husband in ivory and put it in the niche over there. If I happen to look that way I have to lower my eyes. Up to last week I used to regularly put there the flowers of my worship, every morning after my bath. My husband has often chided me over this.

'It shames me to see you place me on a height to which I do not belong,' he said one day.

'What nonsense!'

'I am not only ashamed, but also jealous!'

'Just hear him! Jealous of whom, pray?'

'Of that false me. It only shows that I am too petty for you, that you want some extraordinary man who can overpower you with his superiority, and so you needs must take refuge in making for yourself another "me."'

'This kind of talk only makes me angry,' said I.

'What is the use of being angry with me?' he replied. 'Blame your fate which allowed you no choice, but made you take me blindfold. This keeps you trying to retrieve its blunder by making me out a paragon.'

I felt so hurt at the bare idea that tears started to my eyes that day. And whenever I think of that now, I cannot raise my eyes to the niche.

For now there is another photograph in my jewel case. The other day, when arranging the sitting-room, I brought away that double photo-frame, the one in which Sandip's portrait was next to my husband's. To this portrait I have no flowers of worship to offer, but it remains hidden away under my gems. It has all the greater fascination because kept secret. I look at it now and then with doors closed. At night I turn up the lamp, and sit with it in my hand, gazing and gazing. And every night I think of burning it in the flame of the lamp, to be done with it forever; but every night I heave a sigh and smother it again in my pearls and diamonds.

Ah, wretched woman! What a wealth of love was twined round each one of those jewels! Oh, why am I not dead?

Sandip had impressed it on me that hesitation is not in the nature of woman. For her, neither right nor left has any existence,—she only moves forward. When the women of our country wake up, he repeatedly insisted, their voice will be unmistakably confident in its utterance of the cry: '*I want.*'

'I want!' Sandip went on one day,—this was the primal word at the root of all creation. It had no maxim to guide it, but it became fire and wrought itself into suns and stars. Its partiality is terrible. Because it had a desire for man, it ruthlessly sacrificed millions of beasts for millions of years to achieve that desire. That terrible word 'I want' has taken flesh in woman, and therefore men, who are cowards, try with all their might to keep back this primeval flood with their earthen dykes. They are afraid lest, laughing and dancing as it goes, it should wash away all the hedges and props of their pumpkin field. Men, in every age, flatter themselves that they have secured this force within the bounds of their convenience, but it gathers and grows. Nor is it calm and deep like a lake, but gradually its pressure will increase, the dykes will give way, and the force which has so long been dumb will rush forward with the roar: 'I want!'

These words of Sandip echo in my heart-beats like a war-drum. They shame into silence all my conflicts with myself. What do I care what people may think of me? Of what value are that orchid and that niche in my bedroom? What power have they to belittle me, to put me to shame? The primal fire of creation burns in me.

I felt a strong desire to snatch down the orchid and fling it out of the window, to denude the niche of its picture, to lay bare and naked the unashamed spirit of destruction that raged within me. My arm was raised to do it, but a sudden pang passed through my breast, tears started to my eyes. I threw myself down and sobbed: 'What is the end of all this, what is the end?'

Sandip's Story

IV

When I read these pages of the story of my life I seriously question myself: Is this Sandip? Am I made of words? Am I merely a book with a covering of flesh and blood?

The earth is not a dead thing like the moon. She breathes. Her rivers and oceans send up vapours in which she is clothed. She is covered with a mantle of her own dust which flies about the air. The onlooker, gazing upon the earth from the outside, can see only the light reflected from this vapour and this dust. The tracks of the mighty continents are not distinctly visible.

The man, who is alive as this earth is, is likewise always enveloped in the mist of the ideas which he is breathing out. His real land and water remain hidden, and he appears to be made of only lights and shadows.

It seems to me, in this story of my life, that, like a living planet, I am displaying the picture of an ideal world. But I am not merely what I want, what I think,—I am also what I do not love, what I do *not* wish to be. My creation had begun before I was born. I had no choice in regard to my surroundings and so must make the best of such material as comes to my hand.

My theory of life makes me certain that the Great is cruel. To be just is for ordinary men,—it is reserved for the great to be unjust. The surface of the earth was even. The volcano butted it with its fiery horn and found its own eminence,— its justice was not towards its obstacle, but towards itself. Successful injustice and genuine cruelty have been the only forces by which individual or nation has become millionaire or monarch.

That is why I preach the great discipline of Injustice. I say to every one: Deliverance is based upon injustice. Injustice is the fire which must keep on burning something in order to save itself from becoming ashes. Whenever an individual or nation becomes incapable of perpetrating injustice it is swept into the dust-bin of the world.

As yet this is only my idea,—it is not completely myself. There are rifts in the armour through which something peeps out which is extremely soft and sensitive. Because, as I say, the best part of myself was created before I came to this stage of existence.

From time to time I try my followers in their lesson of cruelty. One day we went on a picnic. A goat was grazing by. I asked them: 'Who is there among you that can cut off a leg of that goat, alive, with this knife, and bring it to me?' While they all hesitated, I went myself and did it. One of them fainted at the sight. But when they saw me unmoved they took the dust of my feet, saying that I was above all human weaknesses. This is to say, they saw that day the vaporous envelope which was my idea, but failed to perceive the inner me, which by a curious freak of fate has been created tender and merciful.

In the present chapter of my life, which is growing in interest every day round Bimala and Nikhil, there is also much that remains hidden underneath. This malady of ideas which afflicts me is shaping my life within: nevertheless a great part of my life remains outside its influence; and so there is set up a discrepancy between my outward life and its inner design which I try my best to keep concealed even from myself; otherwise it may wreck not only my plans, but my very life.

Life is indefinite,—a bundle of contradictions. We men, with our ideas, strive to give it a particular shape by melting it into a particular mould,—into the definiteness of success. All the world-conquerors, from Alexander down to the American millionaires, mould themselves into a sword or a mint, and thus find that distinct image of themselves which is the source of their success.

The chief controversy between Nikhil and myself arises from this: that thought I say 'know thyself,' and Nikhil also says 'know thyself,' his interpretation makes this 'knowing' tantamount to 'not knowing.'

'Winning your kind of success,' Nikhil once objected, 'is success gained at the cost of the soul: but the soul is greater than success.'

I simply said in answer: 'Your words are too vague.'

'That I cannot help,' Nikhil replied. 'A machine is distinct enough, but not so life. If to gain distinctness you try to know life as a machine, then such mere distinctness cannot stand for truth. The soul is not as distinct as success, and so you only lose your soul if you seek it in your success.'

'Where, then, is this wonderful soul?'

'Where it knows itself in the infinite and transcends its success.'

'But how does all this apply to our work for the country?'

'It is the same thing. Where our country makes itself the final object, it gains success at the cost of the soul. Where it recognises the Greatest as greater than all, there it may miss success, but gains its soul.'

'Is there any example of this in history?'

'Man is so great that he can despise not only the success, buy also the example. Possibly example is lacking, just as there is no example of the flower in the seed. But there is the urgence of the flower in the seed all the same.'

It is not that I do not at all understand Nikhil's point of view; that is rather where my danger lies. I was born in India and the poison of its spirituality runs in my blood. However loudly I may proclaim the madness of walking in the path of self-abnegation, I cannot avoid it altogether.

This is exactly how such curious anomalies happen nowadays in our country. We must have our religion and also our nationalism; our *Bhagavadgita* and also our *Bande Mataram*. The result is that both of them suffer. It is like performing with an English military band, side by side with our Indian festive pipes. I must make it the purpose of my life to put an end to this hideous confusion.

I want the western military style to prevail, not the Indian. We shall then not be ashamed of the flag of our passion, which mother Nature has sent with us as our standard into the battlefield of life. Passion is beautiful and pure,—pure as the lily that comes out of the slimy soil. It rises superior to its defilement and needs no Pears' soap to wash it clean.

V

A question has been worrying me the last few days. Why am I allowing my life to become entangled with Bimala's? Am I a drifting log to be caught up at any and every obstacle?

Not that I have any false shame at Bimala becoming an object of my desire. It is only too clear how she wants me, and so I look on her as quite legitimately mine. The fruit hangs on the branch by the stem, but that is no reason why the claim of the stem should be eternal. Ripe fruit cannot for ever swear by its slackening stem-hold. All its sweetness has been accumulated for me; to surrender itself to my hand is the reason of its existence, its very nature, its true morality. So I must pluck it, for it becomes me not to make it futile.

But what is teasing me is that I am getting entangled. Am I not born to rule?—to bestride my proper steed, the crowd, and drive it as I will; the reins in my hand, the destination known only to me, and for it the thorns, the mire, on the road? This steed now awaits me at the door, pawing and champing its bit, its neighing filling the skies. But where am I, and what am I about, letting day after day of golden opportunity slip by?

I used to think I was like a storm,—that the torn flowers with which I strewed my path would not impede my progress. But I am only wandering round and round a flower like a bee,—not a storm. So, as I was saying, the colouring of ideas which man gives himself is only superficial. The inner man remains as ordinary as ever. If some one, who could see right into me, were to write my biography, he would make me out to be no different from that lout of a Panchu, or even from Nikhil!

Last night I was turning over the pages of my old diary .... I had just graduated, and my brain was bursting with philosophy. Even so early I had vowed not to harbour any illusions, whether of my own or others' imagining, but to build my lie on a solid basis of reality. But what has since been its actual story? Where is its solidity? It has rather been a network, where though the thread be continuous, more space is taken up by the holes. Fight as I may, these will not own defeat. Just as I was congratulating myself on steadily following the thread, here I am badly caught in a hole! For I have become susceptible to compunctions.

'I want it; it is here; let me take it.'—this is a clear-cut, straightforward policy. Those who can pursue its course with vigour needs must win through in the end. But the gods would not have it that such journey should be easy, so they have deputed the siren Sympathy to distract the wayfarer, to dim his vision with her tearful mist.

I can see that poor Bimala is struggling like a snared deer. What a piteous alarm there is in her eyes! How she is torn with straining at her bonds! This sight, of course, should gladden the heart of a true hunter. And so do I rejoice; but, then, I am also touched; and therefore I dally, and standing on the brink I am hesitating to pull the noose fast.

There have been moments, I know, when I could have bounded up to her, clasped her hands and folded her to my breast, unresisting. Had I done so, she would not have said one word. She was aware that some crisis was impending, which in a moment would change the meaning of the whole world. Standing before that cavern of the incalculable but yet expected, her face went pale and her eyes glowed with a fearful ecstasy. Within that moment, when it arrives an eternity will take shape, which our destiny awaits, holding its breath.

But I have let this moment slip by. I did not, with uncompromising strength, press the almost certain into the absolutely assured. I now see clearly that some hidden elements in my nature have openly ranged themselves as obstacles in my path.

That is exactly how Ravana, whom I look upon as the real hero of the *Ramayana*, met with his doom. He kept Sita in his Asoka garden, awaiting her pleasure, instead of taking her straight into his harem. This weak spot in his otherwise grand character made the whole of the abduction episode futile. Another such touch of compunction made him disregard, and be lenient to, his traitorous brother Bibhisan, only to get himself killed for his pains.

Thus does the tragic in life come by its own. In the beginning it lies, a little thing, in some dark under-vault, and ends by overthrowing the whole superstructure. The real tragedy is, that man does not know himself for what he really is.

VI

Then again there is Nikhil. Crank though he be, laugh at him as I may, I cannot get rid of he idea that he is my friend. At first I gave no thought to his point of view, but of late it has begun to shame and hurt me. Therefore I have been trying to talk and argue with him in the same enthusiastic way as of old, but it does not ring true. It is even leading me at times into such a length of unnaturalness as to pretend to agree with him. But such hypocrisy is not in my nature, nor in that of Nikhil either. This, at least, is something we have in common. That is why, nowadays, I would rather not come across him, and have taken to fighting shy of his presence.

All these are signs of weakness. No sooner is the possibility of a wrong admitted than it becomes actual, and clutches you by the throat, however you may then try to shake off all belief in it. What I should like to be able to tell Nikhil frankly is, that happenings such as these must be looked in the face— as great Realities—and that which is the Truth should not be allowed to stand between true friends.

There is no denying that I have really weakened. It was not this weakness which won over Bimala; she burnt her wings in the blaze of the full strength of my unhesitating manliness. Whenever smoke obscures its lustre she also becomes confused, and draws back. Then comes a thorough revulsion of feeling, and she fain would take back the garland she has put round my neck, but cannot; and so she only closes her eyes, to shut it out of sight.

But all the same I must not swerve from the path I have chalked out. It would never do to abandon the cause of the country, especially at the present time. I shall simply make Bimala one with my country. The turbulent west wind which has swept away the country's veil of conscience, will sweep away the veil of the wife from Bimala's face, and in that uncovering there will be no shame. The ship will rock as it bears the crowd across the ocean, flying the pennant of *Bande Mataram,* and it will serve as the cradle to my power, as well as to my love.

Bimala will see such a majestic vision of deliverance, that her bonds will slip from about her, without shame, without her even being aware of it. Fascinated by the beauty of this terrible wrecking power, she will not hesitate a moment to be cruel. I have seen in Bimala's nature the cruelty which is the inherent force of existence,—the cruelty which with its unrelenting might keeps the world beautiful.

If only women could be set free from the artificial fetters put round them by men, we cold see on earth the living image of Kali, the shameless, pitiless goddess. I am a worshipper of Kali, and one day I shall truly worship her, setting Bimala on her altar of Destruction. For this let me get ready.

The way of retreat is absolutely closed for both of us. We shall despoil each other: get to hate each other: but never more be free.

Chapter V

Nikhil's Story

IV

Everything is rippling and waving with the flood of August.
The young shoots of rice have the sheen of an infant's
limbs. The water has invaded the garden next to our house.
The morning light, like the love of the blue sky, is lavished
upon the earth.... Why cannot I sing? The water of the
distant river is shimmering with light; the leaves are glistening;
the rice-fields, with their fitful shivers, break into gleams of
gold; and in this symphony of Autumn, only I remain voiceless.
The sunshine of the world strikes my heart, but is not
reflected back.

When I realise the lack of expressiveness in myself, I know
why I am deprived. Who could bear my company day and
night without a break? Bimala is full of the energy of life, and
so she has never become stale to me for a moment, in all these
nine years of our wedded life.

My life has only its dumb depths; but no murmuring
rush. I can only receive; not impart movement. And therefore
my company is like fasting. I recognise clearly to-day that
Bimala has been languishing because of a famine of
companionship.

Then whom shall I blame? Like Vidyapati I can only lament:

It is August, the sky breaks into a passionate rain;
Alas, empty is my house.

My house, I now see, was built to remain empty, because its doors cannot open. But I never knew till now that its divinity had been sitting outside. I had fondly believed that she had accepted my sacrifice, and granted in return her boon. But, alas, my house has all along been empty.

Every year, about this time, it was our practice to go in a house-boat over the broads of Samalda. I used to tell Bimala that a song must come back to its refrain over and over again. The original refrain of every song is in Nature, where the rain-laden wind passes over the rippling stream, where the green earth, drawing its shadow-veil over its face, keeps its ear close to the speaking water. There, at the beginning of time, a man and a woman first met,—not within walls. And therefore we two must come back to Nature, at least once a year, to tune our love anew to the first pure note of the meeting of hearts.

The first two anniversaries of our married life I spent in Calcutta, where I went through my examinations. But from the next year onwards, for seven years without a break, we have celebrated our union among the blossoming water-lilies. Now begins the next octave of my life.

It was difficult for me to ignore the fact that the same month of August had come round again this year. Does Bimala remember it, I wonder?—she has given me to remind. Everything is mute about me.

It is August, the sky breaks into a passionate rain;
And empty is my house.

The house which becomes empty through the parting of lovers, still has music left in the heart of its emptiness. But the house that is empty because hearts are asunder, is awful in its silence. Even the cry of pain is out of place there.

This cry of pain must be silenced in me. So long as I continue to suffer, Bimala will never have true freedom. *I must* free her completely, otherwise I shall never gain *my* freedom from untruth....

I think I have come to the verge of understanding one thing. Man has so fanned the flame of the loves of men and women, as to make it overpass its rightful domain, and now, even in the name of humanity itself, he cannot bring it back under control. Man's worship has idolised his passion. But there must be no more human sacrifices at its shrine....

I went into my bedroom this morning, to fetch a book. It is long since I have been there in the day-time. A pang passed through me as I looked round it to-day, in the morning light. On the clothes rack was hanging a *sari* of Bimala's, crinkled ready for wear. On the dressing-table were her perfumes, her comb, her hair-pins, and with them, still, her vermilion box! Underneath were her tiny gold-embroidered slippers.

Once, in the old days, when Bimala had not yet overcome her objections to shoes, I had got these out from Lucknow, to tempt her. The first time she was ready to drop for very shame, to go in them even from the room to the verandah. Since then she has worn out many shoes, but has treasured up this pair. When first showing her the slippers, I chaffed her over a curious practice of hers: 'I have caught you taking the dust of my feet, thinking me asleep! These are the offerings of my worship to ward the dust off the feet of my wakeful divinity.' 'You must not say such things,' she protested, 'or I will never wear your shoes!'

This bedroom of mine,—it has a subtle atmosphere which goes straight to my heart. I was never aware, as I am to-day, how my thirsting heart has been sending out its roots to cling round each and every familiar object. The severing of the main root, I see, is not enough to set life free. Even these little slippers serve to hold one back.

My wandering eyes fall on the niche. My portrait there is looking the same as ever, in spite of the flowers scattered round it having been withered black! Of all the things in the room their greeting strikes me as sincere. They are still here simply because it was not felt worth while even to remove them. Never mind; let me welcome truth, albeit in such sere and sorry garb, and look forward to the time when I shall be able to do so unmoved, as does my photograph.

As I stood there, Bimal came in from behind. I hastily turned my eyes from the niche to the shelves as I muttered: 'I came to get Amiel's Journal.' What need had I to volunteer an explanation? I felt like a wrong-doer, a trespasser, prying into a secret not meant for me. I could not look Bimal in the face, but hurried away.

V

I had just made the discovery that it was useless to keep up a pretence of reading in my room outside, and also that it was equally beyond me to busy myself attending to anything at all,—so that all the days of my future bid fair to congeal into one solid mass and settle heavily on my breast for good,—when Panchu, the tenant of a neighbouring *zamindar*, came up to me with a basketful of cocoa-nuts and greeted me with a profound obeisance.

'Well, Panchu,' said I. 'What is all this for?'

I had got to know Panchu through my master. He was extremely poor, nor was I in a position to do anything for him; so I supposed this present was intended to procure a tip to help the poor fellow to make both ends meet. I took some money from my purse and held it out towards him, but with folded hands he protested: 'I cannot take that, sir!'

'Why, what is the matter?'

'Let me make a clean breast of it, sir. Once, when I was hard pressed, I stole some cocoa-nuts from the garden here. I am getting old, and may die any day, so I have come to pay them back.'

Amiel's Journal could not have done me any good that day. But these words of Panchu lightened my heart. There are more things in life than the union or separation of man and woman. The great world stretches far beyond, and one can truly measure one's own joys and sorrows when standing in its midst.

Panchu was devoted to my master. I know well enough how he manages to eke out a livelihood. He is up before dawn every day, and with a basket of *pan* leaves, twists of tobacco, coloured cotton yarn, little combs, looking-glasses, and other trinkets beloved of the village women, he wades through the knee-deep water of the marsh and goes over to the *Namasudra* quarters. There he barters his goods for rice, which fetches him a little more than their price in money. If he can get back soon enough he goes out again, after a hurried meal, to the sweetmeat seller's, where he assists in beating sugar for wavers. As soon as he comes home he sits at his shell-bangle making, plodding on often till midnight. All this cruel toil does not earn, for himself and his family, a bare two meals a day during much more than half the year. His method of eating is to begin with a good filling draught of water, and his staple food is the cheapest kind of seedy banana. And yet the family has to go with only one meal a day for the rest of the year.

At one time I had an idea of making him a charity allowance, 'But,' said my master, 'your gift may destroy the man, it cannot destroy the hardship of his lot. Mother Bengal has not only this one Panchu. If the milk in her breasts has run dry, that cannot be supplied from the outside.'

These are thoughts which give one pause, and I decided to devote myself to working it out. That very day I said to Bimal: 'Let us dedicate our lives to removing the root of this sorrow in our country.'

'You are my Prince Siddhartha[1],' Bimala replied with a smile. 'But do not let the torrent of your feelings end by sweeping me away also!'

'Siddhartha took his vows alone. I want ours to be a joint arrangement.'

The idea passed away in talk. The fact is, Bimala is at heart what is called a 'lady.' Though her own people are not well off, she was born a Rani. She has no doubts in her mind that there is a lower unit of measure for the trials and troubles of the 'lower classes.' Want is, of course, a permanent feature of their lives, but does not necessarily mean 'want' to them. Their very smallness protects them, as the banks protect the pool; by widening bounds only the slime is exposed.

The real fact is that Bimala has only come into my home, not into my life. I had magnified her so, leaving her such a large place, that when I lost her, my whole way of life became narrow and confined. I had thrust aside all other objects into a corner to make room for Bimala,—taken up as I was with decorating her and dressing her and educating her and moving round her day and night; forgetting how great is humanity and how nobly precious is man's life. When the actualities of everyday things get the better of the man, then is Truth lost sight of and freedom missed. So painfully important did Bimala make the mere actualities, that the truth remained concealed from me. That is why I find no gap in my misery, and spread this minute point of my emptiness over all the

---

1. The name by which Buddha was known when a Prince, before renouncing the world.

world. And so, for hours on this Autumn morning, the refrain has been humming in my ears:

> It is the month of August, and the sky breaks into a passionate rain;
> Alas, my house is empty.

Bimala's Story

XI

The change which had, in a moment, come over the mind of Bengal was tremendous. It was as if the Ganges had touched the ashes of the sixty thousand sons of Sagar[2] which no fire could enkindle, no other water knead again into living clay. The ashes of lifeless Bengal suddenly spoke up: 'Here am I.'

I have read somewhere that in ancient Greece a sculptor had the good fortune to impart life to the image made by his own hand. Even in that miracle, however, there was the process of form preceding life. But where was the unity in this heap of barren ashes? Had they been hard like stone, we might have had hopes of some form emerging, even as Ahalya, though turned to stone, at last won back her humanity. But these scattered ashes must have dropped to the dust through gaps in the Creator's fingers, to be blown hither and thither by the wind. They had become heaped up. but were never before united. Yet in this day which had come to Bengal, even this collection of looseness had taken shape,

---

2. The condition of the curse which had reduced them to ashes was such that they could only be restored to life if the stream of the Ganges was brought down to them.—Tr.

and proclaimed in a thundering voice, at our very door: 'Here I am.'

How could we help thinking that it was all supernatural? This moment of our history seemed to have dropped into our hand like a jewel from the crown of some drunken god. It had not resemblance to our past; and so we were led to hope that all our wants and miseries would disappear by the spell of some magic charm, that for us there was no longer any boundary line between the possible and the impossible. Everything seemed to be saying to us: 'It is coming; it has come!'

Thus we came to cherish the belief that our history needed no steed, but that like heaven's chariot it would move with its own inherent power.—At least no wages would have to be paid to the charioteer; only his wine cup would have to be filled again and again. And then in some impossible paradise the goal of our hopes would be reached.

My husband was not altogether unmoved, but through all our excitement it was the strain of sadness in him which deepened and deepened. He seemed to have a vision of something beyond the surging present.

I remember one day, in the course of the arguments he continually had with Sandip, he said: 'Good fortune comes to our gate and announces itself, only to prove that we have not the power to receive it,—that we have not kept things ready to be able to invite it into our house.'

'No,' was Sandip's answer. 'You talk like an atheist because you do not believe in our gods. To us it has been made quite visible that the Goddess has come with her boon, yet you distrust the obvious signs of her presence.'

'It is because I strongly believe in my God,' said my husband, 'that I feel so certain that our preparations for his worship are lacking. God has power to give the boon, but we must have power to accept it.'

This kind of talk from my husband would only annoy me. I could not keep from joining in: 'You think this excitement is only a fire of drunkenness, but does not drunkenness, up to a point, give strength?'

'Yes,' my husband replied. 'It may give strength, but not weapons.'

'But strength is the gift of God,' I went on. 'Weapons can be supplied by mere mechanics.'

My husband smiled. 'The mechanics will claim their wages before they deliver their supplies,' he said.

Sandip swelled his chest as he retorted: 'Don't you trouble about that. Their wages shall be paid.'

'I shall bespeak the festive music when the payment has been made, not before,' my husband answered.

'You needn't imagine that we are depending on your bounty for the music,' said Sandip scornfully. 'Our festival is above all money payments.'

And in his thick voice he began to sing:

My Lover of the unpriced love, spurning payments,
Plays upon the simple pipe, bought for nothing,
Drawing my heart away.

Then with a smile he turned to me and said: 'If I sing, Queen Bee, it is only to prove that when music comes into one's life, the lack of a good voice is no matter. When we sing merely on the strength of our tunefulness, the song is belittled. Now that a full flood of music has swept over our country, let Nikhil practise his scales, while we rouse the land with our cracked vices:

My house cries to me: Why go out to lose your all?
My life says: all that you have, fling to the winds!
We must lose our all, let us lose it: what is it worth after all?
If I must court ruin, let me do it smilingly:
For my quest is the death-draught of immortality.

'The truth is, Nikhil, that we have all lost our hearts. None can hold us any longer within the bounds of the easily possible, in our forward rush to the hopelessly impossible.

Those who would draw us back,
They know not the fearful joy of recklessness.
They know not that we have had our call
From the end of the crooked path.
All that is good and straight and trim,—
Let it topple over in the dust.'

I thought that my husband was going to continue the discussion, but he rose silently from his seat and left us.

The thing that was agitating me within was merely a variation of the stormy passion outside, which swept the country from one end to the other. The car of the wielder of my destiny was fast approaching, and the sound of its wheels reverberated in my being. I had a constant feeling that something extraordinary might happen any moment, for which, however, the responsibility would not be mine. Was I not removed from the plane in which right and wrong, and the feelings of others, have to be considered? Had I ever wanted this,—had I ever been waiting or hoping for any such thing? Look at my whole life and tell me then, if I was in any way accountable.

Through all my past I had been consistent in my devotion,—but when at length it came to receiving the boon, a different god appeared! And just as the awakened country, with its *Bande Mataram*, thrills in salutation to the unrealised future before it, so do all my veins and nerves send forth shocks of welcome to the unthought-of, the unknown, the importunate Stranger.

One night I left my bed and slipped out of my room on to the open terrace. Beyond our garden wall are fields of ripening rice. Through the gaps in the village groves to the

North, glimpses of the river are seen. The whole scene slept in the darkness like the vague embryo of some future creation.

In that future I saw my country, a woman like myself, standing expectant. She has been drawn forth from her home corner by the sudden call of some Unknown. She has had no time to pause or ponder, or to light herself a torch, as she rushes forward into the darkness ahead. I know well how her very soul responds to the distant flute-strains which call her; how her breast rises and falls; how she feels she nears it, nay it is already hers, so that it matters not even if she runs blindfold. She is no mother. There is no call to her of children in their hunger, no home to be lighted of an evening, no household work to be done. No; she hies to her tryst, for this is the land of the Vaishnava Poets. She has left home, forgotten domestic duties; she has nothing but an unfathomable yearning which hurries her on,—by what road, to what goal, she recks not.

I, also, am possessed of just such a yearning. I likewise have lost my home and also lost my way. Both the end and the means have become equally shadowy to me. There remain only the yearning and the hurrying on. Ah! wretched wandered through the night, when the dawn reddens you will see no trace of a way to return. But why return? Death will serve as well. If the Dark which sounded the flute should lead to destruction, why trouble about the hereafter? When I am merged in its blackness, neither I, nor good and bad, nor laughter, nor tears, shall be any more!

XII

In Bengal the machinery of time being thus suddenly run at full pressure, things which were difficult became easy, one following soon after another. Nothing could be held back any more, even in our corner of the country. In the beginning our district was backward, for my husband was unwilling to put any compulsion on the villagers. 'Those who make sacrifices for their country's sake are indeed her servants,' he would say, 'but those who compel others to make them in her name are her enemies. They would cut freedom at the root, to gain it at the top.'

But when Sandip came and settled here, and his followers began to move about the country, speaking in towns and market-places, waves of excitement came rolling up to us as well. A band of young fellows of the locality attached themselves to him, some even who had been known as a disgrace to the village. But the glow of their genuine enthusiasm lighted them up, within as well as without. It became quite clear that when the pure breezes of a great joy and hope sweep through the land, all dirt and decay are cleansed away. It is hard, indeed, for men to be frank and straight and healthy, when their country is in the throes of dejection.

Then were all eyes turned on my husband, from whose estates alone foreign sugar and salt and cloths had not been banished. Even the estate officers began to feel awkward and ashamed over it. And yet, some time ago, when my husband began to import country-made articles into our village, he had been secretly and openly twitted for his folly, by old and young alike. When *Swadeshi* had not yet become a boast, we had despised it with all our hearts.

My husband still sharpens his Indian-made pencils with his Indian-made knife, does his writing with reed pens, drinks his water out of a bell-metal vessel, and works at night in the light of an old-fashioned castor-oil lamp. But this dull, milk-and-watery *Swadeshi* of his never appealed to us. Rather, we had always felt ashamed of the inelegant, unfashionable furniture of his reception-rooms, especially when he had the magistrate, or any other European, as his guest.

My husband used to make light of my protests. 'Why allow such trifles to upset you?' he would say with a smile.

'They will think us barbarians, or at all events wanting in refinement.'

'If they do, I will pay them back by thinking that their refinement does not go deeper than their white skins.'

My husband had an ordinary brass pot on his writing-table which he used as a flower-vase. It has often happened that, when I had news of some European guest, I would steal into his room and put in its place a crystal vase of European make.

'Look here, Bimala,' he objected at length, 'that brass pot is as unconscious of itself as those blossoms are; but this thing protests its purpose so loudly, it is only fit for artificial flowers.'

The Bara Rani, alone, pandered to my husband's whims. Once she comes panting to say: 'Oh, brother, have you heard? Such lovely Indian soaps have come out! My days of luxury are gone by; still, if they contain no animal fat, I should like to try some.'

This sort of thing makes my husband beam all over, and the house is deluged with Indian scents and soaps. Soaps indeed! They are more like lumps of caustic soda. And do I not know that what my sister-in-law uses on herself are the European soaps of old, while these are made over to the maids for washing clothes?

Another time it is: 'Oh, brother dear, do get me some of these new Indian pen-holders.'

Her 'brother' bubbles up as usual, and the Bara Rani's room becomes littered with all kinds of awful sticks that go by the name of *Swadeshi* pen-holders. Not that it makes any difference to her, for reading and writing are out of her line. Still, in her writing-case, lies the selfsame ivory pen-holder, the only one ever handled.

The fact is, all this was intended as a hit at me, because I would not keep my husband company in his vagaries. It was no good trying to show up my sister-in-law's insincerity; my husband's face would set so hard, if I barely touched on it. One only gets into trouble, trying to save such people from being imposed upon!

The Bara Rani loves sewing. One day I could not help blurting out: 'What a humbug you are, sister! When your "brother" is present, your mouth waters at the very mention of *Swadeshi* scissors, but it is the English-made article every time when you work.'

'What harm?' she replied. 'Do you not see what pleasure it gives him? We have grown up together in this house, since he was a boy. I simply cannot bear, as you can, the sight of the smile leaving his face. Poor dear, he has no amusement except this playing at shop-keeping. You are his only dissipation, and you will yet be his ruin?'

'Whatever you may say, it is not right to be double-faced,' I retorted.

My sister-in-law laughed out in my face. 'Oh, our artless little Chota Rani!—straight as a schoolmaster's rod, eh? But a woman is not built that way. She is soft and supple, so that she may bend without being crooked.'

I could not forget those words: 'You are his dissipation, and will be his ruin!' To-day I feel,—if a man needs must have some intoxicant, let it not be a woman.

XIII

Suksar, within our estates, is one of the biggest trade centres in the district. On one side of a stretch of water there is held a daily bazar; on the other, a weekly market. During the rains when this piece of water gets connected with the river, and boats can come through, great quantities of cotton yarns, and woollen stuffs for the coming winter, are brought in for sale.

At the height of our enthusiasm, Sandip laid it down that all foreign articles, together with the demon of foreign influence, must be driven out of our territory.

'Of course!' said I, girding myself up for a fight.

'I have had words with Nikhil about it,' said Sandip. 'He tells me, he does not mind speechifying, but he will not have coercion.'

'I will see to that,' I said, with a proud sense of power. I knew how deep was my husband's love for me. Had I been in my senses I should have allowed myself to be torn to pieces rather than assert my claim to that, at such a time. But Sandip had to be impressed with the full strength of my *Shakti*.

Sandip had brought home to me, in his irresistible way, how the cosmic Energy was revealed for each individual in the shape of some special affinity. Vaishnava Philosophy, he said, speaks of the *Shakti* of Delight that dwells in the heart of creation, ever attracting the heart of her Eternal Lover. Men have a perpetual longing to bring out this *Shakti* from the hidden depths of their own nature, and those of us who succeed in doing so at once clearly understand the meaning of the music coming to us from the Dark. He broke out singing:

> My flute, that was busy with its song,
> Is silent now when we stand face to face.
> My call went seeking you from sky to sky
> When you lay hidden;
> But now all my cry finds its smile
> In the face of my beloved.

Listening to his allegories, I had forgotten that I was plain and simple Bimala. I was *Shakti*; also an embodiment of Universal joy. Nothing could fetter me, nothing was impossible for me; whatever I touched would gain new life. The world around me was a fresh creation of mine; for behold, before my heart's response had touched it, there had not been this wealth of gold in the Autumn sky! And this hero, this true servant of the country, this devotee of mine,—this flaming intelligence, this burning energy, this shining genius,—him also was I creating from moment to moment. Have I not seen how my presence pours fresh life into him time after time?

The other day Sandip begged me to receive a young lad, Amulya, an ardent disciple of his. In a moment I could see a new light flash out from the boy's eyes, and knew that he, too, had a vision of *Shakti* manifest, that my creative force had begun its work in his blood. 'What sorcery is this of yours!' exclaimed Sandip next day. 'Amulya is a boy no longer, the wick of his life is all ablaze. Who can hide your fire under your home-roof? Every one of them must be touched up by it, sooner or later, and when every lamp is alight what a grand carnival of a *Dewali* we shall have in the country!'

Blinded with the brilliance of my own glory I had decided to grant my devotee this boon. I was overweeningly confident that none could baulk me of what I really wanted. When I returned to my room after my talk with Sandip, I loosed my hair and tied it up over again. Miss Gilby had taught me a way of brushing it up from the neck and piling it in a knot over my head. This style was a favourite one with my husband. 'It is a pity,' he once said, 'that providence should have chosen poor me, instead of poet Kalidas, for revealing all the wonders of a woman's neck. The poet would probably have likened it to a flower-stem; but I feel it to be a torch, holding aloft the black flame of your hair.' With which he... but why, oh why, do I go back to all that?

I sent for my husband. In the old days I could contrive a hundred and one excuses, good or bad, to get him to come to me. Now that all this had stopped for days I had lost the art of contriving.

Nikhil's Story

VI

Panchu's wife has just died of a lingering consumption. Panchu must undergo a purification ceremony to cleanse himself of sin and to propitiate his community. The community has calculated and informed him that it will cost one hundred and twenty-three rupees.

'How absurd!' I cried, highly indignant. 'Don't submit to this, Panchu. What can they do to you?'

Raising to me his patient eyes like those of a tired-out beast of burden, he said: 'There is my eldest girl, sir, she will have to be married. And my poor wife's last rites have to be put through.'

'Even if the sin were yours, Panchu,' I mused aloud, 'you have surely suffered enough for it already.'

'That is so, sir,' he naïvely assented. 'I had to sell part of my land and mortgage the rest to meet the doctor's bills. But there is no escape from the offerings I have to make the Brahmins.'

What was the use of arguing? When will come the time, I wondered, for the purification of the Brahmins themselves who can accept such offerings?

After his wife's illness and funeral, Panchu, who had been tottering on the brink of starvation, went altogether beyond his depth. In a desperate attempt to gain consolation of some sort he took to sitting at the feet of a wandering ascetic, and succeeded in acquiring philosophy enough to forget that his children went hungry. He kept himself steeped for a time in the idea that the world is vanity, and if pleasure it has none, pain also is a delusion. Then, at last, one night he left his little ones in their tumble-down hovel, and started off wandering on his own account.

I knew nothing of this at the time, for just then a veritable ocean-churning by gods and demons was going on in my mind. Nor did my master tell me that he had taken Panchu's deserted children under his own roof and was caring for them, though alone in the house, with his school to attend to the whole day.

After a month Panchu came back, his ascetic fervour considerably worn of. His eldest boy and girl nestled up to him, crying: 'Where have you been all this time, father?' His youngest boy filled his lap; his second girl leant over his back with her arms round his neck; and they all wept together. 'O sir!' sobbed Panchu, at length, to my master. 'I have not the power to give these little ones enough to eat,—I am not free to run away from them. What has been my sin that I should be scourged so, bound hand and foot?'

In the meantime the thread of Panchu's little trade connections had snapped and he found he could not resume them. He clung on to the shelter of my master's roof, which had first received him on his return, and said not a word of going back home. 'Look here, Panchu,' my master was at last driven to say. 'If you don't take care of your cottage, it will tumble down altogether. I will lend you some money with which you can do a bit of peddling and return it me little by little.'

Panchu was not excessively pleased—was there then no such thing as charity on earth? And when my master asked him to write out a receipt for the money, he felt that this favour, demanding a return, was hardly worth having. My master, however, did not care to make an outward gift which would leave an inward obligation. To destroy self-respect is to destroy caste, was his idea.

After signing the note, Panchu's obeisance to my master fell off considerably in its reverence,—the dust-taking was left out. It made my master smile; he asked noting better than that courtesy should stoop less low. 'Respect given and taken truly balances the account between man and man,' was the way he put it, 'but veneration is overpayment.'

Panchu began to buy cloth at the market and peddle it about the village. He did not get much of cash payment, it is true, but what he could realise in kind, in the way of rice, jute, and other field produce, went towards settlement of his account. In two months' time he was able to pay back an instalment of my master's debt, and with it there was a corresponding reduction in the depth of his bow. He must have begun to feel that he had been revering as a saint a mere man, who had not even risen superior to the lure of lucre.

While Panchu was thus engaged, the full shock of the *Swadeshi* flood fell on him.

VII

It was vacation time, and many youths of our village and its neighbourhood had come home from their schools and colleges. They attached themselves to Sandip's leadership with enthusiasm, and some, in their excess of zeal, gave up their studies altogether. Many of the boys had been free pupils of my school here, and some held college scholarships from me in Calcutta. They came up in a body, and demanded that I should banish foreign goods from my Suksar market.

I told them I could not do it.

They were sarcastic: 'Why, Maharaja, will the loss be too much for you?'

I took no notice of the insult in their tone, and was about to reply that the loss would fall on the poor traders and their customers, not on me, when my master, who was present, interposed.

'Yes, the loss will be his,—not yours, that is clear enough,' he said.

'But for one's country...'

'The country does not mean the soil, but the men on it,' interrupted my master again. 'Have you yet wasted so much as a glance on what was happening to them? But now you would dictate what salt they shall eat, what clothes they shall wear. Why should they put up with such tyranny, and why should we let them?'

'But we have taken to Indian salt and sugar and cloth ourselves.'

'You may do as you please to work of your irritation, to keep up your fanaticism. You are well off, you need not mind the cost. The poor do not want to stand in your way, but you insist on their submitting to your compulsion. As it is, every moment of theirs is a life-and-death struggle for a bare living; you cannot even imagine the difference a few pice means to them,—so little have you in common. You have spent your whole past in a superior compartment, and now you come down to use them as tools for the wreaking of your wrath. I call it cowardly.'

They were all old pupils of my master, so they did not venture to be disrespectful, though they were quivering with indignation. They turned to me. 'Will you then be the only one, Maharaja, to put obstacles in the way of what the country would achieve?'

'Who am I, that I should dare do such a thing? Would I not rather lay down my life to help it?

The M.A. student smiled a crooked smile, as he asked: 'May we enquire what you are actually doing to help?'

'I have imported Indian mill-made yarn and kept it for sale in my Suksar market, and also sent bales of it to markets belonging to neighbouring *zamindars*.'

'But we have been to your market, Maharaja,' the same student exclaimed, 'and found nobody buying this yarn.'

'That is neither my fault nor the fault of my market. It only shows the whole country has not taken your vow.'

'That is not all,' my master went on. 'It shows that what you have pledged yourselves to do is only to pester others. You want dealers, who have not taken your vow, to buy that yarn; weavers, who have not taken your vow, to make it up. Then their wares eventually to be foisted on to consumers who, also, have not taken your vow. The method? Your clamour, and the *zamindars'* oppression. The result: all righteousness yours, all privations theirs!'

'And may we venture to ask, further, what your share of the privation has been?' pursued a science student.

'You want to know, do you?' replied my master. 'It is Nikhil himself who has to buy up that Indian mill yarn; he has had to start a weaving school to get it woven; and to judge by his past brilliant business exploits, by the time his cotton fabrics leave the loom their cost will be that of cloth-of-gold; so they will only find a use, perhaps, as curtains for his drawing-room, even though their flimsiness may fail to screen him. When you get tired of your vow, you will laugh the loudest at their artistic effect. And if their workmanship is ever truly appreciated at all, it will be by foreigners.'

I have known my master all my life, but have never seen him so agitated. I could see that the pain had been silently accumulating in his heart for some time, because of his surpassing love for me, and that his habitual self-possession had become secretly undermined to the breaking point.

'You are our elders,' said the medical student. 'It is unseemly that we should bandy words with you. But tell us, pray finally, are you determined not to oust foreign articles from your market?'

'I will not,' I said, 'because they are not mine.'

'Because that will cause you a loss!' smiled the M.A. student.

'Because he, whose is the loss, is the best judge,' retorted my master.

With a shout of *Bande Mataram* they left us.

Chapter VI

Nikhil's Story

VIII

A few days later, my master brought Panchu round to me. His *zamindar*, it appeared, had fined him a hundred rupees, and was threatening him with ejectment.

'For what fault?' I enquired.

'Because,' I was told, 'he has been found selling foreign cloths. He begged and prayed Harish Kundu, his *zamindar*, to let him sell off his stock, bought with borrowed money, promising faithfully never to do it again; but the *zamindar* would not hear of it, and insisted on his burning the foreign stuff there and then, if he wanted to be let off. Panchu in his desperation blurted out defiantly: "I can't afford it! You are rich; why not buy it up and burn it?" This only made Harish Kundu red in the face as he shouted: "The scoundrel must be taught manners, give him a shoe-beating!" So poor Panchu got insulted as well as fined.'

'What happened to the cloth?'

'The whole bale was burnt.'

'Who else was there?'

'Any number of people, who all kept shouting *Bande Mataram*. Sandip was also there. He took up some of the ashes, crying: "Brothers! This is the first funeral pyre lighted by your village in celebration of the last rites of foreign commerce. These are sacred ashes. Smear yourselves with them in token of your *Swadeshi* vow."'

'Panchu,' said I, turning to him, 'you must lodge a complaint.'

'No one will bear me witness,' he replied.

'None bear witness?—Sandip! Sandip!'

Sandip came out of his room at my call. 'What is the matter?' he asked.

'Won't you bear witness to the burning of this man's cloth?'

Sandip smiled. 'Of course I shall be a witness in the case,' he said. 'But I shall be on the opposite side.'

'What do you mean,' I exclaimed, 'by being a witness on this or that side? Will you not bear witness to the truth?'

'Is the thing which happens the only truth?'

'What other truths can there be?'

'The things that ought to happen! The truth we must build up will require a great deal of untruth in the process. Those who have made their way in the world have created truth, not blindly followed it.'

'And so—'

'And so I will bear what you people are pleased to call false witness, as they have done who have created empires, built up social systems, founded religious organisations. Those who would rule do not dread untruths; the shackles of truth are reserved for those who will fall under their sway. Have you not read history? Do you not know that in the immense cauldrons, where vast political developments are simmering, untruths are the main ingredients?'

'Political cookery on a large scale is doubtless going on, but—'

'Oh, I know! You, of course, will never do any of the cooking. You prefer to be one of those down whose throats the hotchpotch which is being cooked will be crammed. They will partition Bengal and say it is for your benefit. They will seal the doors of education and call it raising the standard. But you will always remain good boys, snivelling in your corners. We bad men, however, must see whether we cannot erect a defensive fortification of untruth.'

'It is no use arguing about these things, Nikhil,' my master interposed. 'How can they who do not feel the truth within them, realise that to bring it out from its obscurity into the light is man's highest aim,—not to keep on heaping material outside?'

Sandip laughed. 'Right, sir!' said he. 'Quite a correct speech for a schoolmaster. That is the kind of stuff I have read in books; but in the real world I have seen that man's chief business is the accumulation of outside material. Those who are masters in the art, advertise the biggest lies in their business, enter false accounts in their political ledgers with their broadest-pointed pens, launch their newspapers daily laden with untruths, and send preaches abroad to disseminate falsehood like flies carrying pestilential germs. I am a humble follower of these great ones. When I was attached to the Congress party I never hesitated to dilute ten per cent of truth with ninety per cent of untruth. And now, merely because I have ceased to belong to that party, I have not forgotten the basic fact that man's goal is not truth but success.'

'True success,' corrected my master.

'May be,' replied Sandip, 'but the fruit of true success ripens only by cultivating the field of untruth, after tearing up the soil and pounding it into dust. Truth grows up by itself like weeds and thorns, and only worms can expect to get fruit from it!' With this he flung out of the room.

My master smiled as he looked towards me. 'Do you know, Nikhil,' he said, 'I believe Sandip is not irreligious,—

his religion is of the obverse side of truth, like the dark moon, which is still a moon, for all that its light has gone over to the wrong side.'

'That is why,' I assented, 'I have always had an affection for him, though we have never been able to agree. I cannot condemn him, even now; though he has hurt me sorely, and may yet hurt me more.'

'I have begun to realise that,' said my master. 'I have long wondered how you could go on putting up with him. I have, at times, even suspected you of weakness. I now see that though you two do not rhyme, your rhythm is the same.'

'Fate seems bent on writing *Paradise Lost* in blank verse, in my case, and so has no use for a rhyming friend!' I remarked, pursuing his conceit.

'But what of Panchu?' resumed my master.

'You say Harish Kundu wants to eject him from his ancestral holding. Supposing I buy it up and then keep him on as my tenant?

'And his fine?'

'How can the *zamindar* realise that if he becomes my tenant?'

'His burnt bale of cloth?'

'I will procure him another. I should like to see any one interfering with a tenant of mine, for trading as he pleases!'

'I am afraid, sir,' interposed Panchu despondently, 'while you big folk are doing the fighting, the police and the law vultures will merrily gather round, and the crowd will enjoy the fun, but when it comes to getting killed, it has be the turn of only poor me!'

'Why, what harm can come to you?'

'They will burn down my house, sir, children and all!'

'Very well, I will take charge of your children,' said my master. 'You may go on with any trade you like. They shan't touch you.'

That very day I bought up Panchu's holding and entered into formal possession. Then the trouble began.

Panchu had inherited the holding of his grandfather as his sole surviving heir. Everybody knew this. But at this juncture an aunt turned up from somewhere, with her boxes and bundles, her rosary, and a widowed niece. She ensconced herself in Panchu's home and laid claim to a life interest in all he had.

Panchu was dumbfounded. 'My aunt died long ago,' he protested.

In reply he was told that he was thinking of his uncle's first wife, but that the former had lost no time in taking to himself a second.

'But my uncle died before my aunt,' exclaimed Panchu, still more mystified. 'Where was the time for him to marry again?'

This was not denied. But Panchu was reminded that it had never been asserted that the second wife had come after the death of the first, but the former had been married by his uncle during the latter's lifetime. Not relishing the idea of living with a co-wife she had remained in her father's house till her husband's death, after which she had got religion and retired to holy Brindaban, whence she was now coming. These facts were well known to the officers of Harish Kundu, as well as to some of his tenants. And if the *zamindar's* summons should be peremptory enough, even some of those who had partaken of the marriage feast would be forthcoming!

IX

One afternoon, when I happened to be specially busy, word came to my office room that Bimala had sent for me. I was startled.

'Who did you say had sent for me?' I asked the messenger.

'The Rani Mother.'

'The Bara Rani?'

'No, sir, the Chota Rani Mother.'

The Chota Rani! It seemed a century since I had been sent for by her. I kept them all waiting there, and went off into the inner apartments. When I stepped into our room I had another shock of surprise to find Bimala there with a distinct suggestion of being dressed up. The room, which from persistent neglect had latterly acquired an air of having grown absent-minded, had regained something of its old order this afternoon. I stood there silently, looking enquiringly at Bimala.

She flushed a little and the fingers of her right hand toyed for a time with the bangles on her left arm. Then she abruptly broke the silence. 'Look here! Is it right that ours should be the only market in all Bengal which allows foreign goods?'

'What, then, would be the right thing to do?' I asked.

'Order them to be cleared out!'

'But the goods are not mine.'

'Is not the market yours?'

'It is much more theirs who use it for trade.'

'Let them trade in Indian goods, then.'

'Nothing would please me better. But suppose they do not?'

'Nonsense! How dare they be so insolent?

'Are you not...'

'I am very busy this afternoon and cannot stop to argue it out. But I must refuse to tyrannise.'

'It would not be tyranny for selfish gain, but for the sake of the country.'

'To tyrannise for the country is to tyrannise over the country. But that I am afraid you will never understand.' With this I came away.

All of a sudden the world shone out for me with a fresh clearness. I seemed to feel it in my blood, that the Earth had lost the weight of its earthiness, and its daily task of sustaining life no longer appeared a burden, as with a wonderful access of power it whirled through space telling its beads of days and nights. What endless work, and withal what illimitable energy of freedom! None shall check it, oh, none can ever check it! From the depths of my being an uprush of joy, like a waterspout, sprang high to storm the skies.

I repeatedly asked myself the meaning of this outburst of feeling. At first there was no intelligible answer. Then it became clear that the bond against which I had been fretting inwardly, night and day, had broken. To my surprise I discovered that my mind was freed from all mistiness. I could see everything relating to Bimala as if vividly pictured on a camera screen. It was palpable that she had specially dressed herself up to coax that order out of me. Till that moment, I had never viewed Bimala's adornment as a thing apart from herself. But to-day the elaborate manner in which she had done up her hair, in the English fashion, made it appear a mere decoration. That which before had the mystery of her personality about it, and was priceless to me, was now out to sell itself cheap.

As I came away from that broken cage of a bedroom, out into the golden sunlight of the open, there was the avenue of bauhinias, along the gravelled path in front of my verandah, suffusing the sky with a rosy flush. A group of starlings beneath the trees were noisily chattering away. In the distance an empty bullock cart, with its nose on the ground, held up its tail aloft,—one of its unharnessed bullocks grazing, the other resting on the grass, its eyes dropping for very comfort, while a crow on its back was pecking away at the insects on its body.

I seemed to have come closer to the heartbeats of the great earth in all the simplicity of its daily life; its warm breath fell on me with the perfume of the bauhinia blossoms; and an anthem, inexpressibly sweet, seemed to peal forth from this world, where I, in my freedom, live in the freedom of all else.

We, men, are knights whose quest is that freedom to which our ideals call us. She who makes for us the banner under which we fare forth is the true Woman for us. We must tear away the disguise of her who weaves our net of enchantment at home, and know her for what she is. We must beware of clothing her in the witchery of our own longings and imaginings, and thus allow her to distract us from our true quest.

To-day I feel that I shall win through. I have come to the gateway of the simple; I am now content to see things as they are. I have gained freedom myself; I shall allow freedom to others. In my work will be my salvation.

I know that, time and again, my heart will ache, but now that I understand its, pain in all its truth, I can disregard it. Now that I know it concerns only me, what after all can be its value? The suffering which belongs to all mankind shall be my crown.

Save me, Truth! Never again let me hanker after the false paradise of Illusion. If I must walk alone, let me at least tread your path. Let the drum-beats of Truth lead me to Victory.

Sandip's Story

VII

Bimala sent for me that day, but for a time she could not utter a word; her eyes kept brimming up to the verge of overflowing. I could see at once that she had been unsuccessful with Nikhil. She had been so proudly confident that she would have her own way,—but I had never shared her confidence. Woman knows man well enough where he is weak, but she is quite unable to fathom him where he is strong. The fact is that man is as much a mystery to woman as woman is to man. If that were not so, the separation of the sexes would only have been a waste of Nature's energy.

Ah pride, pride! The trouble was, not that the necessary thing had failed of accomplishment, but that the entreaty, which had cost her such a struggle to make, should have been refused. What a wealth of colour and movement, suggestion and deception, group themselves round this 'me' and 'mine' in woman. That is just where her beauty lies,—she is ever so much more personal than man. When man was being made, the Creator was a schoolmaster,—His bag full of commandments and principles; but when He came to woman, He resigned His headmastership and turned artist, with only His brush and paint-box.

When Bimala stood silently there, flushed and tearful in her broken pride, like a storm-cloud, laden with rain and charged with lightning, lowering over the horizon, she looked so absolutely sweet that I had to go right up to her and take her by the hand. It was trembling, but she did not snatch it away. 'Bee,' said I, 'We two are colleagues, for our aims are one. Let us sit down and talk it over.'

I led her, unresisting, to a seat. But strange! At that very point the rush of my impetuosity suffered an unaccountable check,—just as the current of the mighty Padma, roaring on in its irresistible course, all of a sudden gets turned away from the bank it is crumbling by some trifling obstacle beneath the surface. When I pressed Bimala's hand my nerves rang music, like tuned-up strings; but the symphony stopped short at the first movement.

What stood in the way? Nothing singly; it was a tangle of a multitude of things,—nothing definitely palpable, but only that unaccountable sense of obstruction. Anyhow, this much has become plain to me, that I cannot swear to what I really am. It is because I am such a mystery to my own mind that my attraction for myself is so strong! If once the whole of myself should become known to me, I would then fling it all away,—and reach beatitude!

As she sat down, Bimala went ashy pale. She, too, must have realised what a crisis had come and gone, leaving her unscathed. The comet had passed by, but the brush of its burning tail had overcome her. To help her to recover herself I said: 'Obstacles there will be, but let us fight them through, and not be down-hearted. Is not that best, Queen?'

Bimala cleared her throat with a little cough, but simply to murmur: 'Yes.'

'Let us sketch out our plan of action,' I continued, as I drew a piece of paper and a pencil from my pocket.

I began to make a list of the workers who had joined us from Calcutta and to assign their duties to each. Bimala interrupted me before I was through, saying wearily: 'Leave it now; I will join you again this evening'; and then she hurried out of the room. It was evident she was not in a state to attend to anything. She must be alone with herself for a while,—perhaps lie down on her bed and have a good cry!

When she left me, my intoxication began to deepen, as the cloud colours grow richer after the sun is down. I felt I had let the moment of moments slip by. What an awful coward I had been! She must have left me in sheer disgust at my qualms—and she was right!

While I was tingling all over with these reflections, a servant came in and announced Amulya, one of our boys. I felt like sending him away for the time, but he stepped in before I could make up my mind. Then we fell to discussing the news of the fights which were raging in different quarters over cloth and sugar and salt; and the air was soon clear of all fumes of intoxication. I felt as if awakened from a dream. I leapt to my feet feeling quite ready for the fray,—*Bande Mataram!*

The news was various. Most of the traders who were tenants of Harish Kundu had come over to us. Many of Nikhil's officials were also secretly on our side, pulling the wires in our interest. The Marwari shopkeepers were offering to pay a penalty, if only allowed to clear their present stocks. Only some Mahomedan traders were still obdurate.

One of them was taking home some German-made shawls for his family. These were confiscated and burnt by one of our village boys. This had given rise to trouble. We offered to buy him Indian woollen stuffs in their place. But where were cheap Indian woollens to be had? We could not very well indulge him in Cashmere shawls! He came and complained to Nikhil, who advised him to go to law. Of course Nikhil's men saw to it that the trial should come to nothing, even his law-agent being on our side!

The point is, if we have to replace burnt foreign clothes with Indian cloth every time, and on the top of that fight through a law-suit, where is the money to come from? And the beauty of it is that this destruction of foreign goods is increasing their demand and sending up the foreigner's profits,—very like what happened to the fortunate shopkeeper whose chandeliers the nabob delighted in smashing, tickled by the tinkle of the breaking glass.

The next problem is,—since there is no such thing as cheap and gaudy Indian woollen stuff, should we be rigorous in our boycott of foreign flannels and merinos, or make an exception in their favour?

'Look here!' said I at length on the first point, 'we are not going to keep on making presents of Indian stuff to those who have got their foreign purchases confiscated. The penalty is intended to fall on them, not on us. If they go to law, we must retaliate by burning down their granaries!—What startles you, Amulya? It is not the prospect of a grand illumination that delights me! You must remember, this is War. If you are afraid of causing suffering, go in for love-making, you will never do for this work!'

The second problem I solved by deciding to allow no compromise with foreign articles, in any circumstance whatever. In the good old days, when these gaily coloured foreign shawls were unknown, our peasantry used to manage well enough with plain cotton quilts,—they must learn to do so again. They may not look as gorgeous, but this is not the time to think of looks.

Most of the boatmen had been won over to refuse to carry foreign goods, but the chief of them, Mirjan, was still insubordinate.

'Could you not get his boat sunk?' I asked our manager here.

'Nothing easier, sir,' he replied. 'But what if afterwards I am held responsible?'

'Why be so clumsy as to leave any loophole for responsibility? However, if there must be any, my shoulders will be there to beat it.'

Mirjan's boat was tied near the landing-place after its freight had been taken over to the market-place. There was no one on it, for the manager had arranged for some entertainment to which all had been invited. After dusk the ·boat, loaded with rubbish, was holed and set adrift. It sank in mid-stream.

Mirjan understood the whole thing. He came to me in tears to beg for mercy. 'I was wrong, sir—' he began.

'What makes you realise that all of a sudden?' I sneered.

He made no direct reply. 'The boat was worth Rs. 2000,' he said. 'I now see my mistake, and if excused this time I will never...' with which he threw himself at my feet.

I asked him to come ten days later. If only we could pay him that Rs. 2000 at once, we could buy him up body and soul. This is just the sort of man who could render us immense service, if won over. We shall never be able to make any headway unless we can lay our hands on plenty of money.

As soon as Bimala came into the sitting-room, in the evening, I said as I rose up to receive her: 'Queen! Everything is ready, success is at hand, but we must have money.'

'Money? How much money?'

'Not so very much, but by hook or by crook we must have it!'

'But how much?'

'A mere fifty thousand rupees will do for the present.'

Bimala blenched inwardly at the figure, but tried not to show it. How could she again admit defeat?

'Queen!' said I, 'you only can make the impossible possible. Indeed you have already done so. Oh, that I could show you the extent of your achievement,—then you would know it. But the time for that is not now. Now we want money!'

'You shall have it,' she said.

I could see that the thought of selling her jewels had occurred to her. So I said: 'Your jewels must remain in reserve. One can never tell when they may be wanted.' And then, as Bimala stared blankly at me in silence, I went on: 'This money must come from your husband's treasury.'

Bimala was still more taken aback. After a long pause she said: 'But how am I to get his money?'

'Is not his money yours as well?'

'Ah, no!' she said, her wounded pride hurt afresh.

'If not,' I cried, 'neither is it his, but his country's, whom he has deprived of it, in her time of need!'

'But how am I to get it?' she repeated.

'Get it you shall and must. You know best how. You must get it for Her to whom it rightfully belongs. *Bande Mataram!* These are the magic words which will open the door of his iron safe, break through the walls of his strong-room, and confound the hearts of those who are disloyal to its call. Say *Bande Mataram*, Bee!'

'*Bande Mataram!*'

Chapter VII

Sandip's Story

VIII

We are men, we are kings, we must have our tribute. Ever since we have come upon the Earth we have been plundering her; and the more we claimed, the more she submitted. From primaeval days we men have been plucking fruits, cutting down trees, digging up the soil, killing beast, bird and fish. From the bottom of he sea, from underneath the ground, from the very jaws of death, it has all been grabbing and grabbing and grabbing,—no strong-box in Nature's storeroom has been respected or left unrifled.

The one delight of this Earth is to fulfil the claims of those who are men. She has been made fertile and beautiful and complete through her endless sacrifices to them. But for this, she would be lost in the wilderness, not knowing herself, the doors of her heart shut, her diamonds and pearls never seeing the light.

Likewise, by sheer force of our claims, we men have opened up all the latent possibilities of women. In the process of surrendering themselves to us, they have ever gained their true greatness. Because they had to bring all the diamonds of their happiness and the pearls of their sorrow into our royal treasury, they have found their true wealth. So for men to accept is truly to give: for women to give is truly to gain.

The demand I have just made from Bimala, however, is indeed a large one! At first I felt scruples; for is it not the habit of man's mind to be in purposeless conflict with itself? I thought I had imposed too hard a task. My first impulse was to call her back, and tell her I would rather not make her life wretched by dragging her into all these troubles. I forgot, for the moment, that it was the mission of man to be aggressive, to make woman's existence fruitful by stirring up disquiet in the depth of her passivity, to make the whole world blessed by churning up the immeasurable abyss of suffering! This is why man's hands are so strong, his grip so firm.

Bimala had been longing with all her heart that I, Sandip, should demand of her some great sacrifice,—should call her to her death. How else could she be happy? Had she not waited all these weary years only for an opportunity to weep out her heart,—so satiated was she with the monotony of her placid happiness? And therefore, at the very first sight of me, her heart's horizon darkened with the rain clouds of her impending days of anguish. If I pity her and save her from her sorrows, what then was the purpose of my being born a man?

The real reason of my qualms is that my demand happens to be for money. That savours of beggary, for money is man's, not woman's. That is why I had to make it a big figure. A thousand or two would have the air of petty theft. Fifty thousand has all the expanse of romantic brigandage.

Ah, but riches should really have been mine! So many of my desires have had to halt, again and again, on the road to accomplishment simply for want of money. This does not become me! Had my fate been merely unjust, it could be forgiven,—but its bad taste is unpardonable. It is not simply a hardship that a man like me should be at his wit's end to pay his house rent, or should have to carefully count out the coins for an Intermediate Class railway ticket,—it is vulgar!

It is equally clear that Nikhil's paternal estates are a superfluity to him. For him it would not have been at all unbecoming to be poor. He would have cheerfully pulled in the double harness of indigent mediocrity with that precious master of his.

I should love to have, just for once, the chance to fling about fifty thousand rupees in the service of my country and to the satisfaction of myself. I am a nabob born, and it is a great dream of mine to get rid of this disguise of poverty, though it be for a day only, and to see myself in my true character.

I have grave misgivings, however, as to Bimala ever getting that Rs. 50,000 within her reach, and it will probably be only a thousand or two which will actually come to hand. Be it so. The wise man is content with half a loaf, or any fraction for that matter, rather than no bread.

I must return to these personal reflections of mine later. News comes that I am wanted at once. Something has gone wrong....

It seems that the police have got a clue to the man who sank Mirjan's boat for us. He was an old offender. They are on his trail, but he should be too practised a hand to be caught blabbing. However, one never knows. Nikhil's back is up, and his manager may not be able to have things his own way.

'If I get into trouble, sir,' said the manager when I saw him, 'I shall have to drag you in!'

'Where is the noose with which you can catch me?' I asked.

'I have a letter of yours, and several of Amulya Babu's.'

I could not see that the letter marked 'urgent' to which I had been hurried into writing a reply was wanted urgently for this purpose only! I am getting to learn quite a number of things.

The point now is, that the police must be bribed and hush-money paid to Mirjan for his boat. It is also becoming evident that much of the cost of this patriotic venture of ours will find its way as profit into the pockets of Nikhil's manager. However, I must shut my eyes to that for the present, for is he not shouting *Bande Mataram* as lustily as I am?

This kind of work has always to be carried on with leaky vessels which let as much through as they fetch in. We all have a hidden fund of moral judgement stored away within us, and so I was about to wax indignant with the manager, and enter in my diary a tirade against the unreliability of our countrymen. But, if there be a god, I must acknowledge with gratitude to him that he has given me a clear-seeing mind, which allows nothing inside or outside it to remain vague. I may delude others, but never myself. So I was unable to continue angry.

Whatever is true is neither good nor bad, but simply true, and that is Science. A lake is only the remnant of water which has not been sucked into the ground. Underneath the cult of *Bande Mataram*, as indeed at the bottom of all mundane affairs, there is a region of slime, whose absorbing power must be reckoned with. The manager will take what he wants; I also have my own wants. These lesser wants form a part of the wants of the great Cause,—the horse must be fed and the wheels must be oiled if the best progress is to be made.

The long and short of it is that money we must have, and that soon. We must take whatever comes the readiest, for we cannot afford to wait. I know that the immediate often swallows up the ultimate; that the Rs. 5000 of to-day may nip in the bud the Rs. 50,000 of to-morrow. But I must accept the penalty. Have I not often twitted Nikhil that they who walk in the paths of restraint have never known what sacrifice is? It is we greedy folk who have to sacrifice our greed at every step!

Of the cardinal sins of man, Desire is for men who are men—but Delusion, which is only for cowards, hampers them.

Because delusion keeps them wrapped up in past and future, but is the very deuce for confounding their footsteps in the present. Those who are always straining their ears for the call of the remote, to the neglect of the call of the imminent, are like Sakuntala[1] absorbed in the memories of her lover. The guest comes unheeded, and the curse descends, depriving them of the very object of their desire.

The other day I pressed Bimala's hand, and that touch still stirs her mind, as it vibrates in mine. Its thrill must not be deadened by repetition, for then what is now music will descend to mere argument. There is at present no room in her mind for the question 'why?' So I must not deprive Bimala, who is one of those creatures for whom illusion is necessary, of her full supply of it.

As for me, I have so much else to do that I shall have to be content for the present with the foam of the wine cup of passion. O man of desire! Curb your greed, and practise your hand on the harp of illusion till you can bring out all the delicate nuances of suggestion. This is not the time to drain the cup to the dregs.

IX

Our work proceeds apace. But though we have shouted ourselves hoarse, proclaiming the Mussulmans to be our brethren, we have come to realise that we shall never be able to bring them wholly round to our side. So they must be suppressed altogether and made to understand that we are the masters. They are now showing their teeth, but one day they shall dance like tame bears to the tune we play.

---

1. Sakuntala, after the king, her lover, went back to his kingdom, promising to send for her, was so lost in thoughts of him, that she failed to hear the call of her hermit guest, who thereupon cursed her, saying that the object of her love would forget all about her.—*Tr.*

'If the idea of a United India is a true one,' objects Nikhil, 'Mussulmans are a necessary part of it.'

'Quite so,' said I, 'but we must know their place and keep them there, otherwise they will constantly be giving trouble.'

'So you want to make trouble to prevent trouble?'

'What, then, is your plan?'

'There is only one well-known way of avoiding quarrels,' said Nikhil meaningly.

I know that, like tales written by good people, Nikhil's discourse always ends in a moral. The strange part of it is that with all his familiarity with moral precepts, he still believes in them! He is an incorrigible schoolboy. His only merit is his sincerity. The mischief with people like him is that they will not admit the finality even of death, but keep their eyes always fixed on a hereafter.

I have long been nursing a plan which, if only I could carry it out, would set fire to the whole country. True patriotism will never be roused in our countrymen unless they can visualise the motherland. We must make a goddess of her. My colleagues saw the point at once. 'Let us devise an appropriate image!' they exclaimed. 'It will not do if you devise it,' I admonished them. 'We must get one of the current images accepted as representing the country,—the worship of the people must flow towards it along the deep-cut grooves of custom.'

But Nikhil's needs must argue even about this. 'We must not seek the help of illusions,' he said to me some time ago, 'for what we believe to be the true cause.'

'Illusions are necessary for lesser minds,' I said, 'and to this class the greater portion of the world belongs. That is why divinities are set up in every country to keep up the illusions of the people, for men are only too well aware of their weakness.'

'No,' he replied. 'God is necessary to clear away our illusions. The divinities which keep them alive are false gods.'

'What of that? If need be, even false gods must be invoked, rather than let the work suffer. Unfortunately for us, our illusions are alive enough, but we do not know how to make them serve our purpose. Look at the Brahmins. In spite of our treating them as demi-gods, and untiringly taking the dust of their feet, they are a force going to waste.

'There will always be a large class of people, given to grovelling, who can never be made to do anything unless they are bespattered with the dust of somebody's feet, be it on their heads or on their backs! What a pity if after keeping Brahmins saved up in our armoury for all these ages,—keen and serviceable,—they cannot be utilised to urge on this rabble in the time of our need.'

But it is impossible to drive all this into Nikhil's head. He has such a prejudice in favour of truth,—as though there exists such an objective reality! How often have I tried to explain to him that where untruth truly exists, there it is indeed the truth. This was understood in our country in the old days, and so they had the courage to declare that for those of little understanding untruth is the truth. For them, who can truly believe their country to be a goddess, her image will do duty for the truth. With our nature and our traditions we are unable to realise our country as she is, but we can easily bring ourselves to believe in her image. Those who want to do real work must not ignore this fact.

Nikhil only got excited. 'Because you have lost the power of walking in the path of truth's attainment,' he cried, 'you keep waiting for some miraculous boon to drop from the skies! That is why when your service to the country has fallen centuries into arrears all you can think of is, to make of it an image and stretch out your hands in expectation of gratuitous favours.'

'We want to perform the impossible,' I said. 'So our country needs must be made into a god.'

'You mean you have no heart for possible tasks,' replied Nikhil. 'Whatever is already there is to be left undisturbed; yet there must be a supernatural result.'

'Look here, Nikhil,' I said at length, thoroughly exasperated. 'The things you have been saying are good enough as moral lessons. These ideas have served their purpose, as milk for babes, at one stage of man's evolution, but will no longer do, now that man has cut his teeth.

'Do we not see before our very eyes how things, of which we never even dreamt of sowing the seed, are sprouting up on every side? By what power? That of the deity in our country who is becoming manifest. It is for the genius of the age to give that deity its image. Genius does not argue, it creates. I only give form to what the country imagines.

'I will spread it abroad that the goddess has vouchsafed me a dream. I will tell the Brahmins that they have been appointed her priests, and that their downfall has been due to their dereliction of duty in not seeing to the proper performance of her worship. Do you say I shall be uttering lies? No, say I, it is the truth—nay more, the truth which the country has so long been waiting to learn from my lips. If only I could get the opportunity to deliver my message, you would see the stupendous result.'

'What I am afraid of,' said Nikhil, 'is, that my lifetime is limited and the result you speak of is not the final result. It will have after-effects which may not be immediately apparent.'

'I only seek the result,' said I, 'which belongs to to-day.'

'The result I seek,' answered Nikhil, 'belongs to all time.

Nikhil may have had his share of Bengal's greatest gift— imagination, but he has allowed it to be overshadowed and nearly killed by an exotic conscientiousness. Just look at the worship of Durga which Bengal has carried to such heights.

That is one of her greatest achievements. I can swear that Durga is a political goddess and was conceived as the image of the *Shakti* of patriotism in the days when Bengal was praying to be delivered from Mussulman domination. What other province of India has succeeded in giving such wonderful visual expression to the ideal of its quest?

Nothing betrayed Nikhil's loss of the divine gift of imagination more conclusively than his reply to me. 'During the Mussulman domination,' he said, 'the Maratha and the Sikh asked for fruit from the arms which they themselves took up. The Bengali contented himself with placing weapons in the hands of his goddess and muttering incantations to her; and as his country did not really happen to be a goddess the only fruit he got was the lopped-off heads of the goats and buffaloes of the sacrifice. The day that we seek the good of the country along the path of righteousness, He who is greater than our country will grant us true fruition.'

The unfortunate part of it is that Nikhil's words sound so fine when put down on paper. My words, however, are not meant to be scribbled on paper, but to be scored into the heart of the country. The Pandit records his *Treatise on Agriculture* in printer's ink; but the cultivator at the point of his plough impresses his endeavour deep in the soil.

X

When I next saw Bimala I pitched my key high without further ado. 'Have we been able,' I began, 'to believe with all our heart in the god for whose worship we have been born all these millions of years, until he actually made himself visible to us?

'How often have I told you,' I continued, 'that had I not seen you I never would have known all my country as One. I know not yet whether you rightly understand me. The gods are invisible only in their heaven,—on earth they show themselves to mortal men.'

Bimala looked at me in a strange kind of way as she gravely replied: 'Indeed I understand you, Sandip.' This was the first time she called me plain Sandip.

'Krishna,' I continued, 'whom Arjuna ordinarily knew only as the driver of his chariot, had also His universal aspect, of which, too, Arjuna had a vision one day, and that day he saw the Truth. I have seen your Universal Aspect in my country. The Ganges and the Brahmaputra are the chains of gold that wind round and round your neck; in the woodland fringes on the distant banks of the dark waters of he river, I have seen your collyrium-darkened eyelashes; the changeful sheen of your *sari* moves for me in the play of light and shade amongst the swaying shoots of green corn; and the blazing summer heat, which makes the whole sky lie gasping like a red-tongued lion in the desert, is nothing but your cruel radiance.

'Since the goddess has vouchsafed her presence to her votary in such wonderful guise, it is for me to proclaim her worship throughout our land, and then shall the country gain new life. "Your image make we in temple after temple."[2] But this our people have not yet fully realised. So I would call on them in your name and offer for their worship an image from which none shall be able to withhold belief. Oh give me this boon, this power.'

Bimala's eyelids drooped and she became rigid in her seat like a figure of stone. Had I continued she would have gone off into a trance. When I ceased speaking she opened wide her eyes, and murmured with fixed gaze, as though still dazed: 'O Traveller in the path of Destruction! Who is there that can

---

2. A line from Bankim Chatterjee's national song '*Bande Mataram.*'

stay your progress? Do I not see that none shall stand in the way of your desires? Kings shall lay their crowns at your feet; the wealthy shall hasten to throw open their treasure for your acceptance; those who have nothing else shall beg to be allowed to offer their lives. O my king, my god! What you have seen in me I know not, but I have seen the immensity of your grandeur in my heart. Who am I, what am I, in its presence? Ah, the awful power of Devastation! Never shall I truly live till it kills me utterly! I can bear it no longer, my heart is breaking!'

Bimala slid down from her seat and fell at my feet, which she clasped, and then she sobbed and sobbed and sobbed.

This is hypnotism indeed,—the charm which can subdue the world! No materials, no weapons,—but just the delusion of irresistible suggestion. Who says 'Truth shall Triumph'?[3] Delusion shall win in the end. The Bengali understood this when he conceived the image of the ten-handed goddess astride her lion, and spread her worship in the land. Bengal must now create a new image to enchant and conquer the world. *Bande Mataram!*

I gently lifted Bimala back into her chair, and lest reaction should set in, I began again without losing time: 'Queen! The Divine Mother has laid on me the duty of establishing her worship in the land. But, also, I am poor!'

Bimala was still flushed, her eyes clouded, her accents thick, as she replied: 'You poor? Is not all that each one has yours? What are my caskets full of jewellery for? Drag away from me all my gold and gems for your worship. I have no use for them!'

Once before Bimala had offered up her ornaments. I am not usually in the habit of drawing lines, but I felt I had to

---

3. A quotation from the Upanishads.

draw the line there.[4] I know why I feel this hesitation. It is for man to give ornaments to woman; to take them from her wounds his manliness.

But I must forget my self. Am I taking them? They are for the Divine Mother, to be poured in worship at her feet. Oh, but it must be a grand ceremony of worship such as the country has never beheld before. It must be a landmark in our history. It shall be my supreme legacy to the Nation. Ignorant men worship gods. I, Sandip, shall create them.

But all this is a far cry. What about the urgent immediate? At least three thousand is indispensably necessary—five thousand would do roundly and nicely. But how on earth am I to mention money after the high flight we have just taken? And yet time is precious!

I crushed all hesitation under foot as I jumped up and made my plunge: 'Queen! Our purse is empty, our work about to stop!'

Bimala winced. I could see she was thinking of that impossible Rs. 50,000. What a load she must have been carrying within her bosom, struggling under it, perhaps, through sleepless nights! What else had she with which to express her loving worship? Debarred from offering her heart

---

4. There is a world of sentiment attached to the ornaments worn by women in Bengal. They are not merely indicative of the love and regard of the giver, but the wearing of them symbolises all that is held best in wifehood,—that constant solicitude for her husband's welfare, the successful performance of the material and spiritual duties of the household entrusted to her care. When the husband dies, and the responsibility for the household changes hands, then all ornaments are cast aside as a sign of the widow's renunciation of worldly concerns. At any other time the giving up of ornaments is always a sign of supreme distress and as such appeals acutely to the sense of chivalry of any Bengali who may happen to witness it.—Tr.

at my feet, she hankers to make this sum of money, so hopelessly large for her, the bearer of her imprisoned feelings. The thought of what she must have gone through gives me a twinge of pain; for she is now wholly mine. The wrench of plucking up the plant by the roots is over. It is now only careful tending and nurture that is needed.

'Queen!' said I, 'that Rs. 50,000 is not particularly wanted just now. I calculate that, for the present, five thousand or even three will serve.'

The relief made her heart rebound. 'I shall fetch you five thousand,' she said in tones which seemed like an outburst of song,—the song which Radhika of the Vaishnava lyrics sang:

For my lover will I bind in my hair
The flower which has no equal in the three worlds!

—it is the same tune, the same song: five thousand will I bring! That flower will I bind in my hair!

The narrow restraint of the flute brings out this quality of song. I must not allow the pressure of too much greed to flatten out the reed, for then, as I fear, music will give place to the questions 'Why?', 'What is the use of so much?', 'How am I to get it?'—not a word of which will rhyme with what Radhika sang! So, as I was saying, illusion alone is real,—it is the flute itself; while truth is but its empty hollow. Nikhil has of late got a taste of that pure emptiness,—one can see it in his face, which pains even me. But it was Nikhil's boast that he wanted the Truth, while mine was that I would never let go illusion from my grasp. Each has been suited to his taste, so why complain?

To keep Bimala's heart in the rarefied air of idealism, I cut short all further discussion over the five thousand rupees. I reverted to the demon-destroying goddess and her worship. When was the ceremony to be held and where? There is a great annual fair at Ruimari, within Nikhil's estates, where hundreds of thousands of pilgrims assemble. That would be a grand place to inaugurate the worship of our goddess!

Bimala waxed intensely enthusiastic. This was not the burning of foreign cloth or the people's granaries, so even Nikhil could have no objection,—so thought she. But I smiled inwardly. How little these two persons, who have been together, day and night, for nine whole years, know of each other! They know something perhaps of their home life, but when it comes to outside concerns they are entirely at sea. They had cherished the belief that the harmony of the home with the outside was perfect. Today they realise to their cost that it is too late to repair their neglect of years, and seek to harmonise them now.

What does it matter? Let those who have made the mistake learn their error by knocking against the world. Why need I bother about their plight? For the present I find it wearisome to keep Bimala soaring much longer, like a captive balloon, in regions ethereal. I had better get quite through with the matter in hand.

When Bimala rose to depart and had neared the door I remarked in my most casual manner: 'So, about the money...'

Bimala halted and faced back as she said: 'On the expiry of the month, when our personal allowances become due...'

'That, I am afraid, would be much too late.'

'When do you want it then?'

'To-morrow.'

'To-morrow you shall have it.'

Chapter VIII

Nikhil's Story

X

Paragraphs and letters against me have begun to come out in the local papers; cartoons and lampoons are to follow, I am told. Jets of wit and humour are being splashed about, and the lies thus scattered are convulsing the whole country. They know that the monopoly of mud-throwing is theirs, and the innocent passer-by cannot escape unsoiled.

They are saying that the residents in my estates, from the highest to the lowest, are in favour of *Swadeshi*, but they dare not declare themselves, for fear of me. The few who have been brave enough to defy me have felt the full rigour of my persecution. I am in secret league with the police, and in private communication with the magistrate, and these frantic efforts of mine to add a foreign title of my own earning to the one I have inherited, will not, it is opined, go in vain.

On the other hand, the papers are full of praise for those devoted son of the motherland, the Kundu and the Chakravarti *zamindars*. If only, say they, the country had a few more of such staunch patriots, the mills of Manchester would have had to sound their own dirge to the tune of *Bande Mataram*.

Then comes a letter in blood-red ink, giving a list of the traitorous *zamindars* whose treasuries have been burnt down because of their failing to support the Cause. Holy fire, it goes on to say, has been aroused to its sacred function of purifying the country; and other agencies are also at work to see that those who are not true sons of the motherland do cease to encumber her lap. The signature is an obvious *nom-de-plume*.

I could see that this was the dong of our local students. So I sent for some of them and showed them the letter.

The B.A. student gravely informed me that they also had heard that a band of desperate patriots had been formed who would stick at nothing in order to clear away all obstacles to the success of *Swadeshi*.

'If,' said I, 'even one of our countrymen succumbs to these overbearing desperadoes, that will indeed be a defeat for the country!'

'We fail to follow you, Maharaja,' said the history student.

'Our country,' I tried to explain, 'has been brought to death's door through sheer fear,—from fear of the gods down to fear of the police; and if you set up, in the name of freedom, the fear of some other bogey, whatever it may be called; if you would raise your victorious standard on the cowardice of the country by means of downright oppression, then no true lover of the country can bow to your decision.'

'Is there any country, sir,' pursued the history student, 'where submission to Government is not due to fear?'

'The freedom that exists in any country,' I replied, 'may be measured by the extent of this reign of fear. Where its threat is confined to those who would hurt or plunder, there the Government may claim to have freed man from the violence of man. But if fear is to regulate how people are to dress, where they shall trade, or what they must eat, then is man's freedom of will utterly ignored, and manhood destroyed at the root.'

'Is not such coercion of the individual will seen in other countries too?' continued the history student.

'Who denies it?' I exclaimed. 'But in every country man has destroyed himself to the extent that he has permitted slavery to flourish.'

'Does it not rather show,' interposed a Master of Arts, 'that trading in slavery is inherent in man—a fundamental fact of his nature?'

'Sandip Babu made the whole thing clear,' said a graduate. 'He gave us the example of Harish Kundu, your neighbouring *zamindar*. From his estates you cannot ferret out a single ounce of foreign salt. Why? Because he has always ruled with an iron hand. In the case of those who are slaves by nature, the lack of a strong master is the greatest of all calamities.'

'Why, sir!' chimed in an undergraduate, 'have you not heard of the obstreperous tenant of Chakravarti, the other *zamindar* close by,—how the law was set on him till he was reduced to utter destitution? When at last he was left with nothing to eat, he started out to sell his wife's silver ornaments, but no one dared buy them. Then Chakravarti's manager offered him five rupees for the lot. They were worth over thirty, but he had to accept or starve. After taking over the bundle from him the manager coolly said that those five rupees would be credited towards his rent! We felt like having nothing more to do with Chakravarti or his manager after that, but Sandip Baby told us that if we threw over all the live people, we should have only dead bodies from the burning-grounds to carry on the work with! These live men, he pointed out, know what they want and how to get it,—they are born rulers. Those who do not know how to desire for themselves, must live in accordance with, or die by virtue of, the desires of such as these. Sandip Baby contrasted them— Kundu and Chakravarti—with you, Maharaja. You, he said, for all your good intentions, will never succeed in planting *Swadeshi* within your territory.'

'It is my desire,' I said, 'to plant something greater than *Swadeshi*. I am not after dead logs but living trees,—and these will take time to grow.'

'I am afraid, sir,' sneered the history student, 'that you will get neither log nor tree. Sandip Babu rightly teaches that in order to get, you must snatch. This is taking all of us some time to learn, because it runs counter to what we were taught at school. I have seen with my own eyes that when a rent-collector of Harish Kundu's found one of the tenants with nothing which could be sold up to pay his rent, he was made to sell his young wife! Buyers were not wanting, and the *zamindar's* demand was satisfied. I tell you, sir, the sight of that man's distress prevented my getting sleep for nights together! But, feel it as I did, this much I realised, that the man who knows how to get the money he is out for, even by selling up his debtor's wife, is a better man than I am. I confess it is beyond me,—I am a weakling, my eyes fill with tears. If anybody can save our country it is these Kundus and these Chakravartis and their officials!'

I was shocked beyond words. 'If what you say be true,' I cried, 'I clearly see that it must be the one endeavour of my life to save the country from these same Kundus and Chakravartis and officials. The slavery that has entered into our very bones is breaking out, at this opportunity, as ghastly tyranny. You have been so used to submit to domination through fear, you have come to believe that to make others submit is a kind of religion. My fight shall be against this weakness, this atrocious cruelty!'

These things, which are so simple to ordinary folk, get so twisted in the minds of our B.A.'s and M.A.'s, the only purpose of whose historical quibbles seems to be to torture the truth!

XI

I am worried over Panchu's sham aunt. It will be difficult to disprove her, for though witnesses of a real event may be few or even wanting, innumerable proofs of a thing that has not happened can always be marshalled. The object of this move, is evidently, to get the sale of Panchu's holding to me set aside.

Being unable to find any other way out of it, I was thinking of allowing Panchu to hold a permanent tenure in my estates and building him a cottage on it. But my master would not have it. I should not give in to these nefarious tactics so easily, he objected, and offered to attend to the matter himself.

'You, sir!' I cried, considerably surprised.

'Yes, I,' he repeated.

I could not see, at all clearly, what my master could do to counteract these legal machinations. That evening, at the time he usually came to me, he did not turn up. On my making inquiries, his servant said he had left home with a few things packed in a small trunk, and some bedding, saying he would be back in a few days. I thought he might have sallied forth to hunt for witnesses in Panchu's uncle's village. In that case, however, I was sure that his would be a hopeless quest....

During the day I forget myself in my work. As the late autumn afternoon wears on, the colours of the sky become turbid, and so do the feelings of my mind. There are many in this world whose minds dwell in brick-built houses,—they can afford to ignore the thing called the outside. But my mind lives under the trees in the open, directly receives upon itself the messages borne by the free winds, and responds from the bottom of its heart to all the musical cadences of light and darkness.

While the day is bright and the world in the pursuit of its numberless tasks crowds around, then it seems as if my life wants nothing else. But when the colours of the sky fade away and the blinds are drawn down over the windows of heaven, then my heart tells me that evening falls just for the purpose of shutting out the world, to mark the time when the darkness must be filled with the One. This is the end to which earth, sky, and waters conspire, and I cannot harden myself against accepting its meaning. So when the gloaming deepens over the world, like the gaze of the dark eyes of the beloved, then my whole being tells me that work alone cannot be the truth of life, that work is not the be-all and the end-all of man, for man is not simply a serf,—even though the serfdom be of the True and the Good.

Alas, Nikhil, have you for ever parted company with that self of yours who used to be set free under the starlight, to plunge into the infinite depths of the night's darkness after the day's work was done? How terribly alone is he, who misses companionship in the midst of the multitudinousness of life.

The other day, when the afternoon had reached the meeting-point of day and night, I had no work, nor the mind for work, nor was my master there to keep me company. With my empty, drifting heart longing to anchor on to something, I traced my steps towards the inner gardens. I was very fond of chrysanthemums and had rows of them, of all varieties, banked up in pots against one of the garden walls. When they were in flower, it looked like a wave of green breaking into iridescent foam. It was some time since I had been to this part of the grounds, and I was beguiled into a cheerful expectancy at the thought of meeting my chrysanthemums after our long separation.

As I went in, the full moon had just peeped over the wall, her slanting rays leaving its foot in deep shadow. It seemed as if she had come a-tiptoe from behind, and clasped the darkness over the eyes, smiling mischievously. When I came near the bank of chrysanthemums, I saw a figure stretched on the grass in front. My heart gave a sudden thud. The figure also sat up with a start at my footsteps.

What was to be done next? I was wondering whether it would do to beat a precipitate retreat. Bimala, also, was doubtless casting about for some way of escape. But it was as awkward to go as to stay! Before I could make up my mind, Bimala rose, pulled the end of her sari over her head, and walked off towards the inner apartments.

This brief pause had been enough to make real to me the cruel load of Bimala's misery. The plaint of my own life vanished from me in a moment. I called out: 'Bimala!'

She started and stayed her steps, but did not turn back. I went round and stood before her. Her face was in the shade, the moonlight fell on mine. Her eyes were downcast, her hands clenched.

'Bimala,' said I, 'why should I seek to keep you fast in this closed cage of mine? Do I not know that thus you cannot but pine and droop?'

She stood still, without raising her eyes or uttering a word.

'I know,' I continued, 'That if I insist on keeping you shackled my whole life will be reduced to nothing but an iron chain. What pleasure can that be to me?'

She was still silent.

'So,' I concluded, 'I tell you, truly, Bimala, you are free. Whatever I may or may not have been to you, I refuse to be your fetters.' With which I came away towards the outer apartments.

No, no, it was not a generous impulse, nor indifference. I had simply come to understand that never would I be free until I could set free. To try to keep Bimala as a garland round my neck, would have meant keeping a weight hanging over my heart. Have I not been praying with all my strength, that if happiness may not be mine, let it go; if grief needs must be my lot, let it come; but let me not be kept in bondage. To clutch hold of that which is untrue as though it were true, is only to throttle oneself. May I be saved from such self-destruction.

When I entered my room, I found my master waiting there. My agitated feelings were still heaving within me. 'Freedom, sir,' I began unceremoniously, without greeting or inquiry, 'freedom is the biggest thing for man. Nothing can be compared to it—nothing at all'

Surprised at my outburst, my master looked up at me in silence.

'One can understand nothing from books,' I went on. 'We read in the scriptures that our desires are bonds, fettering us as well as others. But such words, by themselves, are so empty. It is only when we get to the point of letting the bird out of its cage that we can realise how free the bird has set us. Whatever we cage, shackles us with desire whose bonds are stronger than those of iron chains. I tell you, sir, this is just what the world has failed to understand. They all seek to reform something outside themselves. But reform is wanted only in one's own desires, nowhere else, nowhere else!'

'We think,' he said, 'that we are our own masters when we get in our hands the object of our desire—but we are really our own masters only when we are able to cast out our desires from our minds.'

'When we put all this into words, sir,' I went on, 'it sounds like some bald-headed injunction, but when we realise even a little of it we find it to be *amrita*,—which the gods have drunk and become immortal. We cannot see Beauty till we let go our hold of it. It was Buddha who conquered the world, not Alexander,—this is untrue when stated in dry prose,— oh when shall we be able to sing it? When shall all these most intimate truths of the universe overflow the pages of printed books and leap out in a sacred steam like the Ganges from the Gangotrie?'

I was suddenly reminded of my master's absence during the last few days and of my ignorance as to its reason. I felt somewhat foolish as I asked him: 'And where have you been all this while, sir?'

'Staying with Panchu,' he replied.

'Indeed!' I exclaimed. 'Have you been there all these days?'

'Yes. I wanted to come to an understanding with the woman who calls herself his aunt. She could hardly be induced to believe that there could be such an odd character among the gentle-folk as the one who sought their hospitality. When she found I really meant to stay on, she began to feel rather ashamed of herself. "Mother," said I, "you are not going to get rid of me, even if you abuse me! And so long as I stay, Panchu stays also. For you see, do you not, that I cannot stand by and see his motherless little ones sent out into the streets?"

'She listened to my talks in this strain for a couple of days without saying yes or no. This morning I found her tying up her bundles. "We are gong back to Brindaban," she said. "Let us have our expenses for the journey." I knew she was not going to Brindaban, and also that the cost of her journey would be substantial. So I have come to you.'

"The required cost shall be paid,' I said.

'The old woman is not a bad sort,' my master went on musingly. 'Panchu was not sure of her caste, and would not let her touch the water-jar, or anything at all of his. So they were continually bickering. When she found I had no objection to her touch, she looked after me devotedly. She is a splendid cook!

'But all remnants of Panchu's respect for me vanished! To the last he had thought that I was at least a simple sort of person. But here was I, risking my caste without a qualm to win over the old woman for my purpose. Had I tried to steal a march on her by tutoring a witness for the trial, that would have been a different matter. Tactics must be met by tactics. But stratagem at the expense of orthodoxy is more than he can tolerate!

'Anyhow, I must stay on a few days at Panchu's even after the woman leaves, for Harish Kundu may be up to any kind of devilry. He has been telling his satellites that he was content to have furnished Panchu with an aunt, but I have gone the length of supplying him with a father. He would like to see, now, how many fathers of his can save him!'

'We may or may not be able to save him,' I said; 'but if we should perish in the attempt to save the country from the thousand-and-one snares—of religion, custom and selfishness— which these people are busy spreading, we shall at least die happy.'

Bimala's Story

XIV

Who could have thought that so much would happen in this one life? I feel as if I have passed through a whole series of births, time has been flying so fast, I did not feel it move at all, till the shock came the other day.

I knew there would be words between us when I made up my mind to ask my husband to banish foreign goods from our market. But it was my firm belief that I had no need to meet argument by argument, for there was magic in the very air about me. Had not so tremendous a man as Sandip fallen helplessly at my feet, like a wave of the mighty sea breaking on the shore? Had I called him? No, it was the summons of that magic spell of mine. And Amulya, poor dear boy, when he first came to me—how the current of his life flushed with colour, like the river at dawn! Truly have I realised how a goddess feels when she looks upon the radiant face of her devotee.

With the confidence begotten of these proofs of my power, I was ready to meet my husband like a lightning-charged cloud. But what was it that happened? Never in all these nine years have I seen such a far-away, distraught look in his eyes,—like the desert sky,—with no merciful moisture of its own, no colour reflected even, from what it looked upon.

I should have been so relieved if his anger had flashed out! But I could find nothing in him which I could touch. I felt as unreal as a dream,—a dream which would leave only the blackness of night when it was over.

In the old days I used to be jealous of my sister-in-law for her beauty. Then I used to feel that Providence had given me no power of my own, that my whole strength lay in the love which my husband had bestowed on me. Now that I had drained to the dregs the cup of power and could not do without its intoxication, I suddenly found it dashed to pieces at my feet, leaving me nothing to live for.

How feverishly I had sat to do my hair that day. Oh, shame, shame on me, the utter shame of it! My sister-in-law, when passing by, had exclaimed: 'Aha, Chota Rani! Your hair seems ready to jump off. Don't let it carry your head with it.'

And then, the other day in the garden, how easy my husband found it to tell me that he set me free! But can freedom—empty freedom—be given and taken so easily as all that? It is like setting a fish free in the sky,—for how can I move or live outside the atmosphere of loving care which has always sustained me?

When I came to my room to-day, I saw only furniture—only the bedstead, only the looking-glass, only the clothes-rack—not the all-pervading heart which used to be there, over all. Instead of it there was freedom, only freedom, mere emptiness! A dried-up watercourse with all its rocks and pebbles laid bare. No feeling, only furniture!

When I had arrived at a state of utter bewilderment, wondering whether anything true was left in my life, and whereabouts it could be, I happened to meet Sandip again. Then life struck against life, and the sparks flew in the same old way. Here was truth—impetuous truth—which rushed in and overflowed all bounds, truth which was a thousand times truer than the Bara Rani with her maid, Thako and her sly songs, and all the rest of them who talked and laughed and wandered about....

'Fifty thousand!' Sandip had demanded.

'What is fifty thousand?' cried my intoxicated heart. 'You shall have it!'

How to get it, where to get it, were minor points not worth troubling over. Look at me. Had I not risen, all in one moment, from my nothingness to a height above everything? So shall all things come at my beck and call. I shall get it, get it, get it,—there cannot be any doubt.

Thus had I come away from Sandip the other day. Then as I looked about me, where was it,—the tree of plenty? Oh, why does this outer world insult the heart so?

And yet get it I must; how, I do not care; for sin there cannot be. Sin taints only the weak; I with my *Shakti* am beyond its reach. Only a commoner can be a thief, the king conquers and takes his rightful spoil.... I must find out where the treasury is; who takes the money in; who guards it.

I spent half the night standing in the outer verandah peering at the row of office buildings. But how to get that Rs. 50,000 out of the clutches of those iron bars? If by some *mantram* I could have made all those guards fall dead in their places, I would not have hesitated,—so pitiless did I feel!

But while a whole gang of robbers seemed dancing a war-dance within the whirling brain of its Rani, the great house of the Rajas slept in peace. The gong of the watch sounded hour after hour, and the sky overhead placidly looked on.

At last I sent for Amulya.

'Money is wanted for the Cause,' I told him. 'Can you not get it out of the treasury?'

'Why not?' said he, with his chest thrown out.

Alas! had I not said 'Why not' to Sandip just in the same way? The poor lad's confidence could rouse no hopes in my mind.

'How will you do it?' I asked.

The wild plans he began to unfold would hardly bear repetition outside the pages of a penny dreadful.

'No, Amulya,' I said severely, 'you must not be childish.'

'Very well, then,' he said, 'let me bribe those watchmen.'

'Where is the money to come from?'

'I can loot the bazar,' he burst out, without blenching.

'Leave all that alone. I have my ornaments, they will serve.'

'But,' said Amulya, 'it strikes me that the cashier cannot be bribed. Never mind, there is another and a simpler way.'

'What is that?'

'Why need you hear it? It is quite simple.'

'Still, I should like to know.'

Amulya fumbled in the pocket of his tunic and pulled out, first a small edition of the Gita, which he placed on the table,—and then a little pistol, which he showed me, but said nothing further.

Horror! It did not take him a moment to make up his mind to kill our good old cashier![1] To look at his frank, open face one would not have thought him capable of hurting a fly, but how different were the words which came from his mouth. It was clear that the cashier's place in the world meant nothing real to him; it was a mere vacancy, lifeless, feelingless, with only stock phrases from the Gita,—*Who kills the body kills naught!*

'Whatever do you mean, Amulya?' I exclaimed at length. 'Don't you know that the dear old man has got a wife and children and that his is...'

---

1. The cashier is the official who is most in touch with the ladies of a *zamindar's* household, directly taking their requisitions for household stores and doing their shopping for them, and so he becomes more a member of the family than the others.—*Tr.*

'Where are we to find men who have no wives and children?' he interrupted. 'Look here, Maharani, the thing we call pity is, at bottom, only pity for ourselves. We cannot bear to wound our own tender instincts, and so we do not strike at all;—pity indeed! The height of cowardice!'

To hear Sandip's phrases in the mouth of this mere boy staggered me. So delightfully, lovably immature was he,—of that age when the good may still be believed in as good, of that age when one really lives and grows. The Mother in me awoke.

For myself there was no longer good or bad,—only death, beautiful alluring death. But to hear this stripling calmly talk of murdering an inoffensive old man as the right thing to do, made me shudder all over. The more clearly I saw that there was no sin in this heart, the more horrible appeared to me the sin of his words. I seemed to see the sin of the parents visited on the innocent child.

The sight of his great big eyes shining with faith and enthusiasm touched me to the quick. He was going, in his fascination, straight to the jaws of the python, from which, once inside, there was no return. How was he to be saved? Why does not my country become, for once, a real Mother,—clasp him to her bosom and cry out: 'Oh, my child, my child, what profits it that you should save me, if so it be that I should fail to save you?'

I know, I know, that all Power on earth waxes great under compact with Satan. But the Mother is there, alone though she be, to condemn and stand against this devil's progress. The Mother cares not for mere success, however great,—she wants to give life, to save life. My very soul, to-day, stretches out its hands in yearning to save this child.

A while ago I suggested robbery to him. Whatever I may now say against it will be put down to a woman's weakness.

They only love our weakness when it drags the world in its toils!

'You need do nothing at all, Amulya, I will see to the money,' I told him finally.

When he had almost reached the door, I called him back. 'Amulya,' said I, 'I am your elder sister. To-day is not the Brothers' Day[2] according to the calendar, but all the days in the year are really Brothers' Days. My blessing be with you: may God keep you always.'

These unexpected words form my lips took Amulya by surprise. He stood stock-still for a time. Then, coming to himself, he prostrated himself at my feet in acceptance of the relationship and did me reverence. When he rose his eyes were full of tears.... O little brother mine! I am fast going to my death,—let me take all your sin away with me. May no taint from me ever tarnish your innocence!

I said to him: 'Let your offering of reverence be that pistol!'

'What do you want with it, sister?'

'I will practise death.'

'Right, sister. Our women, also, must know how to die, to deal death!' with which Amulya handed me the pistol.

---

2. The daughter of the house occupies a place of specially tender affection in a Bengali household (perhaps in Hindu households all over India) because, by dictate of custom, she must be given away in marriage so early. She thus takes corresponding memories with her to her husband's home, where she has to begin as a stranger before she can get into her place. The resulting feeling, of the mistress of her new home for the one she has left, has taken ceremonial form as the Brothers' Day, on which the brothers are invited to the married sisters' houses. Where the sister is the elder, she offers her blessing and receives the brother's reverence, and *vice versa*. Presents, called the offerings of reverence (or blessing), are exchanged.—*Tr.*

The radiance of his youthful countenance seemed to tinge my life with the touch of a new dawn. I put away the pistol within my clothes. May this reverence-offering be the last resource in my extremity....

The door to the mother's chamber in my woman's heart once opened, I thought it would always remain open. But this pathway to the supreme good was closed when the mistress took the place of the mother and locked it again. The very next day I saw Sandip; and madness, naked and rampant, danced upon my heart.

What was this? Was this, then, my truer self? Never! I had never before known this shameless, this cruel one within me. The snake-charmer had come, pretending to draw this snake from within the fold of my garment,—but it was never there, it was his all the time. Some demon has gained possession of me, and what I am doing to-day is the play of his activity— it has nothing to do with me.

This demon, in the guise of a god, had come with his ruddy torch to call me that day, saying: 'I am your Country. I am your Sandip. I am more to you than anything else of yours. *Bande Mataram!*' And with folded hands I had responded: 'You are my religion. You are my heaven. Whatever else is mine shall be swept away before my love for you. *Bande Mataram!*'

Five thousand is it? Five thousand it shall be! You want it to-morrow? To-morrow you shall have it! In this desperate orgy, that gift of five thousand shall be as the foam of wine,— and then for the riotous revel! The immovable world shall sway under our feet, fire shall flash from our eyes, a storm shall roar in our ears, what is or is not in front shall become equally dim. And then with tottering footsteps we shall plunge to our death,—in a moment all fire will be extinguished, the ashes will be scattered, and nothing will remain behind.

Chapter IX

Bimala's Story

XV

For a time I was utterly at a loss to think of any way of getting that money. Then, the other day, in the light of intense excitement, suddenly the whole picture stood out clear before me.

Every year my husband makes a reverence-offering of six thousand rupees to my sister-in-law at the time of the Durga Puja. Every year it is deposited in her account at the bank in Calcutta. This year the offering was made as usual, but it has not yet been sent to the bank, being kept meanwhile in an iron safe, in a corner of the little dressing-room attached to our bedroom.

Every year my husband takes the money to the bank himself. This year he has not yet had an opportunity of going to town. How could I fail to see the hand of Providence in this? The money has been held up because the country wants it,—who could have the power to take it away from her to the bank? And how can I have the power to refuse to take the money? The goddess revelling in destruction holds out her blood-cup crying: 'Give me drink. I am thirsty.' I will give her my own heart's blood with that five thousand rupees.

Mother, the loser of that money will scarcely feel the loss, but me you will utterly ruin!

Many a time, in the old days, have I inwardly called the Senior Rani a thief, for I charged her with wheedling money out of my trusting husband. After her husband's death, she often used to make away with things belonging to the estate for her own use. This I used to point out to my husband, but he remained silent. I would get angry and say: 'If you feel generous, make gifts by all means, but why allow yourself to be robbed?' Providence must have smiled, then, at these complaints of mine, for to-night I am on the way to rob my husband's safe of my sister-in-law's money.

My husband's custom was to let his keys remain in his pockets when he took off his clothes for the night, leaving them in the dressing-room. I picked out the key of the safe and opened it. The slight sound it made seemed to wake the whole world! A sudden chill turned my hands and feet icy cold, and I shivered all over.

There was a drawer inside the safe. On opening this I found the money, not in currency notes, but in gold rolled up in paper. I had no time to count out what I wanted. There were twenty rolls, all of which I took and tied up in a corner of my *sari*.

What a weight it was. The burden of the theft crushed my heart to the dust. Perhaps notes would have made it seem less like thieving, but this was all gold.

After I had stolen into my room like a thief, it felt like my own room no longer. All the most precious rights which I had over it vanished at the touch of my theft. I began to mutter to myself, as though telling *mantras: Bande Mataram, Bande Mataram,* my Country, my golden Country, all this gold is for you, for none else!

But in the night the mind is weak. I came back into the bedroom where my husband was asleep, closing my eyes as

I passed through, and went off to the open terrace beyond, on which I lay prone, clasping to my breast the end of the *sari* tied over the gold. And each one of the rolls gave me a shock of pain.

The silent night stood there with forefinger upraised. I could not think of my house as separate from my country: I had robbed my house, I had robbed my country. For this sin my house had ceased to be mine, my country also was estranged from me. Had I died begging for my country, even unsuccessfully, that would have been worship, acceptable to the gods. But theft is never worship,—how then can I offer this gold? Ah me! I am doomed to death myself, must I desecrate my country with my impious touch?

The way to put the money back is closed to me. I have not the strength to return to the room, take again that key, open once more that safe,—I should swoon on the threshold of my husband's door. The only road left now is the road in front. Neither have I the strength deliberately to sit down and count the coins. Let them remain behind their coverings: I cannot calculate.

There was no mist in the winter sky. The stars were shining brightly. If, thought I to myself, as I lay out there, I had to steal these stars one by one, like golden coins, for my country,—these stars so carefully stored up in the bosom of the darkness,—then the sky would be blinded, the night widowed for ever, and my theft would rob the whole world. But was not also this very thing I had done a robbing of the whole world,—not only of money, but of trust, of righteousness?

I spent the night lying on the terrace. When at last it was morning, and I was sure that my husband had risen and left the room, then only with my shawl pulled over my head, could I retrace my steps towards the bedroom.

My sister-in-law was about, with her brass pot, watering her plants. When she saw me passing in the distance she cried: 'Have you heard the news, Chota Rani?'

I stopped in silence, all in a tremor. It seemed to me that the rolls of sovereigns were bulging through the shawl. I feared they would burst and scatter in a ringing shower, exposing to all the servants of the house the thief who had made herself destitute by robbing her own wealth.

'Your band of robbers,' she went on, 'have sent an anonymous message threatening to loot the treasury.'

I remained as silent as a thief.

'I was advising Brother Nikhil to seek your protection,' she continued banteringly. 'Call off your minions, Robber Queen! We will offer sacrifices to your *Bande Mataram* if you will but save us. What doings there are these days!—but for the Lord's sake, spare our house at least from burglary.'

I hastened into my room without reply. I had put my foot on quicksand, and could not now withdraw it. Struggling would only send me down deeper.

If only the time would arrive when I could hand over the money to Sandip! I could bear it no longer, its weight was breaking through my very ribs.

It was still early when I got word that Sandip was awaiting me. To-day I had no thought of adornment. Wrapped as I was in my shawl, I went off to the outer apartments.

As I entered the sitting-room I saw Sandip and Amulya there, together. All my dignity, all my honour, seemed to run tingling through my body from head to foot and vanish into the ground. I should have to lay bare a woman's uttermost shame in sight of this boy! Could they have been discussing my deed in their meeting place? Had any vestige of a veil of decency been left for me?

We women shall never understand men. When they are bent on making a road for some achievement, they think nothing of breaking the heart of the world into pieces to pave it for the progress of their chariot. When they are mad with the intoxication of creating, they rejoice in destroying the creation of the Creator. This heart-breaking shame of mine will not attract even a glance from their eyes. They have no feeling for life itself,—all their eagerness is for their object. What am I to them but a meadow flower in the path of a torrent in flood?

What good will this extinction of me be to Sandip? Only five thousand rupees? Was not I good for something more than only five thousand rupees? Yes, indeed! Did I not learn that from Sandip himself, and was I not able in the light of this knowledge to despise all else in my world? I was the giver of light, of life, of *Shakti*, of immortality,—in that belief, in that joy, I had burst all my bounds and come into the open. Had any one then fulfilled for me that joy, I should have lived in my death. I should have lost nothing in the loss of my all.

Do they want to tell me now that all this was false? The psalm of my praise which was sung so devotedly, did it bring me down from my heaven, not to make heaven of earth, but only to level heaven itself with the dust?

XVI

'The money, Queen?' said Sandip with his keen glance full on my face.

Amulya also fixed his gaze on me. Though not my own mother's child, yet the dear lad is brother to me; for mother is mother all the world over. With his guileless face, his gentle eyes, his innocent youth, he looked at me. And I, a woman,—of his mother's sex—how could I hand him poison, just because he asked for it?

'The money, Queen!' Sandip's insolent demand rang in my ears. For very shame and vexation I felt I wanted to fling that gold at Sandip's head. I could hardly undo the knot of my *sari*, my fingers trembled so. At last the paper rolls dropped on the table.

Sandip's face grew black.... He must have thought that the rolls were of silver.... What contempt was in his looks. What utter disgust at incapacity. It was almost as if he could have struck me! He must have suspected that I had come to parley with him, to offer to compound his claim for five thousand rupees with a few hundreds. There was a moment when I thought he would snatch up the rolls and throw them out of the window, declaring that he was no beggar, but a king claiming tribute.

'Is that all?' asked Amulya with such pity welling up in his voice that I wanted to sob out aloud. I kept my heart tightly pressed down, and merely nodded my head.

Sandip was speechless. He neither touched the rolls, nor uttered a sound.

My humiliation went straight to the boy's heart. With a sudden, feigned enthusiasm he exclaimed: 'It's plenty. It will do splendidly. You have saved us.' With which he tore open the covering of one of the rolls.

The sovereigns shone out. And in a moment the black covering seemed to be lifted from Sandip's countenance also. His delight beamed forth from his features. Unable to control his sudden revulsion of feeling, he sprang up from his seat towards me. What he intended I know not. I flashed a lightning glance towards Amulya,—the colour had left the boy's face as at the stroke of whip. Then with all my strength I thrust Sandip from me. As he reeled back his head struck the edge of the marble table and he dropped on the floor. There he lay awhile, motionless. Exhausted with my effort, I sank back on my seat.

Amulya's face lightened with a joyful radiance. He did not even turn towards Sandip, but came straight up, took the dust to my feet, and then remained there, sitting on the floor in front of me. O my little brother, my child! This reverence of yours is the last touch of heaven left in my empty world! I could contain myself no longer, and my tears flowed fast. I covered my eyes with the end of my *sari*, which I pressed to my face with both my hands, and sobbed and sobbed. And every time that I felt on my feet his tender touch trying to comfort me my tears broke out afresh.

After a little, when I had recovered myself and taken my hands from my face, I saw Sandip back at the table, gathering up the sovereigns in his handkerchief, as if nothing had happened. Amulya rose to his seat, from his place near my feet, his wet eyes shining.

Sandip coolly looked up at my face as he remarked: 'It is six thousand.'

'What do we want with so much, Sandip Babu?' cried Amulya. 'Three thousand five hundred is all we need for our work.'

'Our wants are not for this one place only,' Sandip replied. 'We shall want all we can get.'

'That may be,' said Amulya. 'But in future I undertake to get you all you want. Out of this, Sandip Babu, please return the extra two thousand five hundred to the Maharani.'

Sandip glanced enquiringly at me.

'No, no,' I exclaimed. 'I shall never touch that money again. Do with it as you will.'

'Can man ever give as woman can?' said Sandip, looking towards Amulya.

'They are goddesses!' agreed Amulya with enthusiasm.

'We men can at best give of our power,' continued Sandip. 'But women give themselves. Out of their own life they give birth, out of their own life they give sustenance. Such gifts are the only true gifts.' Then turning to me, 'Queen!' said he 'if what you have given us had been only money I would not have touched it. But you have given that which is more to you than life itself!'

There must be two different persons inside men. One of these in me can understand that Sandip is trying to delude me; the other is content to be deluded. Sandip has power, but no strength of righteousness. The weapon of his which rouses up life smites it again to death. He has the unfailing quiver of the gods, but the shafts in them are of the demons.

Sandip's handkerchief was not large enough to hold all the coins, 'Queen,' he asked, 'can you give me another?'

When I gave him mine, he reverently touched his forehead with it, and then suddenly kneeling on the floor he made me an obeisance. 'Goddess!' he said, 'it was to offer my reverence that I had approached you, but you repulsed me, and rolled me in the dust. Be it so, I accept your repulse as your boon to me, I raise it to my head in salutation!' with which he pointed to the place where he had been hurt.

Had I then misunderstood him? Could it be that his outstretched hands had really been directed towards my feet? Yet, surely, even Amulya had seen the passion that flamed out of his eyes, his face. But Sandip is such an adept in setting music to his chant of praise that I cannot argue; I lose my power of seeing truth; my sight is clouded over like an opium-eater's eyes. And so, after all, he gave me back twice as much in return for the blow I had dealt him,—the wound on his head ended by making me bleed at heart. When I had received Sandip's obeisance my theft seemed to gain a dignity, and the gold glittering on the table to smile away all fear of disgrace, all stings of conscience.

Like me Amulya also was won back. His devotion to Sandip, which had suffered a momentary check, blazed up anew. The flower-vase of his mind filled once more with offerings for the worship of Sandip and me. His simple faith shone out of his eyes with the pure light of the morning star at dawn.

After I had offered worship and received worship my sin became radiant. And as Amulya looked on my face he raised his folded hands in salutation and cried *Bande Mataram!* I cannot expect to have this adoration surrounding me for ever; and yet this has come to be the only means of keeping alive my self-respect.

I can no longer enter my bedroom. The bedstead seems to thrust out a forbidding hand, the iron safe frowns at me. I want to get away from this continual insult to myself which is rankling within me. I want to keep running to Sandip to hear him sing my praises. There is just this one little altar of worship which has kept its head above the all-pervading depths of my dishonour, and so I want to cleave to it night and day; for on whichever side I step away from it, there is only emptiness.

Praise, praise, I want unceasing praise. I cannot live if my wine-cup be left empty for a single moment. So, as the very price of my life, I want Sandip of all the world, to-day.

XVII

When my husband nowadays comes in for his meals I feel I cannot sit before him; and yet it is such a shame not to be near him that I feel I cannot do that either. So I seat myself where we cannot look at each other's face. That was how I was sitting the other day when the Bara Rani came and joined us.

'It is all very well for you, brother,' said she, 'to laugh away these threatening letters. But they do frighten me so. Have you sent off that money you gave me to the Calcutta bank?'

'No, I have not yet had the time to get it away,' my husband replied.

'You are so careless, brother dear, you had better look out....'

'But it is in the iron safe right inside the inner dressing-room,' said my husband with a reassuring smile.

'What if they get in there? You can never tell!'

'If they go so far, they might as well carry you off too!'

'Don't you fear, no one will come for poor me. The real attraction is in your room! But joking apart, don't run the risk of keeping money in the room like that.'

'They will be taking along the Government revenue to Calcutta in a few days now; I will send this money to the bank under the same escort.'

'Very well. But see you don't forget all about it, you are so absent-minded.'

'Even if that money gets lost, while in my room, the loss cannot be yours, Sister Rani.'

'Now, now, brother, you will make me very angry if you talk in that way. Was I making any difference between yours and mine. What if your money is lost, does not that hurt me? If Providence has thought fit to take away my all, it has not left me insensible to the value of the most devoted brother known since the days of Lakshman.[1]

'Well, Junior Rani, are you turned into a wooden doll? You have not spoken a word yet. Do you know, brother, our Junior Rani thinks I try to flatter you. If things came to that pass I should not hesitate to do so, but I know my dear old brother does not need it!'

Thus the Senior Rani chattered on, not forgetting now and then to draw her brother's attention to this or that special delicacy amongst the dishes that were being served. My head was all the time in a whirl. The crisis was fast coming. Something must be done about replacing that money. And as I kept asking myself what could be done, and how it was to be done, the unceasing patter of my sister-in-law's words seemed more and more intolerable.

1. Of the *Ramayana*. The story of his devotion to his elder brother Rama and his brother's wife Sita, has become a by word.

What made it all the worse was, that nothing could escape my sister-in-law's keen eyes. Every now and then she was casting side glances towards me. What she could read in my face I do not know, but to me it seemed that everything was written there only too plainly.

Then I did an infinitely rash thing. Affecting an easy, amused laugh I said: 'All the Senior Rani's suspicions, I see, are reserved for me,—her fears of thieves and robbers are only a feint.'

The Senior Rani smiled mischievously. 'You are right, sister mine. A woman's theft is the most fatal of all thefts. But how can you elude my watchfulness? Am I a man, that you should hoodwink me?'

'If you fear me so,' I retorted, 'let me keep in your hands all I have, as security. If I cause you loss, you can then repay yourself.'

'Just listen to her, our simple little Junior Rani!' she laughed back, turning to my husband. 'Does she not know that there are losses which no security can make good, either in this world or in the next?'

My husband did not join in our exchange of words. When he had finished, he went off to the outer apartments, for nowadays he does not take his mid-day rest in our room.

All my more valuable jewels were in deposit in the treasury in charge of the cashier. Still what I kept with me must have been worth thirty or forty thousand. I took my jewel-box to the Bara Rani's room and opened it out before her, saying: 'I leave these with you, sister. They will keep you quite safe from all worry.'

The Bara Rani made a gesture of mock despair. 'You positively astound me, Chota Rani!' she said. 'Do you really suppose I spend sleepless nights for fear of being robbed by you?'

'What harm if you did have a wholesome fear of me? Does anybody know anybody else in this world?'

'You want to teach me a lesson by trusting me? No, no! I am bothered enough to know what to do with my own jewels, without keeping watch over yours. Take them away, there's a dear, so many prying servants are about.'

I went straight from my sister-in-law's room to the sitting-room outside, and sent for Amulya. With him Sandip came along too. I was in a great hurry, and said to Sandip: 'If you don't mind, I want to have a word or two with Amulya. Would you ...'

Sandip smiled a wry smile. 'So Amulya and I are separate in your eyes? If you have set about to wean him from me, I must confess I have no power to retain him.'

I made no reply, but stood waiting. 'Be it so,' Sandip went on. 'Finish your special talk with Amulya. But then you must give me a special talk all to myself too, or it will mean a defeat for me. I can stand everything, but not defeat. My share must always be the lion's share. This has been my constant quarrel with Providence. I will defeat the Dispenser of my fate, but not take defeat at his hands.' With a crushing look at Amulya, Sandip walked out of the room.

'Amulya, my own little brother, you must do one thing for me,' I said.

'I will stake my life for whatever duty you may lay on me, sister.'

I brought out my jewel-box from the folds of my shawl and placed it before him. 'Sell or pawn these,' I said, 'and get me six thousand rupees as fast as ever you can.'

'No, no Sister Rani,' said Amulya, touched to the quick. 'Let these jewels, be. I will get you six thousand all the same.'

'Oh, don't be silly,' I said impatiently. 'There is no time for any nonsense. Take this box. Get away to Calcutta by the night train. And bring me the money by the day after to-morrow positively.'

Amulya took a diamond necklace out of the box, held it up to the light and put it back gloomily.

'I know,' I told him, 'that you will never get the proper price for these diamonds, so I am giving you jewels worth about thirty thousand. I don't care if they all go, but I must have that six thousand without fail.'

'Do you know, Sister Rani,' said Amulya, 'I have had a quarrel with Sandip Babu over that Rs. 6000 he took from you? I cannot tell you how ashamed I felt. But Sandip Babu would have it that we must give up even our shame for the country. That may be so. But this is somehow different. I do not fear to die for the country, to kill for the country,—that much *Shakti* has been given me. But I cannot forget the shame of having taken money from you. There Sandip Babu is ahead of me. He has no regrets or compunctions. He says we must get rid of the idea that the money belongs to the one in whose box it happens to be,—if we cannot, where is the magic of *Bande Mataram?*'

Amulya gathered enthusiasm as he talked on. He always warms up when he has me for a listener. 'The Gita tells us,' he continued, 'that no one can kill the soul. Killing is a mere word. So also is the taking away of money. Whose is the money? No one has created it. No one can take it away with him when he departs this life, for it is no part of his soul. To-day it is mine, to-morrow my son's, the next day his creditor's. Since, in fact, money belongs to no one, why should any blame attach to our patriots if, instead of leaving it for some worthless son, they take it for their own use?'

When I hear Sandip's words uttered by this boy, I tremble all over. Let those who are snake-charmers play with snakes; if harm comes to them, they are prepared for it. But these boys are so innocent, all the world is ready with its blessing to protect them. They play with a snake not knowing its nature, and when we see them smilingly, trustfully, putting their hands within reach of its fangs, then we understand how terribly dangerous the snake is. Sandip is right when he suspects that though I, for myself, may be ready to die at his hands, this boy I shall wean from him and save.

'So the money is wanted for the use of your patriots?' I questioned with a smile.

'Of course it is!' said Amulya proudly. 'Are they not our kings? Poverty takes away from them their regal power. Do you know, we always insist on Sandip Babu travelling First Class? He never shirks kingly honours,—he accepts them not for himself, but for the glory of us all. The greatest weapon of those who rule the world, Sandip Babu has told us, is the hypnotism of their display. To take the vow of poverty would be for them not merely a penance,—it would mean suicide.'

At this point Sandip noiselessly entered the room. I threw my shawl over the jewel-case with a rapid movement.

'The special-talk business not yet over?' he asked with a sneer in his tone.

'Yes, we've quite finished,' said Amulya apologetically. 'It was nothing much.'

'No, Amulya,' I said, 'we have not quite finished.'

'So exit Sandip, for the second time, I suppose?' said Sandip.

'If you please.'

'And as to Sandip's re-entry...'

'Not to-day. I have no time.'

'I see!' said Sandip as his eyes flashed. 'No time to waste, only for special talks!'

Jealousy! Where the strong man shows weakness, there the weaker sex cannot help beating her drums of victory. So I repeated firmly: 'I really have no time.'

Sandip went away looking black. Amulya was greatly perturbed. 'Sister Rani,' he pleaded, 'Sandip Babu is annoyed.'

'He has neither cause nor right to be annoyed,' I said with some vehemence. 'Let me caution you about one thing, Amulya. Say nothing to Sandip Babu about the sale of my jewels,— on your life.'

'No, I will not.'

'Then you had better not delay any more. You must get away by to-night's train.'

Amulya and I left the room together. As we came out on the verandah Sandip was standing there. I could see he was waiting to waylay Amulya. To prevent that I had to engage him. 'What is it you wanted to tell me, Sandip Babu?' I asked.

'I have nothing special to say—mere small talk. And since you have not the time...'

'I can give you just a little.'

By this time Amulya had left. As we entered the room Sandip asked: 'What was that box Amulya carried away?'

The box had not escaped his eyes. I remained firm. 'If I could have told you, it would have been made over to him in your presence!'

'So you think Amulya will not tell me?'

'No, he will not.'

Sandip could not conceal his anger any longer. 'You think you will gain the mastery over me?' he blazed out. 'That shall never be. Amulya, there, would die a happy death if I deigned to trample him under foot. I will never, so long as I live, allow you to bring him to your feet!'

Oh, the weak! the weak! At last Sandip has realised that he is weak before me! That is why there is this sudden outburst of anger. He has understood that he cannot meet the power that I wield, with mere strength. With a glance I can crumble his strongest fortifications. So he must needs resort to bluster. I simply smiled in contemptuous silence. At last have I come to a level above him. I must never lose this vantage ground; never descend lower again. Amidst all my degradation this bit of dignity must remain to me!

'I know,' said Sandip, after a pause, 'it was your jewel-case.'

'You may guess as you please,' said I, 'but you will get nothing out of me.'

'So you trust Amulya more than you trust me? Do you know that the boy is the shadow of my shadow, the echo of my echo,—that he is nothing if I am not at his side?'

'Where he is not your echo, he is himself, Amulya. And that is where I trust him more than I can trust your echo!'

'You must not forget that you are under a promise to render up all your ornaments to me for the worship of the Divine Mother. In fact your offering has already been made.'

'Whatever ornaments the gods leave to me will be offered up to the gods. But how can I offer those which have been stolen away from me?'

'Look here, it is no use your trying to give me the slip in that fashion. Now is the time for grim work. Let that work be finished, then you can make a display of your woman's wiles to your heart's content,—and I will help you in your game.'

The moment I had stolen my husband's money and paid it to Sandip, the music that was in our relations stopped. Not only did I destroy all my own value by making myself cheap, but Sandip's powers, too, lost scope for their full play. You cannot employ your marksmanship against a thing which is right in your grasp. So Sandip has lost his aspect of the hero; a tone of low quarrelsomeness has come into his words.

Sandip kept his brilliant eyes fixed full on my face till they seemed to blaze with all the thirst of the mid-day sky. Once or twice he fidgeted with his feet, as though to leave his seat, as if to spring right on me. My whole body seemed to swim, my veins throbbed, the hot blood surged up to my ears; I felt

RABINDRANATH TAGORE OMNIBUS III

that if I remained there, I should never get up at all. With a supreme effort I tore myself off the chair, and hastened towards the door.

From Sandip's dry throat there came a muffled cry: 'Whither would you flee, Queen?' The next moment he left his seat with a bound to seize hold of me. At the sound of footsteps outside the door, however, he rapidly retreated and fell back into his chair. I checked my steps near the bookshelf, where I stood staring at the names of the books.

As my husband entered the room, Sandip exclaimed: 'I say, Nikhil, don't you keep Browning among your books here? I was just telling Queen Bee of our college club. Do you remember that contest of ours over the translation of those lines from Browning? You don't?

> She should never have looked at me,
> If she meant I should not love her,
> There are plenty ... men you call such,
> I suppose ... she may discover
> All her soul to, if she pleases,
> And yet leave much as she found them:
> But I'm not so, and she knew it
> When she fixed me, glancing round them.

'I managed to get together the words to render it into Bengali, somehow, but the result was hardly likely to be a "joy forever" to the people of Bengal. I really did think at one time that I was on the verge of becoming a poet, but Providence was kind enough to save me from that disaster. Do you remember old Dakshina? If he had not become a Salt Inspector, he would have been a poet. I remember his rendering to this day....

'No, Queen Bee, it is no use rummaging those bookshelves. Nikhil has ceased to read poetry since his marriage,—perhaps he has no further need for it. But I suppose "the fever fit of poesy," as the Sanskrit has it, is about to attack me again.'

'I have come to give you a warning, Sandip,' said my husband.

'About the fever fit of poesy?'

My husband took no notice of this attempt at humour. 'For some time,' he continued, 'Mahomedan preachers have been about stirring up the local Mussulmans. They are all wild with you, and may attack you any moment.'

'Are you come to advise flight?'

'I have come to give you information, not to offer advice.'

'Had these estates been mine, such a warning would have been necessary for the preachers, not for me. If, instead of trying to frighten me, you give them a taste of your intimidation, that would be worthier both of you and me. Do you know that your weakness is weakening your neighbouring *zamindars* also?'

'I did not offer you my advice, Sandip. I wish you, too, would refrain from giving me yours. Besides, it is useless. And there is another thing I want to tell you. You and your followers have been secretly worrying and oppressing my tenantry. I cannot allow that any longer. So I must ask you to leave my territory.'

'For fear of the Mussulmans, or is there any other fear you have to threaten me with?'

'There are fears the want of which is cowardice. In the name of those fears, I tell you Sandip, you must go. In five days I shall be starting for Calcutta. I want you to accompany me. You may of course stay in my house there,—to that there is no objection.'

'All right, I have still five days' time then. Meanwhile, Queen Bee, let me hum to you my song of parting from your honey-hive. Ah! you poet of modern Bengal! Throw open your doors and let me plunder your words. The theft is really yours, for it is my song which you have made your own—let the name be yours by all means, but the song is mine.' With this Sandip struck up in a deep, husky voice, which threatened to be out of tune, a song in the *Bhairavi* mode:

> In the springtime of your kingdom, my Queen,
> Meeting and partings chase each other in their endless hide and seek,
> And flowers blossom in the wake of those that droop and die in the shade.
> In the springtime of your kingdom, my Queen,
> My meeting with you had its own songs,
> But has not also my leave-taking any gift to offer you?
> That gift is my secret hope, which I keep hidden in the shadows of your flower garden,
> That the rains of July may sweetly temper your fiery June.

His boldness was immense,—boldness which had no veil, but was naked as fire. One finds no time to stop it: it is like trying to resist a thunderbolt: the lightning flashes: it laughs at all resistance.

I left the room. As I was passing along the verandah towards the inner apartments, Amulya suddenly made his appearance and came and stood before me.

'Fear nothing, Sister Rani,' he said. 'I am off to-night and shall not return unsuccessful.'

'Amulya,' said I, looking straight into this earnest, youthful face, 'I fear nothing for myself, but may I never cease to fear for you.'

Amulya turned to go, but before he was out of sight I called him back and asked: 'Have you a mother, Amulya?'

'I have.'

'A sister?'

'No, I am the only child of my mother. My father died when I was quite little.'

'Then go back to your mother, Amulya.'

'But, Sister Rani, I have now both mother and sister.'

'Then, Amulya, before you leave to-night, come and have your dinner here.'

'There won't be time for that. Let me take some food for the journey, consecrated with your touch.'

'What do you specially like, Amulya?'

'If I had been with my mother I should have had lots of *Poush* cakes. Make some for me with your own hands, Sister Rani!'

Chapter X

Nikhil's Story

XII

I learnt from my master that Sandip had joined forces with Harish Kundu, and there was to be a grand celebration of the worship of the demon-destroying Goddess. Harish Kundu was extorting the expenses from his tenantry. Pandits Kaviratna and Vidyavagish had been commissioned to compose a hymn with a double meaning.

My master has just had a passage at arms with Sandip over this. 'Evolution is at work amongst the gods as well,' says Sandip. 'The grandson has to remodel the gods created by the grandfather to suit his own taste, or else he is left an atheist. It is my mission to modernise the ancient deities. I am born the saviour of the gods, to emancipate them from the thraldom of the past.'

I have seen from our boyhood what a juggler with ideas is Sandip. He has no interest in discovering truth, but to make a quizzical display of it rejoices his heart. Had he been born in the wilds of Africa he would have spent a glorious time inventing argument after argument to prove that cannibalism is the best means of promoting true communion between man and man. But those who deal in delusion end by deluding themselves, and I fully believe that, each time Sandip creates a new fallacy, he persuades himself that he has found the truth, however contradictory his creations may be to one another.

However, I shall not give a helping hand to establish a liquor distillery in my country. The young men, who are ready to offer their services for their country's cause, must not fall into this habit of getting intoxicated. The people who want to exact work by drugging methods set more value on the excitement than on the minds they intoxicate.

I had to tell Sandip, in Bimala's presence, that he must go. Perhaps both will impute to me the wrong motive. But I must free myself also from all fear of being misunderstood. Let even Bimala misunderstand me....

A number of Mahomedan preachers are being sent over from Dacca. The Mussulmans in my territory had come to have almost as much of an aversion to the killing of cows as the Hindus. But now cases of cow-killing are cropping up here and there. I had the news first from some of my Mussulman tenants with expressions of their disapproval. Here was a situation which I could see would be difficult to meet. At the bottom was a pretence of fanaticism, which would cease to be a pretence if obstructed. That is just where the ingenuity of the move came in!

I sent for some of my principal Hindu tenants and tried to get them to see the matter in its proper light. 'We can be staunch in our own convictions,' I said, 'but we have no control over those of others. For all that many of us are Vaishnavas, those of us who are Shaktas go on with their animal sacrifices just the same. That cannot be helped. We must, in the same way, let the Mussulmans do as they think best. So please refrain from all disturbance.'

'Maharaja,' they replied, 'these outrages have been unknown for so long.'

'That was so,' I said, 'because such was their spontaneous desire. Let us behave in such a way that the same may become true, over again. But a breach of the peace is not the way to bring this about.'

'No, Maharaja,' they insisted, 'those good old days are gone. This will never stop unless you put it down with a strong hand.'

'Oppression,' I replied, 'will not only not prevent cow-killing, it may lead to the killing of men as well.'

One of them had had an English education. He had learnt to repeat the phrases of the day. 'It is not only a question of orthodoxy,' he argued. 'Our country is mainly agricultural, and cows are...'

'Buffaloes in this country,' I interrupted, 'Likewise give milk and are used for ploughing. And therefore, so long as we dance frantic dances on our temple pavements, smeared with their blood, their severed heads carried on our shoulders, religion will only laugh at us if we quarrel with Mussulmans in her name, and nothing but the quarrel itself will remain true. If the cow alone is to be held sacred from slaughter, and not the buffalo, then that is bigotry, not religion.'

'But are you not aware, sir, of what is behind all this?' pursued the English-knowing tenant. 'This has only become possible because the Mussulman is assured of safety, even if he breaks the law. Have you not heard of the Pachur case?'

'Why is it possible,' I asked, 'to use the Mussulmans thus, as tools against us? Is it not because we have fashioned them into such with our own intolerance? That is how Providence punishes us. Our accumulated sins are being visited on our own heads.'

'Oh, well, if that be so, let them be visited on us. But we shall have our revenge. We have undermined what was the greatest strength of the authorities, their devotion to their own laws. Once they were truly kings, dispensing justice; now they themselves will become law-breakers, and so no better than robbers. This may not go down to history, but we shall carry it in our hearts for all time....'

The evil reports about me which are spreading from paper to paper are making me notorious. News comes that my effigy has been burnt at the river-side burning-ground of the Chakravartis, with due ceremony and enthusiasm; and other insults are in contemplation. The trouble was that they had come to ask me to take shares in a Cotton Mill they wanted to start. I had to tell them that I did not so much mind the loss of my own money, but I would not be a party to causing a loss to so many poor shareholders.

'Are we to understand, Maharaja,' said my visitors, 'that the prosperity of the country does not interest you?'

'Industry may lead to the country's prosperity,' I explained, 'but a mere desire for its prosperity will not make for success in industry. Even when our heads were cool, our industries did not flourish. Why should we suppose that they will do so just because we have become frantic?"

'Why not say plainly that you will not risk your money?'

'I will put in my money when I see that it is industry which prompts you. But, because you have lighted a fire, it does not follow that you have the food to cook over it.'

XIII

What is this? Our Chakua sub-treasury looted! A remittance of Rs. 7500 was due from there to headquarters. The local cashier had changed the cash at the Government Treasury into small currency notes for convenience in carrying, and had kept them ready in bundles. In the middle of the night an armed band had raided the room, and wounded Kasim, the man on guard. The curious part of it was that they had taken only Rs. 6000 and left the rest scattered on the floor, though it would have been as easy to carry that away also. Anyhow, the raid of the dacoits was over; now the police raid would begin. Peace was out of the question.

When I went inside, I found the news had travelled before me. 'What a terrible thing, brother,' exclaimed the Bara Rani. 'Whatever shall we do?'

I made light of the matter to reassure her. 'We still have something left,' I said with a smile. 'We shall manage to get along somehow.'

'Don't joke about it, brother dear. Why are they all so angry with you? Can't your humour them? Why put everybody out?'

'I cannot let the country go to rack and ruin, even if that would please everybody.'

'That was a shocking thing they did at the burning-grounds. It's a horrid shame to treat you so. The Chota Rani has got rid of all her ears by dint of the Englishwoman's teaching, but as for me, I had to send for the priest to avert the omen before I could get any peace of mind. For my sake, dear, do get away to Calcutta. I tremble to think what they may do, if you stay on here.'

My sister-in-law's genuine anxiety touched me deeply.

'And, brother,' she went on, 'did I not warn you, it was not well to keep so much money in your room? They might get wind of it any day. It is not the money,—but who knows...'

To calm her I promised to remove the money to the treasury at once, and then get it away to Calcutta with the first escort going. We went together to my bedroom. The dressing-room door was shut. When I knocked, Bimala called out: 'I am dressing.'

'I wonder at the Chota Rani,' exclaimed my sister-in-law, 'dressing so early in the day! One of their *Bande Mataram* meetings, I suppose.' 'Robber Queen!' she called out in jest to Bimala. 'Are you counting your spoils inside?'

'I will attend to the money a little later,' I said, as I came away to my office room outside.

I found the Police Inspector waiting for me. 'Any trace of the dacoits?' I asked.

'I have my suspicions.'

'On whom?'

'Kasim, the guard.'

'Kasim? But was he not wounded?'

'A mere nothing. A flesh wound on the leg. Probably self-inflicted.'

'But I cannot bring myself to believe it. He is such a trusted servant.'

'You may have trusted him, but that does not prevent his being a thief. Have I not seen men trusted for twenty years together, suddenly developing...'

'Even if it were so, I could not send him to gaol. But why should he have left the rest of the money lying about?'

'To put us off the scent. Whatever you may say, Maharaja, he must be an old hand at the game. He mounts guard during his watch, right enough, but I feel sure he has a finger in all the dacoities going on in the neighbourhood.'

With this the Inspector proceeded to recount the various methods by which it was possible to be concerned in a dacoity twenty or thirty miles away, and yet be back in time for duty.

'Have you brought Kasim here?' I asked.

'No,' was the reply, 'he is in the lock-up. The Magistrate is due for the investigation.'

'I want to see him,' I said.

When I went to his cell he fell at my feet, weeping. 'In God's name,' he said, 'I swear I did not do this thing.'

'I do not doubt you, Kasim,' I assured him. 'Fear nothing. They can do nothing to you, if you are innocent.'

Kasim, however, was unable to give a coherent account of the incident. He was obviously exaggerating. Four or five hundred men, big guns, numberless swords, figured in his narrative. It must have been either his disturbed state of mind or a desire to account for his easy defeat. He would have it that this was Harish Kundu's doing; he was even sure he had heard the voice of Ekram, the head retainer of the Kundus.

'Look here, Kasim,' I had to warn him, 'don't you be dragging other people in with your stories. You are not called upon to make out a case against Harish Kundu, or anybody else.'

XIV

On returning home I asked my master to come over. He shook his head gravely. 'I see no good in this,' said he,—'this setting aside of conscience and putting the country in its place. All the sins of the country will now break out, hideous and unashamed.'

'Who do you think could have...'

'Don't ask me. But sin is rampant. Send them all away, right away from here.'

'I have given them one more day. They will be leaving the day after to-morrow.'

'And another thing. Take Bimala away to Calcutta. She is getting too narrow a view of the outside world from here, she cannot see men and things in their true proportions. Let her see the world,—men and their work,—give her a broad vision.'

'That is exactly what I was thinking.'

'Well, don't make any delay about it. I tell you, Nikhil, man's history has to be built by the united effort of all the races in the world, and therefore this selling of conscience for political reasons,—this making a fetish of one's country, won't do. I know that Europe does not at heart admit this, but there she has not the right to pose as our teacher. Men who die for the truth become immortal: and, if a whole people can die for the truth, it will also achieve immortality in the history of humanity. Here, in this land of India, amid the mocking laughter of Satan piercing the sky, may the feeling for this truth become real! What a terrible epidemic of sin has been brought into our country from foreign lands....'

The whole day passed in the turmoil of investigation. I was tired out when I retired for the night. I left over sending my sister-in-law's money to the treasury till next morning.

I woke up from my sleep at dead of night. The room was dark. I thought I heard a moaning somewhere. Somebody must have been crying. Sounds of sobbing came heavy with tears like fitful gusts of wind in the rainy night. It seemed to me that the cry rose from the heart of my room itself. I was alone. For some days Bimala had her bed in another room adjoining mine. I rose up and when I went out I found her in the balcony lying prone upon her face on the bare floor.

This is something that cannot be written in words. He only knows it who sits in the bosom of the world and receives all its pangs in His own heart. The sky is dumb, the stars are mute, the night is still, and in the midst of it all that one sleepless cry!

We give these sufferings names, bad or good, according to the classifications of the books, but this agony which is welling up from a torn heart, pouring into the fathomless dark, has it any name? When in that midnight, standing under the silent stars, I looked upon that figure, my mind was struck with awe, and I said to myself: 'Who am I to judge her?' O life, O death, O God of the infinite existence, I bow my head in silence to the mystery which is in you.

Once I thought I should turn back. But I could not. I sat down on the ground near Bimala and placed my hand on her head. At the first touch her whole body seemed to stiffen, but the next moment the hardness gave way, and the tears burst out. I gently passed my fingers over her forehead. Suddenly her hands groping for my feet grasped them and drew them to herself, pressing them against her breast with such force that I thought her heart would break.

Bimala's Story

XVIII

Amulya is due to return from Calcutta this morning. I told the servants to let me know as soon as he arrived, but could not keep still. At last I went outside to await him in the sitting-room.

When I sent him off to sell the jewels I must have been thinking only of myself. It never even crossed my mind that so young a boy, trying to sell such valuable jewellery, would at once be suspected. So helpless are we women, we needs must place on others the burden of our danger. When we go to our death we drag down those who are about us.

I had said with pride that I would save Amulya,—as if she who was drowning could save others. But instead of saving him, I have sent him to his doom. My little brother, such a sister have I been to you that Death must have smiled on that Brothers' Day when I gave you my blessing,—I, who wander distracted with the burden of my own evil-doing.

I feel to-day that man is at times attacked with evil as with the plague. Some germ finds its way in from somewhere, and then in the space of one night Death stalks in. Why cannot the stricken one be kept far away from the rest of the world? I, at least, have realised how terrible is the contagion,—like a fiery torch which burns that it may set the world on fire.

It struck nine. I could not get rid of the idea that Amulya was in trouble, that he had fallen into the clutches of the police. There must be great excitement in the Police Office—whose are the jewels?—where did he get them? And in the end I shall have to furnish the answer, in public, before all the world.

What is that answer to be? Your day has come at last, Bara Rani, you whom I have so long despised. You, in the shape of the public, the world, will have your revenge. O God, save me this time, and I will cast all my pride at my sister-in-law's feet.

I could bear it no longer. I went straight to the Bara Rani. She was in the verandah, spicing her betel leaves, Thako at her side. The sight of Thako made me shrink back for a moment, but I overcame all hesitation, and making a low obeisance I took the dust of my elder sister-in-law's feet.

'Bless my soul, Chota Rani,' she exclaimed, 'What has come upon you? Why this sudden reverence?'

'It is my birthday, sister,' said I. 'I have often caused you pain. Give me your blessing to-day that I may never do so again. My mind is so small.' I repeated my obeisance and left her hurriedly, but she called me back.

'You never before told me that this was your birthday, Chotie darling! Be sure to come and have lunch with me this afternoon. You positively must.'

O God, let it really be my birthday to-day. Can I not be born over again? Cleanse me, my God, and purify me and give me one more trial!

I went again to the sitting-room to find Sandip there. A feeling of disgust seemed to poison my very blood. The face of his, which I saw in the morning light, had nothing of the magic radiance of genius.

'Will you leave the room,' I blurted out.

Sandip smiled. 'Since Amulya is not here,' he remarked, 'I should think my turn had come for a special talk.'

My fate was coming back upon me. How was I to take away the right I myself had given. 'I would be alone,' I repeated.

'Queen,' he said, 'the presence of another person does not prevent your being alone. Do not mistake me for one of the crowd. I, Sandip, am always alone, even when surrounded by thousands.'

'Please come some other time. This morning I am...'

'Waiting for Amulya?'

I turned to leave the room for sheer vexation, when Sandip drew out from the folds of his cloak that jewel-casket of mine and banged it down on the marble table. I was thoroughly startled. 'Has not Amulya gone, then?' I exclaimed.

'Gone where?'

'To Calcutta?'

'No,' chuckled Sandip.

Ah, then my blessing had come true, in spite of all. He was saved. Let God's punishment fall on me, the thief, if only Amulya be safe.

The change in my countenance roused Sandip's scorn. 'So pleased, Queen!' sneered he. 'Are these jewels so very precious? How then did you bring yourself to offer them to the Goddess? Your gift was actually made. Would you now take it back?'

Pride dies hard and raises its fangs to the last. It was clear to me I must show Sandip I did not care a rap about these jewels. 'If they have excited your greed,' I said, 'you may have them.'

'My greed to-day embraces the wealth of all Bengal,' replied Sandip. 'Is there a greater force than greed? It is the steed of the great ones of the earth, as is the elephant, Airavat, the steed of Indra. So then these jewels are mine?'

As Sandip took up and replaced the casket under his cloak, Amulya rushed in. There were dark rings under his eyes, his lips were dry, his hair tumbled: the freshness of his youth seemed to have withered in a single day. Pangs gripped my heart as I looked on him.

'My box!' he cried, as he went straight up to Sandip without a glance at me. 'Have you taken that jewel-box from my trunk?'

'Your jewel-box?' mocked Sandip.

'It was my trunk!'

Sandip burst out into a laugh. 'Your distinctions between mine and yours are getting rather thin, Amulya,' he cried. 'You will die a religious preacher yet, I see.'

Amulya sank on a chair with his face in his hands. I went up to him and placing my hand on his head asked him: 'What is your trouble, Amulya?'

He stood straight up as he replied: 'I had set my heart, Sister Rani, on returning your jewels to you with my own hand. Sandip Babu knew this, but he forestalled me.'

'What do I care for my jewels?' I said. 'Let them go. No harm is done.'

'Go? Where?' asked the mystified boy.

'The jewels are mine,' said Sandip. 'Insignia bestowed on me by my Queen!'

'No, no, no,' broke out Amulya wildly. 'Never, sister Rani! I brought them back for you. You shall not give them away to anybody else.'

'I accept your gift, my little brother,' said I. 'But let him, who hankers after them, satisfy his greed.'

Amulya glared at Sandip like a beast of prey, as he growled: 'Look here, Sandip Babu, you know that even hanging has no terrors for me. If you dare take away that box of jewels...'

With an attempt at a sarcastic laugh Sandip said: 'You also ought to know by this time, Amulya, that I am not the man to be afraid of you.'

'Queen Bee,' he went on, turning to me, 'I did not come here to-day to take these jewels, I came to give them to you.

You would have done wrong to take my gift at Amulya's hands. In order to prevent it, I had first to make them clearly mine. Now these my jewels are my gift to you. Here they are! Patch up any understanding with this boy you like. I must go. You have been at your special talks all these days together, leaving me out of them. If special happenings now come to pass, don't blame me.'

'Amulya,' he continued, 'I have sent on your trunks and things to your lodgings. Don't you be keeping any belongings of yours in my room any longer.' With this parting shot, Sandip flung out of the room.

XIX

'I have had no peace of mind, Amulya,' I said to him, 'ever since I sent you off to sell my jewels.'

'Why, Sister Rani?'

'I was afraid lest you should get into trouble with them, lest they should suspect you for a thief. I would rather go without that six thousand. You must now do another thing for me,—go home at once, home to your mother.'

Amulya produced a small bundle and said: 'But, sister, I have got the six thousand.'

'Where from?'

'I tried hard to get gold,' he went on, without replying to my question, 'but could not. So I had to bring it in notes.'

'Tell me truly, Amulya, swear by me, where did you get this money?'

'That I will not tell you.'

Everything seemed to grow dark before my eyes. 'What terrible thing have you done, Amulya?' I cried. 'Is it then...'

'I know you will say I got this money wrongly. Very well, I admit it. But I have paid the full price for my wrong-doing. So now the money is mine.'

I no longer had any desire to learn more about it. My very blood-vessels contracted, making my whole body shrink within itself.

'Take it away, Amulya,' I implored. 'Put it back where you got it from.'

'That would be hard indeed!'

'It is not hard, brother dear. It was an evil moment when you first came to me. Even Sandip has not been able to harm you as I have done.'

Sandip's name seemed to stab him.

'Sandip!' he cried. 'It was you alone who made me come to know that man for what he is. Do you know, sister, he has not spent a pice out of those sovereigns he took from you? He shut himself into his room, after he left you, and gloated over the gold, pouring it out in a heap on the floor. "This is not money," he exclaimed, "but the petals of the divine lotus of power; crystallised strains of music from the pipes that play in the paradise of wealth! I cannot find it in my heart to change them, for they seem longing to fulfil their destiny of adorning the neck of Beauty. Amulya, my boy, don't you look at these with your fleshly eye, they are Lakshmi's smile, the gracious radiance of Indra's queen. No, no, I can't give them up to that boor of a manager. I am sure, Amulya, he was telling us lies. The police haven't traced the man who sank that boat. It's the manager who wants to make something out of it. We must get those letters back from him."

'I asked him how we were to do this; he told me to use force or threats. I offered to do so if he could return the gold. That, he said, we could consider later. I will not trouble you, sister, with all I did to frighten the man into giving up those letters and burn them,—it is a long story. That very night I came to Sandip and said: "We are now safe. Let me have the sovereigns to return them to-morrow to my sister, the Maharani." But he cried, "What infatuation is this of yours? Your precious sister's skirt bids fair to hide the whole country from you. Say *Bande Mataram* and exorcise the evil spirit."

'You know, Sister Rani, the power of Sandip's magic. The gold remained with him. And I spent the whole dark night on the bathing-steps of the lake muttering *Bande Mataram*.

'Then when you gave me your jewels to sell, I went again to Sandip. I could see he was angry with me. But he tried not to show it. "If I still have them hoarded up in any box of mine you may take them," said he, as he flung me his keys. They were nowhere to be seen. "Tell me where they are," I said. "I will do so," he replied, "when I find yur infatuation has left you. Not now."

'When I found I could not move him, I had to employ other methods. Then I tried to get the sovereigns from him in exchange for my currency notes for Rs. 6000. "You shall have them," he said, and disappeared into his bedroom, leaving me waiting outside. There he broke open my trunk and came straight to you with your casket through some other passage. He would not let me bring it, and now he dares call it his gift. How can I tell how much he has deprived me of? I shall never forgive him.

'But, oh sister, his power over me has been utterly broken—And it is you who have broken it!'

'Brother dear,' said I, 'if that is so, then my life is justified. But more remains to be done, Amulya. It is not enough that the spell has been destroyed. Its stains must be washed away. Don't delay and linger, go at once and put back the money where you took it from. Can you not do it, dear?'

'With your blessing everything is possible, Sister Rani.'

'Remember, it will not be your expiation alone, but mine also. I am a woman; the outside world is closed to me, else I would have gone myself. My hardest punishment is that I must put on you the burden of my sin.'

'Don't say that, sister. The path I was treading was not your path. It attracted me because of its dangers and difficulties. Now that your path calls me, let it be a thousand times more difficult and dangerous, the dust of your feet will help me to win through. Is it then your command that this money be replaced?'

'Not my command, brother mine, but a command from above.'

'Of that I know nothing. It is enough for me that this command from above comes from your lips. And, sister, I thought I had an invitation here. I must not lose that. You must give me your *prasad*[1] before I go. Then, if I can possibly manage it, I will finish my duty in the evening.'

Tears came to my eyes when I tried to smile as I said: 'So be it.'

_____

1. Food consecrated by the touch of a revered person.

Chapter XI

Bimala's Story

XX

With Amulya's departure my heart sank within me. In what perilous adventure had I sent this only son of his mother? O God, why need my expiation have such pomp and circumstance? Could I not be allowed to suffer alone without inviting all this multitude to share my punishment? Oh, let not this innocent child fall victim to Your wrath.

I called him back,—'Amulya!'

My voice sounded so feebly, it failed to reach him.

I went up to the door and called again: 'Amulya!'

He had gone.

'Who is there?'

'Rani Mother!'

'Go and tell Amulya Babu that I want him.'

What exactly happened I could not make out,—the man, perhaps, was not familiar with Amulya's name,—but he returned almost at once followed by Sandip.

'The very moment you sent me away,' he said as he came in, 'I had a presentiment that you would call me back. The attraction of the same moon causes both ebb and flow. I was so sure of being sent for, that I was actually waiting out in the passage. As soon as I caught sight of your man, coming from your room, I said: "Yes, yes, I am coming, I am coming at once!"—before he could utter a word. That up-country lout was surprised, I can tell you! He stared at me, open-mouthed, as if he thought I knew magic.

'All the fights in the world, Queen Bee,' Sandip rambled on, 'are really fights between hypnotic forces. Spell cast against spell,—noiseless weapons which reach even invisibe targets. At last I have met in you my match. Your quiver is full, I know, you artful warrior Queen! You are the only one in the world who has been able to turn Sandip out and call Sandip back, at your sweet will. Well, your quarry is at your feet. What will you do with him now? Will you give him the *coup de grâce*, keep him in your cage? Let me warn you beforehand, Queen, you will find the beast as difficult to kill outright as to keep in bondage. Anyway, why lose time in trying your magic weapons?'

Sandip must have felt the shadow of approaching defeat, and this made him try to gain time by chattering away without waiting for a reply. I believe he knew that I had sent the messenger for Amulya, whose name the man must have mentioned. In spite of that he had deliberately played this trick. He was now trying to avoid giving me any opening to tell him that it was Amulya I wanted, not him. But his stratagem was futile, for I could see his weakness through it. I must not yield up a pin's point of the ground I had gained.

'Sandip Babu,' I said, 'I wonder how you can go on making these endless speeches, without a stop. Do you get them up by heart, beforehand?'

Sandip's face flushed instantly.

'I have heard,' I continued, 'that our professional reciters keep a book full of all kinds of ready-made discourses, which can be fitted into any subject. Have you also a book?'

Sandip ground out his reply through his teeth. 'God has given you women a plentiful supply of coquetry to start with, and on the top of that you have the milliner and the jeweller to help you; but do not think we men are so helpless...'

'You had better go back and look up your book, Sandip Babu. You are getting your words all wrong. That's just the trouble with trying to repeat things by rote.'

'You!' shouted Sandip, losing all control over himself. 'You to insult me thus! What is there left of you that I do not know to the very bottom? What...' He became speechless.

Sandip, the wielder of magic spells, is reduced to utter powerlessness, whenever his spell refuses to work. From a king he fell to the level of a boor. Oh, the joy of witnessing his weakness! The harsher he became in his rudeness, the more did this joy well up within me. His snaky coils, with which he used to snare me, are exhausted,—I am free. I am saved, saved. Be rude to me, insult me, for that shows you in your truth; but spare me your songs of praise, which were false.

My husband came in at this juncture. Sandip had not the elasticity to recover himself in a moment, as he used to do before. My husband looked at him for a while in surprise. Had this happened some days ago I should have felt ashamed. But to-day I was pleased,—whatever my husband might think. I wanted to have it out to the finish with my weakening adversary.

Finding us both silent and constrained, my husband hesitated a little, and then took a chair. 'Sandip,' he said, 'I have been looking for you, and was told you were here.'

'I *am* here,' said Sandip with some emphasis. 'Queen Bee sent for me early this morning. And I, the humble worker of the hive, left all else to attend her summons.'

'I am going to Calcutta to-morrow. You will come with me.'

'And why, pray? Do you take me for one of your retinue?'

'Oh, very well, take it that you are going to Calcutta, and that I am your follower.'

'I have no business there.'

'All the more reason for going. You have too much business here.'

'I don't propose to stir.'

'Then I propose to shift you.'

'Forcibly?'

'Forcilby.'

'Very well, then, I will make a move. But the world is not divided between Calcutta and your estates. There are other places on the map.'

'From the way you have been going on, one would hardly have thought that there was any other place in the world except my estates.'

Sandip stood up. 'It does happen at times,' he said, 'that a man's whole world is reduced to a single spot. I have realised my universe in this sitting-room of yours, that is why I have been a fixture here.'

Then he turned to me. 'None but you, Queen Bee,' he said, 'will understand my words,—perhaps not even you. I salute you. With worship in my heart I leave you. My watchword has changed since you have come across my vision. It is no longer *Bande Mataram* (Hail Mother), but Hail Beloved, Hail Enchantress. The mother protects, the mistress leads to destruction,—but sweet is that destruction. You have made the anklet sounds of the dance of death tinkle in my heart. You have changed for me, your devotee, the picture I had of this Bengal of ours,—"the soft breeze-cooled land of pure water and sweet fruit."[1] You have no pity, my beloved. You have come to me with your poison cup and I shall drain it, either to die in agony or live triumphing over death.

---

1. Quotation from the National Song,—*Bande Mataram*.

'Yes,' he continued. 'The mother's day is past. O love, my love, you have made as naught for me the truth and right and heaven itself. All duties have become as shadows: all rules and restraints have snapped their bonds. O love, my love I could set fire to all the world outside this land on which you have set your dainty feet, and dance in mad revel over the ashes.... These are mild men. These are good men. They would do good to all,—as if this all were a reality! No, no! There is no reality in the world save this one real love of mine. I do you reverence. My devotion to you has made me cruel; my worship of you has lighted the raging flame of destruction within me. I am not righteous. I have no beliefs, I only believe in her whom, above all else in the world, I have been able to realise.'

Wonderful! It was wonderful, indeed. Only a minute ago I had despised this man with all my heart. But what I had thought to be dead ashes now glowed with living fire. The fire in him is true, that is beyond doubt. Oh why has God made man such a mixed creature? Was it only to show His supernatural sleight of hand? Only a few minutes ago I had thought that Sandip, whom I had once taken to be a hero, was only the stage hero of melodrama. But that is not so, not so. Even behind the trappings of the theatre, a true hero may sometimes be lurking.

There is much in Sandip that is coarse, that is sensuous, that is false, much that is overlaid with layer after layer of fleshly covering. Yet,—yet it is best to confess that there is a great deal in the depths of him which we do not, cannot understand,—much in ourselves too. A wonderful thing is man. What great mysterious purpose he is working out only the Terrible One[2] knows,—meanwhile we groan under the brunt of it. Shiva is the Lord of Chaos. He is all Joy. He will destroy our bonds.

---

2. Rudra, the Terrible, a name of Shiva.—*Tr.*

I cannot but feel, again and again, that there are two persons in me. One recoils from Sandip in his terrible aspect of Chaos,—the other feels that very vision to be sweetly alluring. The sinking ship drags down all who are swimming round it. Sandip is just such a force of destruction. His immense attraction gets holds of one before fear çan come to the rescue, and then, in the twinkling of an eye, one is drawn away, irresistibly, from all light, all good, all freedom of the sky, all air that can be breathed,—from lifelong accumulations, from everyday cares—right to the bottom of dissolution.

From some realm of calamity has Sandip come as its messenger; and as he stalks the land, muttering unholy incantations, to him flock all the boys and youths. The mother, seated in the lotus-heart of the Country, is wailing her heart out; for they have broken open her store-room, there to hold their drunken revelry. Her vintage of the draught for the immortals they would pour out on the dust; her time-honoured vessels they would smash to pieces. True, I feel with her; but, at the same time, I cannot help being infected with their excitement.

Truth itself has sent us this temptation to test our trustiness in upholding its commandments. Intoxication masquerades in heavenly garb, and dances before the pilgrims saying: 'Fools you are that pursue the fruitless path of renunciation. Its way is long, its time passing slow. So the Wielder of the Thunderbolt has sent me to you. Behold, I the beautiful, the passionate, I will accept you,—in my embrace you shall find fulfilment.'

After a pause Sandip addressed me again: 'Goddess, the time has come for me to leave you. It is well. The work of your nearness has been done. By lingering longer it would only become undone again, little by little. All is lost, if in our greed we try to cheapen that which is the greatest thing on earth. That which is eternal within the moment only becomes shallow if spread out in time. We were about to spoil our infinite moment, when it was your uplifted thunderbolt which came to the rescue. You intervened to save the purity of your own worship,—and in so doing you also saved your worshipper. In my leave-taking to-day your worship stands out the biggest thing. Goddess, I, also, set you free to-day. My earthen temple could hold you no longer,—every moment it was on the point of breaking apart. To-day I depart to worship your larger image in a larger temple. I can gain you more truly only at a distance from yourself. Here I had only your favour, there I shall be vouchsafed your boon.'

My jewel-casket was lying on the table. I held it up aloft as I said: 'I charge you to convey these my jewels to the object of my worship,—to whom I have dedicated them through you.'

My husband remained silent. Sandip left the room.

XXI

I had just sat down to make some cakes for Amulya when the Bara Rani came upon the scene. 'Oh dear,' she exclaimed, 'has it come to this that you must make cakes for your own birthday?'

'Is there no one else for whom I could be making them?' I asked.

'But this is not the day when you should think of feasting others. It is for us to feast you. I was just thinking of making something up[3] when I heard the staggering news which completely upset me. A gang of five or six hundred men, they say, has raided one of our treasuries and made off with six thousand rupees. Our house will be looted next, they expect.'

I felt greatly relieved. So it was our own money after all. I wanted to send for Amulya at once and tell him that he need

---

3. Any dainties to be offered ceremonially should be made by the lady of the house herself.—*Tr.*

only hand over those notes to my husband and leave the explanations to me.

'You *are* a wonderful creature!' my sister-in-law broke out, at the change in my countenance. 'Have you then really no such thing as fear?'

'I cannot believe it,' I said. 'Why should they loot our house?'

'Not believe it, indeed! Who could have believed that they would attack our treasury, either?'

I made no reply, but bent over my cakes, putting in the cocoanut stuffing.

'Well, I'm off,' said the Bara Rani after a prolonged stare at me. 'I must see Brother Nikhil and get something done about sending off my money to Calcutta, before it's too late.'

She was no sooner gone than I left the cakes to take care of themselves and rushed to my dressing-room, shutting myself inside. My husband's tunic with the keys in its pocket was still hanging there,—so forgetful was he. I took the key of the iron safe off the ring and kept it by me, hidden in the folds of my dress.

Then there came a knocking at the door. 'I am dressing,' I called out. I could hear the Bara Rani saying: 'Only a minute ago I saw her making cakes and now she is busy dressing up. What next, I wonder! One of their *Bande Mataram* meetings is on, I suppose. I say, Robber Queen,' she called out to me, 'are you taking stock of your loot?'

When they went away I hardly know what made me open the safe. Perhaps there was a lurking hope that it might all be a dream. What if, on pulling out the inside drawer, I should find the rolls of gold there, just as before?... Alas, everything was as empty as the trust which had been betrayed.

I had to go through the farce of dressing. I had to do my hair up all over again, quite unnecessarily. When I came out my sister-in-law railed at me: 'How many times are your going to dress to-day?'

'My birthday!' I said.

'Oh, any pretext seems good enough,' she went on. 'Many vain people have I seen in my day, but you beat them all hollow.'

I was about to summon a servant to send after Amulya, when one of the men came up with a little note, which he handed to me. It was from Amulya. 'Sister,' he wrote, 'you invited me this afternoon, but I thought I should not wait. Let me first execute your bidding and then come for my *prasad*. I may be a little late.'

To whom could he be going to return that money? Into what fresh entanglement was the poor boy rushing? O miserable woman, you can only send him off like an arrow, but not recall him if you miss your aim.

I should have declared at once that I was at the bottom of this robbery. But women live on the trust of their surroundings,—this is their whole world. If once it is out that this trust has been secretly betrayed, their place in their world is lost. They have then to stand upon the fragments of the thing they have broken, and its jagged edges keep on wounding them at every turn. To sin is easy enough, but to make up for it is above all difficult for a woman.

For some time past all easy approaches for communion with my husband have been closed to me. How then could I burst on him with this stupendous news? He was very late in coming for his meal to-day,—nearly two o'clock. He was absent-minded and hardly touched any food. I had lost even the right to press him to take a little more. I had to avert my face to wipe away my tears.

I wanted so badly to say to him: 'Do come into our room and rest awhile; you look so tired.' I had just cleared my throat with a little cough, when a servant hurried in to say that the Police Inspector had brought Panchu up to the palace. My husband, with the shadow on his face deepened, left his meal unfinished and went out.

A little later the Bara Rani appeared. 'Why did you not send me word when Brother Nikhil came in?' she complained. 'As he was late I thought I might as well finish my bath in the meantime. However did he manage to get through his meal so soon?'

'Why, did you want him for anything?'

'What is this about both of you going off to Calcutta to-morrow? All I can say is, I am not going to be left here alone. I should get startled out of my life at every sound, with all these dacoits about. Is it quite settled about your going to-morrow?'

'Yes,' said I, though I had only just now heard it; and though, moreover, I was not at all sure that before to-morrow our history might not take such a turn as to make it all one whether we went or stayed. After that, what our home, our life would be like, was utterly beyond my ken,—it seemed so misty and phantom-like.

In a very few hours now my unseen fate would become visible. Was there no one who could keep on postponing the flight of these hours, from day to day, and so make them long enough for me to set things right, so far as lay in my power? The time during which the seed lies underground is long— so long indeed that one forgets that there is any danger of its sprouting. But once its shoot shows up above the surface, it grows and grows so fast, there is no time to cover it up, neither with skirt, nor body, nor even life itself.

I will try to think of it no more, but sit quiet,—passive and callous,—let the crash come when it may. By the day after to-morrow all will be over,—publicity, laughter, bewailing, questions, explanations,—everything.

But I cannot forget the face of Amulya,—beautiful, radiant with devotion. He did not wait, despairing, for the blow of fate to fall, but rushed into the thick of danger. In my misery I do him reverence. He is my boy-god. Under the pretext of his playfulness he took from me the weight of my burden. He would save me by taking the punishment meant for me on his own head. But how am I to bear this terrible mercy of my God?

Oh, my child, my child, I do you reverence. Little brother mine, I do you reverence. Pure are you, beautiful are you, I do you reverence. May you come to my arms, in the next birth, as my own child,—that is my prayer.

XXII

Rumour became busy on every side. The police were continually in and out. The servants of the house were in a great flurry.

Khema, my maid, came up to me and said: 'Oh, Rani Mother! for goodness' sake put away my gold necklace and armlets in your iron safe.' To whom was I to explain that the Rani herself had been weaving all this network of trouble, and had got caught in it, too? I had to play the benign protector and take charge of Khema's ornaments and Thako's savings. The milk-woman, in her turn, brought along and kept in my room a box in which were a Benares sari and some other of her valued possessions. 'I got these at your wedding,' she told me.

When, to-morrow, my iron safe will be opened in the presence of these—Khema, Thako, the milk-women and all the rest.... Let me not think of it! Let me rather try to think what it will be like when this third day of Magh comes round again after a year has passed. Will all the wounds of my home life then be still as fresh as ever?...

Amulya writes that he will come later in the evening. I cannot remain alone with my thoughts, doing nothing. So I sit down again to make cakes for him. I have finished making quite a quantity, but still I must go on. Who will eat them? I shall distribute them amongst the servants. I must do so this very night. To-night is my limit. To-morrow will not be in my hands.

I went on untiringly, frying cake after cake. Every now and then it seemed to me that there was some noise in the direction of my rooms, upstairs. Could it be that my husband had missed the key of the safe, and the Bara Rani had assembled all the servants to help him to hunt for it? No, I must not pay heed to these sounds. Let me shut the door.

I rose to do so, when Thako came panting in: 'Rani Mother, oh, Rani Mother!'

'Oh get away!' I snapped out, cutting her short. 'Don't come bothering me.'

'The Bara Rani Mother wants you,' she went on. 'Her nephew has brought such a wonderful machine from Calcutta. It talks like a man. Do come and hear it!'

I did not know whether to laugh or to cry. So, of all things, a gramophone needs must come on the scene at such a time, repeating at every winding the nasal twang of its theatrical songs! What a fearsome thing results when a machine apes a man.

The shades of evening began to fall. I knew that Amulya would not delay to announce himself—yet I could not wait. I summoned a servant and said: 'Go and tell Amulya Babu to come straight in here.' The man came back after a while to say that Amulya was not in,—he had not come back since he had gone.

'Gone!' The last word struck my ears like a wail in the gathering darkness. Amulya gone! Had he then come like a streak of light from the setting sun, only to be gone for ever? All kinds of possible and impossible dangers flitted through my mind. It was I who had sent him to his death. What if he was fearless? That only showed his own greatness of heart. But after this how was I to go on living all by myself?

I had no memento of Amulya save that pistol,—his reverence-offering. It seemed to me that this was a sign given by Providence. This guilt which had contaminated my life at its very root,—my God in the form of a child had left with me the means of wiping it away, and then vanished. Oh the loving gift—the saving grace that lay hidden within it!

I opened my box and took out the pistol, lifting it reverently to my forehead. At that moment the gongs clanged out from the temple attached to our house. I prostrated myself in salutation.

In the evening I feasted the whole household with my cakes. 'You have managed a wonderful birthday feast,—and all by yourself too!'—exclaimed my sister-in-law. 'But you must leave something for us to do.' With this she turned on her gramophone and let loose the shrill treble of the Calcutta actresses all over the place. It seemed like a stable full of neighing fillies.

It got quite late before the feasting was over. I had a sudden longing to end my birthday celebration by taking the dust of my husband's feet. I went up to the bedroom and found him fast asleep. He had had such a worrying, trying day. I raised the edge of the mosquito curtain very very gently, and laid my head near his feet. My hair must have touched him, for he moved his legs in his sleep and pushed my head away.

I then went out and sat in the west verandah. A silk-cotton tree, which had shed all its leaves, stood there in the distance, like a skeleton. Behind it the crescent moon was setting. All of a sudden I had the feeling that the very stars in the sky were afraid of me,—that the whole of the night world was looking askance at me. Why? Because I was alone.

There is nothing so strange in creation as the man who is alone. Even he whose near ones have all died, one by one, is not alone,—companionship comes for him from behind the screen of death. But he, whose kin are there, yet no longer near, who has dropped out of all the varied companionship of a full home,—the starry universe itself seems to bristle to look on him in his darkness.

Where I am, I am not. I am far away from those who are around me. I live and move upon a world-wide chasm of separation, unstable as the dew-drop upon the lotus leaf.

Why do not men change wholly when they change? When I look into my heart, I find everything that was there, still there,—only they are topsy-turvy. Things that were well-ordered have become jumbled up. The gems that were strung into a necklace are now rolling in the dust. And so my heart is breaking.

I feel I want to die. Yet in my heart everything still lives,—nor even in death can I see the end of it all: rather, in death there seems to be ever so much more of repining. What is to be ended must be ended in this life,—there is no other way out.

Oh forgive me just once, only this time, Lord! All that you gave into my hands as the wealth of my life, I have made into my burden. I can neither bear it longer, nor give it up. O Lord, sound once again those flute strains which you played for me, long ago, standing at the rosy edge of my morning sky,—and let all my complexities become simple and easy. Nothing save the music of your flute can make whole that which has been broken, and pure that which has been sullied. Create my home anew with your music. No other way can I see.

I threw myself prone on the ground and sobbed aloud. It was for mercy that I prayed,—some little mercy from somewhere, some shelter, some sign of forgiveness, some hope that might bring about the end. 'Lord,' I vowed to myself, 'I will lie here, waiting and waiting, touching neither food nor drink, so long as your blessing does not reach me.'

I heard the sound of footsteps. Who says that the gods do not show themselves to mortal men? I did not raise my face to look up, lest the sight of it should break the spell. Come, oh come, come and let your feet touch my head. Come, Lord, and set your foot upon my throbbing heart, and at that moment let me die.

He came and sat near my head. Who? My husband! At the first touch of his presence I felt that I should swoon. And then the pain at my heart burst its way out in an overwhelming flood of tears, tearing through all my obstructing veins and nerves. I strained his feet to my bosom,—oh, why could not their impress remain there for ever?

He tenderly stroked my head. I received his blessing. Now I shall be able to take up the penalty of public humiliation which will be mine to-morrow, and offer it, in all sincerity, at the feet of my God.

But what keeps crushing my heart is the thought that the festive flutes which were played at my wedding, nine years ago, welcoming me to this house, will never sound for me again in this life. What rigour of penance is there which can serve to bring me once more, as a bride adorned for her husband, to my place upon that same bridal seat? How many years, how many ages, aeons, must pass before I can find my way back to that day of nine years ago?

God can create new things, but has even He the power to create afresh that which has been destroyed?

Chapter XII

Nikhil's Story

XV

To-day we are going to Calcutta. Our joys and sorrows lie heavy on us if we merely go on accumulating them. Keeping them and accumulating them alike are false. As master of the house I am in an artificial position—in reality I am a wayfarer on the path of life. That is why the true Master of the house gets hurt at every step and at last there comes the supreme hurt of death.

My union with you, my love, was only of the wayside; it was well enough so long as we followed the same road; it will only hamper us if we try to preserve it further. We are now leaving its bonds behind. We are started on our journey beyond, and it will be enough if we can throw each other a glance, or feel the touch of each other's hands in passing. After that? After there is the larger world-path, the endless current of universal life.

How little can you deprive me of, my love, after all? Whenever I set my ear to it, I can hear the flute which is playing, its fountain of melody gushing forth from the flute-stops of separation. The immortal draught of the goddess is never exhausted. She sometimes breaks the bowl from which we drink it, only to smile at seeing us so disconsolate over the trifling loss. I will not stop to pick up my broken bowl. I will march forward, albeit with unsatisfied heart.

The Bara Rani came and asked me: 'What is the meaning, brother, of all these books being packed up and sent off in box-loads?'

'It only means,' I replied, 'that I have not yet been able to get over my fondness for them.'

'I only wish you would keep your fondness for some other things as well! Do you mean you are never coming back home?'

'I shall be coming and going, but shall not immure myself here any more.'

'Oh indeed! Then just come along to my room and see how many things I have been unable to shake off *my* fondness for.' With this she took me by the hand and marched me off.

In my sister-in-law's rooms I found numberless boxes and bundles ready packed. She opened one of the boxes and said: 'See, brother, look at all my *pan*-making things. In this bottle I have catechu powder scented with the pollen of screw-pine blossoms. These little tin boxes are all for different kinds of spices. I have not forgotten my playing cards and draught-board either. If you two are over-busy, I shall manage to make other friends there, who will give me a game. Do you remember this comb? It was one of the *Swadeshi* combs you brought for me....'

'But what is all this for, Sister Rani? Why have *you* been packing up all these things?'

'Do you think I am not going with you?'

'What an extraordinary idea!'

'Don't you be afraid! I am not going there to flirt with you, nor to quarrel with the Chota Rani! One must die sooner or later, and it is just as well to be on the bank of the holy Ganges before it is too late. It is too horrible to think of being cremated in your wretched burning-ground here, under that stumpy banian tree,—that is why I have been refusing to die, and have plagued you all this time.'

At last I could hear the true voice of home. The Bara Rani came into our house as its bride, when I was only six years old. We have played together, through the drowsy afternoons, in a corner of the roof-terrace. I have thrown down to her green *amras* from the tree-top, to be made into deliciously indigestible chutneys by slicing them up with mustard, salt and fragrant herbs. It was my part to gather for her all the forbidden things from the store-room to be used in the marriage celebration of her doll; for, in the penal code of my grandmother, I alone was exempt from punishment. And I used to be appointed her messenger to my brother, whenever she wanted to coax something special out of him, because he could not resist my importunity. I also remember how, when I suffered under the rigorous régime of the doctors of those days,—who would not allow anything except warm water and sugared cardamom seeds during feverish attacks,—my sister-in-law could not bear my privation and used to bring me delicacies on the sly. What a scolding she got one day when she was caught!

And then, as we grew up, our mutual joys and sorrows took on deeper tones of intimacy. How we quarrelled! Sometimes conflicts of worldly interests roused suspicions and jealousies, making breaches in our love; and when the Chota Rani came in between us, these breaches seemed as if they would never be mended, but it always turned out that the healing forces at bottom proved more powerful than the wounds on the surface.

So has a true relationship grown up between us, from our childhood up till now, and its branching foliage has spread and broadened over every room and verandah and terrace of this great house. When I saw the Bara Rani make ready, with all her belongings, to depart from this house of ours, all the ties that bound us, to their wide-spreading ends, felt the shock.

The reason was clear to me, why she had made up her mind to drift away towards the unknown, cutting asunder all her lifelong bounds of daily habit, and of the house itself, which she had never left for a day since she first entered it at the age of nine. And yet it was this real reason which she could not allow to escape her lips, preferring rather to put forward any other paltry excuse.

She had only this one relationship left in all the world, and the poor, unfortunate, widowed and childless woman had cherished it with all the tenderness hoarded in her heart. How deeply she had felt our proposed separation I never realised so keenly as when I stood amongst her scattered boxes and bundles.

I could see at once that the little differences she used to have with Bimala, about money matters, did not proceed from any sordid worldliness, but because she felt that her claims in regard to this one relationship of her life had been overridden and its ties weakened for her by the coming in between of this other woman from goodness knows where! She had been hurt at every turn and yet had not the right to complain.

And Bimala? She also had felt that the Senior Rani's claim over me was not based merely on our social connection, but went much deeper; and she was jealous of these ties between us, reaching back to our childhood.

To-day my heart knocked heavily against the doors of my breast. I sank down upon one of the boxes as I said: 'How I should love, Sister Rani, to go back to the days when we first met in this old house of ours.'

'No, brother dear,' she replied with a sigh, 'I would not live my life again,—not as a woman! Let what I have had to bear end with this one birth. I could not bear it over again.'

I said to her: 'The freedom to which we pass through sorrow is greater than the sorrow.'

'That may be so for you men. Freedom is for you. But we women would keep others bound. We would rather be put into bondage ourselves. No, no, brother, you will never get free from our toils. If you needs must spread your wings, you will have to take us with you; we refuse to be left behind. That is why I have gathered together all this weight of luggage. It would never do to allow men to run too light.'

'I can feel the weight of your words,' I said laughing, 'and if we men do not complain of your burdens, it is because women pay us so handsomely for what they make us carry.'

'You carry it,' she said, 'because it is made up of many small things. Whichever one you think of rejecting pleads that it is so light. And so with much lightness we weigh you down.... When do we start?'

'The train leaves at half-past eleven to-night. There will be lots of time.'

'Look here, do be good for once and listen to just one word of mine. Take a good nap this afternoon. You know you never get any sleep in the train. You look so pulled down, you might go to pieces any moment. Come along, get through your bath first.'

As we went towards my room, Khema, the maid, came up and with an ultra-modest pull at her veil told us, in deprecatingly low tones, that the Police Inspector had arrived with a prisoner and wanted to see the Maharaja.

'Is the maharaja a thief, or a robber,' the Bara Rani flared up, 'that he should be sent upon so by the police? Go and tell the Inspector that the Maharaja is at his bath.'

'Let me just go and see what is the matter,' I pleaded. 'It may be something urgent.'

'No, no,' my sister-in-law insisted. 'Our Chota Rani was making a heap of cakes last night. I'll send some to the

Inspector, to keep him quiet till you're ready.' With this she pushed me into my room and shut the door on me.

I had not the power to resist such tyranny,—so rare is it in this world. Let the Inspector while away the time eating cakes. What if business is a bit neglected?

The police had been in great form these last few days arresting now this one, now that. Each day some innocent person or other would be brought along to enliven the assembly in my office-room. One more such unfortunate, I supposed, must have been brought in that day. But why should the Inspector alone be regaled with cakes? That would not do at all. I thumped vigorously on the door.

'If you are going mad, be quick and pour some water over your head—that will keep you cool,' said my sister-in-law from the passage.

'Send down cakes for two,' I shouted. 'The person who has been brought in as the thief probably deserves them better. Tell the man to give him a good big helping.'

I hurried through my bath. When I came out, I found Bimal sitting on the floor outside.[1] Could this be my Bimal of old, my proud, sensitive Bimal?

What favour could she be wanting to beg, seated like this at my door? As I stopped short, she stood up and said gently with downcast eyes: 'I would have a word with you.'

'Come inside then,' I said.

'But are you going out on any particular business?'

'I was, but let that be. I want to hear...'

'No, finish your business first. We will have our talk after you have had your dinner.'

I went off to my sitting-room, to find the Police Inspector's plate quite empty. The person he had brought with him, however, was still busy eating.

---

1. Sitting on the bare floor is a sign of mourning, and so, by association of ideas, of an abject attitude of mind.—*Tr.*

'Hullo!' I ejaculated in surprise. 'You, Amulya?'

'It is I, sir,' said Amulya with his mouth full of cake. 'I've had quite a feast. And if you don't mind, I'll take the rest with me.' With this he proceeded to tie up the remaining cakes in his handkerchief.

'What does this mean?' I asked, staring at the Inspector.

The man laughed. 'We are no nearer, sir,' he said, 'to solving the problem of the thief: meanwhile the mystery of the theft deepens.' He then produced something tied up in a rag, which when untied disclosed a bundle of currency notes. 'This, Maharaja,' said the Inspector, 'is your six thousand rupees!'

'Where was it found?'

'In Amulya Babu's hands. He went last evening to the manager of your Chakna sub-office to tell him that the money had been found. The manager seemed to be in a greater state of trepidation at the recovery than he had been at the robbery. He was afraid he would be suspected of having made away with the notes and of now making up a cock-and-bull story for fear of being found out. He asked Amulya to wait, on the pretext of getting him some refreshment, and came straight over to the Police Office. I rode off at once, kept Amulya with me, and have been busy with him the whole morning. He refuses to tell us where he got the money from. I warned him he would be kept under restraint till he did so. In that case, he informed me he would have to lie. Very well, I said, he might do so if he pleased. Then he stated that he had found the money under a bush. I pointed out to him that it was not quite so easy to lie as all that. Under what bush? Where was the place? Why was he there? —All this would have to be stated as well. "Don't you worry," he said, "there is plenty of time to invent all that."'

'But, Inspector,' I said, 'why are you badgering a respectable young gentleman like Amulya Babu?'

'I have no desire to harass him,' said the Inspector. 'He is not only a gentleman, but the son of Nibaran Babu, my school-fellow. Let me tell you, Maharaja, exactly what must have happened. Amulya knows the thief, but wants to shield him by drawing suspicion on himself. That is just the sort of bravado he loves to indulge in.' The Inspector turned to Amulya. 'Look here, young man,' he continued, 'I also was eighteen once upon a time, and a student in the Ripon College. I nearly got into gaol trying to rescue a hack driver from a police constable. It was a near shave.' Then he turned again to me and said: 'Maharaja, the real thief will now probably escape, but I think I can tell you who is at the bottom of it all.'

'Who is it, then?' I asked.

'That manager, in collusion with the guard, Kasim.'

When the Inspector, having argued out his theory to his own satisfaction, at last departed, I said to Amulya: 'If you will tell me who took the money, I promise you no one shall be hurt.'

'I did,' said he.

'But how can that be? What about the gang of armed men?...'

'It was I, by myself, alone!'

What Amulya then told me was indeed extraordinary. The manager had just finished his supper and was on the verandah rinsing out his mouth. The place was somewhat dark. Amulya had a revolver in each pocket, one loaded with blank cartridges, the other with ball. He had a mask over his face. He flashed a bull's-eye lantern in the manager's face and fired a blank shot. The man swooned away. Some of the guards, who were off duty, came running up, but when Amulya fired another blank shot at them they lost no time in taking cover. Then Kasim, who was on duty, came up whirling a quarter-staff. This time Amulya aimed a bullet at his legs, and finding himself hit, Kasim collapsed on the floor. Amulya then made the trembling manager, who had come to his senses, open the safe and deliver up six thousand rupees. Finally, he took one of the estate horses and galloped off a few miles, there let the animal loose, and quietly walked up here, to our place.

'What made you do all this, Amulya?' I asked.

'There was a grave reason, Maharaja,' he replied.

'But why, then, did you try to return the money?'

'Let her come, at whose command I did so. In her presence I shall make a clean breast of it.'

'And who may "she" be?'

'My sister, the Chota Rani!'

I sent for Bimala. She came hesitatingly, barefoot, with a white shawl over her head. I had never seen my Bimal like this before. She seemed to have wrapped herself in a morning light.

Amulya prostrated himself in salutation and took the dust of her feet. Then, as he rose, he said: 'Your command has been executed, sister. The money is returned.'

'You have saved me, my little brother,' said Bimal.

'With your image in my mind, I have not uttered a single lie,' Amulya continued. 'My watchword *Bande Mataram* has been cast away at your feet for good. I have also received my reward, your *prasad*, as soon as I came to the palace.'

Bimal looked at him blankly unable to follow his last words. Amulya brought out his handkerchief, and untying it showed her the cakes put away inside. 'I did not eat them all,' he said, 'I have kept these to eat after you have helped me with your own hands.'

I could see that I was not wanted here. I went out of the room. I could only preach and preach, so I mused, and get my effigy burnt for my pains. I had not yet been able to bring back a single soul from the path of death. They who have the power, can do so by a mere sign. My words have not that

ineffable meaning. I am not a flame, only a black coal, which
has gone out. I can light no lamp. That is what the story of
my life shows,—my row of lamps has remained unlit.

XVI

I returned slowly towards the inner apartments. The Bara
Rani's room must have been drawing me again. It had become
an absolute necessity for me, that day, to feel that this life
of mine had been able to strike some real, some responsive
chord in some other harp of life. One cannot realise one's
own existence by remaining within oneself,—it has to be
sought outside.

As I passed in front of my sister-in-law's room, she came
out saying: 'I was afraid you would be late again this afternoon.
However, I ordered your dinner as soon as I heard you
coming. It will be served in a minute.'

'Meanwhile,' I said, 'let me take out that money of yours
and have it kept ready to take with us.'

As we walked on towards my room she asked me if the
Police Inspector had made any report about the robbery. I
somehow did not feel inclined to tell her all the details of
how that six thousand had come back. 'That's just what all
the fuss is about,' I said evasively.

When I went into my dressing-room and took out my
bunch of keys, I did not find the key of the iron safe on the
ring. What an absurdly absent-minded fellow I was, to be
sure! Only this morning I had been opening so many boxes
and things, and never noticed that this key was not there.

'What has happened to your key?' she asked me.

I went on fumbling in this pocket and that, but could give
her no answer. I hunted in the same place over and over again.
It dawned on both of us that it could not be a case of the
key being mislaid. Some one must have taken it off the ring.
Who could it be? Who else could have come into this room?

'Don't you worry about it,' she said to me. 'Get through your dinner first. The Chota Rani must have kept it herself, seeing how absentminded you are getting.'

I was, however, greatly disturbed. It was never Bimala's habit to take any key of mine without telling me about it. Bimal was not present at my meal-time that day: she was busy feasting Amulya in her own room. My sister-in-law wanted to send for her, but I asked her not to do so.

I had just finished my dinner when Bimal came in. I would have preferred not to discuss the matter of the key in the Bara Rani's presence, but as soon as she saw Bimal, she asked her: 'Do you know, dear, where the key of the safe is?'

'I have it,' was the reply.

'Didn't I say so!' exclaimed my sister-in-law triumphantly. 'Our Chota Rani pretends not to care about these robberies, but she takes precautions on the sly, all the same.'

The look on Bimal's face made my mind mis-give me. 'Let the key be, now,' I said. 'I will take out that money in the evening.'

'There you go again, putting it off,' said the Bara Rani. 'Why not take it out and send it to the treasury while you have it in mind?'

'I have taken it out already,' said Bimal.

I was startled.

'Where have you kept it, then?' asked my sister-in-law.

'I have spent it.'

'Just listen to her! Whatever did you spend all that money on?'

Bimal made no reply. I asked her nothing further. The Bara Rani seemed about to make some further remark to Bimala, but checked herself. 'Well, that is all right, anyway,' she said at length, as she looked towards me. 'Just what I used to do with my husband's loose cash. I knew it was no use leaving it with him,—his hundred and one hangers-on would be sure to get hold of it. You are much the same, dear! What a number of ways you men know of getting through money. We can only save it from you by stealing it ourselves! Come along now. Off with you to bed.'

The Bara Rani led me to my room, but I hardly knew where I was going. She sat by my bed after I was stretched on it, and smiled at Bimal as she said: 'Give me one of your *pans*, Chotie darling,—what? You have none! You have become a regular mem-sahib. Then send for some from my room.'

'But have you had your dinner yet?' I anxiously enquired.

'Oh long ago,' she replied,—clearly a fib.

She kept on chattering away there at my bedside, on all manner of things. The maid came and told Bimal that her dinner had been served and was getting cold, but she gave no sign of having heard it. 'Not had your dinner yet? What nonsense! It's fearfully late.' With this the Bara Rani took Bimal away with her.

I could divine that there was some connexion between the taking out of this six thousand and the robbing of the other. But I have no curiosity to learn the nature of it. I shall never ask.

Providence leaves our life moulded in the rough,—its object being that we ourselves should put the finishing touches, shaping it into its final form to our taste. There has always been the hankering within me to express some great idea in the process of giving shape to my life on the lines suggested by the Creator. In this endeavour I have spent all my days. How severely I have curbed my desires, repressed myself at every step, only the Searcher of the Heart knows.

But the difficulty is, that one's life is not solely one's own. He who would create it must do so with the help of his surroundings, or he will fail. So it was my constant dream to draw Bimal to join me in this work of creating myself. I loved her with all my soul; on the strength of that, I could not but succeed in winning her to my purpose,—that was my firm belief.

Then I discovered that those who could simply and naturally draw their environment into the process of their self-creation belonged to one species of the genus 'man,'— and I to another. I had received the vital spark, but could not impart it. Those to whom I have surrendered my all have taken my all, but not myself with it.

My trial is hard indeed. Just when I want a helpmate most, I am thrown back on myself alone. Nevertheless, I record my vow that even in this trial I shall win through. Alone, then, shall I tread my thorny path to the end of this life's journey....

I have begun to suspect that there has all along been a vein of tyranny in me. There was a despotism in my desire to mould my relations with Bimala in a hard, clear-cut, perfect form. But man's life was not meant to be cast in a mould. And if we try to shape the good, as so much mere material, it takes a terrible revenge by losing its life.

I did not realise all this while that it must have been this unconscious tyranny of mine which made us gradually drift apart. Bimala's life, not finding its true level by reason of my pressure from above, has had to find an outlet by undermining its banks at the bottom. She has had to steal this six thousand rupees because she could not be open with me, because she felt that, in certain things, I despotically differed from her.

Men, such as I, possessed with one idea, are indeed at one with those who can manage to agree with us; but those who do not, can only get on with us by heating us. It is our unyielding obstinacy, which drives even the simplest to tortuous ways. In trying to manufacture a helpmate, we spoil a wife.

Could I not go back to the beginning? Then, indeed, I should follow the path of the simple. I should not try to fetter my life's companion with my ideas, but play the joyous pipes of my love and say: 'Do you love me? Then may you grow true to yourself in the light of your love. Let my suggestions be suppressed, let God's design, which is in you, triumph, and my ideas retire abashed.'

But can even Nature's nursing heal the open wound, into which our accumulated differences have broken out? The covering veil, beneath the privacy of which Nature's silent forces alone can work, has been torn asunder. Wounds must be bandaged,—can we not bandage our wound with our love, so that the day may come when its scar will no longer be visible? Is it not too late? So much time has been lost in misunderstanding; it has taken right up to now to come to an understanding; how much more time will it take for the correcting? What if the wound does eventually heal?—can the devastation it has wrought ever be made good?

There was a slight sound near the door. As I turned over I saw Bimala's retreating figure through the open doorway. She must have been waiting by the door, hesitating whether to come in or not, and at last have decided to go back. I jumped up and bounded to the door, calling: 'Bimal.'

She stopped on her way. She had her back to me. I went and took her by the hand and led her into our room. She threw herself face downwards on a pillow, and sobbed and sobbed. I said nothing, but held her hand as I sat by her head.

When her storm of grief had abated she sat up. I tried to draw her to my breast, but she pushed my arms away and knelt at my feet, touching them repeatedly with her head, in obeisance. I hastily drew my feet back, but she clasped them in her arms, saying in a choking voice: 'No, no, no, you must not take away your feet. Let me do my worship.'

I kept still. Who was I to stop her? Was I the god of her worship that I should have any qualms?

Bimala's Story

XXIII

Come, come Now is the time to set sail towards that great confluence, where the river of loves meets the sea of worship. In that pure blue all the weight of its muddiness sinks and disappears.

I now fear nothing,—neither myself, nor anybody else. I have passed through fire. What was inflammable has been burnt to ashes; what is left is deathless. I have dedicated myself to the feet of him, who has received all my sin into the depths of his own pain.

To-night we go to Calcutta. My inward troubles have so long prevented my looking after my things. Now let me arrange and pack them.

After a while I found my husband had come in and was taking a hand in the packing.

'This won't do,' I said. 'Did you not promise me you would have a sleep?'

'I might have made the promise,' he replied, 'but my sleep did not, and it was nowhere to be found.'

'No, no,' I repeated, 'this will never do. Lie down for a while, at least.'

'But how can you get through all this alone?'

'Of course I can.'

'Well, you may boast of being able to do without me. But frankly I can't do without you. Even sleep refused to come to me, alone, in that room.' Then he set to work again.

But there was an interruption, in the shape of a servant, who came and said that Sandip Babu had called and had asked to be announced. I did not dare to ask whom he wanted. The light of the sky seemed suddenly to be shut down, like the leaves of a sensitive plant.

'Come, Bimal,' said my husband. 'Let us go and hear what Sandip has to tell us. Since he has come back again, after taking his leave, he must have something special to say.'

I went, simply because it would have been still more embarrassing to stay. Sandip was staring at a picture on the wall. As we entered he said: 'You must be wondering why the fellow has returned. But you know the ghost is never laid till all the rites are complete.' With these words he brought out of his pocket something tied in his handkerchief, and laying it on the table, undid the knot. It was those sovereigns.

'Don't you mistake me, Nikhil,' he said. 'You must not imagine that the contagion of your company has suddenly turned me honest; I am not the man to come back in slobbering repentance to return ill-gotten money. But...'

He left his speech unfinished. After a pause he turned towards Nikhil, but said to me: 'After all these days, Queen Bee, the ghost of compunction has found an entry into my hitherto untroubled conscience. As I have to wrestle with it every night, after my first sleep is over, I cannot call it a phantom of my imagination. There is no escape even for me till its debt is paid. Into the hands of that spirit, therefore, let me make restitution. Goddess! From you, alone, of all the world, I shall not be able to take away anything. I shall not be rid of you till I am destitute. Take these back!'

He took out at the same time the jewel-casket from under his tunic and put it down, and then left us with hasty steps.

'Listen to me, Sandip,' my husband called after him.

'I have not the time, Nikhil,' said Sandip as he paused near the door. 'The Mussulmans, I am told, have taken me for an invaluable gem, and are conspiring to loot me and hide me away in their graveyard. But I feel that it is necessary that I should live. I have just twenty-five minutes to catch the North-bound train. So, for the present, I must be gone. We shall have our talk out at the next convenient opportunity. If you take my advice, don't you delay in getting away either. I salute you, Queen Bee, Queen of the bleeding hearts, Queen of desolation!'

Sandip then left almost at a run. I stood stock still; I had never realised in such a manner before, how trivial, how paltry, this gold and these jewels were. Only a short while ago I was so busy thinking what I should take with me, and how I should pack it. Now I felt that there was no need to take anything at all. To set out and go forth was the important thing.

My husband left his seat and came up and took me by the hand. 'It is getting late,' he said. 'There is not much time left to complete our preparations for the journey.'

At this point Chandranath Babu suddenly came in. Finding us both together, he fell back for a moment. Then he said, 'Forgive me, my little mother, if I intrude. Nikhil, the Mussulmans are out of hand. They are looting Harish Kundu's treasury. That does not so much matter. But what is intolerable is the violence that is being done to the women of their house.'

'I am off,' said my husband.

'What can you do there?' I pleaded, as I held him by the hand. 'Oh, sir,' I appealed to his master. 'Will you not tell him not to go?'

'My little mother,' he replied, 'there is no time to do anything else.'

'Don't be alarmed, Bimal,' said my husband, as he left us.

When I went to the window I saw my husband galloping away on horseback, with not a weapon in his hands.

In another minute the Bara Rani came running in. 'What have you done, Chotie darling,' she cried. 'How could you let him go?'

'Call the Dewan at once,' she said, turning to a servant. The Ranis never appeared before the Dewan, but the Bara Rani had no thought that day for appearances.

'Send a mounted man to bring back the Maharaja at once,' she said, as soon as the Dewan came up.

'We have all entreated him to stay, Rani mother,' said the Dewan, 'but he refused to turn back.'

'Send word to him that the Bara Rani is ill, that she is on her death-bed,' cried my sister-in-law wildly.

When the Dewan had left she turned on me with a furious outburst. 'Oh, you witch, you ogress, you could not die yourself, but need must send him to his death!...'

The light of the day began to fade. The sun set behind the feathery foliage of the blossoming *Sajna* tree. I can see every different shade of that sunset even to-day. Two masses of cloud on either side of the sinking orb made it look like a great bird with fiery-feathered wings outspread. It seemed to me that this fateful day was taking its flight, to cross the ocean of night.

It became darker and darker. Like the flames of a distant village on fire, leaping up every now and then above the horizon, a distant din swelled up in recurring waves into the darkness.

The bells of the evening worship rang out from our temple. I knew the Bara Rani was sitting there, with palms joined in silent prayer. But I could not move a step from the window.

The roads, the village beyond, and the still more distant fringe of trees, grew more and more vague. The lake in our grounds looked up into the sky with a dull lustre, like a blind man's eye. On the left the tower seemed to be craning its neck to catch sight of something that was happening.

The sounds of night take on all manner of disguises. A twig snaps, and one thinks that somebody is running for his life. A door slams, and one feels it to be the sudden heart-thump of a startled world.

Lights would suddenly flicker under the shade of the distant trees, and then go out again. Horses' hoofs would clatter, now and again, only to turn out to be riders leaving the palace gates.

I continually had the feeling that, if only I could die, all this turmoil would come to an end. So long as I was alive my sins would remain rampant, scattering destruction on every side. I remembered the pistol in my box. But my feet refused to leave the window in quest of it. Was I not awaiting my fate?

The gong of the watch solemnly struck ten. A little later, groups of lights appeared in the distance and a great crowd wound its way, like some great serpent, along the roads in the darkness, towards the place gates.

The Dewan rushed to the gate at the sound. Just then a rider came galloping in. 'What's the news, Jata?' asked the Dewan.

'Not good,' was the reply.

I could hear these words distinctly from my window. But something was next whispered which I could not catch.

Then came a palanquin, followed by a litter. The doctor was walking alongside the palanquin.

'What do you think, doctor?' asked the Dewan.

'Can't say yet,' the doctor replied. 'The wound in the head is a serious one.'

'And Amulya Babu?'

'He has a bullet through the heart. He is done for.'

THE CRESCENT MOON

The Home

I paced alone on the road across the field while the sunset was hiding its last gold like a miser.

The daylight sank deeper and deeper into the darkness, and the widowed land, whose harvest had been reaped, lay silent.

Suddenly a boy's shrill voice rose into the sky. He traversed the dark unseen, leaving the track of his song across the hush of the evening.

His village home lay there at the end of the waste land, beyond the sugar-cane field, hidden among the shadows of the banana and the slender areca palm, the coconut and the dark green jack-fruit trees.

I stopped for a moment in my lonely way under the starlight, and saw spread before me the darkened earth surrounding with her arms countless homes furnished with cradles and beds, mothers' hearts and evening lamps, and young lives glad with a gladness that knows nothing of its value for the world.

On the Seashore

On the seashore of endless worlds children meet. The infinite sky is motionless overhead and the restless water is boisterous. On the seashore of endless worlds the children meet with shouts and dances.

They build their houses with sand, and they play with empty shells. With withered leaves they weave their boats and smilingly float them on the vast deep. Children have their play on the seashore of worlds.

They know not how to swim, they know not how to cast nets. Pearl-fishers dive for pearls, merchants sail in their ships, while children gather pebbles and scatter them again. They seek not for hidden treasures, they know not how to cast nets.

The sea surges up with laughter, and pale gleams the smile of the sea-beach. Death-dealing waves sing meaningless ballads to the children, even like a mother while rocking her baby's cradle. The sea plays with children, and pale gleams the smile of the sea-beach.

On the seashore of endless worlds children meet. Tempest roams in the pathless sky, ships are wrecked in the trackless water, death is abroad and children play. On the seashore of endless worlds is the great meeting of children.

The Source

The sleep that flits on baby's eyes—does anybody know from where it comes? Yes, there is a rumour that it has its dwelling where, in the fairy village among shadows of the forest dimly lit with glow-worms, there hang two shy buds of enchantment. From there it comes to kiss baby's eyes.

The smile that flickers on baby's lips when he sleeps — does anybody know where it was born? Yes, there is a rumour that a young pale beam of a crescent moon touched the edge of a vanishing autumn cloud, and there the smile was first born in the dream of a dew-washed morning—the smile that flickers on baby's lips when he sleeps.

The sweet, soft freshness that blooms on baby's limbs— does anybody know where it was hidden so long? Yes, when the mother was a young girl it lay pervading her heart in tender and silent mystery of love—the sweet, soft freshness that has bloomed on baby's lips.

Baby's Way

If baby only wanted to, he could fly up to heaven this moment.

It is not for nothing that he does not leave us.

He loves to rest his head on mother's bosom, and cannot ever bear to lose sight of her.

Baby knows all manner of wise words, though few on earth can understand their meaning.

It is not for nothing that he never wants to speak.

The one thing he wants is to learn mother's words from mother's lips. That is why he looks so innocent.

Baby had a heap of gold and pearls, yet he came like a beggar on to this earth.

It is not for nothing he came in such a disguise.

This dear little naked mendicant pretends to be utterly helpless, so that he may beg for mother's wealth of love.

Baby was so free from every tie in the land of the tiny crescent moon.

It was not for nothing he gave up his freedom.

He knows that there is room for endless joy in mother's little corner of a heart, and it is sweeter far than liberty to be caught and pressed in her dear arms.

Baby never knew how to cry. He dwelt in the land of perfect bliss.

It is not for nothing he has chosen to shed tears.

Though with the smile of his dear face he draws mother's yearning heart to him, yet his little cries over tiny troubles weave the double bond of pity and love.

The Unheeded Pageant

Ah, who was it coloured that little frock, my child, and covered your sweet limbs with that little red tunic?

You have come out in the morning to play in the courtyard, tottering and tumbling as you run.

But who was it coloured that little frock, my child?

What is it makes you laugh, my little life-bud?

Mother smiles at you standing on the threshold.

She claps her hands and her bracelets jingle, and you dance with your bamboo stick in your hand like a tiny little shepherd.

But what is it makes you laugh, my little life-bud?

O beggar, what do you beg for, clinging to your mother's neck with both your hands?

O greedy heart, shall I pluck the world like a fruit from the sky to place it on your little rosy palm?

O beggar, what are you begging for?

The wind carries away in glee the tinkling of your anklet bells.

The sun smiles and watches your toilet.

The sky watches over you when you sleep in your mother's arms, and the morning comes tiptoe to your bed and kisses your eyes.

The wind carries away in glee the tinkling of your anklet bells.

The fairy mistress of dreams is coming towards you, flying through the twilight sky.

The world-mother keeps her seat by you in your mother's heart.

He who plays his music to the stars is standing at your window with his flute.

And the fairy mistress of dreams is coming towards you, flying through the twilight sky.

Sleep-Stealer

Who stole sleep from baby's eyes? I must know.

Clasping her pitcher to her waist mother went to fetch water from the village near by.

It was noon. The children's playtime was over; the ducks in the pond were silent.

The shepherd boy lay asleep under the shadow of the banyan tree.

The crane stood grave and still in the swamp near the mango grove.

In the meanwhile the Sleep-stealer came and, snatching sleep from baby's eyes, flew away.

When mother came back she found baby travelling the room over on all fours.

Who stole sleep from our baby's eyes? I must know. I must find her and chain her up.

I must look into that dark cave, where, through boulders and scowling stones, trickles a tiny stream.

I must search in the drowsy shade of the *bakula* grove, where pigeons coo in their corner, and fairies' anklets tinkle in the stillness of starry nights.

In the evening I will peep into the whispering silence of the bamboo forest, where fireflies squander their light, and will ask every creature I meet, 'Can anybody tell me where the Sleep-stealer lives?'

Who stole sleep from baby's eyes? I must know.

Shouldn't I give her a good lesson if I could only catch her!

I would raid her nest and see where she hoards all her stolen sleep.

I would plunder it all, and carry it home.

I would bind her two wings securely, set her on the bank of the river, and then let her play at fishing with a reed among the rushes and water-lilies.

When the marketing is over in the evening, and the village children sit in their mothers' laps, then the night birds will mockingly din her ears with:

'Whose sleep will you steal now?'

The Beginning

'Where have I come from, where did you pick me up?' the baby asked its mother.

She answered, half crying, half laughing, and clasping the baby to her breast,—

'You were hidden in my heart as its desire, my darling.

Your were in the dolls of my childhood's games; and when with clay I made the image of my god every morning, I made and unmade you then.

You were enshrined with our household deity, in his worship I worshipped you.

In all my hopes and my loves, in my life, in the life of my mother you have lived.

In the lap of the deathless Spirit who rules our home you have been nursed for ages.

When in girlhood my heart was opening its petals, you hovered as a fragrance about it.

Your tender softness bloomed in my youthful limbs, like a glow in the sky before the sunrise.

Heaven's first darling, twin-born with the morning light, you have floated down the stream of the world's life, and at last you have stranded on my heart.

As I gaze on your face, mystery overwhelms me; you who belong to all have become mine.

For fear of losing you I hold you tight to my breast. What magic has snared the world's treasure in these slender arms of mine?'

Baby's World

I wish I could take a quiet corner in the heart of my baby's very own world.

I know it has stars that talk to him, and a sky that stoops down to his face to amuse him with its silly clouds and rainbows.

Those who make believe to be dumb, and look as if they never could move, come creeping to his window with their stories and with trays crowded with bright toys.

I wish I could travel by the road that crosses baby's mind, and out beyond all bounds;

Where messengers run errands for no cause between the kingdoms of kings of no history;

Where Reason makes kites of her laws and flies them, and Truth sets Fact free from its fetters.

When and Why

When I bring you coloured toys, my child, I understand why there is such a play of colours on clouds, on water, and why flowers are painted in tints—when I give coloured toys to you, my child.

When I sing to make you dance, I truly know why there is music in leaves, and why waves send their chorus of voices to the heart of the listening earth—when I sing to make you dance.

When I bring sweet things to your greedy hands, I know why there is honey in the cup of the flower, and why fruits are secretly filled with sweet juice—when I bring sweet things to your greedy hands.

When I kiss your face to make you smile, my darling, I surely understand what pleasure streams from the sky in morning light, and what delight the summer breeze brings to my body—when I kiss you to make you smile.

Defamation

Why are those tears in your eyes, my child? How horrid of them to be always scolding you for nothing!

You have stained your fingers and face with ink while writing—is that why they call you dirty?

O, fie! Would they dare to call the full moon dirty because it has smudged its face with ink?

For every little trifle they blame you, my child. They are ready to find fault for nothing.

You tore your clothes while playing—is that why they call you untidy?

O, fie! What would they call an autumn morning that smiles through its ragged clouds?

Take no heed of what they say to you, my child.

They make a long list of your misdeeds.

Everybody knows how you love sweet things—is that why they call you greedy?

O, fie! What then would they call us who love you?

The Judge

Say of him what you please, but I know my child's failings. I do not love him because he is good, but because he is my little child.

How should you know how dear he can be when you try to weigh his merits against his faults?

When I must punish him he becomes all the more a part of my being.

When I cause his tears to come my heart weeps with him.

I alone have a right to blame and punish, for he only may chastise who loves.

Playthings

Child, how happy you are sitting in the dust, playing with a broken twig all the morning!

I smile at your play with that little bit of a broken twig.

I am busy with my accounts, adding up figures by the hour.

Perhaps you glance at me and think, 'What a stupid game to spoil your morning with!'

Child, I have forgotten the art of being absorbed in sticks and mud-pies.

I seek out costly playthings, and gather lumps of gold and silver.

With whatever you find you create your glad games. I spend both my time and my strength over things I can never obtain.

In my frail canoe I struggle to cross the sea of desire, and forget that I too am playing a game.

The Astronomer

I only said, 'When in the evening the round full moon gets entangled among the branches of that *Kadam* tree, couldn't somebody catch it?'

But dādā[1] laughed at me and said, 'Baby, you are the silliest child I have ever known. The moon is ever so far from us, how could anybody catch it?'

I said, 'Dādā, how foolish your are! When mother looks out of her window and smiles down at us playing, would you call her far away?'

Still dādā said, 'You are a stupid child! But, baby, where could you find a net big enough to catch the moon with?'

I said, 'Surely you could catch it with your hands.'

But dādā laughed and said, 'You are the silliest child I have known. If it came nearer, you would see how big the moon is.'

I said, 'Dādā, what nonsense they teach at your school! When mother bends her face down to kiss us, does her face look very big?'

But still dādā says, 'You are a stupid child.'

---

1. Elder brother.

Clouds and Waves

Mother, the folk who live up in the clouds call out to me—

'We play from the time we wake till the day ends. We play with the golden dawn, we play with the silver moon.'

I ask, 'But how am I to get up to you?'

They answer, 'Come to the edge of the earth, lift up your hands to the sky, and you will be taken into the clouds.'

'My mother is waiting for me at home,' I say. 'How can I leave her and come?'

Then they smile and float away.

But I know a nicer game than that, mother.

I shall be the cloud and you the moon.

I shall cover you with both my hands, and our housetop will be the blue sky.

The folk who live in the waves call out to me—

'We sing from morning till night; on and on we travel and know not where we pass.'

I ask, 'But how am I to join you?'

They tell me, 'Come to the edge of the shore and stand with your eyes tight shut, and you will be carried out upon the waves.'

I say, 'My mother always wants me at home in the evening—how can I leave her and go?'

Then they smile, dance and pass by.
But I know a better game than that.
I will be the waves and you will be a strange shore.
I shall roll on and on and on, and break upon your lap
with laughter.
And no one in the world will know where we both are.

The Champa Flower

Supposing I became a *champa* flower, just for fun, and grew on a branch high up that tree, and shook in the wind with laughter and danced upon the newly budded leaves, would you know me, mother?

You would call, 'Baby, where are you?' and I should laugh to myself and keep quite quiet.

I should slyly open my petals and watch you at your work.

When after your bath, with wet hair spread on your shoulders, you walked through the shadow of the *champa* tree to the little court where you say your prayers, you would notice the scent of the flower, but not know that it came from me.

When after the midday meal you sat at the window reading *Ramayana*, and the tree's shadow fell over your hair and your lap, I should fling my wee little shadow on to the page of your book, just where you were reading.

But would you guess that it was the tiny shadow of your little child?

When in the evening you went to the cowshed with the lighted lamp in your hand, I should suddenly drop on to the earth again and be your own baby once more, and beg you to tell me a story.

'Where have you been, you naughty child?'

'I won't tell you, mother.' That's what you and I would say then.

Fairyland

If people came to know where my king's palace is, it would vanish into the air.

The walls are of white silver and the roof of shining gold.

The queen lives in a palace with seven courtyards, and she wears a jewel that cost all the wealth of seven kingdoms.

But let me tell you, mother, in a whisper, where my king's palace is.

It is at the corner of our terrace where the pot of the *tulsi* plant stands.

The princess lies sleeping on the far-away shore of the seven impassable seas.

There is none in the world who can find her but myself.

She has bracelets on her arms and pearl drops in her ears; her hair sweeps down upon the floor.

She will wake when I touch her with my magic wand, and jewels will fall from her lips when she smiles.

But let me whisper in your ear, mother; she is there in the corner of our terrace where the pot of the *tulsi* plant stands.

When it is time for you to go to the river for your bath, step up to that terrace on the roof.

I sit in the corner where the shadows of the walls meet together.

Only puss is allowed to come with me, for she knows where the barber in the story lives.

But let me whisper, mother, in your ear where the barber in the story lives.

It is at the corner of the terrace where the pot of the *tulsi* plant stands.

The Land of the Exile

Mother, the light has grown grey in the sky; I do not know what the time is.

There is no fun in my play, so I have come to you. It is Saturday, our holiday.

Leave off your work, mother; sit here by the window and tell me where the desert of Tepāntar in the fairy tale is.

The shadow of the rains has covered the day from end to end.

The fierce lightning is scratching the sky with its nails.

When the clouds rumble and it thunders, I love to be afraid in my heart and cling to you.

When the heavy rain patters for hours on the bamboo leaves, and our windows shake and rattle at the gusts of wind, I like to sit alone in the room, mother, with you, and hear your talk about the desert of Tepāntar in the fairy tale.

Where is it, mother, on the shore of what sea, at the foot of what hills, in the kingdom of what king?

There are no hedges there to mark the fields, no footpath across it by which the villagers reach their village in the evening, or the woman who gathers dry sticks in the forest can bring her load to the market. With patches of yellow grass in the sand and only one tree where the pair of wise old birds have their nest, lies the desert of Tepāntar.

I can imagine how, on just such a cloudy day, the young son of the king is riding alone on a grey horse through the desert, in search of the princess who lies imprisoned in the giant's palace across that unknown water.

When the haze of the rain comes down in the distant sky, and lightning starts up like a sudden fit of pain, does he remember his unhappy mother, abandoned by the king, sweeping the cow-stall and wiping her eyes, while he rides through the desert of Tepāntar in the fairy tale?

See, mother, it is almost dark before the day is over and there are no travellers yonder on the village road.

The shepherd boy has gone home early from the pasture, and men have left their fields to sit on mats under the eaves of their huts, watching the scowling clouds.

Mother, I have left all my books on the shelf—do not ask me to do my lessons now.

When I grow up and am big like my father, I shall learn all that must be learnt.

But just for to-day, tell me, mother, where the desert of Tepāntar in the fairy tale is.

The Rainy Day

Sullen clouds are gathering fast over the black fringe of the forest.

O child, do not go out!

The palm trees in a row by the lake are smiting their heads against the dismal sky; the crows with their draggled wings are silent on the tamarind branches, and the eastern bank of the river is haunted by a deepening gloom.

Our cow is lowing loud, tied at the fence.

O child, wait here till I bring her into the stall.

Men have crowded into the flooded field to catch the fishes as they escape from the overflowing ponds; the rain-water is running in rills through the narrow lanes like a laughing boy who has run away from his mother to tease her.

Listen, someone is shouting for the boatman at the ford.

O child, the daylight is dim, and the crossing at the ferry is closed.

The sky seems to ride fast upon the madly rushing rain; the water in the river is loud and impatient; women have hastened home early from the Ganges with their filled pitchers.

The evening lamps must be made ready.

O child, do not go out!

The road to the market is desolate, the lane to the river is slippery. The wind is roaring and struggling among the bamboo branches like a wild beast tangled in a net.

Paper Boats

Day by day I float my paper boats one by one down the running stream.

In big black letters I write my name on them and the name of the village where I live.

I hope that someone in some strange land will find them and know who I am.

I load my little boats with *shiuli* flowers from our garden, and hope that these blooms of the dawn will be carried safely to land in the night.

I launch my paper boats and look up into the sky and see the little clouds setting their white bulging sails.

I know not what playmate of mine in the sky sends them down the air to race with my boats!

When night comes I bury my face in my arms and dream that my paper boats float on and on under the midnight stars.

The fairies of sleep are sailing in them, and the lading is their baskets full of dreams.

I shall cross the seven seas and the thirteen rivers of
fairyland.

The Sailor

The boat of the boatman Madhu is moored at the wharf of Rajgunj.

It is uselessly laden with jute, and has been lying there idle for ever so long.

If he would only lend me his boat, I should man her with a hundred oars, and hoist sails, five or six or seven.

I should never steer her to stupid markets.

I should sail the seven seas and the thirteen rivers of fairyland.

But, mother, you won't weep for me in a corner.

I am not going into the forest like Ramachandra to come back only after fourteen years.

I shall become the prince of the story, and fill my boat with whatever I like.

I shall take my friend Ashu with me. We shall sail merrily across the seven seas and the thirteen rivers of fairyland.

We shall set sail in the early morning light.

When at noontide you are bathing at the pond, we shall be in the land of a strange king.

We shall pass the ford of Tirpurni, and leave behind us the desert of Tepāntar.

When we come back it will be getting dark, and I shall tell you of all that we have seen.

I shall cross the seven seas and the thirteen rivers of fairyland.

The Further Bank

I long to go over there to the further bank of the river,
Where those boats are tied to the bamboo poles in a
line;
Where men cross over in their boats in the morning with
ploughs on their shoulders to till their far-away fields;
Where the cowherds make their lowing cattle swim across
to the riverside pasture;
Whence they all come back home in the evening, leaving
the jackals to howl in the island overgrown with weeds.
Mother, if you don't mind, I should like to become the
boatman of the ferry when I am grown up.

They say there are strange pools hidden behind that high
bank.
Where flocks of wild ducks come when the rains are over,
and thick reeds grow round the margins where water-birds
lay their eggs;
Where snipes with their dancing tails stamp their tiny
footprints upon the clean soft mud;
Where in the evening the tall grasses crested with white
flowers invite the moonbeam to float upon their waves.
Mother, if you don't mind, I should like to become the
boatman of the ferryboat when I am grown up.

I shall cross and cross back from bank to bank, and all the boys and girls of the village will wonder at me while they are bathing.

When the sun climbs the mid sky and morning wears on to noon, I shall come running to you, saying, 'Mother, I am hungry!'

When the day is done and the shadows cower under the trees, I shall come back in the dusk.

I shall never go away from you into the town to work like father.

Mother, if you don't mind, I should like to become the boatman of the ferryboat when I am grown up.

The Flower-School

When storm-clouds rumble in the sky and June showers come down,

The moist east wind comes marching over the heath to blow its bagpipes among the bamboos.

The crowds of flowers come out of a sudden, from nobody knows where, and dance upon the grass in wild glee.

Mother, I really think the flowers go to school underground.

They do their lessons with doors shut, and if they want to come out to play before it is time, their master makes them stand in a corner.

When the rains come they have their holidays.

Branches clash together in the forest, and the leaves rustle in the wild wind, the thunder-clouds clap their giant hands and the flower children rush out in dresses of pink and yellow and white.

Do you know, mother, their home is in the sky, where the stars are.

Haven't you seen how eager are to get there? Don't you know why they are in such a hurry?

Of course, I can guess to whom they raise their arms: they have their mother as I have my own.

The Merchant

Imagine, mother, that you are to stay at home and I am to travel into strange lands.

Imagine that my boat is ready at the landing fully laden.

Now think well, mother, before you say what I shall bring for you when I come back.

Mother, do you want heaps and heaps of gold?

There, by the banks of golden streams, fields are full of golden harvest.

And in the shade of the forest path the golden *champa* flowers drop on the ground.

I will gather them all for you in many hundred baskets.

Mother, do you want pearls big as the raindrops of autumn?

I shall cross to the pearl island shore.

There in the early morning light pearls tremble on the meadow flowers, pearls drop on the grass, and pearls are scattered on the sand in spray by the wild sea-waves.

My brother shall have a pair of horses with wings to fly among the clouds.

For father I shall bring a magic pen that, without his knowing, will write of itself.

For you, mother, I must have the casket and jewel that cost seven kings their kingdoms.

Sympathy

If I were only a little puppy, not your baby, mother dear, would you say 'No' to me if I tried to eat from your dish?

Would you drive me off, saying to me, 'Get away, you naughty little puppy'?

Then go, mother, go! I will never come to you when you call me, and never let you feed me any more.

If I were only a little green parrot, and not your baby, mother dear, would you keep me chained lest I should fly away?

Would you shake your finger at me and say, 'What an ugrateful wretch of a bird! It is gnawing at its chain day and night'?

Then go, mother, go! I will run away into the woods; I will never let you take me in your arms again.

Vocation

When the gong sounds ten in the morning and I walk to school by our lane,

Every day I meet the hawker crying, 'Bangles, crystal bangles!'

There is nothing to hurry him on, there is no road he must take, no place he must go to, no time when he must come home.

I wish I were a hawker, spending my day in the road, crying, 'Bangles, crystal bangles!'

When at four in the afternoon I come back from the school,

I can see through the gate of that house the gardener digging the ground.

He does what he likes with his spade, he soils his clothes with dust, nobody takes him to task if he gets baked in the sun or gets wet.

I wish I were a gardener digging away at the garden with nobody to stop me from digging.

Just as it gets dark in the evening and my mother sends me to bed,

I can see through my open window the watchman walking up and down.

The lane is dark and lonely, and the street-lamp stands like a giant with one red eye in its head.

The watchman swings his lantern and walks with his shadow at his side, and never once goes to bed in his life.

I wish I were a watchman walking the streets all night, chasing the shadows with my lantern.

Superior

Mother, your baby is silly! She is so absurdly childish! She does not know the difference between the lights in the streets and the stars.

When we play at eating with pebbles, she thinks they are real food, and tries to put them into her mouth.

When I open a book before her and ask her to learn her a, b, c, she tears the leaves with her hands and roars for joy at nothing; this is your baby's way of doing her lesson.

When I shake my head at her in anger and scold her and call her naughty, she laughs and thinks it great fun.

Everybody knows that father is away, but if in play I call aloud 'Father,' she looks about her in excitement and thinks that father is near.

When I hold my class with the donkeys that our washerman brings to carry away the clothes and I warn her that I am the schoolmaster, she will scream for no reason and call me dādā.[1]

Your baby wants to catch the moon. She is so funny; she calls Ganesh[2] Gānush.

Mother, your baby is silly! She is so absurdly childish!

---

1. Elder brother.
2. Ganesh, a common name in India, also that of the god with the elephant's head.

The Little Big Man

I am small because I am a little child. I shall be big when I am as old as my father is.

My teacher will come and say, 'It is late, bring your slate and your books.'

I shall tell him, 'Do you not know I am as big as father? And I must not have lessons any more.'

My master will wonder and say, 'He can leave his books if he likes, for he is grown up.'

I shall dress myself and walk to the fair where the crowd is thick.

My uncle will come rushing up to me and say, 'You will get lost, my boy; let me carry you.'

I shall answer, 'Can't you see, uncle, I am as big as father? I must go to the fair alone.'

Uncle will say, 'Yes, he can go wherever he likes, for he is grown up.'

Mother will come from her bath when I am giving money to my nurse, for I shall know how to open the box with my key.

Mother will say, 'What are you about, naughty child?'

I shall tell her, 'Mother, don't you know, I am as big as father, and I must give silver to my nurse.'

Mother will say to herself, 'He can give money to whom he likes, for he is grown up.'

In the holiday time in October father will come home and, thinking that I am still a baby, will bring for me from the town little shoes and small silken frocks.

I shall say, 'Father, give them to my dādā, for I am as big as you are.'

Father will think and say, 'He can buy his own clothes if he likes, for he is grown up.'

Twelve O'clock

Mother, I do want to leave off my lessons now. I have been at my book all the morning.

You say it is only twelve o'clock. Suppose it isn't any later; can't you ever think it is afternoon when it is only twelve o'clock?

I can easily imagine now that the sun has reached the edge of that rice-field, and the old fisher-woman is gathering herbs for her supper by the side of the pond.

I can just shut my eyes and think that the shadows are growing darker under the *madar* tree, and the water in the pond looks shiny black.

If twelve o'clock can come in the night, why can't the night come when it is twelve o'clock?

Authorship

You say that father writes a lot of books, but what he writes I don't understand.

He was reading to you all the evening, but could you really make out what he meant?

What nice stories, mother, you can tell us! Why can't father write like that, I wonder?

Did he never hear from his own mother stories of giants fairies and princesses?

Has he forgotten them all?

Often when he gets late for his bath you have to go and call him an hundred times.

You wait and keep his dishes warm for him, but he goes on writing and forgets.

Father always plays at making books.

If ever I go to play in father's room, you come and call me, 'What a naughty child!'

If I make the slightest noise you say, 'Don't you see that father's at his work?'

What's the fun of always writing and writing?

When I take up father's pen or pencil and write upon his book just as he does,—a, b, c, d, e, f, g, h, i,—why do you get cross with me then, mother?

You never say a word when father writes.

When my father wastes such heaps of paper, mother, you don't seem to mind at all.
But if I take only one sheet to make a boat with, you say, 'Child, how troublesome you are!'
What do you think of father's spoiling sheets and sheets of paper with black marks all over on both sides?

The Wicked Postman

Why do you sit there on the floor so quiet and silent, tell me, mother dear?

The rain is coming in through the open window, making you all wet, and you don't mind it.

Do you hear the gong striking four? It is time for my brother to come home from school.

What has happened to you that you look so strange?

Haven't you got a letter from father to-day?

I saw the postman bringing letters in his bag for almost everybody in the town.

Only, father's letters he keeps to read himself. I am sure the postman is a wicked man.

But don't be unhappy about that, mother dear.

Tomorrow is market day in the next village. You ask your maid to buy some pens and papers.

I myself will write all father's letters; you will not find a single mistake.

I shall write from A right up to K.

But, mother, why do you smile?

You don't believe that I can write as nicely as father does!

But I shall rule my paper carefully, and write all the letters beautifully big.

When I finish my writing do you think I shall be so foolish as father and drop it into the horrid postman's bag?

I shall bring it to you myself without waiting, and letter by letter help you to read my writing.

I know the postman does not like to give you the really nice letters.

The Hero

Mother, let us imagine we are travelling, and passing through a strange and dangerous country.

You are riding in a palanquin and I am trotting by you on a red horse.

It is evening and the sun goes down. The waste of Joradighi lies wan and grey before us. The land is desolate and barren.

You are frightened and thinking—'I know not where we have come to.'

I say to you, 'Mother, do not be afraid.'

The meadow is prickly with spiky grass, and through it runs a narrow broken path.

There are no cattle to be seen in the wide field; they have gone to their village stalls.

It grows dark and dim on the land and sky, and we cannot tell where we are going.

Suddenly you call me and ask me in a whisper, 'What light is that near the bank?'

Just then there bursts out a fearful yell, and figures come running towards us.

You sit crouched in your palanquin and repeat the names of the gods in prayer.

The bearers, shaking in terror, hide themselves in the thorny bush.

I shout to you, 'Don't be afraid, mother. I am here.'

With long sticks in their hand and hair all wild about their heads, they come nearer and nearer.

I shout, 'Have a care, you villains! One step more and you are dead men.'

They give another terrible yell and rush forward.

You clutch my hand and say, 'Dear boy, for heaven's sake, keep away from them.'

I say, 'Mother, just you watch me.'

Then I spur my horse for a wild gallop, and my sword and buckler clash against each other.

The fight becomes so fearful, mother, that it would give you a cold shudder could you see it from your palanquin.

Many of them fly, and a great number are cut to pieces.

I know you are thinking, sitting all by yourself, that your boy must be dead by this time.

But I come to you all stained with blood, and say, 'Mother, the fight is over now.'

You come out and kiss me, pressing me to your heart, and you say to yourself,

'I don't know what I should do if I hadn't my boy to escort me.'

A thousand useless things happen day after day, and why couldn't such a thing come true by chance?

It would be like a story in a book.

My brother would say, 'Is it possible? I always thought he was so delicate!'

Our village people would all say in amazement, 'Was it not lucky that the boy was with his mother?'

The End

It is time for me to go, mother; I am going.

When in the paling darkness of the lonely dawn you stretch out your arms for your baby in the bed, I shall say, 'Baby is not there!'—mother, I am going.

I shall become a delicate draught of air and caress you; and I shall be ripples in the water when you bathe, and kiss you and kiss you again.

In the gusty night when the rain patters on the leaves you will hear my whisper in your bed, and my laughter will flash with the lightning through the open window into your room.

If you lie awake, thinking of your baby till late into the night, I shall sing to you from the stars, 'Sleep, mother, sleep.'

On the straying moonbeams I shall steal over your bed, and lie upon your bosom while you sleep.

I shall become a dream, and through the little opening of your eyelids I shall slip into the depths of your sleep; and when you wake up and look round startled, like a twinkling firefly I shall flit out into the darkness.

When, on the great festival of *puja*, the neighbours' children come and play about the house, I shall melt into the music of the flute and throb in your heart all day.

Dear auntie will come with *puja*-presents and will ask, 'Where is our baby, sister?' Mother, you will tell her softly, 'He is in the pupils of my eyes, he is in my body and in my soul.'

The Recall

The night was dark when she went away, and they slept. The night is dark now, and I call for her, 'Come back, my darling; the world is asleep; and no one would know, if you came for a moment while stars are gazing at stars.'

She went away when the trees were in bud and the spring was young.

Now the flowers are in high bloom and I call, 'Come back, my darling. The children gather and scatter flowers in reckless sport. And if you come and take one little blossom no one will miss it.'

Those that used to play are playing still, so spend-thrift is life.

I listen to their chatter and call, 'Come back, my darling, for mother's heart is full to the brim with love, and if you come to snatch only one little kiss from her no one will grudge it'.

The First Jasmines

Ah; these jasmines, these white jasmines!
I seem to remember the first day when I filled my hands
with these jasmines, these white jasmines.

I have loved the sunlight, the sky and the green earth;

I have heard the liquid murmur of the river through the
darkness of midnight;

Autumn sunsets have come to me at the bend of a road
in the lonely waste, like a bride raising her veil to accept her
lover.

Yet my memory is still sweet with the first white jasmines
that I held in my hands when I was a child.

Many a glad day has come in my life, and I have laughed
with merrymakers on festival nights.

On grey mornings of rain I have crooned many an idle
song.

I have worn round my neck the evening wreath of *bakulas*
woven by the hand of love.

Yet my heart is sweet with the memory of the first fresh
jasmines that filled my hands when I was a child.

The Banyan Tree

O you shaggy-headed banyan tree standing on the bank of the pond, have you forgotten the little child, like the birds that have nested in your branches and left you?

Do you not remember how he sat at the window and wondered at the tangle of your roots that plunged underground?

The women would come to fill their jars in the pond, and your huge black shadow would wriggle on the water like sleep struggling to wake up.

Sunlight danced on the ripples like restless tiny shuttles weaving golden tapestry.

Two ducks swam by the weedy margin above their shadows, and the child would sit still and think.

He longed to be the wind and blow through your rustling branches, to be your shadow and lengthen with the day on the water, to be a bird and perch on your topmost twig, and to float like those ducks among the weeds and shadows.

Benediction

Bless this little heart, this white soul that has won the kiss of heaven for our earth.

He loves the light of the sun, he loves the sight of his mother's face.

He has not learned to despise the dust, and to hanker after gold.

Clasp him to your heart and bless him.

He has come into this land of a hundred cross-roads.

I know not how he chose you from the crowd, came to your door, and grasped your hand to ask his way.

He will follow you, laughing and talking, and not a doubt in his heart.

Keep his trust, lead him straight and bless him.

Lay your hand on his head, and pray that though the waves underneath grow threatening, yet the breath from above may come and fill his sails and waft him to the haven of peace.

The Gift

I want to give you something, my child, for we are drifting in the stream of the world.

Our lives will be carried apart, and our love forgotten.

But I am not so foolish as to hope that I could buy your heart with my gifts.

Young is your life, your path long, and you drink the love we bring you at one drought and turn and run away from us.

You have your play and your playmates. What harm is there if you have no time or thought for us!

We, indeed, have leisure enough in old age to count the days that are past, to cherish in our hearts what our hands have lost for ever.

The river runs swift with a song, breaking through all barriers. But the mountain stays and remembers, and follows her with his love.

My Song

This song of mine will wind its music around you, my child, like the fond arms of love.

This song of mine will touch your forehead like a kiss of blessing.

When you are alone it will sit by your side and whisper in your ear, when your are in the crowd it will fence you about with aloofness.

My song will be like a pair of wings to your dreams, it will transport your heart to the verge of the unknown.

It will be like the faithful star overhead when dark night is over your road.

My song will sit in the pupils of your eyes, and will carry your sight into the heart of things.

And when my voice is silent in death, my song will speak in your living heart.

The Child-Angel

They clamour and fight, they doubt and despair, they know no end to their wranglings.

Let your life come amongst them like a flame of light, my child, unflickering and pure, and delight them into silence.

They are cruel in their greed and their envy, their words are like hidden knives thirsting for blood.

Go and stand amidst their scowling hearts, my child, and let your gentle eyes fall upon them like the forgiving peace of the evening over the strife of the day.

Let them see your face, my child, and thus know the meaning of all things; let them love you and thus love each other.

Come and take your seat in the bosom of the limitless, my child. At sunrise open and raise your heart like a blossoming flower, and at sunset bend your head and in silence complete the worship of the day.

The Last Bargain

'Come and hire me,' I cried, while in the morning I was walking on the stone-paved road.

Sword in hand, the King came in his chariot.

He held my hand and said, 'I will hire you with my power.'

But his power counted for naught, and he went away in his chariot.

In the heat of the midday the houses stood with shut doors.

I wandered along the crooked lane.

An old man came out with his bag of gold.

He pondered and said, 'I will hire you with my money.'

He weighed his coins one by one, but I turned away.

It was evening. The garden hedge was all aflower.

The fair maid came out and said, 'I will hire you with a smile.'

Her smile paled and melted into tears, and she went back alone into the dark.

The sun glistened on the sand, and the sea waves broke waywardly.

A child sat playing with shells.

He raised his head and seemed to know me, and said, 'I hire you with nothing.'

From thenceforward that bargain struck in child's play made me a free man.